The Two Horizons Old Testament C

J. Gordon McConville and Craig Bartholomew, *General Editors*

Two features distinguish The Two Horizons Old Testament Commentary series: theological exegesis and theological reflection.

Exegesis since the Reformation era and especially in the past two hundred years emphasized careful attention to philology, grammar, syntax, and concerns of a historical nature. More recently, commentary has expanded to include social-scientific, political, or canonical questions and more.

Without slighting the significance of those sorts of questions, scholars in The Two Horizons Old Testament Commentary locate their primary interests on theological readings of texts, past and present. The result is a paragraph-by-paragraph engagement with the text that is deliberately theological in focus.

Theological reflection in The Two Horizons Old Testament Commentary takes many forms, including locating each Old Testament book in relation to the whole of Scripture — asking what the biblical book contributes to biblical theology — and in conversation with constructive theology of today. How commentators engage in the work of theological reflection will differ from book to book, depending on their particular theological tradition and how they perceive the work of biblical theology and theological hermeneutics. This heterogeneity derives as well from the relative infancy of the project of theological interpretation of Scripture in modern times and from the challenge of grappling with a book's message in Greco-Roman antiquity, in the canon of Scripture and history of interpretation, and for life in the admittedly diverse Western world at the beginning of the twenty-first century.

The Two Horizons Old Testament Commentary is written primarily for students, pastors, and other Christian leaders seeking to engage in theological interpretation of Scripture.

Proverbs

Ernest C. Lucas

William B. Eerdmans Publishing Company
Grand Rapids, Michigan / Cambridge, U.K.

Published 2015 by
Wm. B. Eerdmans Publishing Co.
2140 Oak Industrial Drive N.E., Grand Rapids, Michigan 49505 /
P.O. Box 163, Cambridge CB3 9PU U.K.

Printed in the United States of America

21 20 19 18 17 16 15 7 6 5 4 3 2 1

Library of Congress Cataloging-in-Publication Data

Lucas, Ernest.
Proverbs / Ernest C. Lucas.
pages cm. — (The two horizons Old Testament commentary)
Includes bibliographical references and index.
ISBN 978-0-8028-2710-4 (pbk.: alk. paper)
1. Bible. Proverbs — Commentaries. I. Title.

BS1465.53.L83 2015
223'.707 — dc23

2015021794

www.eerdmans.com

To my wife, Hazel, truly an אשת־חיל.

To our sons, Craig and Stuart, each of whom is in their own way a בן חכם.

To their wives, Sevinç and Philippa, each of whom is מיהוה אשה משכלת.

To our grandchildren, Michael, Toby and Christine,
each of whom is a עטרת for us.

Contents

Acknowledgements

This commentary has taken longer than expected to write. A major factor in this has been the increasing demands of teaching, and especially academic administration, in the United Kingdom Higher Education system over the last few years. I am grateful to my series editor, Professor Gordon McConville, for his patience, occasional encouragement and the implied confidence in me. I am also grateful to my colleagues at Bristol Baptist College for their support and encouragement in all my work. Most of all I want to acknowledge the continual understanding, support and encouragement given by my wife, Hazel, even when the writing of the commentary has taken up time that we might have spent together.

Abbreviations

AB	Anchor Bible
AEL	*Ancient Egyptian Literature,* M. Lichtheim. 3 vols. Berkley, CA: University of California Press, 1971-80
AJSL	*American Journal of Semitic Languages and Literatures*
Aq	Aquila's Greek translation of Proverbs
AUSS	*Andrews University Seminary Studies*
BETL	Bibliotheca Ephemeridum Theologicarum Lovaniensium
Bib	*Biblica*
BKAT	Biblischer Kommentar: Altes Testamentum
BNTC	Black's New Testament Commentaries
BTS	*Bible et terre sainte*
BWL	*Babylonian Wisdom Literature,* W. G. Lambert. Winona Lake, IN: Eisenbrauns, 1996
BZAW	Beihefte zur Zeitschrift für die alttestamentliche Wissenschaft
CAD	*The Assyrian Dictionary of the Oriental Institute of the University of Chicago.* Chicago, 1956-2006
CBQ	*Catholic Biblical Quarterly*
COS	*The Context of Scripture.* Edited by W. W. Hallo. Leiden: Brill, 1997-2002
ESV	English Standard Version
ETL	*Ephemerides Theologicae Lovanienses*
EVV	English versions
GKC	*Gesenius' Hebrew Grammar.* Edited by E. Kautzsch. Translated by A. E. Cowley. 2nd ed. Oxford: OUP, 1910
GNB	Good News Bible
HS	*Hebrew Studies*
Int	*Interpretation*

JANESCU	*Journal of the Ancient Near Eastern Society of Columbia University*
JBL	*Journal of Biblical Literature*
JETS	*Journal of the Evangelical Theological Society*
JNSL	*Journal of Northwest Semitic Languages*
Joüon	Joüon, P. A. *A Grammar of Biblical Hebrew.* Translated and revised by T. Muraoka. 2 vols. Subsidia biblical 14/1-2. Rome: Editrice Pontificio Istituto Biblico, 1993 (corrected edition)
JQR	*Jewish Quarterly Review*
JSOT	*Journal for the Study of the Old Testament*
JSOTSup	Journal for the Old Testament: Supplement Series
JTS	*Journal of Theological Studies*
K	Kethibh (the written Hebrew text of the MT)
KJV	King James Version
LXX	Septuagint
ms(s)	manuscript(s)
MT	Massoretic Text
NAB	New American Bible
NCB	New Century Bible
NICOT	New International Commentary on the Old Testament
NIDNTT	*New International Dictionary of New Testament Theology*
NIDOTTE	*New International Dictionary of Old Testament Theology and Exegesis*
NIGTC	New International Greek Testament Commentary
NIV	New International Version
NIVAC	New International Version Application Commentary
NJPSV	New Jewish Publication Society Version (2nd ed.)
NRSV	New Revised Standard Version
NT	New Testament
OT	Old Testament
OTL	Old Testament Library
OTP	*The Old Testament Pseudepigrapha.* J. H. Charlesworth (ed.). 2 vols. Garden City, NY: Doubleday, 1983-85
Q	Qere (the Hebrew text to be read out from the MT)
RB	*Revue biblique*
REB	Revised English Bible
SBFLA	*Studii Biblici Fransiscani Liber Annus*
SBLDS	Society of Biblical Literature Dissertation Series
Sym	Symmachus' Greek translation of Proverbs
Syr	Syriac

Targ	Targum
Theod	Theodotion's Greek translation of Proverbs
TOTC	Tyndale Old Testament Commentary
TynB	*Tyndale Bulletin*
VT	*Vetus Testamentum*
VTSup	Supplements to Vetus Testamentum
Vulg	Vulgate
WMANT	Wissenschaftliche Monographien zum Alten un Neuen Testament
WO	*Die Welt des Orient*
ZAH	*Zeitschrift für Althebräistik*
ZAW	*Zeitschrift für die alttestamentliche Wissenschaft*
ZTK	*Zeitschrift für Theologie und Kirche*

Introduction

Proverbs, Job and Ecclesiastes are usually referred to as the 'wisdom' books of the Hebrew Bible. They differ considerably in literary genres, but together account for most of the occurrences of the various forms of the Hebrew root *ḥkm,* meaning 'wisdom', 'wise', 'to be wise' in the OT. Other words are characteristic of these books but not common outside of them. They also share a common approach to reality, which is 'humanistic' and 'experiential'. Many of the things normally seen as distinctively Israelite are absent from them. The great moments of Israel's history get no mention, nor do the covenants with Abraham, Moses and David. The Temple, its sacrificial system and calendar of feasts are barely mentioned. There is no mention of priest or prophet alongside 'the wise'.

What Is Wisdom?

One way of answering this question is to consider the people who are called 'wise' in the OT. Regarding the construction of the Tabernacle God says to Moses: 'I have given *wisdom* to all the *wise of heart,* so that they may make all that I have commanded you' (Exod. 31:6). These are people skilled in artistic design, metalwork, woodwork, working with precious stones, spinning, weaving and embroidery. Sailors able to navigate across the sea are called 'wise' (Ezek. 27:8). Solomon was given 'wisdom' in response to a prayer for the ability to rule well (1 Kgs. 3:9, 12). 'Wisdom' is also used of cunning (2 Sam. 13:3) and political pragmatism (1 Kgs. 2:6). These examples suggest that, in its widest sense, 'wisdom' in the OT is *the ability to cope with life.* Consideration of the kind of topics covered in Proverbs supports this: marriage and family life, friends and neighbours, care for the poor and needy, agriculture, commerce, behaviour in the law courts and in the royal court.

Within the wisdom literature the meaning of 'wisdom' becomes narrower. Whybray[1] says, 'in Proverbs *ḥokmâ* is always *life*-skill: the ability of the individual to conduct his life in the best possible way and to the best possible effect'. In the wisdom literature 'wisdom' is often coupled with words meaning 'understanding' or 'knowledge', giving it a more 'intellectual' slant. Wisdom is seen as 'an intellectual quality which provides the key to happiness and success, to "life" in its widest sense'.[2] But 'wisdom' in the OT is not to be equated with 'intelligence'. It is always about the skill of coping with life on a practical level. Also, it is something that can be acquired, as the 'prologue' to the Book of Proverbs asserts (Prov. 1:2-6). What is more, true 'wisdom' is rooted in commitment to Yahweh, 'the fear of the LORD' (Prov. 1:7; 9:10; see the comment on 1:7).

What Is a Proverb?

The Hebrew word that is used (in a plural form) in Prov. 1:1, which is translated into English as 'proverb' is מָשָׁל *(māšāl)*. The exact sense of the word is unclear. It could be related to a verb meaning 'to rule' and so mean a word that gives mastery, or a powerful word. Alternatively it could come from a verb meaning 'to be like', and so mean a comparison.[3] In fact only a minority of the sayings in Proverbs are direct comparisons, whether explicit (similes) or implicit (metaphors). In addition, the term *māšāl* is used fairly often in the Hebrew Bible and is applied to sayings, which have a wide variety of literary forms, for example: a satirical poem (Isa. 14:4), a psalm (Ps. 78:2), an allegory (Ezek. 17:2). The word, therefore, does not seem to refer to a specific literary form. Fox[4] argues that the main characteristic of a *māšāl* is that it 'has currency among people.' The saying, 'Is Saul too among the prophets?' became a *māšāl* (1 Sam. 10:12) by repetition so that it gained currency among people. This, he argues, is the meaning of the word *māšāl* in Prov. 1:1, 6; 10:1; 25:1; 26:7, 9.

The Structure of the Book of Proverbs

There are seven headings which clearly divide the book as we have it into sections.

1. Whybray, *Proverbs*, 4.
2. Whybray, *Intellectual Tradition of the Old Testament*, 8.
3. *NIDOTTE* 2:1134-37.
4. Fox, *Proverbs 1–9*, 54-55.

1:1	The proverbs of Solomon son of David, king of Israel.
10:1	The proverbs of Solomon
22:17	Incline your ear, and hear the words of the wise.
24:23	These also are sayings of the wise.
25:1	These also are proverbs of Solomon which the men of Hezekiah, king of Judah, copied.
30:1	The words of Agur son of Jakeh.
31:1	The words of King Lemuel. An oracle that his mother taught him.

The LXX of 22:17 reads, 'To the words of the wise, lend your ear and hear my word.' In the light of this most commentators and translations now emend the Hebrew of this verse to read, 'The words of the wise. Incline your ear and hear my words, and apply your mind to my teaching', so making the 'title' clearer.

There are differences in the form and style of the material which suggests the existence of distinct sections, and some of these coincide with the sections indicated by the headings. Proverbs 10:1–22:16 and 25:1–29:27 consist of 'sentence proverbs'. Each sentence is usually a couplet displaying parallelism between its two halves. Although there are groups of proverbs based on common themes or words, these do not form a reasoned 'discourse'. In 22:17–24:22 the basic unit is a four-part sentence which usually has the form of a command followed by a reason, or motive, for obeying it. Proverbs 24:23-34 also consists mainly of four-part sentences. The material in chs. 1–9 is different again in its form. It contains several connected discourses, poems and speeches. Proverbs 30:15-33 consists, in the main, of a collection of 'number proverbs'. The concluding poem in 31:10-31 stands out as a distinct section, both because of its subject and because in form it is an alphabetic acrostic. Each of the twenty-two verses begins with a letter of the Hebrew alphabet, following their normal sequence.

One area of debate concerns where 'The words of Agur' end. The most obvious break occurs at 30:15, with first of the 'number proverbs'. It is notable that when the LXX deviates in the order of material after 24:22 it treats 30:1-14 as a distinct section. However, whether all of this is intended to be the words of Agur is widely disputed. There is a list of undesirable persons in 30:11-14, with each item beginning, 'There are those . . .'. Verse 10 might precede this because of the catchword 'curse'. There is no obvious link between these verses and what precedes them. The prayer in 30:7-9 is seen by some as a fitting climax to the words of Agur. Others suggest that it is a kind of 'number proverb', which marks the beginning of a collection in which this form of proverb dominates.

There is general agreement that 1:1-7 forms a preface, not just to chs. 1–9, but to the whole book. After the heading (v. 1), the purpose of the book is set out in a series of assertions about the benefits that will accrue from paying heed to its contents. Finally, v. 7 sums up the teaching of the whole book.

With regard to the rest of chs. 1–9 there is general, though not unanimous, agreement that there are ten sections, each of which begins in the same way.[5]

- They are all addressed (in Hebrew) to 'my son' ('sons' in 4:1) as the first or second word.
- The son is commanded to 'hear', 'receive', 'not forget' and so on, the teaching which follows (in 2:1 this is expressed in conditional form, 'if . . .').
- The personal authority of the speaker, the 'father', is asserted.
- The great value and utility of the father's words are asserted or implied.

While the beginnings of these sections are clear (1:8-9; 2:1-4; 3:1-2; 3:21-22; 4:1-2; 4:10; 4:20-21; 5:1-2; 6:20-21; 7:1-3), there is some uncertainty about the ending of some of them. There is a fair degree of agreement on three 'interludes' between some of them.

- 1:20-33, Wisdom's warning.
- 3:13-20, a poem in praise of Wisdom.
- 6:1-19, four admonitions and warnings.

There is no consensus about the reason for the order of the ten sections and the 'interludes'. There is no obvious development of thought or thematic arrangement.

Chapter 8 stands on its own as a speech by Wisdom. The portraits of personified Wisdom (9:1-6) and Folly (9:13-18) form an appropriate climax to this section of the book. There is debate about the nature and function of 9:7-12.

These considerations lead to the following overall structure:

1:1–9:18	The Proverbs of Solomon — I	
	1:1-7	Preface
	1:8-19	Lesson 1
	1:20-33	Wisdom's warning
	2:1-22	Lesson 2
	3:1-12	Lesson 3
	3:13-20	A poem in praise of Wisdom

5. This was first pointed out by Whybray, *Wisdom in Proverbs*. Hesitations about this analysis are expressed by Murphy, *Proverbs*, 8-9.

	3:21-35	Lesson 4
	4:1-9	Lesson 5
	4:10-19	Lesson 6
	4:20-27	Lesson 7
	5:1-23	Lesson 8
	6:1-19	Four admonitions and warnings
	6:20-35	Lesson 9
	7:1-27	Lesson 10
	8:1-36	A speech by Wisdom
	9:1-18	Wisdom and Folly
10:1–22:16	The Proverbs of Solomon — II	
22:17–24:22	The Words of the Wise	
24:23-34	More Words of the Wise	
25:1–29:27	The Proverbs of Solomon — III	
30:1-14	The Words of Agur	
	30:1-3	A profession of ignorance
	30:4	A riddle
	30:5-6	An affirmation about God's word
	30:7-9	A prayer
	30:10	An admonition
	30:11-14	A list of undesirable persons
30:15-33	A Collection of (mainly) Number Proverbs	
31:1-9	The Words of King Lemuel	
31:10-31	The Capable Wife (an alphabetic acrostic poem)	

Luc[6] challenges the consensus that 22:17 and 24:23 are titles. He argues that in the LXX the phrase 'words of the wise' may be merely part of the poetic line, and not a title. It should not be used to 'restore' a title in the MT. He agrees with the LXX translation of 24:23, 'These also are words *for* the wise', and links this with the five 'purpose' statements in 1:2-6, 'to make the wise wiser' (v. 5). Removing these two titles leaves five titles. Luc suggests that the final editor of Proverbs in the MT was deliberately copying the five-fold structure of the Pentateuch. He accepts that, whether or not 22:17 and 24:23 are titles, 22:17–24:22 and 24:23-34 are distinct units within the book.

The strongest of Luc's arguments is his point about 22:17. The emendation of this verse has always been a matter of debate. His translation of 24:23 is less convincing. The appeal to 1:5 is somewhat undermined by the lack of correlation of other sections in the book with the other 'purpose statements'. Finally, the

6. Luc, 'Titles and Structure of Proverbs'.

appeal to a final editorial shaping that seeks to parallel the Pentateuch is not convincing. The sections into which the five titles Luc recognises divide the book are very unequal in length. Two are explicitly attributed to non-Israelites. More importantly, concern for the Torah is not at all evident in Proverbs. If the final editor had wanted to make a link between Wisdom and Torah it is surprising that this was not done more obviously.

On the basis of form, style and content, Skladny[7] argued for a division between chs 10–15 and 16:1–22:16. The proverbs in chs 10–15 are mostly antithetic, while those in 16:1–22:16 are mostly synonymous and progressive. Waltke[8] points out that the change seems to take place at 15:30, and suggests that 15:30-33 is prologue to what follows. Toy[9] pointed out that chs 25–27 consist largely of comparative proverbs, while antithetic and progressive proverbs predominate in chs 28–29. These differences in form do not correlate with changes in theme or topics covered.

Authorship and Date

The study of the structure of Proverbs shows that it is a collection of collections, some of which are attributed to named or unnamed authors other than Solomon. It is likely that Prov. 1:1 is intended to refer to the book as a whole rather than to the collection in Prov. 1–9. To begin with, it is part of what seems to be a prologue to the whole book: 1:1-7. Then, as Kidner[10] points out, 'If chapters 1–9 consisted of proverbs of Solomon we should expect 10:1 to be phrased: "These also are proverbs of Solomon", on the pattern of 24:23 and 25:1.' So, in addition to the collections already discussed, Prov. 1–9 is probably another anonymous, non-Solomonic, collection.

In addition to this there is evidence that the major collections are made up of smaller collections. Besides the evidence of form, style and content that has already been noted, there is the fact that there are some proverbs that are repeated more or less word-for-word, for example Prov. 10:1/15:20; 14:12/16:25; 16:2/21:2. Snell[11] provides an exhaustive list of repeated proverbs of varying degrees of similarity. This is most likely to happen if the bigger collections were made by combining smaller, pre-existing ones. When a work is built up in this

7. Skladny, *Ältesten Spruchsammlungen in Israel.*

8. Waltke, *Proverbs 1–15*, 16.

9. Toy, *Proverbs*, x.

10. Kidner, *Proverbs*, 22.

11. Snell, *Twice-Told Proverbs.*

way, it does not make sense to speak of its 'authorship' in the way in which that term is normally used.

A second factor to bear in mind is that proverbs often arise in an oral context and then may eventually be written down and find their way into a written collection. Wisdom teachers were collectors of material. The preface of the Egyptian *Instruction of Ptahhotep* makes clear that the book includes 'the advice of the ancestors' and 'the utterances of times past'.[12] Ben Sirach tells his students, 'Be ready to listen to every godly discourse, and let no wise proverb escape you' (Sir. 6:35). Proverbs 25:1 tells us that the 'men of Hezekiah' acted as collectors of already existing proverbs. This reference also shows that it is problematic to speak of the date of the Book of Proverbs. Its compilation in the form that we have it took centuries. The phrase 'these also are proverbs of Solomon' in 25:1 implies that at that time there was an already existing collection of 'Solomonic' proverbs.

So what is the meaning of the attributions of proverbs to Solomon in Prov. 1:1; 10:1; and 25:1? They are understandable in the light of the tradition of Solomon's personal wisdom (1 Kgs. 4:29-34). First Kgs. 4:32 says that he 'spoke 3,000 proverbs', which may not mean that he composed them. If we think of his activity with regard to proverbs in a wider sense than that of an originator of new sayings then, as Clifford[13] says, 'There is no reason . . . to doubt that some of the book is "by Solomon", for as king he would have collected, sponsored, or possibly even written, various kinds of writing, including literature *(belles lettres),* as 1 Kings 4:29-31 recognizes.' It is, however, hard to think of Solomon, or anyone in the royal court, as the originator of much of the material in Proverbs. Very little of it refers directly to life at court and none of it seems to verbalise the view-point of a monarch. The most prominent social settings reflected in the book are those of the moderately well-off rural farmer and the urban artisan. It seems likely that the attribution of the book and two collections in it to Solomon serves primarily as noting his foundational role in the collecting of proverbs in Israel, though this does not exclude the reshaping of some proverbs as they were written down, and the creation of some new ones.

If a 'Solomonic' collection began to take shape during his reign (latter part of the tenth century BC) the compilation of the book continued until at least the time of Hezekiah (late eighth century BC). Attempts to date material in the book by various means have led to little in the way of consensus. It is in the nature of proverbs that they do not contain specific historical references by which they can be dated, though references to the king in some proverbs

12. Fox, *Proverbs 1–9,* 57.
13. Clifford, *Proverbs,* 3.

suggests that these are pre-exilic in origin. After a brief survey of a number of linguistic features Clifford[14] concludes that, apart from the fact that the absence of Graecisms suggests a pre-Hellenistic date, 'In sum, the book cannot be dated with certainty from its language.' Most scholars think that Prov. 1–9 and 31:10-31 look as if they have been composed as an introduction and conclusion to the book, and so are the latest parts of it. However, views on the dating of Prov. 1–9 differ widely. On the basis of similarities with Egyptian instructions, Kayatz[15] argued for a pre-exilic dating. Fox[16] thinks that literary form is of little help in dating and considers a Persian or early Hellenistic date likely because, 'Some parts of Prov. 1–9, especially ch. 8, seem to me to be a response to Greek philosophy, though this is an uncertain basis for dating.' Even Waltke,[17] who attributes most of the book to Solomon, accepts that there was a final editing of the book in which Hezekiah's collection and the non-Solomonic material in chs. 30–31 was added to an existing Solomonic work, and that 'This final editor, the real author of the book, not of its sayings, probably lived during the Persian period (ca. 540 B.C.–332 B.C.) or in the Hellenistic era.'

Overall there is a fairly widely held consensus that the Book of Proverbs is a collection of collections, the compilation of which probably stretched over a period of at least five hundred years.

Literary Forms in Proverbs

An appreciation of the different literary forms which occur in Proverbs and their characteristics helps the reader in understanding and interpreting the book. There are two main literary forms, the *instruction* and the *sentence proverb* and a number of other less common forms.

The Instruction Form

McKane[18] carried out a detailed study of Egyptian and Mesopotamian texts. On this basis he was able to define the characteristics of the 'instruction form' in ancient Near Eastern wisdom literature.

14. Clifford, *Proverbs*, 5.
15. Kayatz, *Studien zu Proverbien 1–9*.
16. Fox, *Proverbs 1–9*, 6.
17. Waltke, *Proverbs 1–15*, 37.
18. McKane, *Proverbs*, 51-182.

1. The main element is the imperative or command. This may be either positive or negative. It may be expressed by an imperative, a jussive or a virtual (polite) imperative ('you shall not').
2. There is often a conditional clause. This defines the condition or circumstance in which the imperative applies. It usually precedes the imperative but may follow it.
3. There is usually a motive clause. Its function is to recommend that action of the imperative(s) and show its reasonableness. The motive clause can be developed in various ways to give an 'extended motivation'.
4. There is sometimes a consequence clause. This normally expresses the outcome of obeying the imperative in terms of a desirable objective. The distinction between motive and consequence is not clear-cut.

The 'instruction form' form is to be found in Prov. 1–9; 22:17–24:22; and 31:1-9. A straightforward example of a command followed by motive is provided by Prov. 3:1-2:

Command:	My child, do not forget my teaching, but let your heart keep my commandments;
Motive:	for length of days and years of life and abundant welfare they will give you.

A rather complex example is provided by Prov. 1:10-19.

Condition:	My child, if sinners entice you,
Command:	do not consent.
Condition:	If they say, 'Come with us, let us lie in wait for blood; let us wantonly ambush the innocent; like Sheol let us swallow them alive and whole, like those who go down to the Pit. We shall find all kinds of costly things; throw your lot among us; we will all have one purse' —
Command:	my child, do not walk in their way, keep your foot from their paths;
Motive:	for their feet run to evil, and they hurry to shed blood.
Consequence:	For in vain is the net baited while the bird is looking on; yet they lie in wait — to kill themselves! and set ambush — for their own lives!

Such is the end of all who are greedy for gain;
It takes away the life of its possessors.

This example illustrates the difficulty of distinguishing between motive and consequence clauses. It is possible to take vv. 17-19 as an extension of the motive clause. However, these verses express the negative consequences of the actions of the 'sinners', so are better seen as a negative version of the consequence clause in that they express the consequence of not heeding the commands.

There can be some confusion when people fail to distinguish between the 'instruction form' as defined above and a piece of literature that is 'an instruction book/lecture/unit'. The literary unit begins with an introduction which addresses the reader, often as 'my son', with a call to listen to and heed the teaching that follows. The purpose and value of the teaching may be emphasised. This introduction itself has the instruction form and so does all, or most, of the teaching that follows.

Each lesson in Prov. 1–9 forms an instruction unit. Fox,[19] who calls them 'lectures', divides each of them into three major parts:

1. *Exordium.* The introduction to the lesson, which usually contains an *address* to the son(s), an *exhortation* and a *motivation* to support the exhortation.
2. *Lesson.* The body of the teaching.
3. *Conclusion.* A summary of the teaching, which may end with a *capstone,* a memorable saying that reinforces the teaching.

In the commentary we shall refer to these three sections as the 'introduction', 'main body' and 'conclusion' of each lesson.

The Sentence Proverb

This is the basic unit of Prov. 10:1–22:16 and 25:1–29:27. In most cases the sentence is made up of two 'lines' or 'cola' (singular: colon) and exhibits the parallelism that is a feature of Hebrew poetry. Three types of parallelism are very common in Proverbs.

- **Antithetic parallelism**. In this type the second colon expresses a contrast to the first, for example 'A slack hand causes poverty, but the hand

19. Fox, *Proverbs 1–9*, 45.

of the diligent makes rich' (10:4). Most of the proverbs in chs. 10–15 use antithetic parallelism

- **Synonymous parallelism**. In this case the second colon repeats the essential point of the first, but in different words, for example 'Pride goes before destruction, and a haughty spirit before a fall' (16:18).
- **Progressive parallelism**. In this type the second colon builds on or extends what has been said in the first, for example 'A fool takes no pleasure in understanding, but only in expressing personal opinion' (18:2).

The sentences in Proverbs are usually very terse. The colon often consists of two items juxtaposed without a verb, for example:

> One who loves wrong, one who loves strife:
> One who makes his gate high, one who seeks destruction. (17:19)

Here four items form two pairs. Another example is,

> Hope deferred, a sick heart:
> And/but a tree of life, desire fulfilled. (13:12)

The simple juxtaposition of items may mean that it is unclear which is the subject and which the predicate. One has to rely on the content when determining this.

There is sometimes an implicit comparison in the juxtaposition, for example:

> A city breached without a wall:
> A man who does not control his spirit. (25:28)

Quite often a simple *wāw* (and/but) serves as an implicit comparative particle, for example:

> Cold water upon an exhausted soul:
> And/but (like) good news from a distant land. (25:25)

In similes the comparison is made explicit by the use of particles such as *kî* (like) and *kēn* (so), for example:

> Like a bird wandering from its nest:
> so is a man wandering from his place. (27:8)

> Like snow in summer and like rain in harvest:
> so honour is out of place for a fool. (26:1)

Both implicit comparisons and similes are particularly common in Prov. 25–27.

The sentences can be divided into indicatives (which simply make a statement) and imperatives (usually called 'admonitions'). The admonitions may be either positive (commands) or negative (prohibitions). There are some notable subgroups among the indicative sentences.

The 'Good' Sayings

In fact the majority of these are 'not good' *(lōʾ tôb)* sayings, for example:

> To impose a fine on a righteous man is not good,
> nor to strike the noble for their uprightness. (17:26)

Other examples of this are: 18:5; 19:2; 20:23; 24:23b; 25:27; 28:21. A weaker form of 'not good' is 'not becoming/fitting' *(lōʾ nāʾwâ),* as in 17:7; 19:10; 26:1. The opposite of 'not good' is 'how good' *(mah tôb),* as in 15:23.

The 'Abomination' Sayings

Most of these contrast something that is an 'abomination to the LORD' with what 'delights' him, for example:

> A false balance is an abomination to the LORD,
> but a just weight is his delight. (11:1)

Other examples of this contrast are: 11:1, 20; 12:22; 15:8, 26; 16:5; 20:23; 28:9; 29:27. Proverbs 3:32 and 16:5 lack the contrast, and 6:16 lists 'seven things that are an abomination to the LORD'. The phrase 'abomination to the LORD' occurs only in Proverbs and Deuteronomy.

The 'Better' Sayings

The simple form of these has the form, 'A is better than B', for example:

> Whoever is slow to anger is better than the mighty,
> and he who rules his spirit than he who takes a city. (16:32)

Other examples of this simple form are: 3:14; 8:11, 19; 22:1; 25:7. A more common form has the pattern, 'A with B is better than C with D', for example:

> Better is a little with righteousness,
> than great revenues with injustice. (16:8)

Other examples of this form are: 12:9; 15:16, 17; 16:19; 17:1; 19:1; 27:5, 10b; 28:6.

The 'Beatitudes' or 'Blessings'

These normally begin with the predicative adjective 'blessed/happy' (אַשְׁרֵי/ *ʾašrê*), which points to a state of well-being and contentment, for example:

> Whoever despises his neighbour is a sinner,
> but blessed is he who is generous to the poor. (14:21)

Other examples of beatitudes (also in the second colon) are: 16:20 and 29:18 (see also 8:32, 34).

Structural Units in the Sentence Literature

Yoder[20] expresses the view of many commentators and readers of Proverbs when she says,

> Proverbs 10:1–22:16 consists largely of two-line proverbs, each of which may stand on its own and each of which — at least initially — appears disconnected with the proverbs that precede and follows it . . . this seemingly haphazard arrangement is disorienting . . . proverbs follow one after another in no apparent order of priority.

Not all scholars agree that the arrangement of sentence proverbs in Prov. 10–29 is haphazard. Some have argued for the existence of various kinds of compositional units in this section of the book.

20. Yoder, *Proverbs,* 110.

Proverbial Pairs

Hildebrandt[21] argues that this section of the book contains 'proverbial pairs' bound together by various rhetorical devices. The most common device is catchword repetition. This is particularly significant when the catchwords are low-frequency words, for example:

> For lack of *wood* the *fire* goes out,
> and where there is no whisperer, quarrelling ceases.
> As charcoal is to hot embers and *wood* to *fire,*
> so is a quarrelsome person for kindling strife. (26:20-21)

Another strong indication of an intentional pair is the existence of multi-catchwords, for example:

> Do not withhold discipline from your children;
> if you beat them with a rod, they will not die.
> If you beat them with the rod,
> you will save their lives from Sheol. (23:13-14)

This example shows that bonding by multi-catchwords may also result in bonding by a common theme. Another example of thematic bonding is,

> The righteousness of the blameless keeps their ways straight,
> but the wicked fall by their own wickedness.
> The righteousness of the upright saves them,
> but the treacherous are taken by their schemes. (11:5-6)

Here there is the high-frequency catchword 'righteousness' but the bond is strengthened by the common theme that righteousness leads to success and wickedness to disaster.

Syntactic bonding is less conclusive than catchword or thematic bonding. The two strongest forms of it are direct dependence and linking particles.

> Do not make friends with a man given to anger,
> nor go with a man of wrath,
> lest you may learn his ways
> and entangle yourself in a snare. (22:24-25)

21. Hildebrandt, 'Proverbial Pairs'.

The third-person masculine singular pronominal suffix in 'his ways' points back to 'the man of wrath. There is also the linking word פֶּן (*pen*, 'lest').

Proverb Strings

Hildebrandt[22] subsequently used consideration of various rhetorical devices as the basis for identifying four 'strings' of proverbs in Prov. 10. The identification of 10:1-5 and 10:6-11 as separate 'strings' is convincing. Both are bounded by *inclusios*. The proposed 'strings' in 10:12-21 and 10:22-30 rely on rather convoluted proposed structures which are much less convincing. They seem like unsuccessful attempts to bring together smaller, independent units.

Proverb Poems

Van Leeuwen[23] used structuralist, rhetorical and semantic approaches to study Prov. 25–27. He identified a coherent 'proverb poem' in ch. 25 and three other 'proverb poems' in ch. 26, but could not find a coherent literary unit in ch. 27, concluding that it is a 'proverb miscellany'.

Proverbial Clusters

Heim seeks to identify 'proverbial clusters' in Prov. 10:1–22:16. He provides[24] a valuable survey and critique of scholarly views about the way the sayings are, or are not, organised in Prov. 10:1–22:16. On his part he argues[25] that the primary criteria for the delimitation of cluster should not be 'boundary markers' but linking devices. 'The focus should not be on what *divides* or *separates* groups from their environment, but on features which *link* and *combine* sayings into organic units'. In particular he looks for repetition — such as repetition of consonants, word roots, words, synonyms. The positioning of some linking features makes them boundary markers. Another criterion for distinguishing one cluster from another is the change in linking devices.

Waltke[26] uses 'the mostly single-line rearing (or educative) proverbs' as

22. Hildebrandt, 'Proverbial Strings', 171-85.
23. Van Leeuwen, *Context and Meaning*.
24. Heim, *Like Grapes of Gold Set in Silver*, 7-68.
25. Heim, *Like Grapes of Gold Set in Silver*, 107.
26. Waltke, *Proverbs 1–15*, 21.

a guide to identifying the beginning of what he calls 'units'. He then divides these into 'subunits' which more-or-less correspond to what Heim calls 'clusters'. The criteria he uses[27] in linking proverbs together are such things as *inclusio,* catchwords, structural patterns such as a *chiasmus* and logical or thematic connections.

In this commentary I try to identify 'proverbial clusters' and other structures in the sentence literature using the criteria used by Waltke and Heim. I give a higher priority than Heim does to thematic connections, while recognising that this may introduce a higher degree of subjectivity, and I do not try as hard as Waltke to find logical or thematic connections. I do not assume that they must always be there.

Comparing Clusters

There is not space in the commentary to give a detailed argument for the clusters that are identified. Table 1 on page 17 is a fairly detailed analysis of the clusters that are identified in chs. 10 and 11, and a comparison is made with those identified by Heim[28] and Waltke.[29] From this readers can get a feel for the different approaches and draw their own conclusions about these approaches. The 'commentary' on the clusters is based on my own division of the chapters into clusters and gives some justification for it.

10:1-5. Waltke separates out v. 1 as an introductory 'educative proverb' but recognises the *inclusio* made by the construct form בֶּן *bēn* which delimits vv. 1-5. All three recognise that there is a chiastic pattern of positive and negative statements between pairs of verses, so that the second line of one verse corresponds with the first line of the next. Lucas and Walke recognise a theme of wealth.

10:6-11. Lucas and Heim see the repetition of v. 6b in v. 11b and the righteous/wicked contrast in these verses as delimiting this cluster. Lucas also notes that v. 11a may be a development of v. 6a. The mouth of the righteous passes on the blessings they have received. Waltke sees the mention of 'mouth' in vv. 6b and 14b as forming an *inclusio.* He then divides the cluster into two halves, each of four antithetical proverbs (vv. 6-9, 11-14) with v. 10 as what he calls 'a janus pivot' which looks both backwards and forwards.

27. Waltke, *Proverbs 1–15,* 47.
28. Heim, *Like Grapes of Gold Set in Silver,* 111-46.
29. Waltke, *Proverbs 1–15,* 447-515.

Table 1. Comparing clusters in Proverbs 10 and 11

Waltke		Heim		Lucas
10:1-17				
	10:1	10:1-5		10:1-5
	10:2-5			
	10:6-14	10:6-11		10:6-11
				10:12
	10:15-16	10:12-18		10:13-17
	10:17			
10:18-32				
	10:18-21	10:19-22		10:18-21
		10:22-30		
	10:22-26		10:22-25	10:22-25
			10:26	10:26
	10:27-30		10:27-30	10:27-30
	10:31-32	10:31-32		10:31-32
11:1-8		**11:1-14**		
	11:1-2		11:1	11:1
	11:3-8		11:2-8	11:2-8
11:9			11:9-14	11:9-14
11:10-15				
11:16-22		11:15-21		11:15-21
		11:22-31		
			11:22	11:22
11:23-27			11:23-26	11:23-27
11:28-31			11:27-31	11:28-31

10:12. Heim argues that the repetition of 'hatred' and 'covers/conceals' in vv. 12 and 18 marks off vv. 12-18 as a cluster. However, he recognises that vv. 13-17 are linked by catchwords. Lucas argues that v. 12 is more closely linked to v. 11 than to what follows. There is the catchword link of 'cover/conceals', and it can be seen as giving a specific example of the meaning of v. 11a. It seems preferable to take it as a stand-alone proverb loosely related to its context rather than force it into a cluster.

10:13-17. Heim and Lucas note the catchword links between vv. 13-15 (wisdom/wise/ruin) and vv. 16-17 (life), plus a conceptual link between vv. 15 and 16 (wealth/wage/gain). Lucas sees no coherent theme in the cluster formed by these links. Waltke recognises the conceptual link between vv. 15 and 16, which he treats as a proverb-pair. In his view v. 17 is a single educative proverb which introduces a new section.

10:18-21. For Lucas and Waltke it is the fact that each of these verses refers to organs of speech that makes this a cluster. There is a coherent theme of how speech is used, with emphasis on its bad use in vv. 18-19 and its good use in vv. 20-21. Heim links v. 18 with v. 12 (see above) and so detaches it from v. 19. He thinks v. 22 fits better with what precedes it than with what follows but gives it a pivotal role, closing one cluster and opening the next.

10:22-25. All three see a theme running through these verses, though expressing it slightly differently: fear/hope (Heim), dread/desire (Lucas), pain/pleasure (Waltke).

10:26. Waltke links v. 26 with the preceding verses, arguing that it forms a 'frame' with v. 22 on the grounds of form (both use synthetic parallelism) and paronomasia (עֶצֶב/*'eṣeb,* 'sorrow', in v. 22b and עָצֵל/*'āṣēl,* 'sluggard' in v. 26b). This seems rather forced. Lucas and Heim both see this as a proverb which stands out from its context because of its form (synonymous parallelism and use of simile) and content.

10:27-30. All three see this as a cluster with a similar theme to vv. 22-25, which also begins with a Yahweh proverb.

10:31-32. All three see this as a proverb pair linked by the mention of speech parts in each of the four cola and the righteous/perverse contrast in each verse.

11:1. Lucas and Heim regard this as a stand-alone proverb because of its distinctive content. Waltke argues that it forms a proverb pair with v. 2 because of a common theme of 'dishonest evaluation' since pride is an exaggerated opinion of oneself. This is not a very convincing argument.

11:2-8. Lucas and Heim see in these verses a loose cluster linked by references to destruction/death/perishing on the one hand and being saved on the other. Waltke sees a similar, but more positive, theme of 'security through righteousness' in vv. 3-8.

11:9-14. Waltke regards v. 9 as a janus proverb standing between two clusters, having links with both v. 8 and v. 10. Lucas recognises that v. 9 shares the catchword 'delivered' with v. 8, but thematically the verse goes with what follows, forming a loose cluster on the theme of the relationship of the individual with the community, especially through the use of words. Heim notes the change in subject to speech in these verses but links them in a single cluster with vv. 2-8, arguing that there is a common theme of 'deception', though the justification for this is not clear. Waltke argues that vv. 14-15 form a proverb pair because both 'juxtapose imprudent action which brings disaster with prudent action that gives security'. However, he does class v. 15 as a janus proverb which has links with what follows.

11:15-21. Lucas and Heim note a change in vocabulary with v. 15. Gone is the use of vocabulary in the semantic field of speech. The prominent theme in these verses is the consequences of certain characters or actions.

11:22. Lucas and Heim see this as a stand-alone proverb. Waltke sees it as forming an *inclusio* with v. 16a, which also mentions a woman. However, this is a rather weak linkage.

11:23-27. Lucas and Waltke see here a cluster of proverbs about generosity (vv. 24-26) framed by two proverbs about people's desires, each of which uses the word 'good'. Heim recognises this frame but nevertheless links v. 27 with what follows on the grounds that it opens a cluster which draws conclusions from the observations made in vv. 23-26.

11:28-31. Lucas sees this as a collection of miscellaneous proverbs. Heim argues that these verses contain the theme that altruism is in one's own interest and Waltke sees in them the theme of 'gain and loss'.

From this analysis it can be seen that Heim and Waltke tend to see larger units than I do, but then break them down into subunits which correspond quite closely with the clusters which I identify. There is some encouragement in this degree of agreement to think that the smaller clusters are not just subjective creations by the commentator.

Fox[30] has critiqued Heim's work. He finds it unconvincing for a number of reasons.

1. Heim assumes what is to be proven, that clusters do exist, and this leads to a biased approach. This a fair point, but it is equally biased to assume that there are not any clusters. I have tried to approach the issue without the

30. Fox, 'Like Grapes of Gold Set in Silver'.

expectation that clusters must exist, but with an openness to see whether there are some.

2. Proverbs 10:1–22:16 covers a limited number of subjects. Given the terseness of the language, the multivalence of words and the referential ambiguity of many proverbs, it is not hard to find what may be purely unintended correspondences between proverbs. Heim himself is aware of this danger[31] and seeks to guard against it by looking for 'linkages' of sufficient strength to avoid it. This leads to Fox's next criticism.
3. Heim's approach of looking for literary markers rather than relying primarily on thematic connections, as other commentators have often done, may seem 'objective'. However, the choice of which repetitions and other patterns are important is to some degree subjective, and at times Fox regards Heim's choices as 'idiosyncratic'. I agree with Fox that in some cases Heim seems to be straining to find connections rather than accept that a cluster may not exist. However, this applies to only a minority of cases. One must accept that there is indeed a measure of subjectivity in the choice of criteria for linkages and the application of them. In the natural sciences there is recognition of the importance of 'inter-subjective verification' as a way of ameliorating this. As commented above, the measure of agreement between Heim, Waltke and myself in identifying clusters, using somewhat different approaches, is encouraging for this reason.
4. Heim's approach is too esoteric. It requires a 'skilled and equipped analyst' with plenty of time to devote to the task to uncover the patterns which Heim finds. It is unlikely that the compilers of the collections in Proverbs would put such patterns there and expect the readers to find them. In response it can be said that the compilers were themselves scholars and, according to the prologue in Prov. 1:2-7, intended to address a readership ranging from fellow scholars ('the wise') to the 'simple' reader referred to in the book. They might have put in patterns that only 'the wise' would be able to perceive. This would give the book different levels of meaning for readers of different reading competency. There is, however, a danger of being too esoteric in approach and this is why I have put more emphasis than Heim on the more obvious criterion of looking for thematic or logical connections of meaning while recognising that there might also be other, less obvious, patterns marking out clusters.
5. Although most commentators have recognised the existence of some thematic groups in proverbs above the level of proverb-pairs, few have found

31. Heim, *Like Grapes of Gold Set in Silver*, 55-57.

the preponderance of clusters that Heim does. In his survey of scholars who have denied the existence of coherent clusters Heim points out the existence of various biases which might lead to scholars not recognising such clusters. In any case the history of biblical studies provides examples of the appearance of new ways of reading texts that bring to light things which previous scholars have not noticed. A relevant example is the rise of 'redaction criticism' which has thrown new light on various biblical books, beginning with the NT Synoptic Gospels.

6. Heim's stated goal is to find a way of reading Proverbs that is relevant for a practicing pastor and preacher. Fox finds this 'of doubtful appropriateness to scholarly analysis.' This does not seem a fair criticism. Whatever Heim's goal, the value of it to scholars must be judged by the outcome, not the motivation. Most pastors and preachers probably find redaction criticism a more 'preacher-friendly' way to read the Gospels than some of the other historical-critical approaches, but that does not make it inappropriate as a means of scholarly analysis of the Gospels.

While rejecting what he calls Heim's 'totalising' approach Fox accepts that there is some clustering of proverbs. He thinks that this is the result of 'associative thinking' by the editors of the book. As he explains it,[32] 'When one thought gives rise to another or one word evokes a related one, the result is an associative sequence.' The result is a (small) group of proverbs on the same theme and/or with similar wording. He seems to regard this as a largely unintentional process. This may explain some, probably looser, clusters. However, there is no reason why there should not also be some clusters that are the result of intentional activity by the compilers. It is arguable that good teachers would seek to produce such clusters.

Clusters and Hermeneutics

Where structures exist it is important to consider whether they are more than simply literary constructs. They could be hermeneutically significant. Maybe the sentence proverbs in them should not be interpreted atomistically but in the context of the other sentences that make up the structure. Some scholars reject such an approach. Thus McKane[33] asserts that the wisdom sentence is a complete entity and goes on to say,

32. Fox, *Proverbs 10–31*, 480.
33. McKane, *Proverbs*, 10.

> I am aware that there are editorial principles of different kinds according to which sentences are grouped. I shall call attention to some of these, while maintaining that they are of secondary character and do not contradict the statement that there is, for the most part, no context for the sentence literature.

Commenting on this statement Schwáb[34] asks why the reader should ignore or downplay the 'secondary' or editorial activity of the compiler of Proverbs when interpreting it. He goes on to say, 'After all if someone finds in a book a sentence which was previously used in a different context, he/she would still like to understand that sentence in the book which is in his/her hand.' Again, one can draw attention to the fruitfulness of redaction criticism in the study of other biblical books.

Longman[35] argues against such an approach. He suggests that the randomness of the collections in Proverbs is deliberate, reflecting the messiness of life. Proverbs is not intended to be a 'how-to' fix-it book. However, he admits that this is 'pure speculation as to the conscious strategy of the redactors of the book.' I agree with Heim and Waltke that there is evidence which points to a different conscious strategy being used. Because of his 'speculation' Longman thinks that when two or more proverbs do seem to form a group this has come about unintentionally by a kind of magnetic attraction and is not hermeneutically significant. He says, regarding proverb pairs, 'reading the proverb in context does not change our understanding of either proverb. It doesn't even enrich our understanding.' The readers of this commentary must judge whether or not that is the case when considering the interpretations it gives of proverbs within clusters. Finally, Longman says, 'for a proverb to come alive again, it needs to be spoken orally in the right context.' However, a speaker cannot decide what that right context for a proverb is without having some idea about its possible meaning(s), and this has to arise from reading it in a collection in Proverbs. It is not unreasonable to at least consider whether the compiler(s) have given some help with this by the context in which they have put a proverb. This commentary will explore that possibility.

Rhetorical Devices in Sentence Proverbs

In Hebrew the proverb is a form of poetry and shares the main characteristics of Hebrew poetry. These are: parallelism, terseness and use of figurative language.[36]

34. Schwáb, 'Sayings Clusters in Proverbs', 60.
35. Longman, *Proverbs*, 40-41.
36. Berlin, *Dynamics of Biblical Parallelism*, argues that parallelism and terseness are *the*

Parallelism is the most obvious feature of Hebrew poetry, especially in translation. The basic poetic unit is a sentence (or *bicolon;* plural, *bicola*) consisting of two halves (or *cola*) which can be related to one another in various ways and on a number of levels. The level at which parallelism is most easily appreciated in translation is that of *semantics,* the meaning of the two cola. This has been discussed in the previous section.

Parallelism can occur at the level of sentence structure, or *syntax.* A number of changes can be used to produce parallelism between the cola that make up a sentence:

- A noun clause may replace a verb clause:

  The people curse [verb clause] him who holds back grain,
  but a blessing [noun clause] is on the head of him who sells it. (11:26)

- A statement in one colon may be followed by a question in the next:

  Wrath is cruel, anger is overwhelming,
  but who can stand before jealousy? (27:4)

- The form of the verb may change. A passive verb may be followed by an active one:

  The righteous is delivered [passive] from trouble,
  and the wicked walks [active] into it instead. (11:8)

Parallelism can work in a number of ways at the level of words, the *lexical* level. A major aspect of this is the use of common 'word pairs', such as wise/fool, righteous/wicked, poor/rich, father/mother:

> The tongue of the wise commends knowledge,
> but the mouths of fools pour out folly. (15:2)
>
> A rich man's wealth is his strong city;
> the poverty of the poor is their ruin. (10:15)

These two examples show another form of variation at the lexical level, the use of a singular noun in one colon (wise, rich) and a plural noun in the other (fools, poor). The variation of singular and plural in the Hebrew cannot always be made apparent in English translation:

---

marks of Hebrew poetry. Others give longer lists, for example: Gillingham, *Poems and Psalms of the Hebrew Bible;* Watson, *Classical Hebrew Poetry.*

The wicked [sing.] flee [pl.] when no one pursues,
but the righteous [pl.] are bold [sing] as a lion. (28:1)

A form of parallelism that cannot be preserved in translation is *phonological,* or sound, parallelism. This may involve the repetition of syllables, consonants and/or vowel sounds:

lō' ye' ᵉhab ***lēṣ*** *hôkēaḥ* ***lô***
'el ***ḥᵃkāmîm*** ***lō'*** *yēlēk* (15:12)

A scoffer does not like to be reproved;
he will not go to the wise.

Terseness is achieved in Hebrew poetry in two main ways. One, which is not usually apparent in translation, is by the omission of various Hebrew particles that are common in prose, such as the definite object marker, the prefix that indicates the definite object, and the relative pronoun. The other way of achieving terseness is 'gapping', the omission of words. O'Connor[37] claims that 'gapping' is a major feature of Hebrew poetry and does not occur in prose. A common form of 'gapping' is when the second colon omits the verb used in the first.

A gift in secret averts anger,
and a concealed bribe, strong wrath. (21:14)

When justice is done, it is a joy to the righteous,
but terror to evildoers. (21:15)

In the second example a whole clause is 'gapped'.

Figurative language occurs in prose but it is used much more often, and in greater concentration, in poetry. Hebrew poetry makes use of a wide range of figurative language. Figurative comparisons are particularly common in proverbs. They are a form of 'terseness' since they can enable a brief saying to convey a lot of meaning at several levels. The comparisons may be either explicit (*simile,* using the comparative terms 'like/as') or implicit *(metaphor).* In both cases the things compared are unlike in nature yet have something in common. The distinction between the two forms of comparison is not always kept in English translation. The first example below is a metaphor in Hebrew

37. O'Connor, *Hebrew Verse Structure,* 122-29 and 401-404.

since it does not have the word 'like', whereas the others do, and so are similes. The second example, unusually, spells out the point of comparison.

> [Like] a gold ring or an ornament of gold
> is a wise reprover to a listening ear. (25:12)
>
> Like the cold of snow in the time of harvest
> is a faithful messenger to those who send him;
> he refreshes the soul of his masters. (25:13)
>
> Like snow in summer or rain in harvest,
> so honor is not fitting for a fool. (26:1)

Satire, the use of humour to express ridicule, is used to good effect in some of the proverbs about the 'negative characters' that appear in the book:

> As a door turns on its hinges,
> so does a sluggard in his bed. (26:14)

Paradox is also used to good effect, to make the reader stop and ponder a proverb:

> With patience a ruler may be persuaded,
> and a soft tongue will break a bone. (25:15)

How can something soft break something hard?

Disjointed Proverbs

Fox[38] has drawn attention to 'disjointed proverbs' in which there appears to be a misfit between the two cola because of what he calls a *rhetorical gap,* which is different from the grammatical gap to which the term 'gapping' is normally applied. In these proverbs either the premise or conclusion has been elided in one colon, or sometimes in both. By 'premise' he means 'a principle or a fact on which a conclusion is based'. By 'conclusion' he means 'the consequence of a behaviour defined in the premise or a rule drawn from it'. He discusses the following examples, among others:

38. Fox, 'Rhetoric of Disjointed Proverbs'.

A desire fulfilled is sweet to the soul,
but to turn away from evil is an abomination to fools. (13:19)

At first reading the two cola seem unrelated. Their relationship becomes clear if one supplies the premise 'fools desire evil' for the second colon. It then becomes plain that the first colon is the reason why fools resist turning away from evil — they want to enjoy the sweetness of a desire fulfilled.

A fool despises his father's instruction,
but whoever heeds reproof is prudent. (15:5)

The first colon describes a bad behaviour, but not its consequence. The consequence is implied by the second colon, it is the converse of the claim made in it. So, the fool who despises his father's instruction will be imprudent.

The righteous hates falsehood,
but the wicked man brings shame and disgrace. (13:5)

The mismatch here is that the first colon speaks of an emotion and the second of a consequence. This awkwardness can be resolved by reversing what is said of the righteous to supply a premise for the second colon, and by reversing the consequence in the second colon to supply a conclusion for the first:

The righteous hates falsehood *and brings honor,*
but the wicked *loves falsehood* and brings shame and disgrace.

Fox suggests that these 'disjointed' proverbs may be riddles, which the prologue of Proverbs (1:6) says studying the book will help readers to understand. If read and carefully thought through, the 'disjointed' proverbs not only convey truth, they train the reader in a mode of thinking. They encourage the identifying of behaviour patterns and the association of them with their consequences. They are a way of training the reader to think like 'the wise'.

Using Sentence Proverbs

The sentence proverbs are grounded in experience. They seem to arise from careful observation of life and the world. They are expressed in a brief, easy-to-remember form. Therefore the typical biblical Hebrew proverb can be defined as *'a reflection on life crystallised in a brief, memorable sentence'*.

It is important to recognise some limitations of the proverb as a means of communication and teaching, if it is not to be misused. A proverb arises out of a specific observation or experience and gains its meaning from that context. It is not a universally applicable truth. The reader has to intuit the appropriate context for a proverb. Maybe to remind readers of this the compilers of Proverbs occasionally put two 'opposing' proverbs together, for example Prov. 26:4-5:

> Do not answer a fool according to his folly,
> lest you too become like him. (26:4)
>
> Answer a fool according to his folly,
> lest he be wise in his own eyes. (26:5)

Proverbs have to be used wisely if they are to be of value (see on Prov. 26:1-12).

Many biblical proverbs are simply observations of 'the way it is' and do not contain any explicit evaluation. The statement of a reality need not mean approval of it. It is important to compare proverb with proverb to get a 'rounded' view of what the wisdom teachers were saying.

In expressing 'the way things are' proverbs are observations, not laws. They are *describing the norm,* not *prescribing what must always happen* or *expressing the inevitable.* Life and humans are too complex for a brief sentence to sum up all the truth about a given situation. Those who are wise will use proverbs with due discretion.

Numerical Sayings

Numerical sayings are not found in the extant wisdom literature from Mesopotamia and Egypt,[39] though Roth[40] gives examples of the numerical sequence x/x+1 in parallel lines in Sumerian poetry and Akkadian incantations. There is one numerical saying in *Ahiqar.*[41]

> There are two things which are good,
> and a third which is pleasing to Shamash:
> one who drinks wine and shares it,

39. Murphy, *Wisdom Literature,* 11-12.

40. Roth, 'Numerical Sequence x/x+1 in the Old Testament'. The examples are given on 304-305.

41. Lindenberger, 'Ahiqar', 499.

one who masters wisdom [*and observes it*],
and one who hears a word but tells it not.

Because of its Assyrian setting, it has been widely assumed that the extant Aramaic version of the story of Ahiqar rests on an Akkadian original. In recent years, however, there has been a growing view that the Aramaic text is not a translation, but the original language. The case for an Aramaic original is particularly strong for the collection of sayings. They contain some Aramaic word-plays and few, if any, Akkadian loan words. Some also show a knowledge of West Semitic literary conventions.[42] This leads Lindenberger to conclude that the proverbs in *Ahiqar* originated in northern Syria.[43] There is an example of a numerical saying in the Ugaritic Baal epic.[44]

Two sacrifices Baal abhors,
three the charioteer of the Clouds:
a sacrifice of shame,
and a sacrifice of whoredom,
and a sacrifice of the debauching of handmaidens.

There are also examples of the numerical sequence x/x+1 in parallel lines in Ugaritic poetry.[45] This has led to the suggestion that biblical numerical sayings may be a reflection of Canaanite influence.[46]

Roth[47] has done a detailed study of numerical sayings in the OT. The numerical saying has two constituents: the title line and the list. The title line describes or alludes to the feature or features which the items of the list have in common. There is no rigid form. The number may be anything, but 2, 3 and 7 are particularly common. Some poetical number sayings have the number in the title line in the form x/x+1. Roth calls these 'graded numerical sayings'. They are in the majority in the Book of Proverbs.

Numerical sayings are a form of list. Their distinctive feature is the use of a number in the title line. In reflective sayings the number is used as a device through which a discovered structural order in different phenomena in nature,

42. Lindenberger, 'Ahiqar', 481.

43. Lindenberger, 'Ahiqar', 482.

44. Wyatt, *Religious Texts from Ugarit*, 96.

45. Roth, 'Numerical Sequence x/x+1 in the Old Testament'. The examples are given on 305-306.

46. Nel, 'Genres of Biblical Wisdom Literature', esp. 135, n. 30.

47. Roth, *Numerical Sayings in the Old Testament.*

life, society, and so on, is defined. In hortatory sayings the number serves to fix a given number of requirements in the mind.

The following numerical sayings occur in the Book of Proverbs.

6:16-19	A hortatory graded numerical saying.
30:11-14	Roth suggests that this is a reflection on society that has lost its numerical title line
30:15b-16	A graded numerical saying reflecting on natural phenomena grouped on the basis of insatiability.
30:18-19.	A graded numerical saying reflecting on phenomena in nature that are 'too wonderful' to be understood.
30:21-23	A graded numerical saying reflecting on the order in society.
30:24-28	A graded numerical saying reflecting on four small but wise creatures.
30:29-31	A graded numerical saying reflecting on stately creatures.

Ancient Near Eastern Wisdom Literature

As archaeological discoveries increased our knowledge of the world within which the ancient Hebrews lived, it became clear that Hebrew wisdom literature was a specific example of a much wider, international phenomenon.

Egyptian Wisdom

The Instruction of Hardjedef is thought to be the oldest extant Egyptian instruction, dating from about 2450-2300 BC in the Old Kingdom Period.[48] Hardjedef was the son of Cheops, builder of the Great Pyramid. The fragmentary text concerns setting up a household and funerary arrangements.

The Instruction of Kagemni dates from the same period. It is addressed to Kagemni, a courtier, by an unnamed sage and gives instruction in correct behaviour in the presence of the king.

The Instruction of Ptahhotep is the most important work from the Old Kingdom Period.[49] Ptahhotep is said to be vizier under King Izezi, and the work instructs his son, whom he is preparing to follow him in that office. It has

48. *AEL* 1:58-59.
49. *AEL* 1:61-80.

a prologue, thirty-seven maxims of varying length and an epilogue. It presents the ideal of a quiet, contented humble person, who is contrasted with the hot-tempered, anxious, striving person.

The Instruction for King Merikari comes from the unsettled period between the Old and Middle Kingdoms, dating from about 2100 BC.[50] Merikari's father counsels his son to be patient, to respect people and their property, to protect the powerless, to reject covetousness and favouritism, and to revere the gods and be punctilious in religious observances.

The Instruction of Amenemhet[51] is presented as advice given by Pharaoh Amenemhet I to his son, who succeeded him after he had been assassinated following a palace coup ca. 1960 BC. It therefore appears to come from beyond the grave. Its main, pessimistic, message is not to trust anyone. The date of composition is unclear, but it was in existence prior to 1100 BC.

In *The Instruction of Ani*[52] (ca. 1580-1305 BC), Ani, a scribe in the court of Queen Nefertari, wife of Pharaoh Ahmose, provides advice for his son on family life, avoiding strange women, religious observance, dealing honestly with people, remaining calm and composed. A remarkable epilogue contains a debate between Ani and his son Khonsuhotep about the methods and limits of education.

The Instruction of Amenemope[53] (1250-1100 BC)[54] has attracted particular interest because of similarities with part of the Book of Proverbs (see 'Proverbs 22:17–24:22 and *The Instruction of Amenemope*' below). Its author came from the lower ranks of agricultural officials. The introduction sets out the purpose of the work: to provide training in how to be successful in the royal civil service. Its thirty chapters emphasise the value of a life of moderation and balance in which there is discernment of, and accommodation to, the divine purpose. It develops the contrast between the 'silent man' and the 'heated man', which is implicit in some earlier instructions.

The Instruction of Onchsheshonqy (Ankhsheshonqy)[55] purports to have been written in prison by a priest who was imprisoned because he was implicated in a palace revolt. It is an anthology of some 550 sayings of various kinds, loosely grouped more by format and tone than subject, and expresses strong religious sentiments. It presupposes a rural background rather than the royal court.

50. *COS* 1:61-66; *AEL* 1:97-109.
51. *COS* 1:66-68; *AEL* 1:135-39.
52. *COS* 1:110-115; *AEL* 2:135-46.
53. *COS* 1:115-122; *AEL* 2:146-63.
54. Ray, 'Egyptian Wisdom Literature', 23.
55. *AEL* 3:159-84.

Mesopotamian Wisdom

The Instructions of Shuruppak is the oldest and most widely known Mesopotamian instruction. It is of Sumerian origin. The 'standard version' dates from 1900-1800 BC, but it is known from a version dated to about 2,500 BC.[56] It is named after the father of Ziusudra, the Sumerian equivalent of Noah, who gives his son rules of conduct and wise counsel to enable him to deal effectively with the problems and temptations of life.

Alster has published twenty-eight collections of Sumerian proverbs. Although most are known from texts that date to the Old Babylonian period (1700-1600 BC), he argues that some of the collections come from 2600-2550 BC. He summarises[57] the major topics they cover as, 'a woman's daily routine, family relationships, the good man, the liar, legal proceedings, Fate, the palace, the temples and their gods, as well as historical and ethnic allusions'.

Counsels of Wisdom is a Babylonian collection written in Akkadian and dating from the Kassite period (1500-1200 BC).[58] The beginning is lost but at least part of it is addressed to 'my son'. It contains advice on being guarded in speech, avoiding disputes, treating the poor considerately, avoiding women other than your wife, and acting with piety because it is both proper and beneficial.

Aramaic Wisdom

The story of *Ahiqar* was known from the apocryphal book of Tobit, and in Syriac, Armenian and Arabic versions before an Aramaic version was found at Elephantine in Egypt in the early twentieth century in a papyrus which dates from the fifth century BC. The Aramaic text is fragmentary. It contains about a hundred sayings attached to a narrative about Ahiqar.[59] The narrative tells the story of the disgrace and restoration of Ahiqar, an official in the court of the Assyrian king Sennacherib (704-681 BC) and his son Esarhaddon (680-669 BC). It may have been composed in the seventh century BC. The collection of sayings, some of which may be older than the story, was attached to the story at some later date. Proverbs 23:13-14 is very similar to a saying[60] in *Ahiqar*.

56. *COS* 1:569-70.

57. Alster, *Proverbs of Ancient Sumer. COS* 1:563-567.

58. Lambert, *BWL*, 96-107. A more recent translation can be found in: Foster, *Before the Muses*, 412-15.

59. Lindenberger, *Aramaic Proverbs of Ahiqar;* 'Ahiqar' 479-507.

60. *Ahiqar* lines 81-82, *OTP* 2:498.

The Book of Proverbs

Clifford[61] helpfully summarises the main distinctives of the Book of Proverbs, apart from its theology, as compared to other ancient Near Eastern wisdom literature. Whereas the Egyptian instructions are addressed to a specific person, usually a courtier, the instructions in Prov. 1–9 are intended for a more general audience (Prov. 1:4-5). Compared to both the Egyptian and Mesopotamian instructions those in Proverbs are less specific. They urge readers to seek wisdom rather than to do specific actions. As Clifford puts it, 'Proverbs emphasizes character rather than acts.' In addition, the personification of Wisdom and Folly in these chapters and the vivid descriptions of her other opposites, deceptive men and the 'strange woman', create 'a metaphorical level of discourse that was unknown in earlier wisdom literature'.

The concise saying, or sentence proverb, has taken on a distinctive nature in the Book of Proverbs. The literary forms used are much less diverse than in the Mesopotamian and Aramaic collections. Also, nearly all the sayings in Prov. 10–31 are in the bicolon form, a sentence with two related halves.

Proverbs 22:17–24:22 and The Instruction of Amenemope

In 1923 Budge[62] published the Egyptian 'wisdom' text which came to be known as *The Instruction of Amenemope.*[63] There was immediate recognition that it had a close relationship to a section of the Book of Proverbs: 22:17–24:22. The nature of the relationship has been a matter of some debate ever since.

A wide range of possibilities have been proposed.[64]

1. The author of Prov. 22:17ff. knew *Amenemope* and adapted it to suit his own purpose.
2. The author of *Amenemope* knew Prov. 22:17ff. and made use of it.
3. Both works are based on a now lost Egyptian original.
4. Both works are based on a now lost Hebrew or Semitic original.
5. The two works are not directly connected, although they attest to a general affinity between Egyptian and Hebrew wisdom.

61. Clifford, *Proverbs,* 17-19.

62. Budge, *Facsimiles of Egyptian Hieratic Papyri,* plates I-XIV. The text is British Museum Papyrus 10474.

63. For a modern English translation see: *COS* 1:115-22.

64. Whybray, *Book of Proverbs,* 8.

Although the date of the British Museum papyrus, sixth century BC, made the second option possible, the later discovery of other fragmentary copies of the work made it clear that it existed in the twelfth century BC,[65] so ruling out this option. This early date of the Egyptian work also makes it unlikely that a common Semitic original lies behind it and Prov. 22:17ff. The argument for this had been based primarily on alleged Semitisms in the text and attempts to explain some difficulties in it by appeal to the author's poor translation of a Hebrew or Aramaic original. Williams[66] countered these claims and also pointed out some cases of paronomasia in *Amenemope* which could not have arisen if it were a translation rather than an original Egyptian work. Appeal to a lost common Egyptian original remains pure speculation, so the debate has settled around the first and last options in the list.

Over the decades a wide, though by no means complete, agreement developed among both Egyptologists and biblical scholars that the author of Prov. 22:17ff. knew and made use of *Amenemope*. However, Whybray[67] strongly challenged this view. He deployed several lines of argument.

Proverbs 22:20

He points out that a good deal has been made of the proposed emendation of this verse so that it refers to 'thirty sayings', corresponding to the thirty chapters of *Amenemope*. There is a Q/K variant in this verse. The Q is שָׁלִישִׁים *(šālîšîm)*, which is a term denoting a military rank and, in Whybray's view, clearly inappropriate in context. The K שלשום *(šlšwm)* is usually vocalised as שִׁלְשׁוֹם *(šilšôm)*. This occurs elsewhere only in the idiomatic phrase תְּמֹל שִׁלְשׁוֹם *(tĕmōl šilšôm)*, meaning 'yesterday (and) the day before', but having the sense of 'in the past, formerly'. Whybray thinks that this makes good sense here. He assumes that the single word can stand for the full phrase, and appeals further to the presence of the temporal phrase 'today' in the preceding verse. As a result he sees no need for the widely accepted emendation to *šĕlōšîm* ('thirty'), pointing out that one would expect it to be followed by the word 'words'. He therefore sees no influence from *Amenemope* in this verse.

65. Ray, 'Egyptian Wisdom Literature', 17-29.

66. Williams, 'Alleged Semitic Original', 100-106.

67. Whybray, *Book of Proverbs*, 132-47; Whybray, 'Structure and Composition of Proverbs 22:17–24:22'.

The Number of Units in Prov. 22:17–24:22

Although some scholars have claimed to find thirty sayings in this section, in Whybray's opinion their assessment is mistaken. He claims that they have counted as separate sayings verses that are really the introductions to admonitions (23:12, 19, 22-26; 24:3-4, 13-14). In his view there are not thirty separate units in this section of Proverbs.

The structure of Prov. 22:17–24:22

Whybray agrees with Niccacci[68] that 22:17–23:11 forms a single literary section containing ten admonitions. In Whybray's view the sayings in 23:12–24:22 have not been organised into a single literary unit. They contain diverse material and have been added to 22:17–23:11 piecemeal as unconnected appendices. This, he thinks, militates against the suggestion that the whole section is in some way modelled on *Amenemope*.

The thematic parallels with *Amenemope* are confined to 22:17–23:11. Throughout 22:17–24:22 there are thematic, and even verbal, affinities with the instructions in Prov. 1–9.

Some Egyptologists have expressed doubts about the closeness of the connection between the two texts.

Emerton[69] has made a detailed critique of Whybray's arguments.

Proverbs 22:20

Whybray's interpretation faces problems. The first is his assumption that the word *šilšôm* can mean 'formerly' on its own. There is no evidence for this.[70] Second, there is the fact that none of the versions reads the word before them as meaning this. Finally, it creates the difficulty that the sage is then referring to an earlier private document not available to the readers of the wisdom book. There is no other example of this in the extant wisdom literature. The LXX, Vulg, Syr and Targ all have words meaning 'three times' here, suggesting that they read the Hebrew as the word *šělīšîm,* which occurs in Gen. 6:16; Num.

68. Niccacci, 'Proverbi 22.17–23.11'.

69. Emerton, 'Amenemope and Proverbs XXII 17–XXIV 22'.

70. This is true for Hebrew. In a personal communication (8/8/05) K. A. Kitchen pointed out examples where it does stand on its own in Akkadian. See the examples in *CAD* 17:262b, 268b-69a.

2:24; 1 Sam. 19:21; and 2 Kgs. 1:13 as the masculine plural of the ordinal number 'third'. This implies that the consonantal text before them was that of the Q, *šlyšym* or possibly *šlšym,* as in Gen. 6:16 and so on. The shorter reading could explain the K since in some forms of the Hebrew script *yodh* and *waw* are easily confused. Thus a plausible case can be made for *šĕlōšîm* on text-critical grounds. Whybray's objection, that it ought to have been followed by the word 'words', is not a strong one. In Hebrew, specifications of measure, weight or time are commonly omitted after numerals.[71] The same is true of the word 'things/items' in 2 Sam. 24:12 and, more pertinently, in Prov. 30:7, 15, 18, 21, 29. Whybray's comment that the Q does not make sense in context is valid, but the emendation to 'thirty (things/items)', requiring only a small and understandable consonantal change in the text, makes more sense than the K that he defends.

The Number of Units in Proverbs 22:17–24:22

Emerton examines the analyses presented by several scholars who do find thirty units in this section of Proverbs. Like Niccacci and Whybray they all find ten units in 22:22–23:11. There is also general agreement, including by Whybray, that 24:13-22 contains five units. With regard to 23:12–24:12 Emerton concludes that the most probable analyses of this section lead to dividing it into fourteen or fifteen units, giving a total of twenty-nine or thirty in the section as a whole. Hence there is no basis for Whybray's confident assertion that there are not thirty units here.

The Structure of Proverbs 22:17–24:22 and the Thematic Parallels with Amenemope

Whybray's case with regard to these two issues rests on the assumption that the author of this section of Proverbs intended to produce a work closely modelled on the Egyptian text. However, most of the scholars who have argued for the influence of *Amenemope* on this section of Proverbs have not argued for that. They have argued that the author was seeking to produce his own 'wisdom book' in Hebrew under the influence of the Egyptian text, but drawing on other sources also. In the choice and ordering of the material he had his own aims in mind. Neither the concentration of material parallel to *Amenemope* in 22:17–24:11 nor the diversity of material in the rest of the section militates against this view.

71. GKC §134; Joüon Part 3, §142 n.

The Views of Egyptologists

Whybray refers to a few Egyptologists who have expressed doubts about a direct relationship between this section of Proverbs and *Amenemope*. However, the only detailed discussion he refers to is that by Ruffle.[72] Emerton examines Ruffle's arguments against dependence and finds them unconvincing. A major reason for this is that Ruffle works with the assumption that 'dependence' means that the Hebrew text ought to be a fairly literal translation of the Egyptian. This is not what has been generally advocated.

Conclusion

The kind of theory originally advance by Gressmann,[73] and subsequently taken up and developed by other scholars, that Prov. 22:17–24:22 is a work influenced by *Amenemope,* but which treats the Egyptian work freely, omitting much that is in it and adding material from elsewhere, is still plausible. Recently Fox[74] has suggested how the 'author-editor' of Prov. 22:17–23:11 'worked by scrolling forward and back in the source papyrus, each time picking up material of interest to him and reshaping it in accordance with his goals.'

An Analysis of Proverbs 22:17–24:22

As noted above, there is general agreement about the ten sayings in 22:22–23:11 and the five in 24:13-22. There is considerable agreement in recognising introductions to instructions in 23:12, 19, 26, and somewhat less so regarding 23:15 (see the list on p. 37).

Units 1-10 are marked out by the recurring use of 'Do not', often at the beginning of the saying. The same is true of units 27-29. The use of 'My son' marks out the beginning of units 13, 14, 16, 26, 30. New units are clearly introduced in 23:12 (unit 11) and 23:22 (unit 15). The identification of units 11-16 and 26-30 is reasonably clear. The identification of units 17-25 is more debatable.

The theme of 23:29-35 is drunkenness, and it could be regarded as one unit for this reason. There is a clear link between vv. 29 and 30, since v. 30 answers the questions asked in v. 29. Although it is arguable that the 'Do not' of v. 31

72. Ruffle, 'Teaching of Amenemope'.

73. Gressmann, 'Neugefundene Lehre des Amen-em-ope'.

74. Fox, ''From Amenemope to Proverbs', 91.

Introduction: 22:17-21	16. 23:26-28
1. 22:22-23	17. 23:29-35
2. 22:24-25	18. 24:1-2
3. 22:26-27	19. 24:3-4
4. 22:28	20. 24:5-6
5. 22:29	21. 24:7
6. 23:1-3	22. 24:8
7. 23:4-5	23. 24:9
8. 23:6-8	24. 24:10
9. 23:9	25. 24:11-12
10. 23:10-11	26. 24:13-14
11. 23:12	27. 24:15-16
12. 23:13-14	28. 24:17-18
13. 23:15-18	29. 24:19-20
14. 23:19-21	30. 24:21-22
15. 23:22-25	

introduces a new unit, it follows on very well from vv. 29-30, and it is plausible to see one unit here (unit 17): an instruction consisting of an introduction (a riddle with its answer) followed by an admonition and motive.

There is general agreement that 24:1-2 is a single unit (unit 18). There is disagreement about 24:3-7, which has the general theme of wisdom. However, vv. 3-4 and v. 7 speak of 'wisdom' itself whereas vv. 5-6 speaks of the wise person. This suggest that here there are three separate units (units 19-21).

The next two verses have the common theme of planning evil. They can be taken either as a single unit or as two separate sayings linked by the catch words 'schemer/schemes'. Since each sentence could stand on its own as a proverb the latter view is plausible (units 22-23).

It would be possible to divide the next three verses into either one, two or three sayings. The imperative that opens v. 11 could be the beginning of an instruction, and v. 12 seems to be dependent on it since the 'If . . .' at its beginning makes most sense if it refers back to the previous verse. Because v. 10 makes sense as a complete saying on its own, it is reasonable to see two units here (units 24-25), which are loosely connected by the possibility that v. 11 refers to one example of the 'times of trouble' mentioned in v. 10.

Waltke[75] argues that 22:17-21 should be counted as the first saying. The basis of his argument is that in *Amenemope* the introduction, which has mate-

75. Waltke, *Proverbs 1–15*, 22-24.

rial comparable to Prov. 22:17-21, is counted as the first chapter. He then takes 24:10-12 as a single saying. We have argued above that it is better to take this as two sayings and that this section of Proverbs is only loosely modelled on *Amenemope.*

The Origin of Proverbs

For much of the twentieth-century it was generally maintained that the book of Proverbs, and much of its content, originated among scribal circles associated with the royal court in Jerusalem. The references to Solomon in Prov 1:1 and 10:1 and to the activity of Hezekiah's men collecting Solomonic proverbs in 25:1 seemed to point in this direction. The discovery of links with *Amenemope* gave weight to this view because of the perceived connection between Egyptian instructions and the Egyptian court. By analogy with the situation in Egypt and Mesopotamia it was assumed that there were 'wisdom schools' in Israel and Judah for training scribes and maybe other courtiers, particularly in connection with the court and temple in Jerusalem. Collections of proverbs, it was argued, would have been used for teaching in this context. Malchow's[76] argument that Prov. 27:23–29:27 is 'a manual for future monarchs' could be seen to support this.

However, as early as 1913 Eissfeldt[77] suggested that Proverbs includes some popular sayings that had originally been transmitted orally. He argued that the book contains some single-line proverbs which were 'folk proverbs' but were later expanded into two-line 'wisdom sayings'. There is some support for this in the presence of the narrative books of the OT of such single-line sayings (e.g. 1 Sam. 24:14; 1 Kgs 20:11). Scott[78] later came to much the same conclusions. Westermann[79] too argued that the much of the material in Prov. 10:1–22:16 and 25–29 has its roots in orally transmitted Israelite folk wisdom. He suggested that the level of cultural development in its tribal, premonarchic, period was comparable to that of other pre-literate, tribal cultures, especially African ones, whose proverbs have been collected, and so made available for study.

76. Malchow, 'Manual'.

77. Eissfeldt, *Maschal im Alten Testament.* See also his *Old Testament: An Introduction,* 12, 81-87.

78. Scott, 'Folk Proverbs of the Ancient Near East', reprinted in Crenshaw, *Studies in Ancient Israelite Wisdom,* 417-26; Scott, 'Study of the Wisdom Literature'.

79. Westermann, 'Weisheit in Sprichwort'.

African Proverbs

One of Westermann's students, Golka, carried out some comparative studies of biblical and African proverbs.[80] In one such study he compared the proverbs that refer to the powers and functions of rulers (kings and chiefs) in the Hebrew and African collections. He argued that the interests and sentiments expressed in these 'royal proverbs' indicated that they were not the product of the royal court or of royal scribes but of the common people who observed what went on in the court but did not participate in it. In a wider study he concluded that the African and Hebrew proverbs evidenced much the same concerns. He noted two differences between the two collections of proverbs. There was a lack of any religious element in the African proverbs, except where there was Islamic influence. On the other hand, African traditional proverbs played a part in the administration of justice. They may have been used to support an argument and influence legal decisions.

Naré[81] compared the oral proverbs of the Mossi of Upper Volta with Prov. 25–29. He found that, unlike the material studied by Golka, the religious element was not lacking. The religion of the Mossi is monotheistic, based on belief in a God who created the world and is benevolent and just.

Part of the case put forward by both Westermann and Golka is the argument that the origin of most of the proverbs in chs. 10–29 should be located among the 'simple people' in agrarian villages. Whybray[82] took a similar position. Fox[83] challenges this, arguing that while some of the proverbs may have originated in this setting, it is not the dominant background of the book. He points to proverbs that, he says, these scholars have overlooked, which have references to an urban setting and people of some wealth, such as goldsmithery (17:3; 27:21), fine jewellery (25:11-12), messengers (10:26; 22:21; 25:13), the disciplining of slaves (29:21) and those able to store and distribute considerable stocks of grain (11:26). Fox also disputes Golka's view that the 'royal proverbs' express the outlook of the common people. He argues that many proverbs that Golka regards as being deeply critical of the king do no more than recognise the power of the king, and the damage as well as the good that it can do. Moreover, he says, there is no reason why those close to kings shouldn't see them with critical eyes. Fox calls for a recognition of the diversity of sources and backgrounds of the proverbs.

80. Collected in Golka, *Leopard's Spots.*

81. Naré, *Proverbes salomoniens et proverbes mossi.*

82. Whybray, *Wealth and Poverty in the Book of Proverbs.*

83. Fox, 'Social Location'.

Loader[84] has critically reviewed Golka's work. He argues that Golka's study is biased by his ideological preference for locating the origin of the proverbs among the 'little people' rather than the elite in society. In addition he points out that both Golka and Westermann simply assume that schools did not exist in traditional African tribal cultures. He challenges this assumption, while pointing out that such schools might be quite different from the modern European conception of a school. Nonetheless they provide an institutional didactic setting in which proverbs would have a place. Perhaps most importantly, he challenges Golka's interpretation of many of the African and biblical 'royal proverbs'. He argues that Golka too readily concludes that they are critical of the king or court and that they could not come from those close to the king. In his view Golka has gone too far in the other direction in seeking to counter a one-sided association of the Hebrew proverbs with the royal court.

Golka[85] has responded to Loader's criticisms. The main point in his response is that in his interpretation of the African proverbs he usually relied on the explanation of their meaning given by those who collected them. Sometimes, he said, this explanation was 'surprising' to him, and he accepted that some of them, maybe 20 per cent, might be wrong. Nevertheless he stood by his overall conclusions.

This exchange highlights the need for more depth in comparative studies before reliable conclusions can be drawn. Loader is right to point to the need to investigate what cultural institutions and settings there might be in tribal cultures for the creation and transmission of proverbs. He also makes clear the problem facing biblical scholars of how to arrive at the meaning of a proverb from a different culture with any confidence when they have no expert knowledge of the languages and cultures concerned.

Kimilike's[86] work on proverbs about poverty from an African perspective is discussed in the essay 'Wealth and Poverty in Proverbs.'

Arabic Proverbs

Kassis[87] has made a detailed comparative study of Arabic and biblical proverbs. He classifies the Arabic proverbs as 'classical', 'post-classical' and 'current'. The classical period includes the pre-Islamic and early Islamic eras, before the

84. Loader, 'Wisdom by (the) People for (the) People'.
85. Golka, 'Wisdom by (the) People for (the) People: Einne Antwort'.
86. Kimilike, *Poverty in the Book of Proverbs.*
87. Kassis, *Book of Proverbs and Arabic Proverbial Works.*

expansion of Arabs into other countries and cultures. He admits that the distinction between classical and post-classical proverbs is sometimes not an easy one to make. By 'current' proverbs he means those collected by missionaries, orientalists and nationals since the beginning of the nineteenth century. These proverbs may be expressed in either colloquial or classical Arabic, and are not necessarily of recent origin.

Kassis shows that there is considerable similarity in both form and content between the Arabic and biblical proverbs in Prov. 10:1–22:16 and 25–29, as well as some notable differences. Perhaps one of the most interesting parts of his study it that concerning 'royal proverbs'. He shows that in Arabic this kind of proverb was often used for propagandist purposes, both to support the authority or policies of the Caliph and to foment opposition to them, even rebellion. The proverbs of the later kind, he argues, clearly had their origin among the religious leaders or the common people. However, not all proverbs critical of the Caliph or his court originated among opponents of the ruler. Some originated with rulers themselves, or in their court. A Caliph might produce a proverb that is critical of rulers to express his humility, or to show his compassion and identification with his subjects, perhaps by referring to their sufferings under other unjust rulers. Kassis concludes that his study shows a diversity of origins and functions of royal proverbs. Whether or not a saying is favourable towards, or critical of, the ruler or court is no sure guide to its origin. In his view it is wrong to regard all the royal proverbs as either the product of the court or of the common people.

This study shows the importance of comparing the biblical proverbs with those from more than one culture. Even if Golka's conclusion about royal proverbs in African tribal culture is accepted, Kassis' study shows that things can be different in another culture. This, of course, raises another important issue — which culture is the more appropriate 'model' on the basis of which to understand the biblical material. In favour of giving priority to the Arabic evidence is the closeness geographically, linguistically and culturally between the Arabs and the Hebrews. Part of this closeness is that the extant Arabic proverbs, like those in the Book of Proverbs, cover the transition from a tribally-based culture to a monarchical one.

The Compilation of the Book of Proverbs

Van Leeuwen[88] makes the point that it is important to make clear distinctions between:

88. Van Leeuwen, *Proverbs,* 21-22.

1. the original *sources* of proverbs and collections (whether oral or written);
2. the *persons, processes,* and *places* of literary collection;
3. the editorial *composition* of collections;
4. the final editing of the Book of Proverbs into the form in which we have it.

Sometimes the debate between those advocating a 'folk' origin of proverbs and those favouring a 'school' origin has been confused by the failure to recognise these distinctions.

The conclusion to be drawn from the debate so far seems to be the need to recognise a diversity of origins for the material in Proverbs. Most scholars seem to accept that some of the proverbs have a 'folk' origin. There is then the problem of how to discern these within the extant collection. Eissfeldt, Scott and Westermann all argued that the original folk proverbs were short, one-line sayings and that some of these can be identified in the Book of Proverbs. Williams[89] recognises the difficulty in doing this:

> Of course, it is not always easy to discern whether or not one has a folk saying which has been expanded with the addition of a literary line, or whether it is a really clever folk saying or perhaps a literary creation which the composer has sought to make 'folkish'.

One approach has been to identify two-line proverbs that have one line in common (e.g. 10:2/11:4; 10:6/10:11; 10:15/18:11). However, there is no guarantee that the common line was originally a folk proverb. It is conceivable that the variant proverbs are the result of a deliberate alteration of an original two-line proverb. Kassis[90] argues that there is evidence of the literary development of short sayings in the transmission of Arabic proverbs. He then suggests that finding similar sayings between Hebrew and Arabic proverbs might be a way of identifying original one-line sayings. However, he admits that there is a possible problem in that the similarity might be the result of literary influence one way or the other rather than a common folk saying. There seems to be good grounds for Murphy's comment[91] that, 'it is extremely difficult to make a case for certain sayings as having been popular proverbs before they were collected for the book of Proverbs'.

Whatever the initial origin of the proverbs in the Book of Proverbs, we

89. Williams, 'Power of Form'. The quote is on 49.
90. Kassis, *Book of Proverbs and Arabic Proverbial Works,* 249-64.
91. Murphy, *Wisdom Literature,* 4.

have seen that there is evidence that the book as we have it is a compilation of a number of pre-existing collections. Who was responsible for the collections and for the final compilation? The evidence for the existence of 'wisdom schools' in ancient Israel and Judah is inconclusive.[92] However, in any case, as Fox[93] comments, 'there is nothing in Proverbs to point to a school origin.' Rather, as is pointed out in the commentary on Prov. 1:8-9, the evidence in the book itself suggests the home as the place of instruction. Nor is there much evidence that this instruction was aimed primarily at future courtiers. Despite Malchow's argument, the fact is that, according to Humphreys,[94] there are only about 30 of the 538 sayings in Prov. 10–29 which seem addressed primarily to the courtier. If the home was the place where much of the material in Proverbs was collected and shaped, it was in a particular type of home. The literary quality of many of the sentence proverbs and of the more complex instruction form found particularly, but not solely, in Prov. 1–9, suggests the activity of professional teachers. In Sandoval's[95] view, 'It is difficult to imagine the production (and use) of such didactic collections of proverbs, and certainly an anthology of such collections (a book), in anything other than an elite intellectual environment.' He suggests that the book is the product of a scribal elite. Fox[96] comes to a similar conclusion, and, using the phraseology of Prov. 25:1, he says, 'we may designate the authors and redactors *the king's men*. This term is preferable to the usual *courtier*, which connotes wealth and nobility.' These 'king's men' need not have been particularly high ranking scribes, close to the inner court circles. Whybray[97] points out that many of the Egyptian instructions came from scribes of fairly low rank. The author of *Amenemope* was a scribe of middle, or even lower, social and professional rank. The 'job titles' invoked in it all belong to the middle or lower level of bureaucratic positions.[98] Within Israel these 'learned clerks', as Fox calls them, would have formed a distinct social class, separate from the politically and economically powerful, the urban artisans and the majority rural population. Because of the variety of administrative tasks that they would have fulfilled as a result of their literacy, they would have the opportunity to observe and learn from the behaviour and experience of other groups in Israelite society. As Fox[99] comments, this would account for 'the great diversity and even greater

92. See the brief survey in Lucas, *Psalms and Wisdom Literature*, 82-85.
93. Fox, 'Social Location', 231.
94. Humphreys, 'Motif of the Wise Courtier', 187.
95. Sandoval, *Wealth and Poverty*, 39.
96. Fox, 'Social Location', 236, his italics.
97. Whybray, *Book of Proverbs*, 20.
98. Washington, *Wealth and Poverty*, 50.
99. Fox, 'Social Location', 237.

unity in Proverbs. The diversity comes from the varied sources, the unity from the redactors' own creative activity.' These sages developed their own worldview they present in the material which they have selected to include in the Book of Proverbs. They present it in a way which is didactic and relatively unpolemical. Some scholars compare the rhetoric of Proverbs unfavourably with the fiery rhetoric of the prophets, but there is more than one way of seeking to shape society. In Proverbs the sages seek to do it by education.

Texts and Versions

Hebrew

In many places the MT of Proverbs is free of problems. However, in some places, especially in the 'sentence literature', there are numerous obscurities. These may be the result of the use of rare words — a feature of Hebrew poetry with its frequent use of parallelism. When the only context of a word is a single, brief proverb it is often not easy to determine the meaning. Scholars therefore sometimes resort to comparative philology to suggest meanings based on cognate words in other Semitic languages. This is always a somewhat hazardous approach. Another likely source of some obscurities is copying error.

Two mss from Qumran contain small portions of Proverbs.[100] 4Q102 (= 4QProv^{a}, late first century BC) contains parts of Prov. 1:27–2:1. 4Q103 (= 4QProv^{b}, mid-first century AD) contains fragments of Prov. 13–15. The Hebrew text of these mss is very close to that of the MT.

Greek

The LXX translation of Proverbs is generally dated to the second half of the second century BC, though Cook[101] dates it a bit earlier.

One obvious feature of the LXX of Proverbs is its ordering of the text. Besides some minor variations, there is a major difference in the sequence of the sections after 24:22. Following the Hebrew numbering, the sequence is: 30:1-14; 24:23-34; 30:15-33; 31:1-9; 25:1–29:27; 31:10-31 (with vv. 25-26 in reverse order). The MT order makes sense from a literary point of view. It keeps the sentence literature together in chs. 10-29 and puts a number of short sections of

100. Harrington, *Wisdom Texts from Qumran.*
101. Cook, 'Dating of Septuagint Proverbs'.

various forms and authorship together in chs. 30-31 as 'appendices'. It is hard to find a rationale for the LXX order. The different order in the MT and the LXX may indicate that these units originally circulated as independent collections.

The LXX of Proverbs contains about 130 couplets and thirty partial sentences not present in the MT.[102] On the other hand, it omits about twenty-five verses found in the MT.[103] Some of the extra material occurs in 'doublets'. Fritsch[104] counted about seventy-six of these. They seem to be the result of a more literal rendering of the Hebrew being added to correct a translation that was thought to be too free or inaccurate. Snell[105] suggests that some of the omissions are due to the translator omitting proverbs, or parts of proverbs, that are repeated in the MT.

Scholars differ in their assessment of just how 'free' the original LXX translation was. Gerleman[106] characterised it as 'numbered among the free, sometimes paraphrasing versions'. Cook[107] took a similar view, concluding that the LXX of Proverbs should be seen as an 'exegetical writing'.

Clifford[108] came to a different conclusion. While accepting that the LXX of Proverbs is a fairly free translation, in his view the primary intent of the translator was to render the Hebrew text as accurately as possible, with a 'word for word' translation often being attempted. Fox,[109] in a direct response to Cook, argues that although there are some elements of exegesis in the LXX, they are rarely tendentious. In his view, when its tendency to moralise is allowed for, and the obvious additions and expansions set aside, the LXX translation is a fairly faithful rendering of the original Hebrew. With regard to textual criticism, Fox is more ready than Cook,[110] who urges 'utmost caution', to turn to the LXX for evidence of underlying textual variants in the Hebrew.

Scholars differ over whether or not the LXX gives evidence of a different recension of the Hebrew text from the MT. McKane[111] argues that there is no evidence for this, and Cook[112] agrees. However, Tov[113] argues that the LXX of

102. Fox, *Proverbs 1–9*, 363.
103. Clifford, 'Observations on the Texts and Versions of Proverbs', 61.
104. Fritsch, 'Treatment of the Hexaplaric Signs in the Syro-Hexaplar of Proverbs'.
105. Snell, *Twice-Told Proverbs*, 23-33.
106. Gerleman, *Studies in the Septuagint III*, 12.
107. Cook, *Septuagint of Proverbs*, 12, 35.
108. Clifford, 'Observations on the Texts and Versions of Proverbs'.
109. Fox, *Proverbs 1–9*, 361.
110. Cook, *Septuagint of Proverbs*, 334.
111. McKane, *Proverbs*, 33-47.
112. Cook, *Septuagint of Proverbs*, 334.
113. Tov, 'Recensional Differences'.

Proverbs is based on a Hebrew recension that was parallel to, but different from, that behind the MT. Fox[114] agrees.

The conclusion to be drawn from this discussion is that, once non-textual reasons for different renderings have been taken into account, a small number of variants do remain that need to be considered seriously on a case-by-case basis as possible evidence of a different Hebrew text from that preserved in the MT.

Syriac

The Peshitta translation was made in the second century AD. It is a fairly literal translation of the Hebrew text, while also showing strong influence from the LXX. It omits most of the additional material in the LXX and follows the order of the Hebrew text.

The Syr can be evidence for a textual variant when it diverges from both the MT and the LXX or when it can be back-translated to give the same reading as the LXX, but treats it differently.

Aramaic

The Targ to Proverbs stands out from the other Targumim to the Hagiographa because of its total lack of haggadic and midrashic expansions. There is a general, though not universal, consensus that the Targ of Proverbs is directly dependent on the Syr text. When the Targ diverges from the Syr this can usually be explained by an attempt to render the Hebrew text more literally. The Hebrew text used was very similar to the MT. Numerous agreements between the Targ and the LXX are generally taken to be the result of the reliance of the Targ on the Syr. It is rarely taken as of value in text-criticism.

Those who accept that it makes use of the Syr have suggested dates for the Targ from the third to the eighth century AD.

Latin

Jerome translated a Hebrew text of Proverbs very close to the consonantal MT into Latin in 398 AD. This work was incorporated into the Vulg. He made use

114. Fox, *Proverbs 1–9*, 364.

of the LXX and also of the more literal translations into Greek of Aq, Theod and Sym. Although he also knew the Syr, he rarely followed it rather than the Greek versions. At times he seems to draw on traditional rabbinic or Christian exegesis to make sense of those proverbs with which the Greek translators struggled with only partial success.

Clifford[115] notes that 'Jerome had direct access to important textual witnesses (some no longer extant) and had the training and talent to use them properly.' Therefore, when the Vulg of Proverbs occasionally differs from the MT, or supports another version against the MT, it should be given serious consideration.

115. Clifford, 'Observations on the Texts and Versions of Proverbs,' 60.

Commentary

Proverbs 1

1:1-7 Preface

This is a clear structural unit. The title (v. 1) is linked syntactically with vv. 2-6 by a series of purpose clauses containing verbs in the infinitive construct (v. 5 breaks this pattern). The 'motto' (v. 7) which forms the climax of the section is bound into it by the *inclusio* of the phrase 'wisdom and instruction' which occurs in vv. 2a and 7b. The echo of the motto in 31:30 is an indication that this is a preface to the whole book. The motto is also repeated, with some variation, in 9:10. This indicates that Prov. 1–9 is a discrete section but that it is also an integral part of the whole book.

The title (v. 1) locates the teaching of the book in the mainstream of Israel's wisdom tradition, of which Solomon was seen as the patron. For a fuller discussion of it see 'Authorship and Date' in the introduction.

There is a general similarity between this preface and the introduction of Egyptian instructions. In both cases the author is identified and the purpose of the book is set out using verbs in the infinitive. However, the Egyptian instructions also identify a specific recipient, an aspiring official or courtier. The purpose of the instruction is to enable him to be successful in his career. Proverbs has a much more general readership in mind and therefore its purpose is more general. The purpose is set out by piling up words, many of which recur throughout the book, which indicate the rich content of 'wisdom.' Although the words are not synonyms it is difficult to make clear distinctions between some of them, as comparison of different English translations shows. The intention seems to be to impress the reader with a list of the benefits to be obtained from studying Proverbs.

Wisdom (vv. 2, 7) (חָכְמָה/*ḥokmâ*) is the most inclusive term. In the OT in general 'wisdom' refers to a variety of skills, both intellectual and physical. In Proverbs its meaning becomes somewhat narrower. It always refers to the ability to cope with life in the best way, 'life-skill', and it has an intellectual slant, as its frequent coupling with words like 'knowledge' and 'understanding' indicates. For a fuller discussion see the 'What Is Wisdom?' in the introduction.

Instruction (vv. 2, 3) (מוּסָר/*mûsār*) is a key term in Proverbs, especially in chs 1–9. It always carries the implication of correction or discipline by someone in authority: God, a parent, a teacher. This is why the NIV and some other EVV translate it as 'discipline'. It indicates a process of learning which requires humility and may sometimes be painful.

Words of insight (v. 2) uses the noun (בִּינָה/*bînâ*) from the same root as the preceding verb 'to understand' (הָבִין/*hābîn*). This is a verb which often refers to the insight which comes from knowing something[1] and so the translation 'words of insight' is appropriate rather than just 'words of understanding'.

Wise dealing (v. 3) (הַשְׂכֵּל/*haśkēl*) translates the *hiphil* infinitive absolute of a verb which, as Whybray[2] says, 'carries the implication of an intelligent assessment of situations which can lead to practical decisions'.

Righteousness, justice, and equity (v. 3) (צֶדֶק, מִשְׁפָּט, מֵישָׁרִים/*ṣedeq, mišpāṭ, mêšārîm*) are moral qualities and they may be intended to indicate the way in which 'wise dealing' is to be practiced. Waltke[3] comments, 'since "righteousness" refers to the moral quality that establishes right order and "justice" refers to the moral quality that restores that order when disturbed, they frequently occur together (cf. 2:9)'. The third term is often used in the OT of giving decisions that are honest and fair. In 8:6 and 23:16 it is used of speaking 'what is right'. Brown[4] points out that this trio of moral terms stands at the middle of a chiasm, which makes the point that at the heart of imparting wisdom is the instilling of virtue, not just knowledge.

Prudence (עָרְמָה/*'ormâ*) (v. 4) might be better translated as 'shrewdness' (NRSV, REB). It can be used in a negative sense (most notably in Gen. 3:1 of the serpent) but here is clearly used of the ability to use reason to deal wisely with the problems of life.

Knowledge (דַּעַת/*da'at*) (v. 4) is a very general term, related to the very common verb 'to know' which is discussed below.

Discretion (מְזִמָּה/*mĕzimmâ*) (v. 4) is a noun formed from a verb which

1. *NIDOTTE* 1:652.
2. Whybray, *Proverbs,* 32.
3. Waltke, *Proverbs 1–15,* 98.
4. Brown, *Character in Crisis,* 22-30.

means 'to think, plan, purpose, devise'.[5] It can be used in a negative sense of 'evil devices' (12:2) but when used positively it refers to the ability to walk through life in a way that avoids the pitfalls of evil (2:11-12).

Learning (לֶקַח/*leqaḥ*) (v. 5) is a noun related to a verb meaning 'to receive, take, grasp' which is discussed below. As Atkinson[6] says, it 'means getting a grasp on what the teacher wishes to convey'. Elsewhere in Proverbs it has the connotation of being able to speak in a persuasive way (16:21, 23).

Guidance (תַּחְבֻּלוֹת/*taḥbulôt*) (v. 5) translates a word which occurs only five times in Proverbs and once elsewhere in the OT (Job 37:12). It is related to a word meaning 'rope' (חֶבֶל/*ḥebel*) and may be a term for the steering ropes of a ship, as suggested by the LXX translation (κυβέρνησιν, *kybernēsin*). On this basis it can be taken to refer to the ability to navigate the right course through difficulties. McKane[7] translates the word with the general metaphor 'know the ropes' (cf. 'acquire skill', NRSV, REB). In view of what follows, understanding difficult sayings, the more specific meaning seems appropriate.

This list of terms sums up the attributes or skills which it is claimed the study of the book can impart to the diligent reader. Verse 6 refers to a more specific benefit, the ability to understand particular forms in which wisdom is expressed.

Proverb (מָשָׁל/*māšāl*) is the term used in the title of the book. For a fuller discussion see the introduction. In the OT it is used for so many different types of material that here it is best understood as referring to well-known wisdom sayings, whatever their literary form.

Saying (מְלִיצָה/*mĕlîṣâ*) occurs only here and in Hab. 2:6 in the OT. Presumably it means something more specific than a *māšāl*. Scholars debate its precise meaning. Possible translations other than 'saying' are 'parable' (NIV, REB) and 'figure' (NRSV).

The words of the wise. This occurs as a heading in 22:17 (cf. 24:23) and may refer to collections of wisdom sayings.

Riddles (חִידֹת/*ḥîdōt*) is a common translation of this term, but there are no riddles in the Book of Proverbs. In the OT the word is used of a variety of types of sayings, including the true riddle (e.g. Judg. 14:12-19). It seems to refer to sayings whose meaning is not obvious and which therefore require some insight to be understood. They might be described as 'enigmatic sayings'.

The string of verbs in vv. 2-6 is worth examining in order to understand the purpose of the book.

5. *NIDOTTE* 1:1112-14.

6. Atkinson, *Proverbs*, 25.

7. McKane, *Proverbs*, 211.

To know (v. 2) uses the verb יָדַע/*yāda'*. Although this is very common verb with a wide range of meanings it often implies more than simply intellectual understanding. It can be used to mean 'to have sexual intercourse' (e.g. Gen. 4:1). In Proverbs it can mean 'to acknowledge, to recognise' (e.g. 3:6). With regard to this verb and its related noun Longman[8] comments, 'the only distinctive thing to remark about it is that it probably implies a relationship with the object that is known.'

To understand (vv. 2, 6). According to *NIDOTTE*[9] the verb בִּין/*bîn* is less relational than יָדַע/*yāda'* and 'is used more to refer to the insight that comes from knowing. The verb means 'to perceive through the senses'. Waltke[10] comments that when, as here, it is used in the Hiphil with a direct object 'it denotes the act of giving heed and considering something with the senses in such a way that understanding the object takes place within'.

To receive (v. 3). The verb לָקַח/*lāqaḥ* has the general meaning 'to take, to grasp, to seize'. Murphy[11] notes that it 'has a quite active meaning in sapiential language', and he translates the verb here as 'to take in'. The corresponding noun (see above) indicates 'what is taken in'.

To give (v. 4). The very common verb נָתַן/*nātan,* which means 'to give', moves the focus from the activity of the reader or learner to that of the book or teacher. It follows on naturally from the previous verb. For something to be received it has to be given.

Hear (v. 5). The verb שָׁמַע/*šāma'*, which 'may have the same broad range of meanings as covered by the English word "hearing", in this book signifies to give one's ear to the speaker's words externally and to obey them inwardly'.[12]

The preface refers to two groups of readers. First (v. 4) there are 'the simple' (פְּתָאִים/*pětā'yim*) and 'the youth' (נַעַר/*na'ar*). The 'simple' person is one of the recurrent characters of Proverbs. Those who are 'simple' are inexperienced, untaught, naïve. As a result they can be gullible and easily led astray by those with evil intent (e.g. 14:15). On the other hand they, unlike 'the fool' and 'the scoffer' with whom they are sometimes linked (e.g. 1:22), are teachable so that they might become 'prudent/shrewd' (8:5). The term 'youth' can apply to anyone from a young child to a young adult, but typically refers to an unmarried adolescent[13] which seems to be what it means in Proverbs.

Translations differ in how they treat v. 5. Some (e.g. NIV) treat it as a pa-

8. Longman, *Proverbs,* 97.
9. *NIDOTTE* 1:652.
10. Waltke, *Proverbs 1–15,* 176.
11. Murphy, *Proverbs,* 3-4.
12. Waltke, *Proverbs 1–15,* 178-79.
13. *NIDOTTE* 3:125.

renthesis. Others (e.g. REB) take vv. 5-6 together as addressing a second group of readers, 'the wise' (חָכָם/*ḥākām*) and 'the one who understands' (נָבוֹן/*nābôn*). The second word refers to someone who has בִּינָה/*bînâ* 'insight' (see above). It makes sense to take the two verses together since v. 6 lists activities that seem more appropriate to those involved in advanced study rather than the teaching of those who are immature beginners. These verses make clear that acquiring wisdom is a life-long process. It is not only the young and immature, but also the 'wise', who have more to learn.

In vv. 2-6 wisdom embraces both intellectual knowledge and skills and moral qualities and behaviour. The final verse asserts that wisdom has a theological basis, 'the fear of the LORD'. The word 'beginning' (רֵאשִׁית/*rēʾšît*) can mean: (1) first in time; (2) chief part, principle, essences; (3) the best part. Meaning (1) is to be preferred because nothing in the other thirteen uses of the phrase 'the fear of the LORD' in Proverbs suggests that it is part of wisdom, one of several components, even if the best. Also, the parallel phrase in 9:10a has תְּחִלַּת/*tĕḥillat,* which unequivocally means 'first in time'. This does not mean that 'the fear of the LORD' is an initial stage that can be left behind, but that it is the precondition for knowledge or wisdom. The parallelism in 15:33 supports this, 'The fear of the LORD is instruction in wisdom, and humility comes before honour'. Here humility is the precondition, not the first stage towards, honour (cf. 18:12). Also 'the fear of the LORD' is said to be 'instruction in wisdom', indicating an on-going process, not just a first stage.

'The fear of the LORD/God' is a theme that is found throughout the OT. There are different aspects to it. In Exod. 14:31 and 20:18-21 it refers to a deep sense of religious awe, involving real fear, when confronted with the power and numinous presence of Yahweh. In Deut. 10:12-13, 20 it means having a loyalty and love for Yahweh that is shown in obedience to his commands. In this sense it becomes a motivation for such practical matters as how one treats people (Lev. 19:14, 32). It is this practical, or ethical, aspect that predominates in Proverbs, as expressed in 8:13a, 'The fear of the LORD is hatred of evil.' However, there is no reason to assume that in Proverbs the concept has become purely moral in content and lost the connotation of religious awe and love and devotion to Yahweh. In 2:5 it stands in parallel with 'the knowledge of God' which implies a personal relationship with God, not just intellectual knowledge (see above on '*To know*').

The second half of the verse introduces another of the cast of characters in Proverbs, 'the fool'. There are two words used for 'fool' in Proverbs: אֱוִיל/*ʾĕwîl* (the one used here) and כְּסִיל/*kĕsîl.* Fox[14] sums up the difference in nuance

14. Fox, *Proverbs 1–9*, 41.

between them, 'If the *'ĕwîl* is obtuse by virtue of his moral perversion, the *kĕsîl* is, or probably will become, morally perverse because of his obtuseness'. The fools despise the very thing that Proverbs offers and so are the antithesis of those who fear the LORD. This verse makes clear that education in wisdom is not primarily about acquisition of knowledge or skills but about character formation.[15]

1:8-19 Lesson 1

This is the first of the ten lessons in Prov. 1–9. For the discussion of their form and structure see the section on 'The Instruction Form' in the introduction.

The introduction (vv. 8-9) consists of an address ('Hear, my son') a command (the rest of v. 8) and a motivation (v. 9). The ornament imagery in the motivation may refer to more than just the beauty of the ornaments. The word translated as 'graceful' (חֵן/*ḥēn*) can also mean 'honour', and the garland and pendants (or 'chain' as in NIV, REB) could be marks of honour ('a chain of honour for your neck', REB). Obedience to the parental teaching is not just a good thing in itself, but will lead to the son having a position of respect in the community.

Compared with instructions from Egypt and Mesopotamia, Proverbs gives unusual prominence to the teaching of the mother (see also 6:20; 31:1, 26). Although in the ancient Near East 'father' could be used of a teacher in a school, the reference to both parents here and in 6:20 suggests that the implied setting is education in the home. There may also be, as Fox[16] asserts, the implication that the teaching given in Prov. 1–9 is *parental* teaching, not just that of the father, although he seems to be the teacher. The Egyptian instructions are addressed to a named person, usually a son. The fact that in Proverbs the son is not named generalises the teaching. Although some translations (e.g. NRSV) try to take this further by substituting 'child' for 'son', the fact is that the content of the teaching makes it clear that the person addressed is an adolescent male. The patriarchal setting and gender-specific focus of the teaching in Proverbs, especially chs. 1–9, raises serious questions[17] which can be a stumbling block for those for whom Proverbs is part of Scripture. Van Leeuwen[18] has set out the issues involved:

15. Brown, *Character in Crisis*, 22-49.

16. Fox, *Proverbs 1–9*, 83.

17. See, for example, Brenner, 'Proverbs 1–9: An F Voice?'

18. Van Leeuwen, *Proverbs*, 35.

> Most basic is whether Proverbs 1–9 is merely a patriarchal construct or a revelatory, symbolic representation of reality; whether — despite being subject to the limitations of all human discourse — its metaphors illumine a real order of creation that impinges on humans, to which they are accountable, and within which they may find freedom and life; and, finally, whether God can speak truth about God's own self and reality through the medium of a patriarchal culture.

For those who accept that God has been most fully revealed through incarnation in a particular person who lived in a particular historical situation and culture there is no problem in principle in accepting that Proverbs is a revelatory representation of reality and that God speaks truth through it. All the books of the Bible are 'incarnated revelation' in that they come from, and are addressed to, specific historical and cultural situations. As a result readers who want to apply the message of these books to their lives and situations today have to face the hermeneutic task of 'cultural transposition' of the message. This involves imagining themselves in the place of the original addressee(s) in order to understand what the message of the book is and then considering how it might apply to their situation today in a different historical and cultural setting. The strong gender-specific bias of Proverbs may sometimes make this difficult for women readers, but Bellis[19] has given an example of how it can be done in her transposition of Prov. 7 into an address to her daughters.

One important point that should be recognised in applying the message of these chapters of Proverbs is that the text is not saying that all children should listen unquestioningly to their parents. The parents in these lessons are an ideal couple. They are wise, godly parents. To the extent that real parents are wise and godly they deserve to be listened to, but all real parents are fallible to some degree and therefore open to having their teaching and advice questioned.

The main body (vv. 10-18) has a fairly complex structure. An initial condition and command (v. 10) is followed by another lengthy condition (vv. 11-14) followed by another command (v. 15) supported by a motive (v. 16) and a statement of consequence (vv. 17-18). This first lesson sets the scene for much that is to follow in Proverbs. The youth is faced with the choice between two ways and competing voices calling for his attention and allegiance. In this case the temptation is to get rich quickly by joining a gang of murderous robbers. As well as the lure of riches there is the lure of the camaraderie of the gang. It is a witness to the continuity of human nature and culture that such gangs are as much, if not more, a feature of modern society, especially in cities, as they

19. Bellis, 'Gender and Motives'.

were in ancient Israel. Today such gangs are not the preserve of young men. Female gangs are a feature in some cities.

The father's presentation of the gang leader's speech has a vividness that comes from it being something of a 'cartoon sketch'. It highlights the moral depravity of the gang. They indulge in the wanton killing of those who have done them no harm simply for material gain. The imagery of Sheol (the abode of the dead) as a devouring monster (v. 12) probably has a background in Canaanite mythology. The Ugaritic texts[20] describe the god Mot (Death) as one who swallows his prey. The invitation to 'throw in your lot among us' (v. 14a) means more than it does in modern English idiom ('share our life'). While no doubt including this it also refers to the distribution of land or the spoils of war by casting lots, to ensure fairness in distribution. Enjoying a fair share of booty is what is promised in v. 14b.

The command not to heed this alluring invitation is supported by a moral condemnation of the gang's way of life which is virtually identical to Isa. 59:7a. Because v. 16 is absent from some major LXX mss some suggest that it is a later gloss, copied from Isaiah. While this is possible (vv. 17-18 would then become the supporting motive), equally possible is Fox's[21] suggestion that the verses in Proverbs and Isaiah may both be quoting a common proverb. The meaning of v. 17 is far from clear. In the first place it can be interpreted in two different ways. It may mean *either* that it is pointless to let birds see a trap being set because they will then avoid it *or* that even if birds see a trap being set they are too stupid to avoid it in the face of the lure of the bait. Second, there is the question whether the birds stand for the son, the gang or their victim. Of all the possible interpretations the two most likely seem to be:

1. The son should have more sense than to be lured into the trap that is being set for him, since even a bird has that much sense.
2. The gang have even less sense than birds since they cannot see that their way of life is a trap that will lead to disaster for them.

The second interpretation is to be preferred in the light of v. 18.

Conclusion (v. 19). The lesson ends with a clear declaration of a general principle. It is a statement of the so-called act-consequence nexus in Proverbs. For further discussion see the essay on this topic. The fact that the lessons begin with this warning against 'unjust gain' highlights the ambivalent status of material wealth in Proverbs. It is something that is a 'good' which can enhance

20. Gibson, *Canaanite Myths*, 68.
21. Fox, *Proverbs 1–9*, 87.

life, but it is not an ultimate 'good' to be sought for itself by any means. On this see further the essay 'Wealth and Poverty in Proverbs'.

1:20-33 Wisdom's Warning

In this first 'interlude' in the lessons, personified Wisdom (see the essay 'The Personification of Wisdom in Proverbs') speaks and delivers a severe warning to those who ignore or reject her. This interlude may be a counterpart to the first lesson. In the lesson the father warned of the consequences of giving in to the invitation of sinners. Now there is a warning of the consequences of failing to accept Wisdom's invitation.

The passage begins with an introduction by an unnamed narrator (vv. 20-21), who may be the father of the preceding lesson. Wisdom then calls for attention (vv. 22-23). In the main body of her speech she utters two condemnations, the first in the second person (vv. 24-27) and the second in the third person (vv. 28-31). In the conclusion (vv. 32-33) the fate of those who do not heed her is contrasted with that of those who listen to her. Although some of the vocabulary used is typically sapiential, the picture given of Wisdom crying in the streets and the style and tenor of her speech is more like that of a pre-exilic prophet than a wisdom teacher. Both the early Rabbis and some modern scholars[22] have seen parallels between the portrait of Wisdom here and the prophet Jeremiah.

Introduction (vv. 20-21). The word used for 'Wisdom' here is an unusual apparently feminine plural form (חָכְמוֹת/*ḥokmôt*) although throughout it is construed with feminine singular verb forms. This form is also used of personified Wisdom in 9:1. The only other uses are in Prov. 24:7 (where it is construed as a plural) and Ps. 49:3 [Heb. 4], where it means either 'wisdom' or 'wise words'. The plural here and in 9:1 is usually explained as a plural of intensity or majesty, emphasising the pre-eminence of Wisdom. Albright[23] suggested that it was a Phoenician feminine singular form. Wisdom's behaviour in crying out in the streets would be unusual for a woman in ancient Israel. It emphasises that what she has to offer is for everyone, not just an elite.

Call for attention (vv. 22-23). 'How long' expresses both urgency and frustration at the lack of response. The 'simple' (see on v. 4 above) are linked with 'scoffers' (לֵצִים/*lēṣîm*) and 'fools' (כְּסִיל/*kĕsîl*, see on v. 7 above). The scoffer is another of the cast of characters in Proverbs. He is marked by arrogance (21:24)

22. Fox, *Proverbs 1–9*, 104-105.

23. Albright, 'Some Canaanite-Phoenician Sources', 8.

which makes him unteachable (15:12). Since the other two are both unteachable the primary object of Wisdom's address is the simple ones but lumping them with scoffers and fools acts is a warning to them of the direction in which they are heading if they ignore Wisdom's call. The start of v. 23 is difficult to construe. It can be taken as a conditional phrase without a particle[24] ('If you turn at/respond to my reproof', as in most EVV). Alternatively it can be taken as a simple call for attention ('Give heed to my reproof', NRSV). Either way the main point is the same: those who want to receive the benefits Wisdom offers must respond to her reproof and change their ways.

First condemnation (vv. 24-27). Wisdom says that when calamity strikes those who have rejected her she will laugh at and mock them. There is no hint that Wisdom causes the calamity, she simply assumes that it will happen. Her response to it is harsh, but it should be seen more in terms of rejoicing in the vindication of justice than as an expression of malice.

Second condemnation (vv. 28-31). By the switch to the third person Wisdom now addresses the readers to impress on them the dire situation of those who reject her. Because they have rejected her, they will not find her when they realise they need her and seek for her. This is not revenge, they will simply get their just deserts (v. 31). Fox[25] suggests that this can be understood as meaning that

> When a crisis comes upon the fools, they will desperately wrack their brains for a solution, for a clever idea to get them out of their fix, but they won't come up with one. Their cunning will evaporate, their inner resources crumble. No stratagems will come to mind, no plans to hand.

Conclusion (vv. 32-33). The fates of those who fail to respond positively to Wisdom's call and those who do pay heed to her are starkly contrasted. This underlines the importance and urgency of Wisdom's appeal in this speech.

A striking feature of this speech by Wisdom is that she says things and makes claims that elsewhere are only said or made by God. The promise to 'pour out my spirit' (v. 23) has parallels in God's promises in Isa. 44:3 and Joel 2:28. In Isa. 11:2 the Spirit of the LORD is linked with 'the spirit of wisdom'. The phrase '(I) have stretched out my hand' in v. 24 is similar to Isa. 65:2, 'I have spread out my hands all day to a rebellious people.' The reference to Wisdom laughing and mocking those who have rejected her is reminiscent of Yahweh's laughter and derision of the kings who rebel against him (Ps. 2:4). Perhaps most striking is v. 28. In Deut. 4:29 and Jer. 29:13 Yahweh promises that he will be found by his

24. See GKC §159b-d for this construction.

25. Fox, *Proverbs 1–9*, 105.

people when they seek him wholeheartedly, but in an oracle of judgement in Hos. 5:6 he says that they will seek him and not find him. Finally, there is the fact that whereas in the preaching of the prophets and the exhortatory passages in Deuteronomy the people's fate for good or evil depends on their response to Yahweh and his Law, here it depends on their response to Wisdom (vv. 32-33). Personified Wisdom is clearly presented as standing very close to God and sharing divine authority.

Proverbs 2

2:1-22 Lesson 2

This is a single complex sentence but it has a clear syntactic structure which divides it into logical sections: 'My son, if (v. 1) . . . if (v. 3) . . . if (v. 4) . . . then (v. 5) . . . then (v. 9) . . . to deliver (v. 12) . . . to deliver (v. 16) . . . so (v. 20).' A triple condition (vv. 1-4), if kept, will lead to two consequences (vv. 5-8, 9-11) which, in turn, will lead to two outcomes (vv. 12-15, 16-19) and will culminate in achieving a particular purpose (vv. 20-22). This lesson differs from the others in having conditional clauses instead of imperatives, but this is also true of some Egyptian instructions.[26]

As well as this syntactic structure there is a formal structure. The sentence consists of twenty two couplets (or verses), the number of letters in the Hebrew alphabet. However, it is not a proper acrostic, with each verse beginning with a letter of the alphabet in sequence. Instead, the first letter of the alphabet, *ʾaleph* marks the key sections in the first half of the sentence (vv. 1, 3, 4, 5, 9) and *lāmed,* the letter that begins the second half of the Hebrew alphabet does the same in the second half of the sentence (vv. 12, 16, 20). Another indication of the two-fold structure is that while wisdom is the main topic of vv. 1-11 the theme of 'the two ways', which is introduced in vv. 8-9, becomes the dominant motif of vv. 11-22.

Introduction (vv. 1-11). This lesson has an extended introduction. The three conditional clauses following the address ('My son') (vv. 1-4) amount to an exhortation to obtain wisdom. To achieve this, the son must go beyond attentive listening (vv. 1-2) to an active and persistent seeking, like that of a treasure hunter (vv. 3-4). The next two sections describe the benefits (the 'treasure') that can be obtained. Firstly, there is a deepened relationship with God (v. 5). The 'fear of the LORD is the beginning of wisdom', but as one grows in wisdom, so

26. Kayatz, *Studien zu Proverbien 1–9,* 15-17.

one grows in the fear of the LORD. There is also growth in 'the knowledge of God'. This is not just intellectual knowledge but a personal relationship with God (see on 'knowledge' in the preface above). A paradox is introduced in vv. 6-7a. Instead of being an object attainable by human searching, wisdom is now spoken of as a gift from Yahweh. However, this is only an apparent paradox because Yahweh gives wisdom to those who are serious in their search after it. Human effort and divine grace are not at odds here. The message is much the same as the Apostle Paul's exhortation to Christians, 'work out your own salvation . . . for it is God who works in you' (Phil. 2:12-13). To this benefit is added the promise that Yahweh will guard 'his saints' from going astray (v. 8). This is the only place in Proverbs where the word for 'saint' (חָסִיד/*ḥāsîd*) occurs. It describes those who possess חֶסֶד/*ḥesed,* which is best understood as the love between covenant partners, 'covenant love'. This is a very rare use of covenant language in Proverbs.

The second benefit is a growth in moral understanding (vv. 9-10) and therefore, by implication, in human relationships. This coupling of the relationship to God with human relationships parallels the two parts of the Ten Commandments, and Jesus' summing up of the Law by the two commands to love God with the whole of one's being and one's neighbour as oneself (Mk. 12:29-31). Again there is a promise of protection (v. 11).

The main body (vv. 12-19) gives substance to the promises of protection in vv. 8 and 11. It promises that acquiring wisdom will result in deliverance from 'men of perverted speech' (vv. 12-15) and from 'the forbidden woman' (vv. 16-19). These two examples contain two oppositions, male and female, plural and singular. This suggests that they form a merism, like left and right, which is meant to embrace a whole spectrum by naming its extremes. If so, protection is promised from all kinds of dangerous people, not just the two kinds described.

In fact the evil men are guilty of more than perverse speech. Their basic moral flaw is that they 'forsake the paths of uprightness' (v. 13) and as a result are led into all sorts of evil. The forbidden woman is characterised in a similar way. She is one 'who forsakes the companion of her youth and forgets the covenant of her God' (v. 17). The words which are translated in some modern EVV as 'forbidden' (זָרָה/*zārâ*) and 'adulteress' (נָכְרִיָּה/*nokriyyâ*) have the basic meanings 'strange' and 'foreign'. There has been much scholarly debate about the nature of this woman's strangeness and foreignness. She appears again in 5:1-6; 6:20-35; 7:1-27 and is probably to be identified with[27] 'the woman Folly' in 9:13-18. There is ambiguity in the meaning of both of the words used of her. *Zār* (fem. *zārâ*) can refer to an ethnic foreigner (Isa. 1:7) but most often it refers to someone who is 'out of place' in some way. It is used of lay Israelites in situations

27. Yee, 'I Have Perfumed My Bed with Myrrh', argues for this.

where only priests are allowed (Exod. 29:33; Num. 1:51) or, in the context of the levirate law, someone outside the family (Deut. 25:5). In Prov. 14:10 and 27:2 it means someone other than oneself. In many cases *nokri* (fem. *nokriyyâ*) does refer to what is ethnically foreign (Exod. 2:22; 1 Kgs. 11:1). However, it can have the general sense of 'alien' or 'other' without implying ethnic foreignness (Isa. 28:21; Jer. 2:21). In Prov. 27:2 it is used in parallel with *zār* to mean someone other than oneself. The fact that v. 17 refers to 'her God' rather than Yahweh is sometimes taken as evidence that the woman is not an Israelite. However, in 2:5 'God' is used in parallel with Yahweh and in any case Yahweh could not be used with a pronominal suffix as the grammatical construction here requires. Also, Mal. 2:14 is a very close parallel to Prov. 2:17 and speaks of marriage as a covenant to which Yahweh is witness.[28] The phrase 'covenant of her God' may well be used to indicate that marriage as a covenant is in view since 'covenant of Yahweh' would naturally be taken to refer to the Sinai covenant. An alternative rendering of the phrase takes the noun 'god' to be a mark of the superlative degree[29] and so translates it as 'her sacred covenant' (NRSV). Boström[30] argued that the woman is a devotee of the fertility cult of a foreign goddess and so is luring the Israelite man into an act of sacral prostitution. However, nothing in any of the passages about the strange/foreign woman suggest this interpretation, and if this is what she was doing then presumably she would be *fulfilling* 'the covenant of her God' not *forgetting* it.

The most obvious thing said about this woman is that she is being unfaithful to her husband. This is clear in 6:20-35 and 7:19-20 and is the most likely meaning of 2:17 in the light of Mal. 2:14. She is 'strange' and 'foreign' because she is 'off limits', 'beyond the pale' both morally and socially since she is someone else's wife. This is the justification for modern EVV translating *zārâ* and *nokriyyâ* by 'forbidden woman', 'adulteress', 'loose woman', 'wayward woman'. In Prov. 1–9 this figure operates on two levels. Like the evil men of 2:12-15 she is a real flesh-and-blood person who poses a moral threat to the adolescent son. As such she stands in opposition to a legitimate wife (5:18-20). She is also a personification of evil (6:24) and folly (9:13) and in that role stands in opposition to personified Wisdom, of whom she is in many ways the antithesis,[31] competing with her for the son's attention and devotion. See further the section on 'The Strange/Foreign Woman' in the essay 'The Personification of Wisdom in Proverbs'.

28. Hugenberger, *Marriage as a Covenant*, 296-302.

29. Cf. Gen. 23:6 where 'a prince of god' means 'a mighty prince'.

30. Boström, *Proverbiastudien*, 103-155.

31. On this see Yee, 'I Have Perfumed My Bed with Myrrh'.

Conclusion (vv. 20-23). The purpose of the pursuit of wisdom is set out here in terms of the metaphor of 'the two ways'. Those who pursue wisdom will 'walk. in the way of the good' and 'the paths of the righteous'. As a result they will 'inhabit the land' while the wicked 'will be cut off from the land'. The word for 'land' (אֶרֶץ/*'ereṣ*) has a wide range of meaning. It often refers to Canaan, the Promised Land, and the fact that the verb 'rooted out' in v. 22b occurs in the threat against covenant-breaking in Deut. 28:63, 'you shall be *plucked off* the land' can be taken to support that meaning here. However, since there is no explicit mention of the covenant traditions in Proverbs it is more likely that 'land' here means 'the earth'.[32] In that case what is being expressed here is the recurrent theme in Proverbs of (long) life for the righteous and (early) death for the wicked.

An important aspect of the second lesson is that it presents education as an interactive spiral. The son is urged to seek wisdom in a determined, wholehearted way. In practice this means studying the received wisdom tradition passed on by the teaching of the father (vv. 1-2). However, this human effort on its own will not achieve the desired goal. That is only attainable because Yahweh responds by giving wisdom as a gift (v. 6). The result is that the pursuit of wisdom, which begins on the basis of the fear of the Lord, leads to growth in one's relationship with God (v. 5) and in one's relationship with other people (v. 9). This is an on-going process, which is why even the wise will benefit from studying Proverb (1:5-6).

Proverbs 3

3:1-12 Lesson 3

This consists of six commands each followed by a promissory motivation clause. The content separates vv. 1-4 from what follows, and the resumptive address 'My son' in v. 11, which is also found in Egyptian instructions,[33] suggests that vv. 11-12 form a conclusion.

Introduction (vv. 1-4). These verses urge the son not to abandon his father's teaching. What is promised as a result in v. 3 is something that wisdom also brings (3:16; 9:11), making a close link between the father's teaching and wisdom. The word translated 'peace' (שָׁלוֹם/*šālôm*) means 'a state of wholesome, peaceful well-being, primarily realized in relations among people',[34] hence

32. Fox, *Proverbs 1–9,* 123; Van Leeuwen, *Proverbs,* 45; Waltke, *Proverbs 1–15,* 234.

33. McKane, *Proverbs,* 289.

34. Fox, *Proverbs 1–9,* 143.

translations such as 'abundant welfare' (NRSV) and 'prosperity' (NIV). 'Steadfast love and faithfulness' are often spoken of as attributes of God (e.g. Exod. 34:6-7) but they are also attributes expected of humans, and the context here suggests that they are virtues that the son should display, virtues which flow from keeping the father's teaching. The promise in v. 4 expands on the place in the community implied in v. 3b.

The main body (vv. 5-10) of this lesson deals with the son's relationship to Yahweh. He is exhorted to *trust the Lord* (vv. 5-6), to *fear the Lord* (vv. 7-8) and to *honour the Lord* (vv. 9-10). The promise of 'straight' paths is a promise that the son will reach his goals in life. In the context of the 'two paths' metaphor of Proverbs this may be as much, if not more, a promise of living a morally good life as of material success. Of course the two are often inter-related in Proverbs. In v. 8 there is a promise of physical well-being, and in v. 10 of material prosperity. An important point is made about the nature of true wisdom in vv. 5b, 7: it must go hand-in-hand with humility. Wisdom is not wisdom when it comes from someone who thinks they are wise. Such a person is in reality a fool (26:5, 12).

Conclusion (vv. 11-12). This is not a normal conclusion because it is not a summing up of the lesson. It is more a balancing comment. As Van Leeuwen[35] says, 'Proverbs 3:11-12 presents a direct contradiction to glib "health and wealth" (sub)versions of the gospel, which appeal to vv. 9-10'. Like a good father Yahweh's primary concern for his children is not that they live an easy life, but that they live a good life. This requires discipline. Sometimes the discipline has to take the form of correcting errors. However, sometimes it is more in the nature of training for what lies ahead. Just as athletes sometimes have to undergo training that is painful in order to develop their physical muscles, so we sometimes have to go through painful experiences, unrelated to any mistakes or errors we have made, in order to develop our moral 'muscles'. This is one biblical perspective on the problem of suffering. Deuteronomy 8 and Heb. 12 provide good commentaries on these verses. The imagery used in them is another reminder that education in wisdom is not a purely human endeavour. God plays an active part in it too.

3:13-20 In Praise of Wisdom

This poem encourages the pursuit of wisdom by extolling the value of wisdom. The use of words derived from the Hebrew root אשר/*'šr* as the first and last

35. Van Leeuwen, *Proverbs*, 50.

words of vv. 13-18 forms an *inclusio* binding these verses together, and vv. 19-20 are then linked to them by the use of the pair 'wisdom' and 'understanding' in vv. 13, 19.

Wisdom is personified in v. 16, and there are verbal and thematic links between this poem and those about personified Wisdom in ch. 8 and the ideal wife (another kind of personification of wisdom) in 31:10-31 (8:10-11, 18-19, 22-31, 32, 34; 31:10, 19-20, 28).

The value of wisdom (vv. 13-15) is extolled by proclaiming the good fortune of its possessor (אַשְׁרֵי/*'ašrê;* 'blessed', 'happy'). Wisdom is a better investment than precious metals (v. 14) and more attractive than jewels (v. 15). The specific jewels indicated in v. 15a are unclear (cf. 'rubies', NIV; 'red coral', REB).

The benefits of wisdom (vv. 16-18) are extolled by presenting wisdom as an attractive woman offering valuable gifts. It may be that here Wisdom is depicted in a way that makes her an alternative to the fertility goddesses of the ancient Near East. In particular, Kayatz[36] draws attention to the depictions of the Egyptian goddess Maʿat, goddess of truth and justice, holding the *ankh* (life) sign in her left hand and the *was* sceptre (representing wealth and honour) in her right hand. The worship of the Canaanite fertility goddess was associated with green trees (1 Kgs. 14:23). The 'tree of life' occurs a number of times in Proverbs as a metaphor for the good life offered by wisdom[37] (11:30; 13:12; 15:4). However, see the discussion of Wisdom and various goddesses in the essay 'The Personification of Wisdom in Proverbs'.

Wisdom and creation (vv. 19-20). At first sight this is a rather abrupt change of subject. However, as well as the verbal link with v. 13 there are thematic links with what has gone before. The image of the tree of life evokes the creation story in Genesis. More fundamentally these verses explain why Wisdom can offer the benefits she does. Since Yahweh created the earth and the heavens by wisdom, those who live their lives in accord with wisdom are living in accord with the fundamental structure and purpose of the created order. That is why they will prosper. This is an important theological basis for the teaching of Proverbs.

3:21-35 Lesson 4

This begins with the usual address, 'My son', followed by a command (v. 21) supported by a lengthy motivation (vv. 22-26). The body of the lesson consists of

36. Kayatz, *Studien zu Proverbien 1–9*, 104-105; see also Keel, *Symbolism*, 96.
37. Marcus, 'Tree of Life', 119.

five negative commands, each introduced by the particle אַל/*'al* ('not') followed by a jussive verb (vv. 27-31), the last one having a motivation attached (v. 32). Finally there is a conclusion (vv. 33-34) with a capstone (v. 35).

Introduction (vv. 21-26). The father urges his son to practice the two virtues of 'sound wisdom and discretion' because these will be a source of life and honour for him. Since the Hebrew for 'soul' (נֶפֶשׁ/*nepeš*) also means 'throat' (the 'inside' of the neck) there is an inside/outside parallelism in v. 22. The extended motivation (vv. 23-26) is a promise of divine protection by day (v. 23) and night (v. 24) and from the kind of disaster that may strike the wicked (v. 26).

The main body (vv. 27-32) concerns social relationships. This, presumably, provides specific examples of acting with 'sound wisdom and discretion'. There seem to be three groups of commands dealing with conduct towards (1) a neighbour who has some claim on you (vv. 27-28); (2) a neighbour with whom you are on good terms (vv. 29-30); (3) evil neighbours (vv. 31-32). The change from 'neighbour' to 'a man' (v. 30) shows that 'neighbour' is not construed narrowly (cf. Lk. 10:29-37). The motivation in v. 32 uses a phrase, 'an abomination to the LORD', which occurs a dozen times in proverbs. Clements[38] argues that while the concept of 'abomination' has its origin in the cultic sphere, in proverbs its connotation is ethical, a response of moral outrage. It is often used of behaviour which could not be dealt with readily by the legal system. See the section 'An Abomination to Yahweh' in the essay 'The Spirituality of Proverbs'.

Conclusion (vv. 33-35). This does not sum up the teaching of the lesson but reinforces its motivations. The fate of the wicked and the righteous is contrasted. The general wicked-righteous contrast of v. 33 becomes the more specific scoffer-humble contrast in v. 34. Perhaps picking up on the idea of 'abomination to the LORD' Yahweh is invoked as the guarantor of the fate of the wicked and the righteous. The capstone concerns the standing of the wise and the fools in society, which is appropriate following the concern of the body of the lesson with social relationships.

Proverbs 4

4:1-9 Lesson 5

This lesson is unusual in having the plural address 'sons'. It is also the only lesson which lacks a conclusion, which may be the result of its unique content.

38. Clements, 'Abomination'.

It begins with the father's reminiscence of his own education (vv. 1-4a) and the main body of it is a quotation of his father's words (vv. 4b-9).

Introduction (vv. 1-4a). This gives a glimpse of education in ancient Israel. The reference to both father and mother (v. 3; cf. 1:8) strongly suggests that the setting was home. The father's reminiscence of his own education and quotation of his father's teaching has two rhetorical effects. First, it builds a bond of empathy with his sons — reminding them that he has been in their position. He provides them with a model of what he is exhorting them to do, to pay attention to, and to adhere to, his teaching. He has done that with regard to his father's teaching. Second, it gives his teaching the weight and authority of a tradition that has been passed down the generations from father to son. It is not the mere antiquity of the tradition which gives it authority, but the fact that it is a tradition which has been lived out and tested down the years.

The main body (vv. 4b-9) consists of two parts, which are united by the command to get wisdom and insight (vv. 5, 7; on the use of the verb קָנָה/*qānâ* in these verses see the essay 'Wealth and Poverty in Proverbs'). The first part is an exhortation to hold firm to the grandfather's words (vv. 4b-5). This makes clear that wisdom is not a once-for-all attainment. It is a process and unless there is continuing effort there can be regress.

The second part (vv. 6-9) speaks about Wisdom in the third person. She is personified and spoken about as a woman to be loved, prized and embraced and who rewards her lover. Commentators differ over whether she is being spoken of as a patron (which fits with the promises of rewards) or as a bride (which makes more sense of the erotic tone of the language). In support of her being a bride one might point to the benefits which the ideal wife brings to her husband (31:11-12, 23) and the practice of crowning a bridegroom (Song 3:11).

The REB omits v. 7 because it is not in the LXX and seems to break the flow of thought. Also it is not easy to translate. It seems odd to say that the beginning of wisdom is to get wisdom. Fox[39] resolves this by suggesting that wisdom is being used in two senses here. Its first use refers to the wisdom possessed by the wise person. The second use refers to the content of the knowledge that is being taught. Possession of that is the initial and necessary stage towards becoming a wise person. Another way of resolving is indicated by the NIV, 'Wisdom is supreme; therefore get wisdom'. This takes the word for 'beginning' to mean 'the best part/supreme' (see on 1:7). The second half of the verse stresses that wisdom/insight is to be obtained above all else. It amounts to saying, 'If necessary, sell all you have to get it!' Whichever way v. 7a is understood, the meaning of the verse is not such that it does not make

39. Fox, *Proverbs 1–9*, 175.

sense in context. It leads in quite well to what follows. The LXX translator may have left it out because it is awkward rather than because it was missing from his Hebrew text.

4:10-19 Lesson 6

This sets out starkly the metaphor of 'the two ways' and is an exhortation to hold to the right path and shun the evil one.

Introduction (v. 10). The usual address is followed by a command to accept the father's teaching because it will lead to a long life.

The main body (vv. 11-17) is composed of two parts. The first (vv. 11-13) deals with 'the paths of uprightness'. The implication of v. 11 is that the son has already embarked on this path under his father's tuition. It is a safe path, free of treacherous obstructions (v. 12; contrast v. 19). The way to ensure one remains on the right road is to 'Keep hold of instruction' (v. 13). The fact that in v. 13b 'instruction' is personified as feminine, even though the noun is masculine, indicates that this verse looks back to v. 12 and that 'instruction' is being treated as a synonym for 'wisdom'.

'The path of the wicked' is set out in vivid terms in vv. 14-17. The repeated admonitions and verbs used in vv. 14-15 imply that the choice to be made is not a once-for-all one. It is as if the path of the wicked is, at least sometimes, close enough to the right path to be a tempting alternative to it. It requires determined, active choice to avoid it. The teacher does not describe the path itself, but those who are on it. They are painted as disgusting, abhorrent characters, presumably to deter the son from thinking of joining them. Evil has become their sleeping pill, without having done some crime they cannot sleep at night, and evil deeds are their food and drink (vv. 16-17). As Waltke[40] puts it, they are 'evilholics'.

Conclusion (vv. 18-19). Many commentators[41] think these verses should be transposed to avoid the change of subject from the wicked to the righteous and then back again. However, as Fox[42] points out, the transition creates a *caesura* which marks off these verses as a distinct unit. They form a conclusion which underlines the contrast between the 'two ways' using the contrast of light and darkness. The imagery of v. 18 once again implies that gaining wisdom is a dynamic process of growth. The light-darkness contrast is found in the NT, par-

40. Waltke, *Proverbs 1–15*, 286.
41. E.g. Toy, *Proverbs*, 93; Whybray, *Proverbs*, 80.
42. Fox, *Proverbs 1–9*, 182.

ticularly in the Johannine literature where Jesus is the light that has come into the world but is shunned by the wicked who prefer the darkness (Jn. 3:19-21).

4:20-27 Lesson 7

This lesson stresses the importance of vigilance if one is to remain on the right path. It is, as Hubbard[43] puts it, 'a lesson in the anatomy of discipleship' since it refers to many body parts. In v. 22b the father's words are said to be able to bring healing to 'all the flesh' of those who find them. There is no Hebrew word for 'body' so this is a way of referring to 'the whole body' (NIV). The lesson then refers to various organs: ear, eye, heart, mouth (v. 24a, see NIV), lips (v. 22b, see NIV), eyeball or eyelid (the word translated 'gaze' in v. 25 probably means some part of the eye), feet.

Introduction (vv. 20-22). The address is followed by two commands, the second being followed by a motivation. The son is called on to use his ear, eyes (in v. 21a 'your sight' is literally 'your eyes') and heart (or mind, as in REB, see further below) to take in the father's teaching, which is then to be lived out through his whole being, as the references to the various organs of the body in what follows makes clear.

The main body (vv. 23-26). The key verse in this lesson is v. 23. To understand it is necessary to understand how the word 'heart' (לֵב/*lēb*, occasionally לֵבָב/*lēbāb*) is used in Hebrew. It is used of the physical organ that beats in the chest but is frequently used in a metaphorical sense which is different from its metaphorical sense in English. In English it is used of the centre of the emotions, especially love. In Hebrew it is used of the inner person, especially the centre of thinking, willing and feeling. As Waltke[44] comments, there is no one English word which 'combines the complex interplay of intellect, sensibility and will'. Because it is frequently linked with thinking and willing, often the most appropriate translation is 'mind'. So, in v. 21b, which is a command to memorise the father's words, the REB has 'keep them fixed in your mind'. In v. 23a the REB uses the word 'heart' because 'mind' would be too narrow. Perhaps 'inner self' would be a good way to translate 'heart' here. The inner self is the source of life (the way one lives) which is expressed through the bodily members mentioned in the following verses. It must therefore be kept guarded against any evil inclinations and intentions. One aspect of this is the memorising of the father's teaching (v. 21), but the memorising must lead to a genuine 'internalising' so

43. Hubbard, *Proverbs*, 88.
44. Waltke, *Proverbs 1–15*, 91.

that the teaching affects thought and behaviour. Verse 24 stresses the 'defensive' aspect of the guarding, avoiding various forms of evil before returning to positive commands to give careful consideration to how one lives (vv. 25-26). The Apostle Paul's use of the metaphor of running a race (Phil. 3:12-14) is a good Christian commentary on v. 25.

Conclusion (v. 27). This assumes that the son is on the right path and sums up the thrust of the lesson.

Proverbs 5

5:1-23 Lesson 8

The topic here is the dangers of the adulterous 'strange/forbidden' (v. 3) woman (see on 2:12-19). The main body of the lesson is bracketed by mentions of her which act as an *inclusio* (vv. 3a, 20a). The father warns the son that while sexual intercourse with a woman outside marriage may seem to promise great pleasure, in reality it will lead to great pain. He then moves from the negative warning to a positive encouragement to enjoy sexual intercourse with his own wife. Mention of 'the path to Sheol' and 'the path of life' (vv. 5-6) indicates that this lesson sets out a concrete example of the two paths that have been a theme in earlier lessons.

Introduction (vv. 1-2). The father exhorts his son to pay heed to his words and to be careful about how he uses his lips. On the surface this refers to speech, but in the light of the next verse there is a double meaning.

The main body (vv. 3-20) is made up of three sections. In the first (vv. 3-6) the father warns against the fatal attraction of illicit sex. There is a double meaning to v. 3. On one level it can be read as referring to the seductive words of the woman. In Song 4:11 the imagery of v. 3a refers to kisses, and the word translated 'speech' in v. 3b (חֵךְ/*ḥēk*) means 'palate' (ESV footnote), so on another level the verse can be read as referring to intimate kisses. There is a similar double meaning in v. 5 since 'feet' in Hebrew can be euphemism for the sex organs (e.g. Exod. 4:25; Deut. 28:57). The son is warned that yielding to the seductress's offer of pleasure will end in pain and will constitute embarking on the path to Sheol, the place of the dead.

The second section depicts the consequences of adultery (vv. 7-14) as a way of deterring the son from it. The picture painted in vv. 9-10 is rather undefined and impressionistic. The adulterer will lose his honour, length of life, strength and the fruits of his labour to an undefined cast of characters: 'others', 'the merciless' (possibly the woman's husband, cf. 6:34), 'strangers' and 'foreigners' (both indicating people outside his extended family). Verse 11b would most naturally refer to disease, possibly venereal disease.[45] The overall point being made is that sexual promiscuity is life-sapping and leads to poverty and loss of reputation. This is driven home by the father putting into the mouth of the adulterer a confession in which he admits the folly of what he has done (vv. 12-14).

The teaching takes a positive turn as the father commends the joys of sex within marriage (vv. 15-20). The use of water imagery in relation to life is common in the OT and has its background in the climate of Canaan. For most of the year it is arid, and fertility depends heavily on the seasonal rains which replenish the cisterns, which collect and store the run-off, and the underground aquifers, which feed the wells and springs. It is not surprising that the woman, as a source of life, is spoken of in the Song of Songs as 'a garden fountain, a well of living water, and flowing streams from Lebanon' (4:15). There is debate about how the imagery is used in vv. 15-18. It clearly refers to the woman in vv. 15 and 18, but its referent in v. 16 is unclear. There is also the question whether this verse is to be taken as a statement, 'Let . . .' (KJV), or as a negative question, 'should . . . ?' (ESV, NIV, NRSV), taken as equivalent to a negative command (REB). There are three main ways in which this verse has been understood. Some take it to be a statement that the husband's sexual fidelity will be rewarded by numerous offspring, whereas those that result from an illicit relationship will belong to others (v. 17). Another possibility is that it is a warning that if the son has sex with another's wife, other men will have sex with his, perhaps because neglect of his wife will lead her to seek satisfaction elsewhere (cf. Job 31:9-10). The commonest understanding has been that the reference is to a man's promiscuity, with the water imagery referring to male sperm. Although this requires a change in the referent of the imagery from woman to man and back again, in the context this seems the best understanding. The use of animal imagery of the beloved has its parallel in Song 2:9, 17; 8:14, as does the language of being intoxicated with love (Song 4:10). Given the delights available in marriage, to seek the deadly pleasures of illicit sex is folly (v. 20).

Conclusion (vv. 21-23). The ultimate motivation for not embarking on the wrong path is that God is watching and upholds the moral order. Verses 22-23 indicate that this generally happens through people reaping the consequences of their own decisions and actions. The general nature of this conclusion, with its use of the path imagery, suggests that this lesson is a specific example of the 'two paths' theme. If this is so, it is probably valid to see behind the opposition of the strange woman and the legitimate wife the opposition of Folly and Wisdom.

In both the conclusion and the son's confession this lesson makes clear

45. Fox, *Proverbs 1–9*, 197 quotes references to venereal disease in Akkadian sources.

that people must take responsibility for the life-choices that they make. It is hypocritical to pray, 'Lead us not into temptation' and not take active steps to avoid it (v. 8) and to resist it (v. 15).

The limited portrayal of women in this lesson, and indeed in Prov. 1–9, as either desirable wife or desirable temptress is troubling to some readers. In part it follows from the nature of the proverb genre. The sentence proverb, because of its brevity, generally works with bipolar oppositions, black and white rather than shades of grey. This seems to carry over to the instructions. There is also concern that the book does not explicitly protest against the exploitation of women which may lead to prostitution. Because of the male-oriented focus of the teaching the causes of female prostitution and adultery are beyond its horizon except inasmuch as male behaviour makes them possible. Clearly, if males heeded the exhortations to be faithful in marriage and avoid illicit sex a major cause of prostitution and adultery would be removed. The primary concern of the lessons is the damage that male sexual promiscuity can do to family, self and society. Women can transpose the teaching into their situation by replacing the honey-lipped woman by a sweet-talking man on the prowl for a one-night stand.

Proverbs 6

6:1-19 Four Epigrams

These short epigrams differ in form and content from what precedes and follows them. The first two (vv. 1-5, 6-11) are on the theme of folly and are linked by references to sleep and slumber. The third and fourth are on the theme of evil and are linked by the use of lists of body parts. There is no clear reason why these two pairs of sayings are put together nor why they occur here, apart from a possible catchword link in the use of the verb לָכַד/*lākad* in 5:22a ('ensnare') and 6:2b ('caught').

On standing surety (vv. 1-5). This has the 'instruction' form, with an address, 'My son', followed by a condition (vv. 1-2) and a command (vv. 3-5). It warns, in strong terms, against standing surety for a non-family member, a theme that recurs in Proverbs. As 22:26-27 shows, what is in mind is a financial pledge which could lead to the loss of the guarantor's property. Proverbs encourages giving generously to the poor (e.g. 28:27), but loans are regarded as too risky. Israelites were forbidden to charge one another interest on loans, though they could do this to foreigners (Deut. 23:19-20). There are no laws about standing as surety for a loan and no information elsewhere in the OT about this.

There are different possible ways to understand v. 1. The words 'neighbour' and 'stranger' may both refer to the debtor, in which case the terms may serve as a merism, implying everyone or anyone. Alternatively, v. 1a can be translated 'put up security to your neighbour', in which case the surety is given to the 'neighbour' for a loan he has made to the 'stranger'. This seems a rather unlikely situation. In any case, putting up security for a loan is seen as getting into a self-imposed trap out of which one should get as soon as possible, sparing no effort in the process. The word translated 'hasten' in v. 3b is probably better translated as 'humble yourself' (ESV footnote). It is better to lose your dignity than lose your property.

The similes in v. 5 underline the seriousness of the situation of the guarantor of a loan. The end of v. 5 lacks the words 'of the hunter' (ESV). An alternative to adding those words is to emend the Hebrew word 'hand' (יָד/*yad*) to the word for 'hunter' (צַיָּד/*ṣayyād*), which requires adding just one letter to the consonantal text.

On laziness (vv. 6-11). The sluggard is one of the cast of recurrent characters in Proverbs, and is sometimes contrasted with the diligent person (e.g. 12:24, 27). Here the contrast is with the diligence and prudence of the ant. The teacher does not present an animal fable (an invented tale in which an animal is given human characteristics) but a straightforward piece of observation. This is an example of one of the ways in which wisdom principles were derived. In v. 10 the teacher may be mimicking the words of the sluggard ('I'm just having a little rest') in satirical fashion. The saying ends with a warning that laziness will lead to poverty. The exact meaning of the words translated 'robber' and 'armed man' in v. 11 is uncertain (cf. REB: 'footpad', 'hardened ruffian') but the overall meaning is clear.

On the worthless person (vv. 12-15). 'A worthless person' is more literally 'a man of belial'. The phrase 'a man/son/daughter of belial' (cf. 1 Sam. 25:25, KJV) is used of a variety of evildoers in the OT. Fox[46] sums up its meaning as referring to people 'of shoddy moral character, prone to wickedness and simple nastiness, and devoid of good sense and moral compunctions'. Here the 'man of belial' is depicted as someone whose wickedness is expressed through his bodily members: mouth (v. 12, NIV), eyes, fingers, feet and heart (significantly the climax of the list). He is an example of what the Apostle Paul said should not be the case, 'Do not present your members to sin as instruments for unrighteousness' (Rom. 6:13). The meaning of the actions described in v. 13 is uncertain. The verse seems to refer to body language that communicates his malevolence.[47] Clifford[48]

46. Fox, *Proverbs 1–9*, 219.

47. Bryce, 'Omen-Wisdom', 31-33 argues for some magical significance.

48. Clifford, *Proverbs*, 76.

sums up the portrait of this person when he says that these verses 'describe the wicked person in his essence (v. 12a), demeanour (vv. 12b-13), inner life (v. 14a), effect upon society (v. 14b), and destiny (v. 15)'. The final verse is the main point of this section. Its assurance that shifty, wicked people like this character will not escape punishment is a warning not to be like him.

On what the Lord hates (vv. 16-19). This is the only numerical proverb in the book outside ch. 30. See the 'Numerical Sayings' in the introduction on this form of proverb and on 3:32 for the meaning of 'an abomination to the Lord'.

The list of seven things includes five body parts and two kinds of people. As in the previous section, the heart has a significant position, this time at the centre of the list, as befits the word for the 'inner self' that is the source of life (4:23). The two kinds of people listed are ones whose evil actions are destructive of true community both in wider society (v. 19a) and in the family (v. 19b) which is its basic unit.

6:20-35 Lesson 9

This lesson is the second of three on the subject of adultery. The first (5:1-23) supported its warning against adultery positively by an exhortation to enjoy the love of a legitimate wife. Now the warning is supported in a negative way by a description of the serious consequences of adultery.

Introduction (vv. 20-24). After the address ('My son'), for the second time in the lessons (cf. 1:8) the son is called upon to heed the teaching of his mother as well as that of his father. There is similarity of both word and content between vv. 21-22 and Deut. 6:6-8; 11:18-19. The imagery of v. 23 is the same as that of Ps. 119:105, a 'torah psalm'. It is not clear that there is any direct dependence involved here, and if there is in which direction it lies. Rather, this may be evidence of a shared area of thought between jurists and sages, both being concerned with the transmission of Israelite traditions in the context of the family.

The verbs in v. 22 are all feminine singular but there is no obvious feminine singular antecedent. One possible explanation is that the parents' commandment and teaching are being taken as constituting wisdom, which is the implicit subject of the verbs. The son is urged to hold fast to these teachings and value them because they will illuminate the way of life for him. A particular example of this is then introduced in v. 24: they will preserve him from adultery by protecting him against the seductive words of an adulteress. In v. 24a the MT has 'the evil woman' (אֵשֶׁת רָע/*'ēšet rāʿ*) but a change of vowels leads to the reading 'the wife of a neighbour' (אֵשֶׁת רֵעַ/*'ēšet rēaʿ*) (ESV footnote, NRSV, REB, following the LXX). In v. 24b she is called 'the foreign woman' (see discussion on 2:16).

The main body (vv. 25-33). The son is now given three reasons for avoiding adultery. First (vv. 25-26) he is warned not to be lured by the woman's beauty by drawing a comparison between the cost of prostitution and that of adultery. The Hebrew of v. 26a is enigmatic, literally 'for on behalf of a woman, a harlot, up to a loaf of bread'. By a variety of different routes most scholars come to the meaning given in the ESV, 'for the price of a prostitute is only a loaf of bread', though some favour the NIV translation, 'for the prostitute reduces you to a loaf of bread'. Either way the point being made is the contrast between the cost of prostitution (at the most financial ruin) and of adultery (your life). What this means is spelt out in more detail in what follows. There is no reason to take this contrast as in any way condoning prostitution, especially in the light of the stress on marital fidelity in the previous lesson.

The second reason for avoiding adultery is expressed using vivid imagery (vv. 27-29). Adultery is playing with fire, and those who indulge in it will get burned. There are sexual overtones in the use of the words 'chest' (literally, 'bosom') and 'feet' (see on 5:5).

What the punishment referred to in v. 29b is begins to become clear in the third reason for avoiding adultery (vv. 30-32). Translations of v. 30a differ depending on whether it is taken as a negative question (REB, 'Is not a thief contemptible . . . ?') or as a negative statement (ESV, 'A thief is not contemptible . . .'). The sentence lacks any interrogative marker. The relatively lenient attitude to theft prompted by hunger is found in the Targ: 'It is not fitting to be astonished at the thief who steals that his appetite might be satisfied because he is hungry', and also in the Egyptian story of 'The Eloquent Peasant'.[49] The implication in each case is that desperate need is what is driving the thief. The seven-fold retribution (v. 31a) goes beyond what is demanded in the Mosaic Law (Exod. 22:1-4, 6-8 [Heb. 21:37; 22:1-3, 5-7]) but here may be an idiom meaning 'pay dearly' as the second half of the verse shows. Again, the main point is made by the contrast. If the thief who is driven by a 'legitimate' appetite suffers the loss of all his possessions (which might be replaceable) it is sheer stupidity to commit adultery to satisfy an illegitimate appetite because you will lose yourself. What this means begins to be spelt out in v. 33: physical suffering, dishonour and permanent disgrace.

Conclusion (vv. 34-35). This expands on v. 33. It explains why the punishment will be severe and inevitable. It will be the result of the jealous fury of the adulteress's husband. Exactly what is envisaged depends on the understanding of the final phrase in v. 34, which is literally 'the day of vengeance' (בְּיוֹם נָקָם/ *bĕyôm nāqām*). Peels[50] argues that, 'Whereas the word-group *nqm* nowhere

49. *AEL* 1:174.

50. Peels, 'Passion or Justice?', 271.

in the OT indicates private blood-revenge, many texts can be found where the action of *nqm* is placed in the framework of justice and jurisdiction'. He therefore concludes that here 'the day of vengeance' is the day on which the husband makes the case public after which the community is to execute the sentence. In the Mosaic Law adultery is punishable by death (Lev. 18:20; 20:10; Deut. 22:22). In other cases of the death penalty it could be commuted to a ransom payment (כֹּפֶר/*kōper*, the word translated 'compensation' in v. 35a) if the offended party agreed. According to v. 35a the husband will not agree to this. The meaning of v. 33b is probably that he will not accept any bribe (NRSV), however large, to cover the matter up and not make it public. This is why the parents speak of adultery as a matter of life and death (vv. 26, 32).

An important aspect of this lesson is its recognition of the need for discipline (v. 23b) with regard to one's 'desire' (v. 25a) or 'lust' (NIV). James warns of the role that 'desire' can play in leading to sinful actions (Jas. 1:13-15). Jesus radicalises the message of this lesson this in Matt. 5:27-30.

Proverbs 7

7:1-27 Lesson 10

The substance of this final lesson is a vividly told moral tale illustrating the lure of illicit sex for the unwary and its tragic consequence.

Introduction (vv. 1-5). The father again calls on his son to remember and heed his teaching. There are strong similarities with the introductions of earlier lessons, especially 3:1-3 and 6:20-21, 24. What is distinctive here is the command in v. 4, in which wisdom is personified. In Song 4:9-10, 12; 5:1 'sister' is a term of endearment put in parallel with 'bride'. It may well be that the son is being urged to develop an intimate relationship with Woman Wisdom as a protection against an illicit relationship with the adulteress (again 'the foreign woman'; see on 2:16).

The main body (vv. 6-23). The natural narrator of the story would be the father who is delivering the lesson. However, because the motif of 'the woman at the window' is a narrative type scene in the OT (Judg. 5:28; 2 Sam. 6:16; 2 Kgs. 9:30-33) and is depicted in some Samarian ivories,[51] some scholars suggest that the speaker is the mother,[52] although in the other type scenes the woman is a negative figure in the story. In the LXX the verbs in vv. 6-7 are all third person

51. Keel and Uehlinger, *Gods, Goddesses,* 210.

52. For example, Brenner and van Dijk-Hemmes, *On Gendering Texts,* 57.

feminine. Boström[53] took this to be the original text with the adulteress as the subject of the verbs. This has found little support because as part of the lesson one would expect a piece of first person autobiographical observation by the teacher.

In vv. 6-9 the teacher describes a young man who is both 'simple' and 'lacking in sense'. The meaning of vv. 8-9 is not clear. Is the young man deliberately heading for the adulteress's house? It would be more in character with someone who is 'simple' in Proverbs (see on 1:4) if he was unwittingly putting himself in harm's way by not taking care of where he walked at a dangerous time of the day. Also, what follows suggests that the meeting with the woman is a chance encounter.

Suddenly the woman appears and the narrator describes her (vv. 10-13). Quite what is meant by 'dressed as a prostitute' is unclear. In Gen. 38:14 a harlot's outfit includes a veil. Maybe the woman wore this to hide her identity. On the other hand the narrator may be saying that she was provocatively dressed, rather than referring to a particular type of clothing. With the omniscience of a narrator we are given a portrait of her character in terms of her behaviour (vv. 11-12). She is uninhibited and flouts the mores of society. There is a double meaning in v. 11b since 'feet' can be a euphemism for the genitalia. She goes looking for men to seduce. When she meets the young man she accosts him in a shameless and brazen way.

The speech by which she seduces the young man is recounted in vv. 14-20. The reference to sacrifices (literally, 'peace offerings') and vows in v. 14 has been the subject of much discussion. Boström's[54] interpretation of this verse is an important basis for his interpretation of the 'foreign woman' as a non-Israelite cult prostitute, a devotee of a pagan fertility goddess. In this case sexual intercourse with the young man would be the fulfilment of her vow to her goddess. However, if that were the meaning here it is surprising that there is no hint of censure or warning with regard to religious apostasy in the lesson. Also, it is unlikely that such encounters would be common enough to be made the basis of a lesson like this. It seems more natural to take the verses as referring to the peace offering made in connection with a vow. Part of the animal was burnt on the altar but most of it was returned to the offerer to be eaten on the same day or the following day (Lev. 7:16-18). The woman's words would then be taken to mean that she was inviting him to a sumptuous meal. What follows adds further enticement. She flatters the youth by implying that she has come looking for him in particular and then paints a picture of the luxurious couch she has

53. Boström, *Proverbiastudien,* 120-27.

54. Boström, *Proverbiastudien,* 103-55.

prepared for them. It is covered with expensive and exotic linen and perfumed with equally exotic and expensive spices. The three spices mentioned in v. 17 occur together in Song 4:14 in an erotic context. She ends with an invitation to a night of love-making. She reassures the youth that there is nothing to fear because her husband is away on a business trip and will not be home for some days or weeks.

The final part of the tale (vv. 21-23) tells of the youth's response. Assailed by her seductive speech he suddenly gives way and follows her home. The animal imagery of vv. 22-23 casts a new light on vv. 14 — the youth becomes the sacrificial animal. The MT of v. 22c makes little sense in context and is generally regarded as corrupt and in need of amending[55] along the lines found in the ESV text. These similes brand the youth as indeed 'lacking sense', having no more intelligence than one of these animals that go unwittingly to their death. How, or in what way, the night of adultery cost the youth his life is not explained.

Conclusion (vv. 24-27). The lesson ends with a warning to take to heart the moral of the tale and not get involved with the adulteress. She is described as a warrior who has slain many victims and her house as the entrance to the realm of the dead. It may be that behind vv. 26-27 there is imagery related to a goddess of love and war such as Anat of Ugarit, Ishtar of Babylon and Inanna of Sumer.

The reference to personified Wisdom in v. 4 suggests that this lesson is to be read on two levels. It is a warning against adultery, but it also has a wider application. It is a call to choose Wisdom rather than Folly as a way of life and so prepares the way for the following chapters.

In this lesson we have another example of the place of observation in the way in which wisdom principles were derived (cf. 6:8-11). The tale is no doubt fictional in its detail (the narrator is unlikely to have overheard the woman's word from his window), but based on real life observation.

Proverbs 8

8:1-36 Wisdom's Self-Praise

This second speech by personified Wisdom is a counterpart to the first in 1:20-33. Whereas that was a speech addressed to the simple, scoffers and fools and had the negative tone of a reproof (1:22-23), this speech is addressed to everyone, including the simple and fools (8:4-5) and has a positive tone as Wisdom

55. Driver, 'Problems in "Proverbs"', 143.

commends herself — though it does end with a warning to those who fail to find her (8:36, cf. 1:32). In the more immediate context Wisdom appears in this chapter as a contrast to the adulteress of the previous chapter and earlier lessons. Whereas she accosts a 'simple' youth stealthily in the street by night (7:7-9, 13) and seduces him by deceitful words (7:21) offering him love that in fact leads to death because her house is the way to death (7:27), Wisdom appears in broad daylight in public (8:2-3) addressing everyone, including the 'simple', in truthful words (8:6-9) offering them love (8:17) which, if they frequent her house, will lead to life (8:34-35). This implicit contrast prepares the way for the explicit contrast between Wisdom and Folly in ch 9.

In vv. 4-36 Wisdom boasts of her character, power and authority and of the gifts she can bestow. Self-praise by a deity is well-attested in Ancient Near Eastern religious texts,[56] and in the OT Yahweh occasionally speaks in self-praise (e.g. Isa. 42:8-9; 44:24-28; 45:5-7). However, in this speech Wisdom is not presented as a deity but as an attribute or agent of Yahweh to whom certain powers have been delegated with regard to Yahweh's relationship with human beings. For further discussion of the possible background to this chapter see the essay 'The Personification of Wisdom in Proverbs'.

Following a scene-setting introduction (vv. 1-3) Wisdom speaks, and the speech can be divided into four main sections: an opening exhortation (vv. 4-11); an assertion of Wisdom's character, power and benefits (vv. 12-21); Wisdom's role in relation to Yahweh and the created world (vv. 22-31); a closing exhortation (vv. 32-36).

8:1-3 Introduction

An unidentified voice (probably that of the father of the lessons) introduces Woman Wisdom and calls attention to her speech. She is said to cry out at various locations in the city (cf. 1:20-21). Three places seem to be specified: a high point (possibly the acropolis where the temple, and possibly palace, would be situated); the crossroads; outside the city gates (cf. Absalom situating himself here to ingratiate himself with people, 2 Sam. 15:2). These are all busy public places where she would be seen and heard by crowds of people. The picture that is created is of Wisdom addressing the inhabitants of a bustling city. There is no doubt a symbolic meaning here: 'the city is the culture-shaped world of humans, a reflection in miniature of the world itself'.[57]

56. Kayatz, *Studien zu Proverbien 1–9*, 77-98; Lang, *Wisdom and the Book of Proverbs*, 56ff.
57. Van Leeuwen, *Proverbs*, 89.

8:4-11 An Exhortation to Listen

Wisdom's appeal is universal (vv. 4-5). She addresses humanity in general, even fools. Her invitation is not limited to Israelites, the wise, the wealthy or males. The 'simple' are normally seen as untaught but open to instruction (see on 1:4); the 'fool', however, is usually presented as unteachable (see on 1:7). The address to them here may indicate that they are not beyond all hope, or it may be that Wisdom, like the prophets (Isa. 6:8-10; Ezek. 2:3-5) has a duty to address even those who will not respond so that they are left without excuse.

Two motivations are given for listening to Wisdom's words. The first is their character, they are honest and truthful (vv. 6-9). The word translated as 'noble' in v. 6, נְגִידִים/*nĕgîdîm,* should probably be revocalised[58] to נְגָדִים/*nĕgādîm,* with the sense 'that which is straightforward, right' in view of the parallelism in the verse. There is, as noted above, a contrast here with the words of the strange woman and the adulteress. Wisdom loathes their kind of speech. Those who follow Wisdom's words will not be lead astray. Those who are already on the path to truth will recognise the moral quality of Wisdom's words. The second motivation is that Wisdom's instruction is more valuable than anything else (vv. 10-11, cf. 3:14-15). Since v. 11 speaks about Wisdom in the third person in a speech that is otherwise in the first person it may well be a gloss added by a scribe based on 3:15. In this part of her speech Wisdom does not offer any specific teaching, but offers herself as a trustworthy and valuable teacher.

8:12-21 Wisdom's Benefits

This part of the speech can be divided into three sections dealing with her character, her benefits to society and her benefits to individuals.

Woman Wisdom proclaims her virtues both in positive terms (v. 12) and negatively by saying what she hates (v. 13). Some scholars find the language of Wisdom 'dwelling' with prudence and 'finding' knowledge strange and so re-point the verbs to give the reading found in the REB: 'I bestow shrewdness and show the way to knowledge and discretion'. However, there is nothing odd in saying that Wisdom is intimately related to these virtues but distinct from them. Also, as Waltke[59] points out, by expressing things in this way 'wisdom herself models the role of a believing seeker after virtue'. A reason for the slight distancing of Wisdom from 'prudence' and 'discretion' may be the fact that

58. Grollenberg, 'Prov. VII,6 et XVII,27'.

59. Waltke, *Proverbs 1–15,* 400.

in themselves these are morally neutral and can be used for good or evil (see on 1:4). The repudiation of evil in v. 13 makes clear that in the case of Woman Wisdom they are used only for good. Because v. 13 is unusual in having three lines most commentators regard v. 13a as a later addition to the speech, either echoing 3:7 or 16:6 (although the wording is not identical) or to make a link with the Ideal Wife (31:30, but this seems a bit subtle). It certainly serves to explicitly identify Wisdom with Yahwistic piety.

In vv. 14-16 Wisdom asserts that it is she who gives rulers the attributes and powers they need to rule rightly. This is reminiscent of Yahweh giving Solomon wisdom so that he might rule Israel well (1 Kgs. 3:5-14). It is significant that the attributes which Wisdom claims for herself in v. 14 are attributed to God in Job 12:13 and are those bestowed on the ideal Davidic king by the Spirit of Yahweh (Isa. 11:2). Wisdom, therefore, is presented here as the mediator between God and human rulers. Of course not all rulers actually rule wisely, but these verses assert that Wisdom gives the ability to rule justly and effectively. To claim this is to claim that wisdom is the basis for a stable and just society.

The phrase 'those who love me' acts as an *inclusio* for vv. 17-21. These verses speak of the benefits that Wisdom bestows on those who love her. The greatest of these is Wisdom's own love (v. 17). With the expression of mutual love an erotic element surfaces, as it will again in the conclusion of the speech. Although the benefits include material wealth and success there is a clear moral emphasis. Wisdom bestows righteousness as well as wealth (v. 18). Wealth can corrupt unless it is held and used within a moral code. Also, the pursuit of wealth for itself is a form of idolatry and so leads to corruption, which is why the pursuit of Wisdom must be put above that of wealth (vv. 19-20). The imagery of 'the two ways' is alluded to in v. 20. Because Wisdom bestows her benefits only in morally right ways, those who are wise will only acquire and use their wealth in ways that are morally right.

8:22-31 Wisdom and Creation

So far in her speech Wisdom has spoken of herself and her actions in the present. In this section she speaks of the past, of her origins before the creation of the earth (vv. 22-26) and of her presence during its creation (vv. 27-31). It has been the centre of much debate both because the meaning of key words is unclear and because it has been caught up in doctrinal disputes.

The focus now shifts from Wisdom as the central character to Yahweh. This is signalled by his name standing as the opening word of v. 22. He is the subject of the active verbs in vv. 22-29, and Wisdom's status is defined in relation to him and his actions.

The meaning of the second word of v. 22 (קָנָנִי/*qānānî*) has been a matter of dispute since the early versions. The LXX, Targ and Syr translated it as 'created me' (so NRSV, REB) whereas the Vulg has 'possessed me' (so ESV, NIV). There is no doubt that in the OT[60] and in Proverbs the verb *qānâ* nearly always means 'to acquire, to possess' (e.g. 1:5 'obtain'; 4:5, 7 'get'), often by purchase (e.g. 20:14). There is a handful of passages in which the meaning 'to create' is possible[61] (Gen. 4:1; 14:19, 22; Deut. 32:6; Ps. 139:13; Prov. 8:22) and in Ps. 104:24 the derivative קִנְיָן/*qinyān* seems to mean 'creatures'. With the exception of Gen. 4:1 God is always the subject of the verb in these examples. It is arguable that just as in a number of cases the context suggests a narrowing of meaning from 'to acquire' to 'to purchase' (one specific way of acquiring) so in these cases the context suggests the more specific meaning 'to create'. In fact in Gen. 4:1; Deut. 32:6; and Ps. 139:13 the context of parenthood suggests the meaning 'to procreate'. This rendering can be supported by the epithet *qnyt 'lm* ((pro-)creator of the gods) which is applied five times to Asherah in Ugaritic texts.[62]

The following verses in Prov. 8 use the imagery of procreation. In vv. 24-25 Wisdom says 'I was brought forth' (חוֹלָלְתִּי/*ḥôlāltî*) using a verb which denotes a mother's birth labours (e.g. Isa. 13:8; 23:4) and so usually refers to birth. It is used of Yahweh in Deut. 32:18 and Ps. 90:2 but never of human males. The verb translated 'set up' (נִסַּכְתִּי/*nissaktî*) in v. 23 is problematic. It is usually taken to be from a verb *nsk* 'to be poured out', giving the literal meaning 'I was poured out', which makes little sense here. In Ps. 2:6 the same verb is used of the appointment of the king, presumably alluding to the pouring out of oil in the anointing of a king. That derived sense does not seem appropriate here. This has led to the suggestion that here the word is derived from another verb *skk* meaning 'to weave, form'[63] (REB, NIV footnote). That verb is used in Ps. 139:13b of God 'knitting together' the embryo in the mother's womb. In context, then, it seems best to translate v. 22 as 'The LORD gave birth to me' (cf. ESV footnote 'fathered') and see a consistent birth imagery running through vv. 22-25.[64] This imagery is, of course being used figuratively. It does present Yahweh in a female role (making the gender of the ESV footnote inappropriate), as is the case elsewhere in the OT (e.g. Deut. 32:18; Isa. 46:3-4; 66:13).

In v. 22a the phrase רֵאשִׁית דַּרְכּוֹ/*rē'šît darkô* (literally, 'the beginning of

60. *NIDOTTE* 3:941.
61. Waltke, *Proverbs 1–15*, 408-409.
62. Clifford, *Proverbs*, 96.
63. *NIDOTTE* 3:253-54.
64. Irwin, 'Where Shall Wisdom Be Found?'

his way') stands in apposition to 'me' and so the REB translation 'the first of his works' is better than the ESV's 'at the beginning of his work', as it makes clear that Wisdom was the first of Yahweh's creative acts, as the parallel in v. 22b says. The term 'his way' is used of God's creative activity in Job 26:14; 40:19. The following verse emphasises that Wisdom was brought into being before God began to create the earth. This is expanded on in vv. 24-26. The negative formulation of these verses stressing what did not exist when Wisdom came into being ('When there were no . . .', 'Before . . .') is a feature of the opening of ancient Near Eastern creation stories such as the Babylonian *Enuma Elish*. The enumeration of features of the cosmos moves generally upwards from the waters in the depths (v. 24a) to the springs that bring it to the earth's surface (v. 25b), to the settling of the roots of the mountains (v. 25a, see REB), to the surface of the earth. The concern of vv. 22-26 is not the *how* of Wisdom's origin, despite all the debate that that has engendered, but the *when* — that it occurred before the creation of the earth.

In vv. 27-31 the focus changes from Wisdom's origins to her presence with Yahweh as he created the earth. Despite this the upward movement in the description of features of the cosmos continues and moves up to the sky (v. 27a), to the horizon (v. 27b), and then the clouds (v. 28a, see the REB). The movement then descends to the wellsprings (v. 28b), to the sea-shore (v. 29ad) and finally the foundations of the earth (v. 29c). As Fox[65] comments, 'This systematic movement (noted by Meinhold) impresses on the reader creation as a coherent panorama rather than just an assemblage of phenomena.'

Behind this description (put in simplified terms)[66] is the cosmos seen as consisting of three levels: the underworld, the earth and the heavens. Each level is supported by 'pillars'. The mountains and the earth rest on such pillars. The sky is a dome, with the horizon as a band between the earth and the sky. The primeval ocean or abyss surrounds this cosmos. Wellsprings feed the underground waters to the earth and seas. Floodgates in the sky control the upper waters to give rain.

Verse 30 is the centre of much debate because the third word in the MT (אָמוֹן/*'āmôn*) occurs only here in the OT and its meaning is uncertain. The uncertainty goes back to the early versions. The following are the more likely possibilities.

1. Most commentators and EVV (e.g. ESV, NRSV, NIV) take it to mean 'artisan' or 'craftsman', a view that goes back to the Syr and Vulg and

65. Fox, *Proverbs 1–9*, 281-82.

66. For a detailed discussion see Keel, *Symbolism*, 16-60.

possibly the LXX. This is also how the author of the *Wisdom of Solomon* understood it (Wis. 7:21; 8:6). Most scholars now think the word is a loanword from Akkadian *ummānu* via Aramaic. They appeal to the word אָמָּן/*'ommān* in Song 7:1 [Heb 7:2] which seems to mean 'master craftsman'. The Akkadian word means a skilled craftsman (though it can mean a court expert or counsellor). The weakness with this meaning is that in the context nothing is said about Wisdom doing anything in the process of creation.

2. Some accept the meaning 'craftsman' but take the word as in apposition to the pronominal suffix, so that it refers to God, not Wisdom: 'I was beside him, the craftsman.' While grammatically possible this seems odd in context where some further description of Wisdom would seem appropriate.
3. Clifford[67] accepts that the word is a loanword from the Akkadian *ummānu* and re-vocalises it as *'ommān* but argues that the background is the Babylonian mythology about the post-flood sages who were the bringers of culture to the human race. They were called *ummānu*. He therefore takes Wisdom to be saying 'I was at his side as a (heavenly) sage', that is as a heavenly figure who mediates to humans the knowledge they need in order to live as the Creator intends they should. The weakness with this proposal is that the evidence Clifford provides that this mythology was widely enough known outside Babylon for a Hebrew author to allude to it and expect to be understood is limited.
4. Some, following Aq, take the word to mean something like 'nursling', 'cherished child' (e.g. REB, NRSV footnote). This requires emending the MT to אָמוּן/*'amûn*, taking it as a *qal* passive participle. It is argued that this fits the context well, coming after the account of Wisdom's birth and before the reference to her playing like a child. However, one might expect a feminine form of the passive participle since a feminine form of the *qal* active participle occurs in 2 Sam. 4:4 and Ruth 4:16. Also what follows need not refer to a child's play.
5. Fox[68] advocates a variant of the previous view by proposing that the word as it stands in the MT is a *qal* infinitive absolute meaning 'being raised/growing up' and acting as an adverbial complement to the main verb. Waltke[69] argues that this is grammatically questionable since the *qal* infinitive is active, meaning 'raising' and so Fox's meaning would presumably require the passive *niphal* stem.

67. Clifford, *Proverbs*, 23-28.

68. Fox, '*'amon* Again', 699-702; *Proverbs 1–9*, 287.

69. Waltke, *Proverbs 1–15*, 419.

6. Sym, Theod, and Targ understood the word as coming from the Hebrew root *'mn* meaning 'to be firm, faithful' and this leads to the possible translation 'I was beside him faithfully', taking the word as a *qal* infinitive absolute from that root. It is debatable how grammatically probable this is.[70]

None of these possibilities is totally compelling. Despite its wide popularity (1) faces the serious objection that in this section of the speech it is Yahweh, not Wisdom, who is active in creation. On balance, and it is a fine judgement, (3) seems to fit the context best. It prepares the way for what is said about Wisdom's role in instructing humans in vv. 32-35. It does require the assumption that the background mythology was well enough known, at least among the Hebrew sages, for the meaning of the loanword to be known. Even if the mythology was forgotten, or unknown, the meaning 'court expert/counsellor'[71] for *ummānu* may have been known and would, on its own, present much the same picture of Wisdom. As time went on that meaning was forgotten and the word became a puzzle.

The words 'delight' (שַׁעֲשֻׁעִים/*šaʿăšuʿîm,* the plural form probably implies 'totally given to delight') and 'rejoicing' (מְשַׂחֶקֶת/*měśaḥeqet*) are sometimes used to support the view that Wisdom is depicted as a child at play. However, as Whybray[72] comments, 'this interpretation is entirely dependent on the view that *'āmôn* in this verse means "little child" or the like, and finds no support in the meaning of these words themselves'. The word for 'delight' is used repeatedly in Ps. 119 to declare the author's delight in Yahweh's laws. The word for 'rejoicing' can be used of joyful behaviour in general (Jer. 15:17; 30:19) or of something more specific such as telling jokes (Prov. 26:19) or singing and dancing by adults (1 Sam. 18:7; 2 Sam. 6:5, 21). It is unclear whether it is Yahweh (ESV, NRSV, REB) or Wisdom (NIV) who is taking delight in v. 30b. The word 'his' is not there in the MT (as ESV, NRSV note). The parallel in v. 31b favours the NIV translation. Wisdom takes delight in seeing Yahweh's work of creation and celebrates before him. This is reminiscent of the heavenly beings singing and shouting for joy at the creation of the world in Job 38:7 and of David's celebrating 'before the LORD' (2 Sam. 6:5) when bringing the Ark of the Covenant to Jerusalem.

The emphasis in this section of the speech is on Wisdom as an observer as God creates the world. She delights in what she sees, and in particular delights in human beings. The implication of this is that she is well-placed to

70. See Fox, *Proverbs 1–9*, 286 and Waltke, *Proverbs 1–15*, 420 for the detailed arguments.

71. *AHw* 3.1415-16.

72. Whybray, *Proverbs*, 136.

play a mediating role between God and humans. This is made explicit in the conclusion to her speech (vv. 32-36) where she speaks as a teacher, in the way the father has in the preceding lessons. She urges humans to pay heed to her because those who accept and act on her instruction will be blessed — finding life and favour from the LORD. Those who reject her plea are warned that they are harming themselves and allying themselves with death rather than life. In these verses the imagery of 'the two ways' with their contrasting ends, alluded to in v. 20, appears again. The significance of the imagery in v. 34 is unclear: are the sons waiting at the door courtiers waiting for royal favour, or servants waiting to do their mistress's bidding, or pupils waiting to receive instruction, or suitors seeking admission to their beloved? The last seems the most likely, harking back to v. 17 and also preparing the way for the invitation of Wisdom's banquet in her house in 9:1-6.

The significance of vv. 22-31 in this speech is that they support Wisdom's claim to be able to provide the benefits promised in vv. 12-21 and are the basis for the appeal in vv. 32-36. This is because they establish the position and authority of Wisdom in various ways. First of all she is shown to have an intimate relationship with Yahweh. She is his child and was at his side when he created the cosmos. If 'sage, counsellor' is the right translation of *'āmôn* in v. 30a then this may be a comment on 3:19 and Wisdom's role in creation. She embodies the principles and plan used in the creation. Second, the fact that she came into existence before anything else gives her a place of precedence over all created beings. It also implies that she has superior knowledge to all other beings, as Eliphaz's taunt to Job indicates: 'Are you the first man who was born? Or were you brought forth before the hills? Have you listened in the council of God? And do you limit wisdom to yourself?' (Job 15:7-8). Third, her presence throughout, and observation of, the process of creation fits her to be the one who teaches humans how to live rightly in that creation. She has unique knowledge of how the cosmos was made and so of how it works (cf. Yahweh's question to Job, 'Who is this that darkens counsel with words without knowledge? . . . Where were you when I laid the foundations of the earth?', Job 38:2-4). As Kidner[73] puts it,

> the only wisdom by which you can handle everyday things in conformity with their nature is the wisdom by which they were divinely made and ordered. Proverbs 8, which states this superlatively, is therefore far from being a non-functional pinnacle of the book's eloquence, but is rather an exposure of the main framework of its thought.

73. Kidner, *Proverbs,* 32.

Fourth, for all these reasons, it is only Wisdom who is fit to be the mediator between the Creator and his human creatures, a task in which she delights.

For a discussion of the role that Prov 8 has played in doctrinal controversy see the essay 'Wisdom and Christology'.

Proverbs 9

9:1-18 Wisdom and Folly

This chapter provides a fitting conclusion to Prov. 1–9. The themes of the contrast between the wise and the foolish, the 'two ways' with their contrasting ends and personified Wisdom and the 'strange woman'/adulteress, reach a climax in two contrasting portraits (vv. 1-6, 13-18) of Woman Wisdom and Woman Folly each inviting the 'simple' into her house to enjoy a meal. There are both similarities and differences in the portraits. The effect is to close this section of the book by presenting the student with the challenge to make a decision between the ways of wisdom and folly. The place and role of vv. 7-12 in this chapter is much debated and will be discussed below.

9:1-6 Wisdom's Invitation

The word for Wisdom in v. 1 is the same unusual plural form as in 1:20 (see on that verse). There have been numerous suggestions[74] as to the nature of Wisdom's house and its seven pillars. Whybray[75] divides them into three main categories: the cultic, the cosmological and the literal. He points out that the interpretations in the first two categories are based more on hypotheses about the nature of the figure of Wisdom than on the information in this verse. The literal meaning seems the most likely (though there may be a double meaning too), especially since there is archaeological evidence of houses with pillars supporting the portico which extended into the central courtyard.[76] Seven pillars would indicate a large house, but here the number may be primarily symbolic, signifying completeness and perfection. The mention of meat and wine (probably mixed with spices; see Song 8:2) indicates a sumptuous meal. The motif of a banquet recurs in ancient Near Eastern literature, and some have proposed

74. See the list given by Murphy, *Proverbs*, 58.

75. Whybray, *Proverbs*, 142.

76. Lang, *Wisdom and the Book of Proverbs*, 90-93.

links between Prov. 9 and specific texts.[77] However, as Murphy[78] notes the verbal similarities are not surprising given the common subject matter. Biblical parallels such as 1 Kgs. 8:65-66; Isa. 55:1-2; 64:11-14 may be more relevant.

Some find vv. 3-5 problematic because, although the young women are sent out to invite people to the meal, the wording of the invitation implies that Wisdom herself is speaking. However, as Fox[79] says, in the ancient Near East 'Messages were formulated as the sender's words, not the messenger's. . . . The maids convey the message, but the message is Wisdom's and spoken in her voice'. The invitation is addressed to the 'simple', those who are untaught, and therefore gullible, but open to instruction (see on 1:4). It comes with a condition (v. 5). They are called upon to change their way of life, leaving their 'simple ways' to follow 'the way of insight', which is the way to life. The invitation is a call to conversion.

There are erotic overtones in Wisdom inviting men to a meal, implying an intimate relationship. This follows the erotic language used of Wisdom in 3:18; 7:4; 8:17.

9:7-12 Wisdom Sayings

Because of the change in literary style, and because they separate the two portraits of Wisdom and Folly, most scholars regard these verses as a secondary intrusive addition to this chapter. None has given an explanation for the intrusion that has found general acceptance. The fact that Wisdom seems to speak in v. 11 has led some to move it to follow v. 6.

Murphy comments[80] that our problem with these verses may arise from modern concepts of what is logical and aesthetic. The original author may have thought differently. He says, 'Indeed, we may rightly assume that the architect of this final contrast regarded, or would have regarded, the intervening verses as somehow necessary or at least fitting. In that case, can we legitimately conclude that they are an insertion?'

Byargeon[81] has argued that this section has a coherent literary structure. The use of the noun 'scoffer' and the verb 'to scoff' in vv. 7, 12 forms an *inclusio.* Not all the details of his argument are compelling, but there does seem to be a chiastic structure.

77. Lichtenstein, 'Banquet Motif'; Clifford, *Proverbs,* 103.

78. Murphy, *Proverbs,* 57-58.

79. Fox, *Proverbs 1–9,* 298.

80. Murphy, *Proverbs,* 61.

81. Byargeon, 'Structure and Significance', 368-72.

A1 vv. 7-8. The consequences for the wise of correcting the scoffer.
B1 v. 9. Instruction multiplies the learning of the wise.
C. v. 10 Motto.
B2 v. 11. Wisdom will multiply the years of the wise.
A2 v. 12. The consequences to oneself of being wise or a scoffer.

These verses contain echoes of words and themes from Prov. 1, most notably the motto of 1:7a, and so form an *inclusio* for chs. 1–9. If that is their purpose it is not clear why they occur here and not at the end of the chapter. It may be that the portrait of Folly was considered a more fitting climax to the whole section. They express starkly the contrast between the 'two ways' of v. 6 and in that sense provide a preparation for the figure of Folly as a contrast to that of Wisdom.

Verses 7-8 speak about the incorrigibility of the scoffer (see on 1:22), warning that those who try to teach them engage in a fruitless, and dangerous, task. There is uncertainty about the meaning of v. 7b. Translated literally it says, 'And whoever reproves a wicked man, blemish (מוּמוֹ/*mûmô*).' The last word can refer to a moral blemish or a physical blemish or injury. The REB takes it to mean acquiring the scoffer's faults, but the parallel with v. 7a leads most translations to take it to refer to insult (NIV) or injury (ESV, NRSV). The following verse reinforces v. 7 and also introduces the scoffer/wise contrast, which reappears in v. 12 in the reverse order.

Verse 10a repeats the motto of 1:7a with 'wisdom' replacing 'knowledge.' The two words are not synonymous, but overlap sufficiently in meaning (as the use of 'knowledge' in v. 7b indicates) for the two forms of the motto to say the same thing (see on 1:7 for discussion of the meaning). 'The Holy One' in v. 7b is literally 'the holy ones.' In Hos. 11:12 [Heb. 12:1] the same plural word clearly has a singular meaning as it is used in parallel with 'God.' As with the Hebrew word for 'God' the plural form is probably a 'plural of excellence/majesty.'[82]

The first-person voice of v. 11 could be that of the parent/teacher, presumably the speaker of vv. 1-3. However, the association of wisdom with life in 3:16, 18; 4:13; 8:35; 9:6 makes it more likely that the speaker is Wisdom. This leads a few commentators[83] to take this whole section as a continuation of Wisdom's speech in vv. 4-6. However, the change from invitation to instruction is abrupt and there is little link in subject matter.

There is an apparent contradiction between what is said in v. 12 and the clear theme in Proverbs that wisdom can be passed on to other people, and

82. Joüon §136d.

83. For example, Hubbard, *Proverbs*, 134.

indeed that the behaviour of scoffers can affect others adversely. As with other proverbs, this is a consequence of the inherent limitation of the proverbial form. The emphasis of this proverb is on the effect of a life-choice on the person who makes it. People must bear the responsibility for the choices they make.

9:13-18 Folly's Invitation

'The Woman Folly' translates אֵשֶׁת כְּסִילוּת/*'ēšet kĕsîlût*. The second word occurs only here in the OT in this form. The *-ût* ending can express the abstract meaning of its root,[84] making the literal meaning of the phrase 'woman of foolishness' (NRSV 'the foolish woman'). However, the obvious personification and contrast with Woman Wisdom requires the meaning Woman Folly.[85] The meaning of v. 13b is unclear. The first part can be taken to mean either that she is seductive (ESV) or that she is ignorant (NRSV, ESV footnote), and the second part can be translated as 'she knows nothing' (ESV, NRSV) or as 'she cares for nothing' (REB). Woman Folly is depicted as having many of the traits of the 'strange'/adulterous woman of the earlier chapters: she is noisy (7:11), lacking in knowledge (5:6), she invites men to secret meals (7:15-20), her path leads to death (2:18; 5:5; 7:27).

Woman Folly is said to have a house, but there is no mention of her building it. The contrast with Woman Wisdom is significant in light of 14:1: 'The wisest of women builds her house, but folly with her own hands tears it down.' Wisdom is presented as constructive, Folly is destructive. Both women issue their invitation from 'the highest places in the town' (vv. 3b, 14b). They use identical words (vv. 4, 16) but their invitations differ profoundly. As Clifford[86] puts it,

> One demands that her guests leave behind their ignorance, whereas the other trades on their ignorance. Folly offers only clandestine pleasure ('stolen water,' 'food eaten in secret') but it ends in death. Wisdom offers food and discipline that enables her guests to live.

As noted in commenting on 5:16-18, water imagery can have sexual connotations.

Longman[87] takes 9:3 to imply that Wisdom's house is built on the highest

84. Joüon §88j.
85. Whybray, *Proverbs,* 147 takes the genitive as explicative, giving the same result.
86. Clifford, *Proverbs,* 105.
87. Longman, *Proverbs,* 222.

point of the city and says, 'In the ancient Near East, only one house is built on the high place of a city, and that is the temple. It is not a stretch, therefore, to suggest that Wisdom is not only the personification of Yahweh's wisdom but also of Yahweh himself.' He takes v. 14 to imply that Folly's house is also at the highest point of the city, and takes this to mean that she is a personification of the pagan gods and goddesses who desire to lure Israel away from Yahweh. Perdue[88] comes to a similar conclusion regarding the meaning of the Wisdom/Folly opposition, but on the basis of seeing the description of Wisdom's house as implying that it is a temple. If this metaphorical interpretation of the meaning of the contrast is valid, then it brings the various oppositions of Prov 1–9 to a climax which underlines the motto of 1:7a and 9:10a that 'The fear of Yahweh is the beginning of knowledge/wisdom' and the seriousness of the constant call to 'get wisdom' above all else.

Proverbs 10

10:1-5 Wise and Foolish Sons

On the heading in v. 1a see the sections 'The Structure of Proverbs' and 'Authorship' in the introduction.

The wise-foolish contrast in v. 1 provides a link to ch. 9, and the use of father/mother/son makes a link to 1:8. By this means the collection of sentence proverbs is presented as continuing the teaching of the parents in chs. 1–9.

Use of the construction 'son of X' twice in vv. 1 and 5 forms an *inclusio,* which is made clearer by coming at the beginning of v. 1b and at the end of v. 5. There is a chiastic pattern of positive-negative statements between pairs of verses. There is a coherence of thought in this cluster of proverbs. The general statement in v. 1 that the character of a son has an effect on his parents is supported by a specific reason in v. 2, that ill-gotten wealth does not give ultimate security. Only righteousness does that. In the context of the cluster the security concerned is not just that of the son, but the family's longer-term future. The proverb asserts that righteousness is better than wealth. The reason for this is given in v. 3: Yahweh will ensure that the righteous will not starve and that the appetite of the wicked is not satisfied. Verse 4 introduces a fairly common theme in Proverbs: laziness leads to poverty and diligence to wealth. This prepares the way for v. 5, which gives a concrete example of what it might mean for the sons of v. 1 to be wise or foolish.

88. Perdue, *Proverbs,* 149-54

It is unclear what is meant by 'death' in v. 2. The Targ explains it as 'evil death', presumably an untimely, premature death. This may be because the wise will not get themselves into situations which might have that outcome. However, 'death' here may not mean just the event which ends life, but a power which diminishes the quality of life. There is little evidence of any concept of 'eternal life' in Proverbs (see the section 'Theological Considerations' in the essay 'Acts and Consequences in Proverbs').

The compilers of Proverbs knew that righteous people do sometimes go hungry, and there are proverbs which recognise this (15:16; 16:8). So, in v. 3 we face one of the factors which readers of proverbs must recognise. Van Leeuwen[89] puts it well: 'One proverb is never adequate to describe all of reality; here we find a statement of God's fundamental and usual mode of dealing with humans. Other sayings . . . show that the situation is more complex.'

10:6-11 The Righteous and the Wicked

The repetition of v. 6b in v. 11b together with the righteous-wicked contrast in both verses suggests that they form an *inclusio* for a cluster. Some scholars question whether v. 6b is the original second half of this proverb because of a lack of parallelism between head-mouth and between the *fate* of the righteous–the *behaviour* of the wicked. They suggest that it has been imported from v. 11b where it seems to fit better. Clifford[90] disagrees, arguing that 'mouth' is to be taken as parallel to 'head' (as part standing for the whole) and that the verb יְכַסֶּה/*yěkasseh*, can mean either 'cover, conceal' or 'fill'. Taken in the second sense it does speak of the fate of the wicked (NIV, 'but violence overwhelms the mouth of the wicked').

There is also debate about v. 10b (which in the MT is identical to v. 8b). It does not provide a good parallel to v. 10a, and so here the NRSV follows the reading of the LXX, 'but the one who rebukes boldly makes peace' (cf. REB). This provides a reasonable antithesis to the first line (see below).

The idea of 'blessing' links vv. 6 and 7, with v. 7 giving a specific example of the more general statement in the previous verse. The esteem in which a righteous person is held lives on after death, but the memory of a wicked person disappears with the rotting of their corpse. The parallelism between the two halves of v. 8 is not clear, but the meaning of v. 8b may be that the fool is too busy expressing his own opinions to accept learning in the way the wise person

89. Van Leeuwen, *Proverbs*, 107.

90. Clifford, *Proverbs*, 113.

does. Verse 9 stands at the heart of the cluster and is a general statement about the two ways exemplified by the righteous/wicked and wise/fool contrasts in the preceding verses. The significance of the winking of the eye in v. 10a is unclear (cf. 6:13). If it refers to some deceitful or insincere gesture, then the reading of the LXX in v. 10b provides a reasonable antithesis to it. The verse then gives a specific example of the general contrast made in v. 9. While v. 11b repeats v. 6b, v. 11a may be a development of v. 6a: the mouth (words) of the righteous passes on the blessing they have received. Apart from the words of the righteous, three things are said to be a fountain of life in Proverbs: the teaching of the wise (13:14), the fear of the LORD (14:27), and good sense (16:22).

10:12 Hate and Love

Heim[91] argues that the repetition of 'hatred' and 'covers/conceals' in v. 18 means that vv. 12-18 are marked off as a cluster. However, he accepts that the delimitation of this supposed cluster is unclear. His interpretation of it as a cluster seems forced. Verse 12 seems more closely linked to v. 11 than to what follows. There is the catchword link of 'covers/conceals', and it can be seen as a specific example of the meaning of v. 11a. To 'cover all offences' means to forgive them, as in Ps. 85:2 [Heb. 85:3]. Clifford[92] notes, that the basic antithesis in this proverb is between pacifying and provoking. Exercising love in forgiveness promotes communal harmony, whereas expressions of hatred disrupt it.

10:13-17 Miscellaneous Proverbs

There are catchword links between vv. 13-15 (wisdom/wise/ruin). The ideas of 'wealth' and 'wage, gain' give a conceptual link between vv. 15 and 16, and the word 'life' links vv. 16 and 17. Despite the verbal links there is no coherent theme in these verses.

The parallelism between the two halves of v. 13 is not obvious. This may be an example of a 'disjointed proverb'[93] in which a conclusion has been elided from the first colon. The meaning would then be that the person of understanding knows what to say and when to say it and so does not provoke the correction or punishment that the person who lacks sense does. Verse 14 supports this

91. Heim, *Like Grapes of Gold Set in Silver,* 120.
92. Clifford, *Proverbs,* 114.
93. Fox, 'Disjointed Proverbs'.

meaning: because the wise have stored up knowledge their speech has a positive effect, whereas that of the fool brings disaster.

The link between vv. 14 and 15 is verbal ('ruin') not thematic. Clifford[94] notes that the word ruin (מְחִתַּת/*mĕḥittat*) is used in Ps. 89:40 [Heb. 89:41] of a ruined city. If that is intended here it strengthens the parallelism of this proverb. The statement in v. 15 simply reflects the reality of life. A rich person can cope with a rise in food prices without much difficulty, whereas it may drive a poor person into starvation, or into petty crime to try and avoid it. Elsewhere Proverbs has more to say about the rich and the poor, and in general the references to 'the rich' (עָשִׁיר/*'āšîr*) are hostile.[95] Here v. 16 may be a check against a wrong interpretation of v. 15. It asserts that only wealth that is gained by righteous means is life-enhancing. The contrast between 'life' and 'sin' is unusual. Some commentators and translations take it as a reference to the harmful consequences of sin ('but the income of the wicked brings them punishment', NIV; 'the earnings of the wicked make for a bad end', REB). Others[96] take the Hebrew word חַטָּאת/*ḥaṭṭā't* not to mean 'sin' but 'missing/falling short', meaning that the wicked fail to attain 'life' (cf. the use of the cognate verb in 20:2 to mean '[he] forfeits his life').

The difference between the NRSV ('Whoever heeds instruction is on the path to life, but one who rejects reproof goes astray', cf. REB) and the NIV ('He who heeds discipline shows the way to life, but whoever ignores correction leads others astray') arises from disagreement about the rendering of the first and last words in the proverb. The opening word in the MT (אֹרַח/*'ōraḥ*) is a noun meaning 'path, way' and leads to the literal translation, 'He who heeds discipline is the way to life' and hence the NIV translation. Re-pointing it as a Qal participle (אֹרֵחַ/*'ōrēaḥ*) 'is on the way to' gives the NRSV translation. The last word (מַתְעֶה/*mat'eh*) is a *hiphil* participle and can be taken to mean either 'leads astray' or 'goes astray'. Since the causative meaning of a *hiphil* is more common, and the MT reading gives a good parallel to this, the NIV translation seems preferable. It then forms a counterpart to v. 16 by referring to the effect that the behaviour of the righteous and the wicked have on the fate of others, not just their own fate.

10:18-21 Bad and Good Speech

Each of these verses refers to organs of speech (lips, tongue), and there is also a 'many/little/many' alternation in vv. 19-21. There is a coherent thread of how

94. Clifford, *Proverbs*, 114-15.
95. Whybray, *Wealth and Poverty*, 22-23.
96. Clifford, *Proverbs*, 115; Whybray, *Proverbs*, 166.

speech is used, with an emphasis on its bad use in vv. 18-19 and its good use in vv. 20-21.

Verse 18 stands out by not having the clear antithetic parallelism that predominates in this section of Proverbs. It is not clear what is the subject and what the object in v. 18a, hence the different translations in the ESV ('The one who conceals hatred has lying lips'; cf. NIV) and the NRSV and REB ('Lying lips conceal hatred'). The meaning is much the same in either case, but the ESV translation gives a better formal parallelism with v. 18b: one who conceals hatred is a liar// one who slanders is a fool. Both cola refer to a form of dishonesty. Some commentators[97] argue that the proverb is better construed as a single sentence: 'Both the one who conceals hatred with lying lips and the one who spreads slander is a fool'. However v. 18 is construed, v. 19 can be taken as a comment on it. 'Many words' are needed both to conceal hatred and to spread slander. Both evils, and others, can be avoided by restricting oneself to a few well-chosen words.

The next two verses expand on the positive statement of v. 19b. The 'tongue' or 'lips' is paired with 'heart' a number of times in Proverbs. Clifford[98] sums up the significance of this pairing: 'Heart and tongue stand, respectively, for knowledge and its verbal expression. Together, tongue and heart symbolize the person as a communicating being'. Following on from v. 19, v. 20 asserts that the words of the righteous are scarce (choice) and valuable (like silver) whereas those of the wicked are worthless (כִּמְעָט/*kimʿāṭ*, an emphatic form of the word for 'little').[99] This evaluation is supported by v. 21, which stresses the beneficial effects of the words of the wise for others. The verb רָעָה/*rāʿâ* ('feed'), means to tend a flock like a shepherd. In the OT it is used of the care that God or a king, or other leader, shows for people. Only here is it used of the righteous. Their wisdom nourishes many people. By contrast the fools cannot even look after themselves.

10:22-25 Dread and Desire

The message of v. 22, that it is Yahweh who brings blessing, sets the tone for the next few verses. The REB brings out the emphasis of the Hebrew of v. 22a: 'The blessing of the LORD is what brings riches'. Verse 22b can be construed in two ways. The ESV and NRSV footnote renderings are to be preferred: 'and toil adds nothing to it'. Otherwise, as Fox[100] comments, v. 22b would be banal, as one

97. See the syntactic argument of Waltke, *Proverbs 1–15*, 466, n. 4.
98. Clifford, *Proverbs*, 115.
99. GKC §118x.
100. Fox, *Proverbs 10–31*, 525.

would not expect a blessing to include misery. That human effort cannot add to Yahweh's blessing does not contradict 10:4b or denigrate human effort (any more than 21:30 contradicts the constant call to seek wisdom), but recognises that no human effort can succeed without Yahweh (cf. 16:3).

Verse 23 defines the moral character of the fool and the 'man of understanding'. The Hebrew of v. 23b is elliptical, 'but wisdom to a man of understanding', and needs something to be supplied to complete the sense. The word translated 'joke' in the first colon (שְׂחוֹק/*śĕḥôq*) also has the more general sense 'pleasure', and this fits well in the second colon. Despite the entertainment the wicked get from doing wrong they have an underlying dread (v. 24a), presumably that the consequences of their evil might catch up with them. The righteous, because of their moral character, have desires that are good and that will be granted by Yahweh, who is to be taken as the implied subject of the verb in v. 24b. This is an example of the 'blessing of the LORD' mentioned in v. 22a. This short cluster is concluded by v. 25, which gives an example of what people dread: a (probably metaphorical) tempest. The wicked will not survive it, but the righteous will. Jesus' parable about the two houses in Matt. 7:24-27 could be an expansion of this proverb.

10:26 The Sluggard

This proverb stands out in its context because of its form (synonymous parallelism and use of a double simile) and content. Sloth or laziness is a frequent topic in Proverbs and is personified in the figure of the sluggard (עָצֵל/*'āṣēl*), who is usually the subject of sarcasm and scorn. The point here is the irritation and damage that his laziness causes to those who send him to do a task (his 'employers', NRSV).

10:27-30 Contrasting Destinies

Another Yahweh proverb (v. 27) introduces a new cluster of proverbs which contrast the destinies of the righteous and the wicked (on 'the fear Yahweh' see on 1:7). It sets the scene for what follows by asserting that a person's destiny depends on their relationship to Yahweh. As usual with a proverb, it states what is generally true, not what always happens in the complexity of life. Verse 28 refers to people's inner expectations: the righteous will find that theirs are realised whereas those of the wicked will be dashed. The reason for this difference in experience is given in v. 29. The phrase 'the way of the LORD' is ambiguous.

It could mean the way the 'blameless' live, the way of wisdom and the fear of the LORD, or it could mean the Yahweh's way of acting, his protection of the righteous and punishment of evildoers. The latter meaning makes good sense here. If the first sense is adopted the meaning of the second colon is not clear. The message of this cluster is summed up in v. 30. The result of right conduct is stability and security, and the result of wickedness is loss of both (on the 'land' in Proverbs see on 2:21-22). Psalm 37 can be read as a commentary on this cluster, and on v. 30 in particular.

10:31-32 More on Words

Here the body parts mouth/tongue/lips are a poetic way of referring to the whole person involved in a particular activity. The use of them links these two verses, as does the use of the word 'perverse'. The verb used in v. 31a for 'bring forth' (נוּב/*nûb*) is rare in the OT and has an agricultural background.[101] This suggests that an agricultural metaphor is being used in this verse. The righteous produce the fruits of wisdom but the perverse do not (the implication is that they produce folly)[102] and so are cut down like a worthless plant. The reason for the difference in fruit-bearing is given in v. 32. The righteous know how to use words properly ('suit words to the occasion', REB) whereas the wicked misuse them perversely.

Proverbs 11

11:1 Business Ethics

This verse stands out in context because of its content. It is linked to 10:32 by the catchword רָצוֹן/*rāṣôn* ('acceptable', 'delight'). The use of false weights is condemned in OT law (Deut. 25:14-15; Lev. 19:35-36) and by the prophets (Ezek. 45:10; Hos. 12:7 [Heb. 12:8]; Amos 8:5; Mic. 6:10-11). It is also dealt with in Prov. 16:11; 20:10, 23. In Egyptian wisdom literature[103] dishonest weights are said to displease the gods. On the meaning of 'abomination', see on 3:32.

101. *NIDOTTE* 3:52.
102. Fox, 'Disjointed Proverbs', 172-73.
103. See for example *AEL* 2:156-57.

11:2-8 True and False Security

These verses are loosely linked by recurring references to destruction/death/perishing on the one hand and being saved on the other.

The word for 'humble' in v. 2 (צְנוּעִים/*ṣĕnûʿîm*) occurs only here in the OT. It is probably best translated as 'modesty' (REB) in the sense of a proper self-assessment. The proud and the modest differ in their openness to learn from advice and from their mistakes. The proud are doomed to repeat their errors and so end up in disgrace.

Words such as 'upright', 'righteousness' and 'treacherous' recur in vv. 3-6, which expresses in various ways the belief that the virtues of the upright protect them from disaster whereas the moral failings of the wicked lead to their ruin. This is stated as a general principle in v. 3. Verse 4b repeats 10:2b but the verse as a whole makes a more general statement that riches are not an ultimate basis for security. In the OT prophets 'the day of wrath' usually has an eschatological meaning but here it probably refers to any disaster that threatens death, as in Job 21:30; Ezek. 7:19; Zeph. 1:15. The metaphor of the two ways appears in v. 5, which is similar in meaning to v. 3. A specific cause of the downfall of the wicked is given in v. 6, their 'lust' or 'evil desires' (NIV).

Textual and philological problems in v. 7 make its meaning uncertain. The first colon seems too long and includes the phrase 'wicked man'. Some scholars think that 'wicked' is a later addition to the text (it is missing from two Hebrew mss)[104] and omit it. The second main area of debate concerns the meaning of אוֹנִים/*ʾônîm* in v. 7b. It might come from a noun, אוֹן/*ʾôn,* which has a wide range of meanings[105] of which the most likely are either 'wealth' (ESV, REB) or 'strength/power' (NIV). The NRSV ('the expectation of the godless comes to nothing') assumes that it comes from a different noun אָוֶן/*ʾāwen* meaning 'evil', but this makes the two halves of the proverb say almost exactly the same thing. Even if the word 'wicked' is omitted from v. 7a it is probably to be inferred that it is wicked people who are in mind, with v. 7b specifying one of their major sources of hope. Less likely is the meaning that death brings an end to all hopes, and that not even wealth/power survive death.

Van Leeuwen[106] rightly points to two biblical examples of the meaning of this proverb: Haman being hanged on the gallows he had prepared for Mordecai (Est. 7:10) and Daniel's enemies being thrown into the lions' den to suffer the fate they had planned for Daniel (Dan. 6:24).

104. Waltke, *Proverbs 1–15,* 481, n. 67.
105. *NIDOTTE* 1:315.
106. Van Leeuwen, *Proverbs,* 118.

11:9-14 Speech and Community

The theme of the relationship of the individual to the community, especially through the use of words, runs through these proverbs but they are not a carefully structured cluster. The LXX enhances the communal aspect by translating 'neighbour' in vv. 9, 12 as 'citizen'.

Although v. 9 shares the catchword 'delivered' with v. 8, thematically it goes with the following verses. Grammatically v. 9b is ambiguous. Although most EVV take it to mean that the knowledge the righteous have saves them from the attempts of the godless to ruin others, it can be taken to mean that their knowledge delivers the 'neighbours' whom the godless are seeking to ruin. This provides a better contrast with the first colon and coheres with the communal theme. The rather free translation of the REB ('By their words the godless try to ruin others, but when the righteous plead for them they are saved') seems to put this specifically into a judicial context.

Both vv. 10 and 11 are concerned with the benefits which the righteous bring to a community, specified as a city. Verse 11 provides the explanation for the rejoicing in v. 10. The nature of the 'blessing' in v. 11a is undefined. It is also unclear whether it refers to the blessing God bestows on the upright or the blessing which the upright impart to others. Perhaps the distinction is unimportant since the one will lead to the other. However, the unusual parallel between 'blessing' and 'mouth' may indicate that it is particularly the prayers and counsel of the upright that are implied.

Alliteration between their last words, 'overthrown' (תֵּהָרֵס/*tēhārēs*) and 'remains silent' (יַחֲרִישׁ/*yaḥărîš*) links vv. 11 and 12, but vv. 12 and 13 clearly form a pair in terms of their content: the importance of self-restraint in speech in contrast to the destructive effects on the community of derogatory comments. 'Slandering' in v. 13a gives a specific example of what it means to 'belittle' a neighbour (v. 12a). The NIV and NRSV translate רָכִיל/*rākîl* as 'gossip' rather than 'slanderer', but Kidner[107] notes that, 'Other Old Testament references to the *talebearer* (apart from the indeterminate 20:19) portray him as malicious rather than indiscreet; he is an informer out to hurt'. The secrets (סוֹד/*sôd*) he betrays may refer to either the deliberations of some body (so LXX, 'counsel in an assembly') or the confidences of friends (e.g. 3:32; Job 19:19; Ps. 25:14). The latter seems more appropriate here.

Verse 14 is a general statement about the importance of good counsel for a community. Since the word for 'safety' (תְּשׁוּעָה/*tĕšûʿâ*) can mean 'victory' and because v. 14b recurs in 24:6b following a reference to waging war, it is possible

107. Kidner, *Proverbs*, 91.

to translate this verse as the REB does: 'For want of skilful strategy an army is lost; victory is the fruit of long planning'. However, it is more likely that, 'this verse offers a metaphor from waging war applicable to daily life'[108] and that the more general sense given by the translations of the ESV, NIV and NRSV is appropriate.

11:15-21 Reaping What You Sow

A prominent theme of these verses is the consequences of certain characters or actions. (On the theme of not acting as a guarantor for a loan [v. 15] see on 6:1-5.)

It is difficult to identify the essential antithesis in v. 16. Is it between gentle and violent ways of achieving one's ends (ESV, 'A gracious woman gets honor, and violent men get riches'), between honour and riches (REB, 'A gracious woman gets honour; a bold man gets only a fortune'; cf. NIV) or between women and men? The longer LXX text followed by the NRSV is probably an attempt to interpret the unclear Hebrew text. Van Leeuwen[109] takes the adjective חֵן/*ḥēn* not as 'gracious' but as 'beautiful' (a sense it often has when describing women) and the proverb as simply an observation on the way the world is: beautiful women get honour, violent men get riches.

Verse 17 expresses the paradox that when people do something out of concern for others they sometimes gain benefit from it, and those who harm others may harm their own interests. Verses 18-21 expand on this paradox. In vv. 18-19, 21 the consequences of righteous actions are satisfaction, life and safety, whereas the wicked experience disappointment, death and punishment. In the MT v. 21b has 'the seed of the righteous'. The NIV and NRSV take this to mean 'those who are righteous'. The ESV and REB follow its more usual sense 'the offspring of the righteous', implying that the deeds of the righteous provide security not only for themselves, but also their children (cf. 13:22; 14:26; 20:7).

11:22 Beauty without Wisdom

Beauty without wisdom being incongruous[110] is the message of this proverb. It may be advice to a young man looking for a wife. Beauty is not worth the

108. Clifford, *Proverbs*, 123.
109. Van Leeuwen, *Proverbs*, 118-119.
110. Murphy, *Proverbs*, 83.

problems that an indiscreet wife might cause. The proverb gains impact from the fact that Israelite women wore nose rings (Gen. 24:47; Isa. 3:21) and the pig was an unclean animal.

11:23-27 Generosity

Generosity is the theme of vv. 24-26, which are flanked by two proverbs about people's desires, both of which use the word *ṭôḇ* ('good').

Verse 23 is a variant of 10:28, which prompts the REB, following the LXX, to emend the final word from 'wrath' to 'nothingness' — an unnecessary harmonisation. The point of this verse, and v. 27, is the contrast between the righteous and the wicked in what they desire and in the outcome of their desires.

Verse 24 states a paradox similar to that of v. 17. As Van Leeuwen[111] puts it, 'Generosity would seem to diminish one's resources but, in God's economy, brings gain' — the reverse is true for those who are miserly (cf. 2 Cor 9:6). Verse 25 reinforces v. 24a. The first colon can be translated literally as, 'the throat of blessing will grow fat', and the proverb may refer to generosity in giving food and drink.[112] This would lead in well to v. 26a, which condemns those who seek to manipulate the food market (perhaps in times of scarcity) for personal gain.

11:28-31 Miscellaneous Proverbs

There is no clear theme in these proverbs.

Verse 28 does not condemn wealth but, implicitly, trust in wealth instead of God (cf. 11:4; 1 Tim. 6:17). The NRSV improves the parallelism by emending יִפֹּל/*yippōl* ('fall') to יִבֹּל/*yibbōl* ('wither'), but the versions do not support this.

The subject of v. 29 is the mismanagement of a household and its resources. 'Inherit the wind' probably means 'become insolvent'. The message of v. 29b is that 'Incompetency of any kind leads to slavery'.[113]

Verse 30a promises that righteousness leads to life (on 'the tree of life' see on 3:18). Verse 30b is difficult to interpret because elsewhere in the OT the phrase 'to capture souls' means 'to take away life'. The NRSV and REB therefore emend 'wise' (חָכָם/*ḥākām*) to 'violence' (חָמָס/*ḥāmās*) with some support from the LXX. The Targ, however, takes the phrase in a positive way: 'The winner

111. Van Leeuwen, *Proverbs,* 119.
112. Clifford, *Proverbs,* 125 takes it this way.
113. Murphy, *Proverbs,* 84.

of his soul is wisdom' (cf. NJPSV, 'A wise man captivates people'), and some scholars[114] argue that the context here requires a positive reading of the colon along the lines that the righteous give life to others.

It is not easy to understand the 'If . . . how much more' argument of v. 31. It probably means: since even the righteous are repaid for those sins they commit (cf. 20:9), how much more will the wicked get their due in this life? This seems to be how the LXX understood it (1 Pet. 4:18 quotes its paraphrase).

Proverbs 12

12:1-3 Fundamental Truths

Fundamental truths that underlie the teaching of the sages are expressed in these three proverbs.

The sages regarded willingness to learn through correction as crucial in gaining wisdom. Quoting Bonhoeffer, Van Leeuwen[115] comments that 'Paradoxically, discipline is a "station on the way to freedom".' Those who reject discipline are characterised as בַּעַר/*bāʿar* (v. 1), a word which refers to a person 'who does not have the rationality that differentiates men from animals (Ps. 73:22)'.[116] Because the LORD upholds the moral order (v. 2) the ultimate destinies of the wicked and the righteous are assured. The 'root of the righteous' refers to the stable foundation which endures to succeeding generations.

12:4 The Excellent Wife

The 'excellent wife' is a recurrent theme in Proverbs, addressed as it is to young males. What is said on this theme is meant to motivate care in the choice of a spouse. The imagery used here may allude to the crowns worn by bride and groom in the wedding ceremony of the time.[117] The antithesis in v. 4b does not define in what way a wife might 'bring shame' to her husband. The imagery used can be paraphrased in modern terms as 'cancer' (REB).

114. Clifford, *Proverbs,* 127; Heim, *Like Grapes of Gold Set in Silver,* 145-46; Irwin, 'Metaphor'; Waltke, *Proverbs 1–15,* 513.

115. Van Leeuwen, *Proverbs,* 124.

116. *NIDOTTE* 1:691.

117. Clifford, *Proverbs,* 130.

12:5-7 The Two Ways

The two ways seen worked out in the sequence of plan-action-consequence is the theme of this small group of proverbs. The parallelism in v. 5 shows that the first colon refers to 'plans' (NIV; a common meaning of מַחְשְׁבוֹת/*maḥšĕbôt*) and not just general 'thoughts'. Some commentators[118] see a judicial setting behind v. 6, but the language of v. 6a could be a metaphor of wider applicability. As in 12:3 the consequences of the plans and actions of the righteous are presented as bringing security to their family, not just themselves.

12:8-12 Life and Work

Clifford[119] says of v. 8, 'What is hidden (in the mind) will eventually come out — and merit praise or blame.' The next verse may be a specific illustration of what has just been said. Re-pointing of עֶבֶד/*'ebed* to עֹבֵד/*'ōbēd* (suggested by the LXX) allows a change of meaning from 'have a servant' (ESV, NIV, NRSV) to 'earn one's living' (REB). Either way, the point of the proverb is that substance is more important than appearance.

Farming is the background to vv. 10-11. There is an oxymoron in v. 10b: even the attempted kindness of the wicked toward their domesticated animals is a form of cruelty. This proverb may imply that people's sensitivity (or lack of it) to the needs of the animals that work for them is an indication of how they will treat other people. The theme of diligence leading to prosperity is common in Proverbs (e.g. 10:4-5) but here, unusually, the contrast is not with laziness but with energy misdirected to undefined 'worthless pursuits' (v. 11b). They might vary from seemingly harmless 'displacement activities' which prevent one getting on with the task in hand to addictive activities which waste time, energy and money.

Text-critical and philological problems abound in v. 12. The ESV stays fairly close to the MT of v. 12a : 'The wicked man desires the hunting nets of the evildoers'. Various transpositions and emendations of the MT have been proposed, including that reflected in the REB: 'The stronghold of the wicked crumbles like clay'. After assessing several of them McKane[120] concludes, 'v. 12a remains a puzzle'. In the MT v. 12b reads, 'The root of the righteous *will give*', and it is the meaning of the verb that is the puzzle. One way of dealing with it

118. Murphy, *Proverbs*, 89; Whybray, *Proverbs*, 192.
119. Clifford, *Proverbs*, 130.
120. McKane, *Proverbs*, 450.

is to take the phrase as elliptical and supply some object for the verb, like 'fruit' in the ESV. The REB follows the LXX in reading 'will endure' rather than 'will give', resulting in 'the righteous will take lasting root'. Unfortunately, given the state of the text the exact nature of the contrast being made between the wicked and the righteous is unclear.

12:13-25 Words: Character and Consequences

With the exception of vv. 20-21, 24 these proverbs are about speech, its consequences and the ways in which speech reveals the speaker's character.

Verse 13a is a statement of the principle of retribution. Those who commit sins of speech will find that they cause trouble for themselves. The righteous, by contrast, presumably because their speech is truthful, can get themselves out of troublesome situations. Verse 14 extends the meaning of v. 13. People cannot escape the consequences of both their words and their actions. In this case they are the good consequences appropriate to the words and actions of the righteous.

The next two proverbs are about the fool. The first returns to the theme of 12:1, the importance of teachability. As well as being unteachable, the fool lacks self-control. Instant reaction to an insult gives the insulter the satisfaction of knowing that they have gained a victory. The prudent person refuses to give that satisfaction.

The word used for 'speaks' in v. 17a (יָפִיחַ/*yāpîaḥ*) in its other uses in Proverbs means 'testify in court' (6:19; 14:5, 25; 19:5, 9), and the word used for 'witness' in v. 17b (עֵד/*'ēd*) often has a legal sense. So, the setting of this proverb is the courtroom. On the face of it, this seems tautologous. However, it may be addressing the question, 'How can one evaluate courtroom testimony?'[121] The answer is that one should examine the way the witnesses use speech in their ordinary use of speech. The warning about the harm that rash words can do (v. 18) may also have legal testimony in mind, but the proverb is also of more general relevance. Verse 19 asserts that truth will endure but that lies will be found out. Again, legal testimony may be in mind.

There is no clear antithesis in v. 20. This may be a 'disjointed proverb'[122] in which the consequence of the action (presumably the opposite of the 'joy' of v. 20b) has been elided from the first colon. This would fit with the suggestion[123]

121. Clifford, *Proverbs*, 132.
122. Fox, 'Disjointed Proverbs'.
123. McKane, *Proverbs*, 447.

that the implied antithesis requires the 'deceit' to be self-deception. Those who devise evil delude themselves and so suffer when the plan rebounds on them. Those who plan for the common good share in the well-being they help to achieve. The following verse expands this into a general principle, which is not to be taken as an invariable rule.

Verse 22 returns to the theme of speech, making clear that good and bad uses of speech have the consequences they do because the LORD delights in the one and abhors the other. On 'abomination to the LORD' see on 3:32. Verse 23 is a more general statement of what was said in v. 16: the wise know when to speak and what to say but fools cannot control their speech, and so show that they are fools.

There is irony in v. 24. Hard workers achieve positions of authority where they do not need to work, but the lazy end up doing forced labour for others.

Words can be a power for good, as v. 25 asserts. There may be a contrast here between the anxiety and depression that comes from within and the encouragement and uplift that comes from outside through the words of another.

12:26-28 Three Miscellaneous Proverbs

These three proverbs, which contain textual difficulties, conclude this chapter.

Comparison of different EVV shows that the MT of v. 26a is obscure and open to various interpretations. No generally acceptable solution has been found despite various suggested emendations.

> ESV: 'One who is righteous is a guide to his neighbour.' (cf. NRSV)
> NIV: 'A righteous man is cautious in friendship.'
> REB: 'The righteous are freed from evil.'

Despite uncertainties in the MT the main point of v. 27 is clear. It discourages laziness and encourages diligence. The first colon pillories the lazy by saying either that they cannot catch any game or that they do not even cook it when they have caught it. The second colon is enigmatic: 'The wealth of a man is precious, a diligent person.' The translation of the ESV, 'but the diligent man will get precious wealth' seems reasonable.

The translations of v. 28b in the NIV ('along that path is immortality') and the REB ('but there is a well-worn path to death') indicate the range of possible interpretations. These arise because the MT is clearly corrupt. It reads 'but the way of the path (נְתִיבָה/*nĕtîbâ*) no (אַל/*'al*) death'. None of the ancient versions read the word 'of the path', and most commentators agree that it is a textual error, but there is no agreement on what should replace it. Also, the form of the word for 'no' is that used with verbs, not nouns. Most re-point it as the preposition אֶל/*'el* meaning 'to'. A reading such as that of the REB gives a parallelism which reflects the 'two ways' imagery that is common in Proverbs. The textual uncertainty is too great to make this the one verse in Proverbs which reflects a belief in the after-life, as the NIV translation does.

Proverbs 13

13:1-6 Speech

Speech is the main theme of these verses. Verses 2-4 are linked by the root נפשׁ/*npš* which is translated variously as 'desire' (v. 2), 'life' (v. 3) and 'soul' (v. 4). The righteous-wicked contrast links vv. 5 and 6.

The first colon of v. 1 lacks a verb. The ESV and NIV supply 'listen' from the second colon whereas the NRSV and REB emend the word 'father' (אָב/*'āb*) to 'loves' (אֹהֵב/*'ohēb*) in line with 12:1. See comment on 12:1 on the importance of teachability (a theme repeated in 13:10, 13, 18) and on 1:22 on the scoffer.

Proverbs 13:2a asserts that people will reap the consequences of their words (cf. 12:14a). The antithesis is not exact but clearly implies that the words of v. 2a are good ones. Clifford[124] takes נֶפֶשׁ/*nepeš* in v. 2b in the sense 'throat' (as an organ of speech, i.e. 'words') to give a better parallel. The parallelism implies that the 'violence' rebounds on the speaker. Van Leeuwen[125] comments, 'Verse 3 follows logically upon v. 2. Since speech bears good or bad fruit, the organs of speech must be carefully controlled'. The wide-open lips of v. 3b represent an unguarded mouth. In v. 4 נֶפֶשׁ/*nepeš* is best translated as 'appetite' as in NRSV. This verse is an extension of v. 2a in the same way as 12:14b extends 12:14a, that people must face the consequences of their actions as well as of their words. On the sluggard see the comment on 6:6-11.

Verse 5b does not say how the wicked bring shame, but presumably it is because, in contrast to the righteous, they love falsehood.[126] The verbs in the second colon can be taken intransitively as in the NRSV ('acts shamefully') or, more likely, causatively as in the ESV ('brings shame'). Whybray[127] suggests that v. 6 is 'intended to constitute a comment on v. 5; both the righteous and

124. Clifford, *Proverbs*, 136.
125. Van Leeuwen, *Proverbs*, 131.
126. Fox, 'Disjointed Proverbs', 172.
127. Whybray, *Proverbs*, 202.

the wicked respectively reap the fruits of their own conduct'. If so, it reinforces vv. 2-4.

13:7-11 Wealth and Poverty

The occurrence of הוֹן/*hôn* ('wealth') and the root רב/*rb* ('great', 'increase') in vv. 7, 11 forms an *inclusio* for these verses.

Although phrased as a statement of the way things are, v. 7 is sufficiently ambiguous to be open to various interpretations, such as: 'appearances are deceptive' and 'people can be deluded about their true situation'. Apart from the substitution of 'a poor man' for 'a scoffer', v. 8b is identical to v. 1b, but in view of the different context provided by v. 8a, most commentators take the noun גְּעָרָה/*gĕʿārâ* to mean 'threat' here. The proverb is then a statement that while the wealthy have the resources to get themselves out of certain kinds of trouble (perhaps kidnapping or blackmail are in mind) the poor person's lack of wealth means that they are not subject to such threats.

'Light' in v. 9 is a metaphor for life-force (cf. 20:20; 24:20). The normal meaning of the verb יִשְׂמָח/*yiśmāḥ* in the first colon is 'rejoices' (ESV, NRSV). Some take it to mean 'shine brightly' (NIV, REB) on the basis of cognate verbs.[128] Taken in its context this general statement is a comment on the previous verse: true security is not in either wealth or poverty but in righteousness.

A literal translation of the MT of v. 10a is 'By arrogance he gives only strife', which is reflected by the ESV and NIV. The reading of the NRSV, 'By insolence the heedless make strife' (cf. REB), results from re-pointing רַק/*raq* ('only') as רֵק/*rēq* ('empty-headed').[129] Again, a general statement might be taken in context as preparing the way for the verse which follows since those who get rich quickly have a tendency to arrogance.

The MT of v. 11a reads, 'Riches dwindle *from nothingness/impermanence*' (מֵהֶבֶל/*mēhebel,* a word that means 'vapour'). The NIV translation, 'Dishonest money dwindles away' is argued for by Waltke:[130] 'The metaphor of getting money from a vapour suggests what English speakers call "easy money", including tyranny, injustice, extortion, lies and windfalls, at the expense of others.' Most commentators emend the text to מְבֹהָל/*mĕbōhāl* 'hastily acquired' following the LXX (ESV, NRSV, REB). The suspicion of hastily gained wealth is repeated in 20:21; 28:20, 22.

128. See Clifford, *Proverbs,* 135; Whybray, *Proverbs,* 203-204.
129. McKane, *Proverbs,* 453-454.
130. Waltke, *Proverbs 1–15,* 561.

13:12-19 The Benefits of Wisdom

The phrase 'a desire fulfilled' in vv. 12 and 19 makes these verses a frame for this section, and the similarity in meaning of vv. 13 and 18 strengthens this frame. Yoder[131] sees a chiasm here with vv. 14 and 17 about people whose speech is live-giving or deadly and vv. 15 and 16 being about good sense. The theme running through vv. 13-18 is the benefits which wisdom brings.

Verse 12 is a psychological observation, not a piece of advice. On the imagery of the tree of life see comment on 3:18. Verse 13 repeats a common theme in Proverbs (see on 12:1). There is some debate as to whether the 'word' and 'commandment' here are human or divine. McKane[132] overdoes the distinction since in Proverbs the authoritative teaching of the father often seems to be presented as an extension of Yahweh's commands.[133] The 'reward' in v. 13b is made clear in the next two proverbs. Murphy[134] comments that life in v. 14a 'is to be understood in its total meaning: not just being spared from imminent or unexpected death, but also embracing a high quality of life'. Verse 14b underlines this. One aspect of a high quality of life is being well-regarded in one's community (v. 15a). In v. 15b the MT reads, 'The way of the treacherous is enduring (אֵיתָן/*'êtān*)'. The NIV takes 'enduring' in the sense of 'firm, hard' in order to obtain the negative sense that seems required. The ESV, NRSV and REB emend the text to אֵידָם/*'êdām,* 'ruin' in line with the LXX reading.

The NIV takes the 'all' in v. 16a as qualifying 'prudent person', whereas the other versions take it as the object of the verb. The proverb is an interesting variant of 12:23. The prudent may keep quiet while fools babble on, but they show their wisdom by what they do.

In a largely oral culture messengers played a very important role. They were needed to convey messages safely and accurately, and sometimes acted as intermediaries and negotiators. A messenger who acted out of malice or self-interest could do great harm. As the MT of v. 17a stands it means that the wicked messenger does harm to himself (ESV, NIV). To get a better parallelism with the second colon some emend the verb יִפֹּל/*yippōl* ('falls') to the causative *(hiphil)* form יַפִּל/*yappīl* ('cause to fall'), hence the NRSV, 'A bad messenger brings trouble' (cf. REB). The nature of the 'trouble' and 'healing' is left open.

The theme of the importance of teachability returns in v. 18 (cf. 21:11; 13:1, 13). Verse 19a is similar to v. 13b. While most commentators see little correla-

131. Yoder, *Proverbs,* 150.

132. McKane, *Proverbs,* 454.

133. Longman, *Proverbs,* 288.

134. Murphy, *Proverbs,* 97.

tion between the cola of this verse, Fox[135] regards v. 19 as a disjointed proverb in which the premise 'fools desire evil' has to be supplied in the second colon. It then becomes clear that the reason why fools resist turning away from evil is given in the first colon, they want the sweetness of having their evil desire fulfilled.

13:20-25 Encouragement to Be Good

Encouragement to be good is given in these verses by setting out the rewards of goodness.

The sages were aware that the instruction given through classroom learning, at home or school, is not enough. We are influenced by those with whom we associate, and therefore we need to choose our companions carefully. The REB follows the K of v. 20a: 'Walk with the wise and learn wisdom'; whereas other EVV follow the Q by replacing the imperatives with imperfects to give a closer parallelism with the verb forms in the second colon: 'Whoever walks with the wise becomes wise' (ESV). There is no great difference in meaning.

Verses 21 and 22 are linked by a striking chiastic pattern in that v. 21 begins and ends with 'sinners . . . good' and v. 22 with 'good . . . sinner'. The previous verse stressed the importance of seeking the right companions. Verse 21 states the retribution principle in the unusual form that what people pursue pursues them, so that they get what they deserve. This is then supported by a concrete example in v. 22. In a society where there was no clear idea of life beyond death it was particularly important to leave a good inheritance to future generations. The good person is assured that this will be so, whereas the sinner is warned that, in some unspecified way, the wealth they accumulate will not benefit their descendants but pass to the righteous. This provided one answer to the apparent injustice of sinners sometimes gaining wealth. Matters will be sorted out in future generations. The thinking here is clearly communal and not individualistic.

Translation problems in v. 23 make its meaning uncertain. The EVV give the most probable meaning of the MT. This acts as counter to a too rigid application of vv. 20-22. It recognises that some people are poor, not because they are sinners, but because of injustice, the sins of others.

The importance of discipline in the pursuit of wisdom has been emphasised in vv. 1, 10, 18. A specific example is given in v. 24. Physical punishment was taken for granted in the ancient Near East and is mentioned frequently in Egyptian literature. Statements like this proverb trouble some today, given the

135. Fox, 'Disjointed Proverbs', 168-69.

legitimate concerns about violent parents and child abuse. However, this should not stop us taking serious the issue with which it deals, what Van Leeuwen[136] calls the paradox of 'tough love'. He says, 'If human nature has been distorted by sin, to let a child do as it pleases is no kindness. To let a child grow up with no sense of boundaries or consequences is cruel'. We have to discern the best way to establish and inculcate those boundaries today and what are appropriate methods of discipline.

Verse 25 echoes the sentiment of 10:3. See the comment on that verse.

Proverbs 14

14:1-3 Wisdom and Folly

Wisdom and folly occur in chiastic order in vv. 1 and 3 and form a frame for this group of verses.

The ESV gives a fairly literal translation of the MT of v. 1a. Because, apart from the word 'women', the consonantal text is identical to that of 9:1, and the word seems to make the colon overlong, some scholars delete it and translate the colon in the same way as 9:1. They understand the verse as personifying wisdom and folly as in ch. 9. However, the text makes sense as it stands. It presents, not a personification of wisdom and folly, but their incarnation in women as home-makers. Given the wide range of meanings of the word 'house' in Hebrew there is no need to insist that this verse refers to the building of the physical structure of a house. The excellent wife of 31:10-31 is the epitome of 'the wisest of women' of v. 1a. In the context of Proverbs as a whole the purpose of this proverb is to stress that care is needed in choosing a spouse. The following verse serves to equate wisdom and folly with a person's attitude to Yahweh. Since the Hebrew word for 'uprightness' can also mean 'straight' there is a contrast with 'devious' which is not apparent in English translation. On 'the fear of the LORD' see on 1:7. Verse 3 gives an example of folly and wisdom in the realm of words, which provides a transition to the following proverbs. The NJPSV follows the MT in its translation of v. 3a, 'In the mouth of a fool is a rod of haughtiness'. In its only other occurrence in the OT the word translated as 'haughtiness' (חֹטֶר/*ḥōṭer*) means 'shoot' (Isa. 11:1), so the idea here might be of pride growing from the mouth of the fool. Pride, of course, will lead to disaster (16:8). The ESV emends the word for 'haughtiness' (גַּאֲוָה/*ga'ăwâ*) to the word for 'back' (גֵּוֹה/*gēwōh*). The meaning then is that the fool's speech will bring punishment or

136. Van Leeuwen, *Proverbs*, 135.

other pain on him. This produces a stricter antithesis with the second colon, but there is no textual support for this emendation.

14:4 An Agricultural Proverb

Although Heim[137] argues that this verse belongs with those which follow it, it seems to stand alone. The ESV gives a translation of the MT in the first colon, 'Where there are no oxen the manger is clean', and the meaning of the proverb then seems to be, 'although the farmer can save himself work or expense by not keeping oxen, that is a false economy'. The NRSV translation, 'Where there are no oxen, there is no grain', results from emending the word for 'manger' (אֵבוּס/*'ēbûs*) to the negative particle אֶפֶס/*'epes* and translating the word בָּר/*bār* as 'grain' rather than 'empty' (it has both meanings). The second colon then becomes an explanation of the first, and the meaning might be that you have to spend in order to get produce. Whichever meaning is adopted the proverb's message can be applied beyond the application to farming.

14:5-9 Wisdom and Speech

As Heim[138] points out, all these verses except v. 8 have terms directly related to speech, and all except v. 5 have intellectual vocabulary.

Verse 5 is similar to 12:17. See the comment there.

Verses 6-8 are linked by the catchwords 'wisdom', 'knowledge' and 'fool'. For Whybray[139] the point of v. 6 is 'that wisdom is not a commodity which anyone may acquire whenever he feels the need for it: it only comes to those who by their way of life have disposed themselves to receive it'. Since the scoffer is arrogant (21:24) and refuses to accept rebuke (15:12) he is unteachable. Those with understanding are in a position to gain more wisdom (1:5). Although the early versions and some modern scholars find v. 7b difficult, the ESV makes good sense of the MT. It follows on from the previous verse as a comment on where not to seek wisdom. Verse 8 is also a comment on v. 6, using the motif of the two ways. The wise person is able to discern the right way. Because the fool has a distorted view of reality (13:19) and will not listen to others (12:15), the way that they think is right will lead them astray.

137. Heim, *Like Grapes of Gold Set in Silver*, 175.
138. Heim, *Like Grapes of Gold Set in Silver*, 174-75.
139. Whybray, *Proverbs*, 213.

The MT of v. 9 is literally, 'Fools scorn (singular) guilt(-offering); and between upright persons favour'. Various emendations have been suggested to cope with the difficulties this presents.[140] Despite the lack of concord the ESV takes the plural noun 'fools' as the subject of the singular verb. This can be justified as a 'distributive singular'[141] giving the sense, 'every fool mocks at the guilt offering'.[142] The REB brings out the probable meaning, 'Fools are too arrogant to make amends'. The ESV translation of v. 9b, 'but the upright enjoy acceptance', leaves open the question of who does the 'accepting'. The NIV puts the emphasis on the upright themselves (probably reflecting the word 'between' in the MT), 'but goodwill is found among the upright'. The NRSV takes God as the implied subject, 'but the upright enjoy God's favour'. The REB has, 'the upright know what reconciliation means', which makes a strong antithesis with the first colon but probably stretches the meaning too far.

14:10-14 Proverbs about the Heart

Proverbs about the heart (vv. 10, 13, 14) seem to mark these verses out as a group, but it is difficult to see an overarching theme. On the meaning of 'heart' in Hebrew as 'the inner person' see on 4:23.

Verse 10 is one of a number of proverbs which seem to be primarily psychological observations (e.g. 12:25; 13:12). Van Leeuwen[143] puts its meaning well, saying that however close we come to other people, 'we remain individual persons, unique centres of consciousness and responsibility, each with his or her own hiddenness. In its depths this hiddenness lies open only to God (15:11; 17:3).'

There is an affinity between v. 11 and 11:28 and 12:7 in the contrast between the consequences of wicked and righteous ways of life. There is irony in the contrast between the apparently solid 'house' of the wicked and the seemingly flimsy 'tent' of the righteous.

Verses 12 and 13 are linked by the catchword 'end'. The REB translation of יָשָׁר/*yāšār* as 'straightforward' is to be preferred to the ESV's 'right'. The proverb is open to different interpretations. Taken in conjunction with v. 11 it can be seen as a comment on the misconceived choices of the wicked (cf. 12:15; 14:8). Taken on its own, or in conjunction with v. 13, it can be seen as a more general statement about the uncertainties of life, 'A road may seem straight-

140. See the discussion in Whybray, *Proverbs*, 214-15.

141. GKC §145l. A number of 'undoubted examples' of this in Proverbs are listed, but not this verse.

142. Cf. Kidner, *Proverbs*, 107.

143. Van Leeuwen, *Proverbs*, 140.

forward, yet end as a way to death' (REB). If that is its meaning then, as Murphy[144] comments, it is one of the proverbs which show that, 'The sages were aware of the incalculables in human existence, even if they did not sharpen them in the style of Qoheleth'. Its link with v. 13 would then be not only the catchword but the implicit warning that appearances can mislead. Verse 13 is another psychological observation. The NRSV takes it as a statement of fact, but the other EVV are probably right to take the imperfect form of the verb as having a modal nuance here, '. . . may ache, . . . may be grief'. The proverb expresses the complexity of life: experiences can be 'bittersweet' and what seems a cause of joy can lead to grief. As such it is also a warning not to judge by appearances alone.

Verse 14 is another statement of the principle that peoples' actions rebound on them (cf. 12:14; 13:2). The Hebrew of verse 14b is awkward, as reflected in the NIV, 'The faithless will be fully repaid for their ways, and the good man rewarded for his' (the ESV seems to be a paraphrase of this sense). The NRSV 'smooths' the sense by emending מֵעָלָיו/*mēʿālāyw*, 'from upon him(self)' to מַעֲלָלָיו/*maʿălālāyw* ('from his deeds'): 'and the good what their deeds deserve'.

14:15-18 Proverbs about the Simple and the Prudent

These verses (15, 18) frame two proverbs that can be taken to define the traits of the simple and the prudent more closely (vv. 16-17). On the meaning of 'simple' and 'prudent' in Proverbs see on 1:4.

Verse 15 states a fundamental difference between the simple and the prudent. The simple are credulous, blindly accepting what others say. The prudent think carefully about how they should behave. The first colon of v. 16 picks up on this aspect of prudence. It can be construed in two ways. The Hebrew uses the verb 'to fear' (יָרֵא/*yārē'*). The NIV takes this as a shorthand for 'fears the LORD', which leads people to turn away from evil (3:7; 8:13). The ESV and NRSV take 'fear' in the weakened sense of 'be cautious' but still give their behaviour a moral tone by saying that they turn away from 'evil'. The word translated 'evil' (רָע/*rāʿ*) can also mean 'misfortune', and the REB takes it in this sense: 'One who is wise is cautious and avoids trouble.' Given the tendency to moral evaluation when contrasting the wise and foolish, the ESV/NRSV translation is probably better. The fool's impetuosity (v. 16b) is picked up in v. 17a. The loss of control that goes with being quick-tempered leads to

144. Murphy, *Proverbs*, 105.

foolish behaviour. In v. 17b the ESV reflects the MT: 'and a man of evil devices is hated' (cf. NIV, NRSV). Some scholars argue that one would expect an antithesis to v. 17a and that the word for 'evil devices' (מְזִמּוֹת/*mĕzimmôt*) is often used in Proverbs in the neutral sense of 'cleverness, discretion' which would give a contrast to being quick-tempered. However, they then have to emend the verb from 'hated' (יִשָּׂנֵא/*yiśśānēʾ*) to 'is lifted up' (יִשָּׂא/*yiśśēʾ*). This leads to the REB translation, 'advancement comes by careful thought.' However, Clifford[145] points out that while *mĕzimmôt* on its own can be used positively the phrase 'man of *mĕzimmôt*' is only used negatively (12:2; 24:8). There is no reason why this proverb has to be antithetical. Taken as it stands in the MT there is an intensification of meaning between the cola, a movement from the person who acts impetuously, and therefore foolishly, to the one who acts with premeditated malice, which provokes hatred. The cluster ends with a general statement which serves to commend prudence. The ESV and NIV follow the MT in v. 18a: 'The simple inherit folly.' In their translations the NRSV and REB emend the verb 'inherit' (נָחֲלוּ/*nāḥălû*) to a verb meaning 'to adorn' (נֶחֱלוּ/*neḥĕlû*). This gives a better parallelism with v. 18b ('The simple are adorned with folly', NRSV) but the emendation is purely conjectural. The MT makes good sense if 'inherit' is taken in this context to mean that simplemindedness naturally produces folly — because, as the previous proverbs have shown, it is characterised by credulity, impetuosity, lack of self-control and possibly malice. By contrast prudence produces knowledge, which is like a crown because it leads to people being recognised and honoured for it.

14:19-22 Wealth and Poverty

The catchwords 'good' and 'evil' link vv. 19 and 22, making them a frame for two proverbs linked by the words 'poor' and 'neighbour'.

Verse 19 is a blunt statement, in synonymous parallelism, that the wicked will end up subservient to the good, indeed begging at their door. As with other 'black-and-white' proverbs it has to be taken as a statement of general principle and balanced by others that recognise that in the complexity of life the reality is sometimes different. The story of Joseph (Gen. 37, 42) can be taken as an illustration of this proverb, and that of the rich man and Lazarus illustrates that the reality seen in the context of this life alone is sometimes different (Lk. 16:19-31).

The proverb pair in vv. 20-21 may be an illustration of the general prin-

145. Clifford, *Proverbs*, 146.

ciple in v. 19,[146] dealing with one kind of behaviour. Verse 20 is an observation on human nature. People prefer to be with those from whom they might gain benefit than those who make demands on them. On its own it could be seen as an amoral statement which gives encouragement to seek wealth. The link with v. 21 passes a negative judgement on the behaviour it describes. In this verse the REB follows the LXX and emends 'his neighbour' (רֵעֵהוּ/*rēʿēhû*) to 'the hungry' (רָעֵב/*rāʿēb*). This is unnecessary, and the LXX translators may have made the change because they thought it improved the parallelism (cf. Isa. 58:7).

The consequences of good and evil behaviour are the theme of v. 22. The second colon lacks a second verb to link the good with 'steadfast love and faithfulness'. Parallelism would suggest supplying 'are/show' (REB). However, some scholars suggest that, since 'steadfast love and faithfulness' are often spoken of as attributes of Yahweh, he is the implied giver of these to the good, and so supply the verb 'find' (NIV, NRSV) or 'meet' (ESV). Parallelism with receiving blessing in v. 21b may also support this interpretation.

14:23-24 Work and Words

This proverb pair commends hard work as the route to prosperity — a common theme in Proverbs (e.g. 10:4; 12:11). Since in Proverbs in general words are regarded as powerful (for good or ill) the force of 'the word of the lips' in v. 23a is rightly understood as 'mere words' by the EVV. Verse 24 identifies the behaviours in v. 23 with the wise and fools. The NRSV breaks this link by emending עָשְׁרָם/*ʿošrām* ('their wealth') to עָרְמָתָם/*ʿormātām* ('their cleverness') following the LXX. However, the MT makes good sense, especially as in 3:16 and 8:18 wealth is among the gifts given by Wisdom. The ESV translation of v. 24b, 'But the folly of fools brings folly' (cf. NIV); follows the MT. Because this seems tautologous the NRSV and REB emend the first occurrence of 'folly' (אִוֶּלֶת/*ʾiwwelet*) to 'garland' (לִוְיַת/*liwyat*) to improve the parallelism: 'but folly is the garland of fools' (cf. 4:9). However, the ineffectiveness of the folly of fools in the MT provides a parallel to the ineffectiveness of words in v. 23b.

14:25 Perjury in Court

Perjury in court and its possible life and death effects is the topic of this proverb, as of some others. See the comment on 14:5.

146. Heim, *Like Grapes of Gold Set in Silver,* 181.

14:26-27 The Fear of the LORD and Its Consequences

On the meaning of 'the fear of the LORD' see on 1:7.

The first colon of v. 26 lacks a verb, and as a result there is no antecedent for 'his' in the second colon. The REB deals with this by changing the adjective 'strong' (עֹז/*'ōz*) to the noun 'strong person' (עָז/*'āz*): 'One who is strong and trusts in the fear of the LORD will be a refuge for his children'. The other EVV preserve the MT and supply an antecedent by adding 'one has' in v. 26a: 'In the fear of the LORD one has strong confidence, and his children will have a refuge' (ESV). The point of the proverb is clearly that reverence for Yahweh has benefits down the generations. This might refer both to the effect of the teaching and example of the parents and to promises such as Exod. 20:5-6 and Deut. 5:9. Verse 27 is identical to 13:14 (see comment there) except that there it is 'the teaching of the wise' that is the fountain of life. The sages recognised that humans can mediate divine blessing.

14:28 A Royal Proverb

Heim[147] argues that because of the repetition of 'people' in v. 34 and 'king' in v. 35 these verses form a frame for vv. 28-35. However, there is no clear thematic unity in these verses. This proverb seems a banal statement of the obvious, that the reputation of a kingdom is related to its size and resources, of which the population is an important element. However, in a world where the emphasis was usually on the dependence of the people on the king (e.g. 1 Sam. 8:4-5; 2 Sam. 2:7; Lam. 4:20) it provides a different perspective.

14:29-30 The Danger of Uncontrolled Emotion

The danger of uncontrolled emotion is the theme of this pair of proverbs. In v. 29 the social consequences are in mind, and in v. 30 the consequences for the individual are to the fore. The stress on self-restraint is common in Egyptian wisdom literature[148] with the 'heated man' being contrasted unfavourably with the 'silent man'. Verse 30 shows that the sages were aware of what would now be called 'psychosomatic illness'. Longman[149] comments, 'The first colon states that an emotionally healthy person enjoys physical well-being; the second colon

147. Heim, *Like Grapes of Gold Set in Silver*, 187.
148. See for example *AEL* 2:146-53.
149. Longman, *Proverbs*, 307.

observes that psychological turmoil results in physical illness.' On the meaning of 'heart' see comment on 4:23. Murphy[150] points out the aptness of the link of envy with rot, or cancer, in the bones because 'envy eats away at a person.'

14:31 Generosity to the Poor

Generosity to the poor is commended in v. 21b. Here an additional reason is given for it. Poor people, like everyone else, are created by God. How we treat them reflects our attitude towards the Creator. This observation is strengthened by the recognition that all humans are made in the image of God (Gen. 1:27).

14:32 Another Proverb about Consequences

The MT of v. 32b reads, 'but a righteous person seeks refuge in his death'. What this means is unclear. The NRSV translation, 'but the righteous find a refuge in their integrity' (cf. REB) follows the LXX and Syr and emends בְּמוֹתוֹ/*bĕmôtō* ('in his death') to בְּתֻמּוֹ/*bĕtûmmô* ('in his integrity'). However, the LXX may be trying to make the best of a difficult text. McKane[151] points out that the verb in v. 32b means 'to seek refuge' rather than 'to find refuge', and Van Leeuwen[152] notes that it is the LORD who is usually the object of such seeking. The meaning then may be that the righteous seeks refuge in Yahweh even when facing death (cf. NIV). Whether, taken this way, it hints at an afterlife is unclear, but Ps. 16 might express similar ideas.

14:33 Wisdom's Home among Humans

Wisdom's home is the subject of this proverb, but the meaning of v. 33b is unclear. The MT, followed by the ESV and NIV, 'supposes the idea that wisdom speaks to all people alike'.[153] While it is possible that there is the implication here that the wise and the fools respond differently to wisdom[154] most scholars find the statement so contrary to what is generally said about fools and wisdom that they follow the LXX and insert a negative into the colon: 'but it is not known in the heart of fools' (NRSV, cf. REB).

150. Murphy, *Proverbs*, 107.
151. McKane, *Proverbs*, 475
152. Van Leeuwen, *Proverbs*, 144.
153. Van Leeuwen, *Proverbs*, 144.
154. Waltke, *Proverbs 1–15*, 610-11.

14:34-35 Nations and Kings

It may be that v. 34 is a comment on v. 28. Clifford[155] notes that whereas nations are usually evaluated by such considerations as wealth, military might, territorial expansion, this proverb affirms that the key factor is 'righteousness', being in a right relationship with God. If this is so, then the character of its leadership, the king in ancient Israel, is important. Verse 35 speaks of the king's ability to judge others and favour wise courtiers.

Proverbs 15

15:1-4 The Power of Words

Commenting on 15:1 Clifford[156] says, 'Paradoxically, where words are concerned, soft is hard, that is, effective, and hard is soft, that is, ineffective.' The word 'anger' provides a link with 14:35. In context, 15:2 identifies the two uses of words in the previous verse with the wise and the foolish. There is an additional thought that the wise not only reply in a manner that is effective in a particular situation, but also provide valuable insight into it. The translation 'commends' (ESV, NIV) renders the MT (תֵּיטִיב/*têṭîb*) whereas 'dispense' (NRSV) and 'spread' (REB) reflect an unnecessary conjectural emendation (תַּטִּיף/*taṭṭîp*). Verse 3 is linked to v. 2 by the use of the same Hebrew root, here translated 'good', as is used in 'commends' in v. 2. In context this general statement of Yahweh's omniscience gives encouragement to use words wisely and not foolishly. The use of the word 'tongue' in v. 4 links it to v. 2, but it is similar to v. 1 in giving another example of the power of words. They can promote life or weaken it by bringing despair (on the meaning of 'the tree of life' see on 3:18). The adjective (מַרְפֵּא/*marpē'*) used to describe the tongue may mean either 'gentle' (ESV, NIV) or 'healing' (NRSV), depending on which Hebrew root underlies it.[157]

15:5-12 Openness to Correction

Openness to correction, an essential aspect of teachability, is frequently commended in Proverbs (e.g. 5:12; 12:1; 13:1), and this theme in vv. 5 and 12 frames

155. Clifford, *Proverbs*, 148.
156. Clifford, *Proverbs*, 150.
157. On the interchange between ל״ה and ל״א verbs see Joüon §79l.

this section, though there is no consistent theme running through it. Another common theme, the different outcomes of the efforts of the righteous and the wicked is found in v. 6 (cf. 10:2, 16; 11:4). Here it can be seen as a motive for heeding reproof and becoming wise. Verse 7 might give a reason for the different outcomes of v. 6. The footnote to v. 7b in the ESV and the REB translation reflect the fact that the final words (לֹא־כֵן/*lōʾ-kēn*) can be translated as either 'not so' or 'not reliable'.

Verses 8 and 9 are linked by the phrase 'an abomination to the LORD' (on its meaning see on 3:32). As v. 9 makes clear, the essential contrast in v. 8 is not between different acts of piety, but between the lifestyles of the worshippers. A sacrifice, however costly, is repugnant to God if offered by someone whose lifestyle he hates. By contrast, the simple prayer of a righteous person is acceptable. Verse 10 picks up on the word 'way' in v. 9a and is a warning to the wicked of the serious consequences that lie ahead if they do not change their lifestyles. There is a semantic link between 'die' in v. 10b and v. 11a. 'Abaddon', like 'Sheol', is a name for the abode of the dead (Job 28:22; Prov. 27:20). The point of this proverb in context is that there is no way the wicked can escape the consequence of their way of life because their inner thoughts, not just their deeds, are open to God — which is why their sacrifices are unacceptable. This verse extends the 'every place' of v. 3 to the underworld.

15:13-17 Emotions and Their Consequences

This cluster is tied together by catchwords. In the MT the word 'heart' is the first word of vv. 13 and 14, and the word 'better' (literally, 'good') is the first word of vv. 16 and 17. In v. 15 'cheerful of heart' is literally 'good of heart', so binding the surrounding pairs together. On the meaning of 'heart' see the comment on 4:23.

Verse 13 is a psychological observation about the effect of a person's mental and emotional states on themselves. Verse 13a notes that their inner state affects their outward appearance. By contrast v. 13b refers to the effect of one inner disposition on another, the sorrowful heart leading to despondency or depression. However, this too might affect a person's outward demeanour. There is a double contrast between the two cola of v. 14. The 'heart-mouth' contrast implies a contrast in depth between the wise and the fool, and this is supported between the 'seeking-eating' contrast — the fool takes in whatever is available before him but the wise goes looking for what is worthwhile. Maybe v. 14a indicates one way in which gladness of heart can be attained. Verse 15 picks up on v. 13. It asserts that one's inner attitude can alleviate the sufferings caused by external circumstances.

The pair of 'better than' proverbs shows that the sages were aware of the paradoxes of real life. The fear of the LORD does not always lead to prosperity, but may sometimes lead one to choose scarcity (v. 16). A concrete example is given in v. 17. The enjoyment of good personal relationships is worth more than the enjoyment of good food. The feast motif here may throw light on the source of the 'feast' of v. 15b: good relationships with both God and one's neighbours.

The *Instruction of Amenemope* 9:5-8 has sayings similar to vv. 16-17: 'Better is poverty in the hand of the god, than wealth in the storehouse'; 'Better is bread with a happy heart, than wealth with vexation.'[158]

15:18 Self-Control

Self-control was an important virtue for the sages (14:29; 16:32) in both Israel and Egypt (see on 14:29). Being 'slow to anger' is one of the characteristics of Yahweh (Exod. 34:6-7).

15:19 The Two Ways

The 'two ways' motif is expressed in the unusual pairing of the sluggard (see on 6:6-11) and the righteous. The REB follows the LXX and emends 'righteous' (יְשָׁרִים/*yĕšārîm*) to 'diligent' (חָרוּצִים/*ḥārûṣîm*). However, the unusual linkage may be deliberate, implying that the diligent (13:4) are upright. It is unclear what the 'hedge of thorns' is. In 22:13 the obstacles in the sluggard's way are a figment of his imagination created by his own disposition.

15:20-23 Words and Joy

A Hebrew root meaning 'glad/joy' occurs in vv. 20, 21, 23. Verse 20 is a variant of 10:1, and that parallel probably prompts the REB to say 'young fool' in v. 20b. The genuine reason for joy in v. 20 is contrasted with the senseless joy of a person who is amused by the trivialities of life in v. 21a. A person with true understanding is not distracted by them. Verse 22 is a variant of 11:14. The sages emphasised taking advice, but v. 23 makes the point that it is important not only for the content of advice to be correct, but it must also be given at the correct time if it is to be effective.

158. *AEL* 2:152.

15:24-27 Life

'Life' in vv. 24 and 27 may mark this out as a unit. Verses 25 and 26 are Yahweh proverbs, and 'house' in v. 25 links with v. 27. The 'two ways' motif is used in v. 24, and the 'up/down' imagery could be taken in the eschatological sense of 'heaven/hell'. However, it is much more likely that here it is used in the same way as in Deut. 28:13 to indicate success and failure in life. The Yahweh proverbs may be intended as examples of what the contrasting ways involve. In Israel's subsistence economy preserving the ancestral land of a family was vitally important, and that meant preserving the boundary marks (Deut. 19:14; 27:17). Powerless people, like widows, would be particularly vulnerable to encroachment on their land, and Yahweh had promised to protect them from mistreatment (Exod. 22:22-24). Pride sometimes leads to oppression, and v. 25 is a warning against it. The meaning of v. 26b is unclear, as the different rendering of the ESV/NRSV as compared with that of the NIV/REB shows, but the overall sense is clear. Wicked thoughts are contrasted with pure words as things which Yahweh finds repugnant (on 'abomination' see on 3:32) or pleasing. Verse 27a may look back to v. 25 since one form of unjust gain was appropriating other people's land (Isa. 5:8-9; Hos. 5:10). Bribing judges enabled the rich to oppress the poor and make unjust gains (Deut. 16:18-20; Amos 5:12).

15:28-33 References to Seeing and Hearing

Verse 28 is similar to v. 2 with the righteous/wicked contrast replacing that of the wise/fools. It highlights the importance of a considered answer as compared to the malicious babblings of the wicked.

The parallelism of v. 29 implies that the LORD does not respond to the prayers of the wicked because of their wickedness (cf. v. 8). The motif of God being far off recurs in the OT. As Waltke[159] says, 'Assertions about the LORD's presence or distance are not theological statements that restrict his omnipresence but religious statements about the availability of his favour.'

Verse 30 is another psychological observation. The meaning of 'the light of the eyes' is uncertain but the NIV has probably caught the sense: 'A cheerful look brings joy to the heart' (cf. REB). If that is so, then both cola of the proverb are about how external things can affect a person's internal disposition for good. The first refers to non-verbal communication and the second to a verbal message.

159. Waltke, *Proverbs 1–15*, 639.

The mention of the ear in v. 31 may be prompted by the mention of the eye in the previous verse. As noted on vv. 5-12, the issue of how people respond to reproof is a common theme in Proverbs. These are further proverbs which encourage a positive response by asserting the benefits reproof brings.

Verse 33 takes up the theme of 'the fear of the LORD' from 1:7 (see the comment there) and 9:10 as essential to acquiring wisdom. The second colon links in with vv. 31-32 because pride is a major stumbling block to receiving reproof and instruction (cf. 11:2), therefore growth in wisdom requires humility, especially in terms of reverence towards Yahweh.

Proverbs 16

16:1-9 Divine Sovereignty and Human Planning

Divine sovereignty and human planning form the theme of vv. 1 and 9 also an *inclusio* for this cluster. Their opening words have a chiastic arrangement: 'Of *man* the arrangements of the *heart*' (v. 1), 'The *heart of man* plans his way' (v. 9). All these verses except v. 8 are Yahweh proverbs.

Although v. 1 is sometimes taken to mean[160] 'Man proposes, God disposes', it is more nuanced than that. As Clifford[161] points out, the antithesis of heart and tongue is one way of expressing the totality of human activity. The proverb, then, does not denigrate human planning but stresses that human dependence on God is needed for success in carrying out plans. The following verses develop this. Since God knows our true motivations better than we do (v. 2) we should be humble with regard to our plans and actions, as the Apostle Paul was: 'I am not aware of anything against myself, but I am not thereby acquitted. It is the Lord who judges me' (1 Cor. 4:4). The unexpected order of works/plans makes a complementary emphasis to v. 1. The whole process of a project must be submitted to God if it is to be completed successfully. Verse 4 asserts that even the actions of the wicked, who do not commit their work to God, come under the sovereignty of God. The syntax of v. 4a is ambiguous. The NIV, 'The LORD works out everything for his own ends', suggests that God's sovereignty enables him to use even the deeds of the wicked for good (cf. Rom. 8:28). It is more likely that the proverb is saying that God's sovereign control will ensure that those who behave wickedly will be punished. It is not saying that God predestines certain individuals to act wickedly so that they will be punished.

160. For example, Toy, *Proverbs*, 320.
161. Clifford, *Proverbs*, 157.

Verses 5-8 expand on v. 2a by describing behaviours of which Yahweh does and does not approve. See on 3:32 for the meaning of 'an abomination to the LORD' (v. 5). Because arrogance prevents a person depending on God it is hateful to Yahweh. By contrast, steadfast love and faithfulness, whether expressed towards God or fellow human beings (3:3-4), are an expression of reverence towards Yahweh ('the fear of the LORD', see on 1:7). They keep a person from doing evil, and make forgiveness possible if they do sin. Sacrifices for atonement are only effective if offered in the right spirit (e.g. 1 Sam. 15:22; Hos. 6:6). One of the outcomes of being in a right relationship with Yahweh is a harmonious relationship with other people (v. 7). Verse 8 is similar to 15:16, a Yahweh proverb, but has a more explicit ethical tone in its righteousness-injustice contrast. It gives an example of a 'way' that pleases Yahweh.

Verse 9 rounds off this cluster by returning to the theme of v. 1, but expands its application from individual projects to a person's whole way of life, 'his way/steps'.

16:10-15 The King

The king is the subject of all these proverbs except v. 11. In Israel the king was seen as Yahweh's regent ruling Yahweh's people, and so it is appropriate that a group of proverbs about the king should follow a group of Yahweh proverbs.

It is only in v. 10 that the word קֶסֶם/*qesem* ('oracle') is used in a positive sense. Elsewhere in the OT it refers to a forbidden form of divination. Commentators differ over whether the word is being used here metaphorically[162] or to refer to use of a 'divine lot' in some legal cases.[163] Either way, the proverb asserts that God gives the king the ability to make just decisions. The same word (מִשְׁפָּט/*mišpāṭ*) is used for 'judgement' (v. 10) and 'just' (v. 11). The two verses are also linked because the king was meant to uphold just measures (cf. 2 Sam. 14:16). Like 11:1 this proverb expresses Yahweh's concern for honesty in business. 'Accuracy of scales and balances is the LORD's concern; all the weights in the bag are his business' (REB).

Verses 12 and 13 form a pair. Both (in Hebrew) speak of 'kings' and use the word 'righteous(ness)'. In v. 12 the NRSV implies that it is the kings who do evil. The more open REB translation is to be preferred: 'Wrongdoing is abhorrent to kings'. Psalm 101 might be seen as a commentary on this verse, with the king expressing his determination to do away with evildoers in his kingdom and to

162. Waltke, *Proverbs 15–31*, 17.
163. Van Leeuwen, *Proverbs*, 160.

have ministers who 'walk in the way that is blameless' (Ps. 101:6). A particular example of the righteousness which gives stability to a kingdom is given in vv. 13 — just and honest speech.

The next two proverbs are realistic observations on the power of an absolute monarch. They refer to 'a king' in the singular and have the common word pair life/death. His wrath or favour can be a matter of life or death, so the wise courtier needs to know how to appease wrath (15:1). The metaphor in v. 15b reflects the climatic conditions of Canaan, where the spring rains were important for a good harvest.

16:16-19 Wise Behaviour

Wise behaviour is the theme of this group of proverbs, framed by two 'better than' sayings. As already noted, such proverbs recognise the complexities of life.

Verse 16 echoes the words of Woman Wisdom (8:10, 19), and the justification for its claim is given in 3:13-18. Another justification appears in v. 17, which uses the metaphor of life as a journey and gives wisdom an ethical meaning. Wisdom keeps people on the right path and guards against danger. Verses 18 and 19 are a proverb pair which deals with one particular danger, pride. It expands on 11:2 (see comment there). The phrase 'divide the spoil' suggests a background in warfare. Victory in battle can prompt pride in the victors as they attribute success purely to their own efforts. Alternatively, pride may lead to ill-gotten gains (see on 15:25).

16:20-24 Speech

Speech of various kinds is the subject of these verses. The interpretation of v. 20 depends on how דָּבָר/*dābār* is understood. It can mean 'matter/business', as in the REB: 'He who is shrewd in business will prosper'. It is more likely that it means 'word' in this context. This could be the teaching of sages, 'Whoever gives heed to instruction prospers' (NIV), or the word of the Lord — though that might come through the sages. The REB takes the proverb to be antithetical, but most scholars take it as synonymous parallelism, indicating that human effort (in business or learning) should be combined with dependence on God.

The Hebrew of v. 21a is difficult. The REB translation, 'The sensible person seeks advice from the wise', results from emending the verb יִקָּרֵא/*yiqqārē'* ('is called') to יִקְרָא/*yiqrāʾ* ('call upon'). However, the MT makes reasonable sense, and if it is accepted the proverb means that effective speech needs to be both discerning and 'sweet' (possibly 'eloquent' or 'kindly').

Like 'the mouth of the righteous' (10:11), 'the teaching of the wise' (13:14) and 'the fear of the LORD' (14:27), 'good sense' (16:22, 'understanding' NIV, 'wisdom' NRSV) is 'a fountain of life', a source of vitality and blessing, to those who have it. The second colon is terse and enigmatic. It could mean 'but folly brings punishment to fools' (NIV; cf. NRSV, REB), or it could mean that to try to instruct fools is folly[164] (ESV).

Verse 23, like v. 21, is about effective speech. This time the point is that speech reflects the inner person. That is why the speech of the wise is effective.

Verse 24 picks up the theme of sweetness from v. 21. If words are 'gracious' (ESV; 'kind', REB; 'pleasant', NIV, NRSV) they are a powerful force for good. They are compared to honey, which was prized both for its pleasant taste and its medicinal value.[165] They bring inner refreshment and healing. The NIV 'bones' reflects the MT and is better than 'body', because in Hebrew idiom the 'bones' refer to the core of one's being.

16:25

This is identical to 14:12. See the comment there.

16:26 The Need to Eat Motivates People to Work

Here 'mouth' stands for 'appetite' instead of 'speech'. This is a 'neutral' saying, a very similar, but more negative one, is Eccles. 6:7.

16:27-30 Evil People and the Effects of Their Speech

Verses 27-29 each begin with the phrase 'a man of X' in Hebrew, and v. 30 is linked to them by the catchwords 'dishonest' (v. 28a), 'lips' (v. 27b, Heb.) and 'evil' (v. 27a).

The verb in v. 27a is 'digs', which leads to the REB paraphrase: 'A scoundrel rakes up evil gossip'. However, the sense is probably that he digs a pit to

164. McKane, *Proverbs*, 490.
165. *NIDOTTE* 3:784.

trap people, so 'plots evil' (ESV) is better. It is unclear whether v. 28 refers to one kind of person or two. Perhaps the 'whisperer' (ESV; 'gossip', NIV) is a sub-group of those who are dishonest. The REB translation of this verse hides the pattern of the Hebrew by replacing the types of people by types of action: 'disaffection', 'tale-bearing'. Verse 29 is reminiscent of 1:10-19. The precise nature of the facial expressions in v. 30 is unclear (cf. 6:13; 10:10). The point of the verse is probably that, for the observant, the body language of those planning evil gives them away.

16:31 Old Age and Wisdom

These themes were commonly linked in the ancient Near East. Other things being equal, an older person is more likely to be wise than a younger one because experience, reflected on properly, is one way of gaining wisdom. The second colon is an explanation of the first. The glory comes 'not from a long life as such but from a long *righteous* life'.[166] Of course modern Western culture adds a different element to this. As Waltke[167] notes, old age is now 'often achieved through amoral and even immoral technology, not through virtue'.

16:32 Self-Control

Self-control is commended by this 'better than' proverb, as it is several times in Proverbs (12:16; 14:29-30; 15:18). Clifford[168] sums up this proverb well: 'Conquest of self is better than conquest of others.'

16:33 The Sovereignty of God

This proverb is a return to the theme of vv. 1-9. Yahwism recognised one kind of 'sacred lot' as valid, at least in the earlier period, the use of the Urim and Thumim (Exod. 28:30 and 1 Sam. 23:1-6 describes its use; it is not mentioned after the time of David). The land was allocated by lots by Joshua (Num. 26:55-56; Josh. 14:2), and Saul was chosen by lot (1 Sam. 10:17-27). The basic point of this proverb is that it is God, not humans, who is in control of the future.

166. Clifford, *Proverbs,* 162.
167. Waltke, *Proverbs 15–31,* 36.
168. Clifford, *Proverbs,* 162.

Proverbs 17

17:1-9 Some Miscellaneous Proverbs

It is difficult to discern clear groupings or clusters of proverbs in this chapter.

Verse 1 asserts that good fellowship is better than a good feast (cf. 15:17). There is perhaps irony in the fact that the word here for 'feast' is literally 'sacrifices'. It is used of the 'peace offering' (Lev. 3), most of which was cooked and eaten by the offerer's family and friends.

Character may sometimes win out over natural ties is the message of v. 2. This proverb is a warning to young men not to presume on the privileges of birth but to pull their weight in the family. What 'acting shamefully' means is not defined but probably refers to a refusal to play a proper role in supporting the family, like the son who is too lazy to help with harvesting (10:5).

Precious metals are melted so that impurities can be poured off, and this provides an analogy for God testing, and by implication refining, the human character (v. 3; on the meaning of 'heart' see 4:23). This may come about as God lets them experience difficult situations (cf. Zech. 13:9).

Many proverbs condemn wrong and harmful uses of speech. Verse 4 condemns those who listen to harmful words. The meaning may be either that what you listen to influences the kind of person you become or, more likely, that what you enjoy listening to reveals the kind of person you are.

Verse 5, like 14:31, is a reminder that a poor person deserves the same respect as anyone else, because all humans are made by God. The second colon widens the application to anyone who suffers any kind of calamity, not just poverty. This is one of those proverbs which balances others that present poverty as the consequence of laziness or wickedness.

In verse 6 the terms used in 16:31 for the *'crown of glory'* of the aged are distributed among the generations: Grandchildren are a *crown* of the aged and fathers are the *glory* of their children. The actions of family members may reflect either glory or shame on their kin. This proverb speaks of the ideal family. Verses 21 and 25 recognise that this is not true of all families.

The exact meaning of the phrase שְׂפַת־יֶתֶר/*śĕpat-yeter* (v. 7) is debated, but most take it to mean 'lips of excellence', hence the ESV translation ('fine speech') is to be preferred to the NIV ('arrogant lips'). It is not fitting for fools to be able to speak well, because that only increases the possibility of their words doing harm. It is even less fitting for those in positions of power and leadership to speak dishonestly. Proverbs which speak of things that are 'not fitting' imply that such things do sometimes happen, and are another indication that the sages were aware that life is more complex than the black-and-white nature that some proverbs might imply.

It is important to recognise that v. 8 is written from the perspective ('in the eyes of') of the briber (the less literal translations of the NIV and REB obscure this). There is no clear evaluation of this perspective, but the proverb may be given an ironic, even pejorative, tone by the phrase 'a magic stone' (v. 7a, ESV). Other proverbs (e.g. v. 23) condemn bribery.

Making and keeping friends is the subject of v. 9. Friendship will not grow where there is unwillingness to overlook the occasional failings and faults of the other person. If those failings and faults are gossiped about to others, it will destroy the friendship. Other proverbs recognise that there is a time and place for friends to confront one another (27:5-6).

17:10-16 Danger, Beware!

Two proverbs about the inability of fools to learn (vv. 10, 16) frame a group about dangerous people or actions.

Openness to rebuke and correction (v. 10a) is frequently urged in Proverbs. The second colon uses exaggeration in depicting the incorrigibility of fools (the law limited beating to forty lashes, Deut. 25:3).

With two or three exceptions the word for 'rebellion' (מְרִי/*mĕrî*) in v. 11a is always used of rebellion against God.[169] The passive verb in v. 11b is then best taken as a 'divine passive', with God as the sender of the messenger. The messenger could be some natural calamity or a person. The adjective אַכְזָרִי/*'akzārî* is probably better translated as 'merciless' (NIV, REB) rather than 'cruel' (ESV, NRSV) (cf. Prov. 12:10; Jer. 6:23; 50:42).

Verse 12 uses humorous exaggeration in comparing the damage a fool can do with that done by an enraged she-bear. Throughout the OT the bear is presented as a dangerous animal, and the phrase 'like a she-bear robbed of her cubs' seems to have been a common simile for a dangerous enemy (2 Sam. 17:8; Hos. 13:8). This is a graphic warning not to associate with fools (cf. 13:20b).

Verse 13 expresses the principle of just retribution. The evil that is done by someone who has the ingratitude to turn on a benefactor and do them harm will rebound on the perpetrator. Indeed it will affect his entire family. This might be because his attitude will affect family relationships.

The first colon of v. 14 is quite terse: 'One who releases water, beginning

169. Waltke, *Proverbs 15–31*, 52.

of quarrelling'. Starting a quarrel can be like opening sluice gates, and once water has poured out there is no way of getting it back. So, beware of starting a quarrel! It's better to keep the sluice closed and avoid it. Water was a precious commodity in Israel, with its heavy dependence on seasonal rains, so the metaphor is particularly apt. That background probably prompted the REB translation of v. 14a, 'stealing water starts a quarrel', but this takes a metaphor too literally.

Verse 15 describes actions that are the direct opposite of how a judge should behave in a legal case (Deut. 25:1). That is why the behaviour is 'an abomination' (on this see on 6:16). The NIV makes the legal setting clear: 'Acquitting the guilty and condemning the innocent — the LORD detests them both'.

There is irony and humour in the description of the fool in v. 16, though the sense is ambiguous. It may be saying that the fool lacks the ability to benefit from teaching even if he can get it (ESV) or that he lacks the desire to be taught even if given the opportunity (NIV). Some take this verse as evidence that there were professional wisdom teachers in ancient Israel, but there is no clear evidence of this before the Hellenistic period.

17:17-18 Friends and Neighbours

In Hebrew רֵעַ/*rēaʿ* can mean either friend or neighbour. It is unclear whether the parallelism in v. 17 is antithetical or synonymous, as in the EVV. The latter is probably right. As Longman[170] says, 'The relationship between the cola seems to be one of intensifying and particularizing, but not contrasting.' On giving security for a friend or neighbour (v. 18) see the comment on 6:1-5.

17:19 Arrogance

Arrogance may be the theme of this enigmatic proverb. It is not clear which is the subject and which the predicate in v. 19a. The REB ('One who likes giving offence likes strife') seems preferable to the NIV ('He who loves a quarrel loves sin'). More difficult to understand is the meaning of the imagery of the high door in v. 19b. The most likely suggestion is that it refers to arrogance. The link between the two cola is also unclear, but arrogance often causes offence.

170. Longman, *Proverbs*, 348

17:20 Dishonesty

Dishonesty is not the best policy is the message of this proverb. The person who is morally twisted inside will speak with a twisted (dishonest) tongue. This will ultimately lead to disaster.

17:21-25 Foolishness

Foolishness in its various forms is a theme of this group of verses which is framed by two proverbs about the grief a foolish son brings to his parents. Verses 21 and 25 are an expansion of the theme of 10:1a. See the comment on that verse. They may be addressed either to the parents (make sure you inculcate wisdom into your child) or to the child (don't be a fool and cause your parents grief).

Joy and sorrow link v. 22 with v. 21. This is another psychological observation (cf. 14:30; 15:13). It makes the point that one's emotional state has physical effects.

Verse 23 makes clear that bribery, especially in the judicial process, is wrong. The context may imply that those who employ it are also foolish. The law explicitly forbids such bribery to pervert justice (Deut. 16:19).

The difference between the wise and foolish person in v. 24 is that the wise keep focussed on wisdom whereas the fool is unfocussed, easily distracted.

17:26 Perversion of the Legal System

The theme here is the same as in v. 23. There are some uncertainties in translation as comparison of the ESV and NIV shows: fine/punish in v. 26a; noble/official in v. 26b. However, the meaning is clear: it is 'not good' that innocent people should be punished.

17:27-28 Self-Control in Speech

In v. 27 it is unclear what is the subject and what the predicate in both cola. The ESV and NIV go different ways on this. However, the meaning is clear: knowledge and understanding are paired with self-control, especially in speech. This is a common theme in Proverbs (e.g. 10:19; 11:12; 13:3; 14:29; 15:18; 16:32). There is humour and irony in v. 28. It says that the best chance that fools have of being thought wise is to say nothing — but that is something they find impossible, as words just pour out of them (15:2)!

Proverbs 18

18:1-3 Three Antisocial People

The exact meaning of v. 1 is unclear because the meaning of some words is uncertain. The subject is a 'separated person' (נִפְרָד/*niprād*) who might be isolated by exclusion or by choice. The latter seems more likely as this fits better with 'seeks his own desire'. Such a person 'breaks out against' (ESV) or 'quarrels with' (REB) what his community accepts as its general norms, 'sound judgement'. The moral is that one cannot become wise by isolating oneself. The fool isolates himself by refusing to listen to the wisdom of others and delighting only in expressing his own views (v. 2).

The two cola of v. 3 can be taken either as standing in parallel, in which case both say that evil behaviour leads to rejection by the community, or there may be a progression from one to the other, in which case wickedness is depicted as resulting in a growing alienation from others: contempt, dishonour, disgrace.

18:4 An Enigmatic Saying

There is no connective between the two cola of this proverb, as the ESV indicates. Despite this the NIV and REB add a 'but' taking them as antithetical. Waltke[171] takes v. 4a to refer to 'the concealing speech of the ordinary person, which even he cannot fully plumb because of his depraved motives'. This stands in contrast to the words of the wise. However, he admits that the lack of a disjunctive in v. 4b 'favors interpreting the parallels as synthetic descriptions of wisdom's speech'. If this is accepted, v. 4b specifies further what is said of the 'words' in the first colon: they become a source of wisdom to others, and the proverb then applies only to the speech of the wise.

18:5 The Perversion of Justice

Compare 17:23, 26. It is another proverb about what is 'not good', like 17:26. The partiality spoken of here is condemned in Lev. 19:15.

171. Waltke, *Proverbs 15–31*, 71.

18:6-7 The Harmful Effects of Foolish Talk

These verses are linked by a chiastic word order: lips — mouth — mouth — lips. Verse 6 asserts that foolish words cause conflict. The ESV takes v. 6b to mean that this may rebound on the fool ('his mouth invites a beating'). The REB ('his words provoke blows') reflects the more open-ended nature of the Hebrew. In v. 7 the focus is on the harm the fool's words do to himself. The exact nature of that harm is left undefined.

18:8 The Whisperer

The 'whisperer' or 'gossip' (NIV) has been met in 16:28, where the subject was the divisive effect of slanderous gossip. This proverb is a realistic observation on its attractiveness. Van Leeuwen [172]observes that 'Gossip is like junk food (see 16:28), delicious to taste before it settles inside to do its destructive work.' The proverb is an implicit warning to the listeners not to aid and abet the gossip.

18:9 Laziness

Laziness is often condemned in Proverbs (e.g. 10:4-5; 12:24, 27). This saying lacks the satirical bite of the proverbs about the sluggard, the embodiment of laziness (see on 6:6-11). It is nonetheless a strong condemnation of laziness and so a warning against it. Lethargy can be as destructive as active wrongdoing.

18:10-11 True Security

This proverb pair is linked by the word 'strong' and the words 'safe' (v. 10) and 'high' (v. 11) which both use forms of the *niphal* participle from the Hebrew root שׂגב/*śgb*.

There are echoes of the language of the Psalms in v. 10. Reliance on the name of the LORD is found in Pss. 20:7 [Heb. 8] and 124:8; and the LORD is called a 'strong tower' in Ps. 61:3 [Heb. 4]. To speak of the name of the LORD is to refer to his character, which is expressed by the name. The righteous can seek refuge with Yahweh because he looks after them in various ways (e.g. 10:3; 15:29; 16:7). Verse 11a is a repeat of 10:15a and is probably a comment on it. That

172. Van Leeuwen, *Proverbs*, 173.

verse made the realistic comment that their wealth gives the rich some protection from the vicissitudes of life. Verse 11b makes the point that sometimes this proves to be merely a figment of the imagination (cf. Lk. 12:15-21). By its juxtaposition to v. 11, the preceding verse is also a comment on 10:15a, saying that true security can be found only by trusting Yahweh.

18:12 Pride

Pride can be prompted by wealth, and that might be a link between this verse and v. 11. Verse 12a is a compressed version of 16:18, and v. 12b repeats 15:33b (see comments on those verses).

18:13 The Fool

The fool's refusal to listen to others (15:5), love of expressing his self-opinionated views (12:15) and lack of self-control (14:29) are all summed up in this proverb. Verse 12 can be seen as a comment on the pride that leads the fool to ignore other's views and be self-opinionated.

Speech is a form of communication, and true communication requires dialogue. This means listening in order to understand what the other is saying. That is what the fools do not do. They do not listen to the question before giving their answer. They interrupt others to say whatever has come into their mind, which in their view must be more important than what anyone else has to say. The result is that they expose their folly and bring shame on themselves (ESV, NIV, NRSV). The REB takes 'shame' in the sense of 'insult' and so describes the fools' behaviour as insulting to the person they interrupt.

18:14 A Psychological Observation

This verse has clear links with 15:13 and 17:22. All these proverbs recognise the close psychosomatic links between one's emotional, mental and physical health. Whereas 15:13 and 17:22 contrast a positive state with the negative one of 'a crushed spirit', 18:14 contrasts two states of different degrees of negativity. One is endurable, the other not. It is not easy to define when a spirit, a person's inner psychical vitality, is 'crushed', though 15:13b gives one way in which a spirit may be 'crushed.'

18:15 A Predisposition to Learn

A predisposition is needed if one is actually to learn. In this proverb both the inner ('heart', i.e. 'mind') and outer ('ear') organs involved in learning in a largely oral culture need to be receptive (cf. 2:2). The mind needs to be 'intelligent' (ESV) or, better, 'discerning' (NIV, REB), and the ears eager to take in knowledge. Both halves of this proverb have a similarity to 15:14a.

18:16-19 Legal Processes

Legal processes seem to be the subject of vv. 17-18, and probably of the surrounding verses too. Even so, the principles they express are applicable to disputes in general.

Like 17:8, v. 16 is a simple observation without an explicit evaluation. The 'gift' here need not be a bribe given for a specific purpose, but rather a way of ingratiating oneself with influential people. However, the context of what follows suggests that a desire to influence a legal process is implied. In an Israelite context this was unacceptable (cf. 17:23). The language used in v. 17 indicates that its subject is legal proceedings. It is a warning against hasty judgements made before all the facts have been heard and examined. Apart from v. 18 there is no reference in the OT to lots being used to settle a legal dispute (see on 16:33). In the light of the previous verse Van Leeuwen's[173] suggestion seems plausible: 'Perhaps the lot was used when the arguments of each side seemed equally matched.' The point of v. 18b is probably that lingering disputes between influential people are particularly disruptive to a community, and so need to be settled by any acceptable means. There are grammatical problems in v. 19 but the general sense is clear. It is a warning against letting disputes become intractable to the point where people are locked into unyielding defensive positions (cf. 17:14). Although 'brother' in Hebrew can have a wider meaning than a blood relative, the fact is that family feuds can become particularly bitter and difficult to settle.

18:20-21 The Consequences of Speech

These consequences are expressed through the metaphor of 'fruit' (the word forms an *inclusio*), which binds this pair of proverbs together. Verse 20a is a

173. Van Leeuwen, *Proverbs*, 174.

variant of 12:14a and 13:2a, and makes the same point: that people will reap the consequences of their words. The second colon underlines this. Although the proverb could be taken literally — those who speak well can earn their living by it — it is more likely that it should be taken figuratively. The word translated 'stomach' is used figuratively in 18:8 of the inner depths of one's being. The use of words can give one intellectual and spiritual satisfaction in the way that food gives physical satisfaction.

The meaning of v. 21 is a matter of debate, even though there are no translation problems. Overall the meaning seems to be the same as v. 20, with an added emphasis in the first colon on the power of words for good or ill. The problem is in understanding the second colon. Here 'it' is feminine in Hebrew and most naturally refers back to 'the tongue' (a feminine noun). But what does it mean to 'love the tongue'? McKane[174] takes it to refer to those who 'are in love with language; they use it fastidiously, they search for chaste expression and precise meaning, and they have an end in view which they will reach because they know what language is for and how it can best be used to achieve its purpose'. Whybray,[175] however, takes it to refer to 'those who like to chatter or to express their opinions . . . [and] such people will be faced with the consequences of their loquacity.' He thinks that bad consequences are implied. It may be that v. 21b is meant to be ambiguous. The 'fruits' (life or death) will depend on the kind of 'tongue' one loves (cf. 15:2, 4).

18:22 A Good Wife

A good wife (the proverb seems to presuppose the 'good', cf. 12:4) is seen as a good gift from God. Clifford[176] comments that this is one of those proverbs which puts human (finding) and divine work (granting favour) side by side without attempting to explain how they are related. Aitken[177] points out that in this proverb, 'The first line echoes and the second line repeats the words of Lady Wisdom in 8:35 . . . as if to say that finding a good wife is on a par with finding wisdom.' The proverb is just as applicable to women finding good husbands.

174. McKane, *Proverbs,* 514-15.
175. Whybray, *Proverbs,* 273.
176. Clifford, *Proverbs,* 174.
177. Aitken, *Proverbs,* 153.

18:23 The Disadvantages of the Poor

These disadvantages are the subject of a number of observations in proverbs (e.g. 10:15; 13:23; 14:20). This one notes that they have to watch their tongues while the rich can say what they like. In particular, the poor have to plead for help but may receive a brusque response from the rich. There may be implicit criticism of the rich here (cf. 14:31; 17:5).

18:24 Friendship

Friendship of various kinds is clearly the subject of this proverb, but the meaning of the first colon is obscured by uncertainties in the Hebrew. The meaning of the second colon is clear: there is a kind of friend who is utterly reliable. To what kind of friend is this one being compared?

One issue is whether the first word in the MT of v. 24a should be emended from אִישׁ/*'îš* ('man') to יֵשׁ/*yēš* ('there is') to give a strict parallel with v. 24b. This, however, does not change the sense greatly. More important is how the verb הִתְרֹעֵעַ/*hitrō'ēa'* is understood. The ESV and NIV derive it from the root רעע/*r''* meaning 'to be harmful', so that the colon says that relying on many (presumably, superficial) friends can lead to disaster. The REB derives it from the root רוע/*rw'*, which normally means 'to shout' but can have the weaker sense 'to chatter'. The colon then means that some friends are only good to socialise with. The NRSV derives the verb from the root רעה/*r'h* 'to be a companion' (this requires a slight emendation of the MT) resulting in the meaning that some friends are only 'fair weather friends'.

Proverbs 19

19:1-3 Way Imagery

This group of proverbs begins with another 'better than' saying (v. 1): poverty with integrity is to be preferred to dishonesty. The REB emends the word 'fool' (כְּסִיל/*kĕsîl*) to 'rich' (עָשִׁיר/*'āšîr*) to give a better parallel with the first colon (cf. 28:6). This follows the reading of the Syr, but that might be an assimilation to 28:6. There is some 'shock value' in the unexpectedness of the MT text, which implies that the fool is probably a rich person. Verse 2 gives another example of folly — both cola warn against impulsive activism which lacks careful forethought. In one case the impulse is inner desire, in the other it is hastiness. Verse

3 is probably a comment on v. 2, and possibly v. 1b. When people's folly leads them to disaster they blame God instead of recognising their own culpability. 'Folly and blasphemy are closely linked here.'[178]

19:4-10 Wealth and Poverty

Several of these loosely related proverbs are simply observations of the effects of wealth and poverty without any explicit evaluation.

The effect of wealth and poverty on friendship is set out starkly in v. 4. While the wealthy gain many friends the poor person is likely to loose his one friend (cf. 14:20).

Verse 5 is one of a number of proverbs about perjury (e.g. 6:19; 12:17; 14:5, 25). Clearly this was a serious issue in ancient Israel. It was severely punished (Deut. 19:16-21), and the proverb asserts that the perjurer will not escape punishment. It may be that v. 5 is placed where it is as a reminder that wealth (especially 'gifts', v. 6) must not be used to pervert justice

Verses 6 and 7 are a pair that pick up on v. 4, with v. 6 expanding on v. 4a and v. 7 on v. 4b. The word נָדִיב/*nādîb* in v. 6a can mean either 'a ruler' (NIV, REB) or 'a generous person' (ESV, NRSV). The latter gives better parallelism with v. 6b, though a double meaning may be intended. The meaning of the first two cola of v. 7 is clear, but the third colon is obscure. The MT is probably corrupt. A literal translation is, 'pursuing words, not they' (K) or 'pursuing words, they (are) his' (Q). The ancient versions are no help here. The NRSV makes the best sense of a bad text: 'When they call after them, they are not there.'

Self-interest can be a strong motivation and is appealed to in v. 8 to encourage the pursuit of wisdom. To 'discover good' (ESV) is rightly interpreted by the other EVV as 'prosper'. This proverb may be here as a reminder that there is something more important than material wealth, namely wisdom (16:16), and that wisdom promises enduring wealth (8:18-19).

Verse 9 repeats v. 5, with one verbal change that does not affect the meaning.

Verse 10 is another proverb about what is 'not fitting' (see on 17:7). Most EVV take תַּעֲנוּג/*ta'ănûg* in its usual sense of 'luxury'. The REB derives the sense 'control' (hence, 'at the helm') from an Arabic cognate, without any evidence for this meaning in Hebrew. This may seem to give a better parallel with the second colon, but as it stands the proverb makes a similar contrast to that in

178. Whybray, *Proverbs*, 276.

30:22. Prosperity is properly the outcome of being wise, and so it is unfitting for a fool. Why it is even worse for a slave to rule over princes is not explained.

19:11-12 Anger

Self-control, including being slow to anger, is a recurrent theme in Proverbs (see on 16:32). In v. 11 it is linked with not reacting to provocation when someone causes offence. This increases the wise person's 'glory' (or 'reputation') perhaps because it reflects Yahweh's forgiveness and restraint of anger (Mic. 7:18). Verse 12 contrasts a king's wrath, as dangerous and deadly as a lion's, with his favour, which is as life-giving as the dew. In the arid summer of Palestine the dew is vital for the survival of vegetation. Taken in isolation v. 12 could be simply an observation about the power kings wield, with an implicit message to the wise not to arouse the ruler's anger. Where it is, v. 11 may be an implicit criticism of rulers who are too readily aroused to anger.

19:13-14 Domestic Matters

Domestic matters seen from a male perspective (but easily translated into a female one) link this pair of proverbs, as do the words 'father(s)' and 'wife'. Verse 13 is about things which cause domestic unhappiness. The foolish son appears also in 10:1; 17:21, 25 (see the comments there), and 27:15-16 expands on the imagery used of the nagging wife in v. 13b. Verse 14 balances the previous one by speaking about what brings domestic happiness, including the prudent wife. Within v. 14 there is a double contrast, between what comes of right (house and wealth) from a human source (his father) and what comes as gift (a prudent wife) from the LORD. In v. 14a there is an echo of 18:22, and 31:10-31 provides a portrait of the prudent wife. No doubt there is the implication that the gift from the LORD is of greater importance than the inheritance. Without a good spouse the house and wealth cannot be enjoyed, as v. 13b points out.

19:15 Laziness

Laziness and its harmful consequences are a frequent topic in proverbs (see on 18:9). The topic may appear here as an example of something that is not prudent and also because the mention of sleep in v. 15a has an echo of what is said of the foolish son in 10:5, and so links back to 19:13.

19:16-23 Miscellaneous Proverbs on the Theme of Education

The language of v. 16 is reminiscent of chs. 1–9.[179] Most scholars take 'the commandment' to refer to the instruction of the teacher (cf. NIV) and take 'his ways' to refer to the way of life of the learner. The proverb is then an encouragement to heed the teaching of the sages and take care to live by it. It is possible that this proverb refers to the commandments of Yahweh, and the REB adopts this meaning, making it explicit by replacing 'his way' by 'the way of the LORD' in the second colon.

Generosity to the poor is urged in 14:31 because it honours God, and in 14:21 those who are generous to the poor are promised 'blessing'. In v. 17 the blessing is made more concrete by describing what is given to the poor as a loan to Yahweh, which he will repay. Whether this will be by material or spiritual blessings is not stated.

The next three proverbs are admonitions, an unusual form in 10:1–22:16. Verse 18 is addressed to fathers and calls on them to discipline their sons. The 'hope' is no doubt that of improvement in their character and behaviour. The discipline would have included corporal punishment (13:24). There are different interpretations of v. 18b. The REB takes it as a warning: 'only be careful not to flog him to death'. This might be taken as a humorous, exaggerated way of saying, 'don't overdo the punishment'. The ESV's 'do not set your heart on putting him to death' may be an allusion to the law in Deut. 21:18-21 which prescribes death by stoning for a 'stubborn and rebellious son'. It is the parents who invoke this law. A more likely view than either of these is that the 'death' referred to is the outcome of a wayward life and that the father is being urged not to let this happen, hence the NIV's 'do not be a willing party to his death'.

The meaning of v. 19a is clear: those who give way to violent anger will bear the (presumably painful) consequences. The meaning of v. 19b is unclear. It may be a warning that attempts to help them get out of whatever predicament their anger gets them into is futile, because they will do it again. The REB goes beyond this: 'try to save him, and you make matters worse'. This is a possible meaning, and may imply that the person has to suffer the painful consequences to the full if they are to learn from the experience and amend their ways.

Verse 20 is an admonition typical of the introductions to the lessons in chs. 1–9, though expressed in less personal terms. The second colon recognises that attaining wisdom is a process. Verse 21 is a reminder that human

179. On this passage expressing the theme of education, see Heim, *Like Grapes of Gold,* 262.

wisdom has limits and that Yahweh's purposes may overrule human plans (cf. 16:1, 9).

The meaning of v. 22a is uncertain. The word חַסְדּוֹ *ḥasdô* would normally be taken to refer to 'steadfast love' but might come from a rare word meaning 'shame'. Also the word 'desire' might be taken in either a positive or negative sense. Hence the two options: 'What is desired in a man is steadfast love' (ESV) and 'Greed is a disgrace to a man' (REB). The REB rendering gives a better counterpart to the 'better than' saying in v. 22b: that it is better to be poor than dishonest (cf. 19:1).

Verse 23a is similar to 10:27a and 14:27a (see comments there). The Hebrew of v. 23b is difficult, literally, 'a satisfied (person) spends the night not visited by harm'. The NIV probably gets the sense intended: 'then one rests content untouched by trouble'.

19:24-29 Bad Characters of Various Kinds

As laziness personified, the sluggard does not have the energy even to feed himself (v. 24; cf. 19:15). As an object of the sages' satire he is a warning to others. The difference between the 'scoffer' and the 'simple' (v. 25) is that the scoffer is incorrigible but the simple is teachable and so will learn from seeing the scoffer physically chastised. A verbal rebuke alone is enough for the 'man of understanding' to learn his lesson.

Honouring parents is enjoined in the Ten Commandments (Exod. 20:12). The son in v. 26 does the opposite and so brings shame and disgrace on his family. One cause of such behaviour is given in the ironical admonition in v. 27, ceasing to heed parental instruction.

The punishment of perjurers has been promised in 19:5, 9. Verse 28 deals with their motivation — they 'devour iniquity' which, as Whybray[180] comments, 'probably means something like "gets pleasure from iniquity." ' The REB's 'fosters mischief' depends on a meaning for the verb postulated on the basis of an Arabic cognate.

Verse 29 may be a warning that the worthless witness of v. 28 will meet with punishment. The REB obtains stricter parallelism between the two cola by following the reading of the LXX in v. 29a and emending שְׁפָטִים/*šĕpāṭîm* (condemnations/penalties) to שְׁבָטִים/*šĕbāṭîm* ('rods').

180. Whybray, *Proverbs*, 287.

Proverbs 20

20:1-4 Unwise Behaviour

In v. 1 wine and 'strong drink' (probably 'beer', NIV) are personified according to the effects that overindulgence in them produces. The second colon may mean either that the drunken person behaves unwisely or that the wise do not get drunk. Verse 2a is a variant of 19:12a with a stronger word for 'anger'. The proverb warns of the deadly danger of provoking such anger. The REB adopts an alternative meaning of the verb in v. 2b, 'to ignore', which seems less appropriate. Verse 3 is one of several proverbs about avoiding or calming strife rather than getting involved in it (e.g. 15:18; 17:14; 18:6). Paradoxically it promises that more honour comes from avoiding a fight than winning it when communal harmony is at stake.[181] That figure of fun, the sluggard, makes another appearance in v. 4, expecting a harvest despite being too lazy to do the preparatory work for it. Ploughing in Palestine was done after the early autumn rains of October-November had softened the ground and before the end of the rainy season in March.

20:5-13 Discernment of Character

Verse 5 states the need for such discernment.[182] The imagery of 'deep water' could refer to what is hidden, but more probably in this context refers to the profundity of human thoughts and motives (cf. 16:2; 18:4). The wise person has the discernment to understand what is beneath the surface and express it in appropriate words.

The terms 'steadfast love' and 'faithful' in v. 6 express similar virtues and are often paired (e.g. 16:6a; 20:28) so what is being contrasted here is not these qualities but the public profession of them and the reality in practice. Use of the question form in v. 6b implies that the truly faithful person is difficult, or impossible, to find. Verse 7 may be a qualifying comment on v. 6: such people do exist and are a blessing to their descendants. This may be because of the example they set for, and the values they inculcate in, their children.

'The throne is established by righteousness' (16:12). If this is so, then the king has to judge righteously. Psalm 72:1-2 is a prayer that Yahweh will enable

181. Clifford, *Proverbs,* 182.

182. On this passage expressing the theme of character, see Whybray, *Composition,* 115, though he does not include v. 13.

him to do so. Verse 8 gives a picture of this ideal king. He has the discernment to recognise evil and the will to remove it like chaff from grain.

The question form of v. 9 implies a negative answer, 'No one'. This proverb shows the sages' awareness that the normally seemingly black and white polarisations of righteous (or wise) and wicked (or foolish) are a simplification (cf. 16:2). Real life is more complex. Acceptance of the truth of this proverb, however, did not stop them seeking the ideal of righteousness and urging others to do so.

Like 11:1 and 16:11, v. 10 expresses Yahweh's concern for honesty in business (see on those verses). 'Unequal weights' means using different weights for selling and for buying to gain commercial advantage. This proverb may be here as a warning that the LORD can discern what is hidden to humans — the falsity of the weights.

The verb יִתְנַכֶּר/*yitnakker* in v. 11a can mean either 'to make oneself known' (ESV) or 'to dissemble' (NJPSV, ESV footnote). Taken in the first sense the proverb is a version of 'by their fruits you shall know them' and may be advice to parents to discern the character of a child so that any remedial training can be begun early. If taken in the second sense it is a warning that appearances can be deceptive, and so discernment is needed to determine the true character of the child.

The import of the statement that the ear and eye, the two organs used in discernment, are made by the LORD is probably that humans should therefore use them properly for the purpose for which they were given. This will mean beginning with the 'fear of the LORD' who made them (1:7). Verse 13 is linked to verse 12 by the catchword 'eye' and taken on its own is another warning against laziness (see on 19:15). It may be put here to bring out the implicit message of v. 12, the importance of making the effort to use the ear and eye properly.

20:14-19 Commerce or Commercial Imagery

Verse 14 is a humorous proverb based on the bartering for goods in the marketplaces of the ancient Near East. The buyer deprecates the quality of the goods in order to keep the price down, but having bought them boasts that he has got a good bargain. The point of the proverb may be that words are not to be taken at face value, but their use is to be judged according to context. The use of words is the subject of v. 15. It is a variant of the teaching that wisdom is more valuable than precious metals and jewels (see on 16:16). Here wise words ('lips of knowledge') are said to be more valuable than gold or precious stones and a better adornment than jewels.

Verse 16 is another warning against standing surety for a loan (see on 11:15). In this case it is particularly strong because it is a loan to a stranger. Deuteronomy 24:10-13, 17 allows clothes to be given in pledge for a loan, but puts restrictions on this practice. The proverb is probably ironical: anyone who stands pledge for a loan to a stranger is acting stupidly, and their pledge is as good as forfeit from the outset. The Q has 'strange woman' (probably influenced by the use of this term in chs. 1–9) in v. 16b. The NIV follows this text but the ESV and most other EVV follow the K and read 'foreigners', which makes better sense.

The same Hebrew root (עבר/*'br*) lies behind the word 'security' in v. 16 and the word 'sweet' in v. 17, so linking the two verses. Verse 17 uses a vivid metaphor to say that the benefits gained by deceit will provide deceptive rewards. This may be a comment on the business dealings that are the subject of vv. 14 and 16.

Verses 18-19 are loosely linked to vv. 14-17 by the repetition of the root (עבר/*'br*) in the word 'associate' in v. 19. The general principle of v. 18a, that it is wise to take counsel from others before acting (cf. 11:14; 15:22), could apply to business deals, though v. 18b applies it to warfare. In context, the point of the warning in v. 19 may be that sometimes plans need to be kept confidential if they are to be successful. This proverb is a variant of 11:13.

20:20-25 Yahweh's Relationship with Humans

This group of verses includes three Yahweh proverbs.

In the law codes, cursing parents, flouting the command to honour them, is punishable by death (Exod. 21:17; Lev. 20:9; cf. Deut. 27:16). The imagery of the extinguished lamp is expressed more starkly in v. 20 than in 13:9, no doubt to emphasise the seriousness of the offence. Verse 21 probably gives an example of one way in which parents may be dishonoured: by a child somehow precipitating gaining their inheritance. The second colon fits in with a general theme in Proverbs that getting rich quickly will lead to disappointment (11:18; 13:11; 21:5). Verse 23 adds weight to the assurances in vv. 20-21 that wrongdoing will be punished. Yahweh will ensure this. Given the number of proverbs on legal matters this one should not be taken as advising people to 'wait on the LORD' as an alternative to proper legal action. It advises against taking the law into one's own hands, and also gives comfort when legal action is not possible. On v. 23 see the comment on v. 10. In this context it further underlines Yahweh's support of what is right. The main point of v. 24 is Yahweh's sovereignty, belief in which is essential if one is to trust him to uphold the moral order. Proverbs, like the rest of the OT, holds in tension belief in God's sovereignty and human responsibility. Here, as in 16:1, 9, recognition of God's sovereignty acts as a counter to human hubris. It means that there is an element of uncertainty and mystery in life, but that is no excuse for not thinking and planning ahead (15:22; 16:3; 20:18). Because human understanding is limited, the sages warn against acting in hasty and unconsidered ways (14:16-17; 16:20; 18:13). Verse 25 applies this to the specific case of vows, commitments made to God. One's relationship with God needs to be taken seriously and given due consideration. To do anything else is to dishonour God, and might have serious consequences.

20:26–21:4 The Relationship of Yahweh with the King, and of Both with People in General

These verses include three Yahweh proverbs and three royal proverbs. The imagery of the lamp marks this section (20:27; 21:4) and links it with the previous one (20:20).

Verse 26, defines a characteristic of a wise king, his discerning and sifting out the wicked (cf. v. 8). The wheel in v. 26b probably refers to the use of cart wheels in threshing (Isa. 28:27-28). The REB interpretation of it as the 'wheel of fortune' is unlikely. Verse 27 complements v. 26, speaking of Yahweh's ability to discern the inner thoughts and motives of humans, including kings. 'Spirit' (or 'breath', ESV footnote) is the word used in Gen 2:7 for the 'breath' of life (נִשְׁמַת/*nišmat*) which made Adam a living being. Verse 27a can be understood in two ways. Either 'the lamp of the LORD' is equated with 'the spirit of man' (ESV) or it searches it out (NIV). The latter reads the verb in the second colon back into the first — which is possible but less likely. In either case, the overall meaning of the proverb is clear. In v. 28 steadfast love and faithfulness are personified as guardians of the king. They could refer to the king's own virtues, but it is more likely that the reference is to Yahweh's upholding of the king, with v. 28b speaking of the king's responsibility to reflect Yahweh's character in his rule. The NRSV and REB follow the LXX in replacing 'steadfast love' in v 28b with 'righteousness/justice', but the LXX may be assimilating the colon to 16:12b.

Verse 29 may simply state characteristics of different stages of life. However, given the high valuation of wisdom in Proverbs there probably is an element of comparison. Murphy[183] comments, 'While the strength of youth is not to be disdained, he has a future to face, and it is there that a true judgment of a person lies'. The sages certainly did not share the modern veneration of youthfulness over age. The story of Rehoboam's folly (1 Kgs. 12:1-20) provides a lesson for a king of the value of wisdom over the 'macho' tendency of youthfulness.

183. Murphy, *Proverbs*, 154.

The meaning of the word תַּמְרִיק/*tamrîq* (K; the Q has תַּמרוּק/*tamrûq*) in v. 30a is problematic. However, the overall meaning is probably as conveyed by the EVV and summed up by Van Leeuwen:[184] 'The external discipline of the body affects the inmost being' and, in the sages' view, affects it for good (cf. 13:24).

Proverbs 21

21:1-4 Continuing the Theme of 20:26-30

Verse 1 uses the imagery of a farmer's control of his irrigation channels. Isaiah 32:1-2 compares the influence of good rulers to the effect of such channels. Here the point is God's sovereignty even over seemingly free and powerful kings. On verse 2 see comment on 16:2, of which it is a variant. Here it adds to v. 1 the reminder that God knows people better that they know themselves. He knows what lies behind outward acts of homage to him, and v. 3 specifies what he looks for (cf. 15:8). It expresses a view found in the prophets (e.g. Hos. 6:6; Mic. 6:6-8). This is not a rejection of sacrificial worship, but a condemnation of its misuse.

The meaning of v. 4b is debatable. The word נִר/*nir* can mean either 'lamp' or 'fallow ground'. The NJPSV adopts the second meaning, 'the tillage of the wicked is sinful' (cf. ESV footnote), meaning 'haughty looks, a proud heart' form cultivatable ground that can produce only what is sinful. Most EVV adopt the more common meaning 'lamp' but commentators debate the exact import of the imagery 'the lamp of the wicked'. There is probably a contrast with 'the lamp of the LORD' in 20:27. The meaning of the proverb may then be that pride distorts a person's inner being resulting in a false light that produces sin. The REB of v. 4b, 'These sins brand the wicked', adopts a very speculative meaning of *nir* based on an Arabic cognate.[185]

21:5-6 The Acquisition of Wealth

Although elsewhere haste is linked with some form of evil (e.g. 15:28; 19:2; 28:20) there is no explicit moral connotation to it in v. 5, which simply asserts that impulsiveness leads to poverty. The recipe for sure success is diligence and patience. Another deceptive root to wealth is dishonesty (v. 6). The MT of v. 6b is literally 'a fleeting vapour *for those who seek* (מְבַקְשֵׁי/*mĕbaqšê*) death'.

184. Van Leeuwen, *Proverbs,* 188.
185. Driver, 'Problems in the Hebrew Text', 185.

Most EVV follow the LXX, Vul and some Hebrew MSS in emending the text to וּמוֹקְשֵׁי/*ûmôqšê*, '*and snares* of death'.

21:7-8 Bad and Good Conduct

Because they ignore justice, those who act violently will find it rebounds on them. The rare verb used in v. 7a is used in Hab. 1:15 of catching fish in a net.

Most EVV understand v. 8 as contrasting the way of the guilty and the pure (or 'innocent', NIV). However, the meaning of וָזָר/*wāzār* (which occurs only here) as 'guilty' is uncertain. The Syr, Vulg and Targ seem to have read it as וְזָר/*wězār* 'and strange'. This is adopted by the NJPSV: 'The way of a man may be tortuous and strange,/Though his actions are blameless and proper.' This is preferred by Longman,[186] who takes it to mean, 'Appearances can be deceiving.'

21:9-19 A Collection of Miscellaneous Proverbs

These are bracketed by proverbs about a quarrelsome wife/woman (vv. 9, 19).

The 'better than' proverb in v. 9 is duplicated in 25:24 and has a variant in v. 19 (cf. 19:13; 27:15). Its basic point is that it is difficult to live with someone always ready to pick a fight. As Whybray[187] comments, both 'a corner of a roof top' here and 'a desert land' in v. 19 should be taken as 'examples of humorous fantasy'. The meaning of the phrase 'a house shared' is uncertain. On the basis of Akkadian cognates Clifford[188] prefers 'a house of noise'. Clearly this proverb is just as applicable to a quarrelsome husband.

Verse 10 is an observation about the psychology of the wicked. The soul (נֶפֶשׁ/*nepeš*) here is the organ of appetite (cf. 13:2, 4), and v. 10a speaks of someone obsessed with doing evil. They are so addicted to it that if anyone stands in the way of fulfilling their desire, they will suffer as a result.

The syntax of v. 11 is complex, making two readings possible depending on who is taken as the subject of the second verb in v. 11b. If it is the wise (ESV), then the two cola contrast the simple, who learns through seeing the fate of the scoffer, with the wise, who is open to accept the teaching of the sages (cf. 19:25). The REB takes the simple as the subject, so that the proverb is about two ways in which they can learn: 'simpletons learn wisdom when the insolent are

186. Longman, *Proverbs*, 392.
187. Whybray, *Proverbs*, 310.
188. Clifford, *Proverbs*, 190.

punished; when the wise prosper they draw a lesson from it'. The REB takes הַשְׂכִּיל/*haśkîl* to mean 'prosper' (as in 17:8) rather than 'instruct'. This word, taken in the sense 'observe', and the idea of punishment make a link with v. 12. Most commentators take 'the righteous' in v. 12a to refer to God (cf. Isa. 24:16) since nowhere else in Proverbs does the righteous person do anything to the wicked. It is God who brings calamity on them.

Verse 13 gives an example of the lack of mercy spoken of in v. 10. It promises judgement on the 'eye for an eye' principle. It also expresses the concern for the poor which is a theme in Proverbs (14:21, 31; 17:5; 19:17; 22:9, 22-23; 28:27).

Like 17:8 and 18:16, v. 14 is simply an observation about the use of bribes. For an evaluation of their use see 15:27; 17:23. Verse 15 may be intended as a comment on v. 14, implying that bribes pervert justice. Although the EVV use a passive translation 'when justice is done' many commentators prefer an active sense, 'The doing of justice', so that the proverb refers to behaviour, not just observation.

The metaphor of the 'two ways' which pervades Proverbs and is particularly prominent in chs. 1–9 is picked up in v. 16, 'This verse says in a few words what is developed at length in chaps. 1–9.'[189] Failure to heed the teaching of the wise is to join the way that leads to a premature and/or unhappy death. One example of 'wandering' off the right path is an excessive indulgence of pleasure (v. 17). The first colon states the general principle and the second makes it more specific by reference to feasting (oil was used cosmetically on such occasions, Ps. 104:15; Isa. 61:3). Here hedonism is a cause of poverty, which Proverbs more often attributes to laziness (e.g. 10:4; 14:23).

The meaning of v. 18 is unclear. If 'ransom' is taken in its normal sense the proverb is full of difficulties. If the righteous need a ransom they must have done something wrong, so are they righteous? Is it just for the wicked to be punished in their place? The least unsatisfactory understanding may be Toy's:[190] 'The thought appears to be simply that the bad and not the good suffer, a fact which is poetically represented as a substitution of the former for the latter' (cf. 11:8).

On v. 19 see comment on v. 9.

21:20-23 The Benefits of Wisdom

Hedonism leads to poverty (v. 17) but those who gain wisdom will enjoy the pleasures of life (v. 20). The NRSV of v. 20a follows the LXX in omitting the

189. Van Leeuwen, *Proverbs*, 193-94.

190. Toy, *Proverbs*, 406.

word 'oil' and adding the verb 'remains': 'Precious treasure remains in the house of the wise.' On the basis of an Arabic cognate[191] the REB re-points the word for 'oil' (שֶׁמֶן/*šemen*) as an adjective (שָׁמִין/*šāmîn*) meaning 'costly': 'The wise man has a houseful of fine and costly treasures.' These changes seem unnecessary. Oil was a symbol of wealth, as in v. 17. Just as the pursuit of wisdom leads to prosperity, so the pursuit of virtue (v. 21) leads to 'life, righteousness and honour'. Some scholars find the presence of 'righteousness' in the second colon odd after its use in the first. Following the LXX the NRSV omits it. The NIV and REB give it the somewhat forced meaning 'prosperity'. Taken together these verses have a similar message to Matt. 6:33.

Verse 22 is a mini-narrative making the point that wisdom, no doubt in the form of a well-planned stratagem, is superior to military might (cf. 16:32; Eccles. 9:14-16).

Verse 23 is an expanded variant of 13:3a (see comment there) and picks up the general theme of the value of reticence (e.g. 10:19; 12:23; 17:27-28).

21:24-29 Wicked People

The pride which characterises the scoffer (v. 24) is a vice frequently condemned in Proverbs (e.g. 11:2; 16:5; 18:12; 21:4). The second colon is not tautologous, but a rhetorical intensification, as in 'boys will be boys'.[192]

The picture of the sluggard in v. 25 is similar to that in 19:24. His desire to be lazy (6:9-11) means that he never works to get the necessities of life, and so it will lead to his death. Verse 26 has no definite subject, and most EVV take it to refer back to the sluggard. His selfish, unfulfilled cravings are contrasted with the generosity of the righteous person. The NRSV follows the LXX by inserting 'the wicked' as the subject, making it a self-contained proverb contrasting the greed of the wicked with the generosity of the righteous.

Verse 27 is a variant of 15:8. The 'how much more' at the start of the second colon is the normal meaning of אַף כִּי/*'ap kî,* but it is difficult to imagine the wicked would ever offer a sacrifice without 'evil intent'. The colon may be a rhetorical flourish, or it may be that in this case the phrase should be translated as 'for', as in the LXX.

Perjury is condemned throughout Proverbs, and v. 28a is a variant of 19:5a, 9a. However, the second colon changes the focus from the person of the false witness to his words. The EVV understand 'a man who hears' in v. 28b in

191. McKane, *Proverbs,* 552-53.
192. Van Leeuwen, *Proverbs,* 194.

various ways. The NRSV has 'A good listener will testify successfully', which can be taken as a reference to a reliable witness. The REB takes 'perish' in the first colon in the sense of 'be cut short' and translates the second as 'but a truthful witness will speak on'. The false witness will be recognised as such and silenced but the true witness will be given a full hearing. The NIV's 'and whoever listens to him will be destroyed for ever' takes the verb דָּבַר *dābar* in v. 28b to have the rare meaning 'to destroy' and so is the least likely rendering.

In v. 29a the EVV follow the Q (יָבִין/*yābîn*, 'discern') and the LXX rather than the K (יָכִין/*yākîn*, 'establish', 'direct aright') which has the support of the Targ and Vulg. The Q contrasts the stubbornness of the wicked with the willingness of the upright to think about his ways and, by implication, change them. The K might contrast the wicked defiantly going off on their own course with the upright maintaining the right course. These meanings do not differ greatly.

21:30-31 Two Yahweh Proverbs

The first asserts the superiority of Yahweh's wisdom over all human wisdom. This follows from the 'motto' of 1:7. True wisdom flows from Yahweh, and so any 'wisdom' that seeks to oppose him is false and will fail. Verse 31 applies this to the field of battle. These proverbs are among those which show that the sages were aware of the limitations of human wisdom and understanding of life because of the sovereignty of Yahweh. Von Rad[193] says of these proverbs, their aim is

> to put a stop to the erroneous concept that a guarantee of success was to be found simply in practicing human wisdom and in making preparations. Man must always keep himself open to the activity of God, an activity which completely escapes all calculation.

Proverbs 22:1-16

22:1-5 Wealth and Danger

Verse 1 relativises wealth. A good reputation and public approval are a firmer basis for a good life in society than wealth (cf. 3:4; Eccles. 7:1). The imagery used here is also used of wisdom (16:16), but gaining wisdom is the way to gain favour

193. von Rad, *Wisdom in Israel,* 101.

with people (3:4-5; 13:15a). Verse 2 relativises wealth in another way, by dealing with the status of the rich and the poor. Whybray[194] comments that the verb 'meet together' should 'probably be understood figuratively as meaning that rich and poor have something in common: their status as Yahweh's creatures'. If so, then although no explicit moral lesson is drawn, the proverb may imply what is said in 14:31 and 17:5, that the rich are to treat the poor with respect and compassion.

Verse 3 is a mini-narrative stressing the importance of prudence, or shrewdness/cleverness (REB/NRSV), for avoiding danger and its consequences, into which the 'simple' walk. unawares.

Riches are also relativised in v. 4. The syntax of the first colon is ambiguous. There is no 'and' in it, so it is possible to take 'the fear of the LORD' as part of the 'reward for humility', as the REB does. However, it seems better to take the two phrases in v. 4a as in apposition[195] (i.e. the kind of humility concerned is that based on the fear of the LORD) and v. 4b as the 'reward'. The first colon then gives the condition for gaining enduring riches.

Although the meaning of the first word in v. 5 is uncertain, the overall meaning is clear. A person concerned about their well-being will keep clear of 'crooked' people because their way of life leads them into difficult and dangerous situations.

22:6-16 Miscellaneous Proverbs

This collection includes a frame provided by pairs of proverbs about child discipline and poverty (vv. 6-7, 15-16).

The first colon of v. 6 is literally, 'Dedicate a child according to his way'. The EVV rightly understand the second phrase to mean 'the way he should go' (ESV, NIV) or 'the right way' (NRSV, REB). In Rabbinic Hebrew the verb חָנַךְ/*ḥānak* means 'instruct, train', which makes sense here, but the nuance of 'dedicating' the child to a way of life also makes sense. Proverbs are statements of what normally happens 'other things being equal', and v. 6b is not a promise but an expectation. Influences other than the parent might prevent the expected from happening.

Taken at face value v. 7 is simply an observation on the harsh realities of life. However, it is an implicit warning against falling into debt.

The principle of just retribution is expressed in v. 8a using agricultural

194. Whybray, *Proverbs*, 318.

195. Waltke, *Proverbs 15–31*, 193.

imagery, which may extend to v. 8b, where the 'rod' could be a threshing flail.[196] The meaning of v. 8b is unclear. The REB takes the owner of the 'rod' to be God and re-points the verb יִכְלֶה/*yikleh* ('it will fail') as יְכַלֵּהוּ/*yĕkallēhû* ('will destroy him'): 'the rod of God's wrath will destroy him'. However, ESV's literal translation, 'the rod of his fury will fail', does make sense if the rod 'refers to the instrument by which the wicked manifest their "injustice," and the failure of such is one way in which they harvest evil'.[197] Isaiah 14:5-6 provides a parallel, with God breaking the rod with which the oppressive Babylonian king has struck people in wrath.

Verse 9 provides a counterpoint to both the previous verses. In contrast to v. 8 the principle of just retribution is applied to a good action, generous sharing with the poor rather than making them go into debt by taking a loan (contrast v. 7).

Verse 10 reveals another characteristic of the scoffer to complement his pride (21:24) — his quarrelsome and abusive nature which provokes strife. He has to be banished to protect the harmony of the community.

The Hebrew grammar of v. 11 is difficult. The ESV, NRSV and NIV all give fairly literal translations which make reasonable sense. The REB takes Yahweh as the subject of the first colon (as does the LXX, though it has a different reading of the verse overall): 'The LORD loves a person to be sincere.' The second colon, 'by attractive speech a king's friendship is won', then seems to stand in contrast to this, saying that kings are susceptible to flattery. This is a rather speculative translation.

Most commentators take 'knowledge' in v. 12a to be a shorthand for '(the words of) the knowledgeable' to provide a parallel with 'the words of the traitor' in v. 11b. The REB interprets it as referring to a judicial context: 'the LORD keeps watch over every claim at law, and upsets the perjurer's case'. The more general and straightforward translations of the other EVV are preferable.

Verse 13 gives another humorous and satirical portrait of the sluggard and his excuses for inaction (see on 21:5). The purpose of the sages' ridicule is to deter others from being lazy.

The 'strange woman', so prominent in chs. 1–9 (see on 2:16-19), appears only in v. 14 in the sentence proverbs — in the plural as the ESV indicates. Her mouth, which in chs. 1–9 utters seductive words to lead young men astray, is depicted as a trap one might fall into. Here she appears as an instrument of God's wrath.

The need for discipline in the training of children is a common theme in

196. Clifford, *Proverbs*, 197.

197. Longman, *Proverbs*, 406, n. 4.

Proverbs (e.g. 13:24; 19:18; 22:6). The first colon is often taken to imply that there is an innate folly in children but Van Leeuwen[198] may be right in suggesting that the proverb should be taken as an implicit conditional sentence: 'If folly is . . .'

The Hebrew of v. 16 is very succinct and its syntax difficult, which makes it hard to interpret with certainty. The lack of a connective between the two cola allows the differing translations of the REB ('Oppression of the poor brings gain, but giving to the rich only leads to penury') and the ESV ('Whoever oppresses the poor to increase his wealth, or gives to the rich, will only come to poverty'). The ESV's interpretation is more in line with other proverbs about the rich and the poor. The oppression of the poor might be through tax farming or usury. The gifts to the rich are presumably attempts to curry favour with them. How these strategies to get rich will lead to poverty is not spelt out.

Proverbs 22:17–24:22

See the section in the introduction on 'Proverbs 22:17–24:22 and *The Instruction of Amenemope*' for a discussion of the relationship of this section to the Egyptian work and its overall structure.

22:17-21 Introduction

The LXX begins v. 17 with, 'Incline your ear to the words of the wise and hear my word.' This variant from the MT, plus the clear heading in 24:23a, has led to the suggestion that an original title, 'The words of the wise', has been copied into the MT and the LXX in different places. The NRSV accepts this: 'The words of the wise: Incline you ear and hear my words.'

'Thirty sayings' in v. 20 is an emendation of the MT. The K (שִׁלְשׁוֹם/*šilšôm*) is usually taken to mean 'formerly', though in its other uses in this sense it always occurs in conjunction with תְּמוֹל/*tĕmôl* or its variants.[199] The Q (שָׁלִישִׁים/*šālîšîm*) 'officers' does not makes sense, and a suggested figurative sense 'noble things' is unlikely. A slight emendation of the text to שְׁלֹשִׁים/*šĕlōšîm* 'thirty' has been adopted by most scholars on the basis of the ancient versions, which read the word 'three times' (the same consonants as 'thirty') here, and a reference in

198. Van Leeuwen, *Proverbs,* 199.

199. Though its Akkadian cognate could be used in this sense on its own (*CAD* 17:268b-69a). This leads K. A. Kitchen to suggest that Prov. 22:20 is an archaic use of the Hebrew word in this sense (private communication).

the final lines of *Amenemope*[200] to that work having 'thirty chapters'. Since the meaning 'formerly' seems strange, referring to a document not available to the readers of Proverbs, and many scholars do find thirty sayings in this section, the emendation seems reasonable. The fact that there is no specification of the thing enumerated ('sayings') in the MT is not a strong objection since this is common in Hebrew.[201]

Verses 17-18 contain many echoes of the introductions to the lessons in chs. 1–9 (e.g. 2:2, 10; 4:20-21; 5:1-2) and also of *Amenemope*[202] in the call to pay heed to the words of the teacher and to memorise them so that they are ready for use. The Hebrew of v. 18a says literally, 'keep them in your belly', which is similar to the phrase 'Let them rest in the casket of your belly' in *Amenemope.* The 'pleasantness' that will follow if the teachings are internalised is given as a motivation for learning them. Verse 19 is at the centre of the introduction and expresses a distinctly Israelite theological motivation for the teaching: to promote trust in Yahweh. This can be related to the 'motto' of 1:7. The final section of the introduction (vv. 20-21) states a desired 'learning outcome' that is not entirely clear. There is a similarity between v. 21b and a statement of purpose in *Amenemope:* 'To know how to return an answer to him who said it, and to direct a report to one who has sent him.'[203] This may be a reference to being a reliable messenger[204] or other public official. The reference to the teaching having been written down (v. 20a) is notable.

22:22-23 Saying 1

This prohibition against mistreating the poor and its motivation, that Yahweh is their protector, is in line with other proverbs (14:31; 17:5) and the OT laws (Exod. 22:21-23; 23:6; Deut. 24:14-15). Mention of 'the gate' applies this to a legal setting, since legal disputes were settled by the elders sitting in the public space by the city gate (e.g. Ruth 4:1-2). The first admonition after the prologue of *Amenemope* is similar: 'Beware of robbing a wretch, Of attacking a cripple.'[205] Later there is reference to the treatment of the poor in court: 'Do not incline to

200. 27:6f. *COS* 1:116.

201. Joüon §142n.

202. 'Give your ears, hear the sayings, Give your heart to understand them: It profits your heart; Woe to him who neglects them! Let them rest in the casket of your belly; May they be bolted in your heart. When there rises a whirlwind of words, They'll be a mooring for your tongue.' III.9-16, *COS* 1.116.

203. I.5-6, *COS* 1:116.

204. Murphy, *Proverbs,* 170.

205. IV.4-5, *COS* 1:116.

the well-dressed man, and rebuff the one in rags', and the motivation given is that Ma'at 'saves the poor from his tormentor'.[206]

22:24-25 Saying 2

From the first lesson (1:10-19) onwards Proverbs warns against associating with various bad characters. One of these is the person given to anger (e.g. 14:17; 15:18). Here the motivation given evokes the image of the 'two ways'. To learn the wrong way is to court disaster. *Amenemope* also warns against association with the angry person.[207]

22:26-27 Saying 3

This admonition fits in with Proverbs' consistent warnings against acting as guarantor for a loan (see on 20:16). The motivation given here, with a rather humorous picture of having your bed snatched from under you, is the danger of losing your personal property. Beds were something of a luxury in ancient Israel, but someone who gave surety for a loan would be relatively wealthy.

22:28 Saying 4

On the importance of the ancient boundary markers see comment on 15:25. *Amenemope* has similar admonitions.[208]

22:29 Saying 5

This saying breaks the pattern of admonitions with a rhetorical question which draws the reader into a didactic observation. This is similar to the proverbs encouraging diligence (12:11, 24, 27; 13:4; 14:23), but adds the element of the

206. XXI.1-8, *COS* 1:120.

207. 'Don't start a quarrel with a hot-mouthed man. . . . Withdraw from him, leave him alone' 5.10ff, *COS* 1:117. 'Do not befriend the heated man, nor approach him for conversation' 11:13-14, *COS* 1:118.

208. 'Do not move the markers at the borders of the fields, nor shift the position of the measuring-cord. Do not be greedy for a cubit of land, nor encroach on the boundaries of the widow', VII:11ff., *COS* 1:117.

need for skill. Those who have both qualities will succeed in their careers. No particular career is implied here, unlike the proverb in *Amenemope* which says, 'The scribe who is skilled in his office, he is found worthy to be a courtier.'[209]

23:1-3 Saying 6

The topic of table etiquette occurs in Egyptian instructions, including *Amenemope:* 'Do not eat in the presence of an official and then set your mouth before him. . . . Look at the bowl that is before you, and let it serve your needs. An official is great in his office, as a well is rich in drawings of water.'[210] Seemingly, behaviour at meals could be a testing time for an ambitious courtier. In v. 1b it is not clear whether the courtier should pay careful attention to the food that is before him or the person in whose presence he eats — probably both are meant. Verse 2a is an idiom meaning 'curb your appetite'. Restraint in various forms is a theme in Proverbs. In v. 3 the food is probably called 'deceptive' because the meal is not simply an opportunity to enjoy good food, it is a test taken under the eyes of the ruler.

23:4-5 Saying 7

Elsewhere in Proverbs wealth is a reward for diligence (10:4-5; 12:27; 13:4). This proverb is about a fixation with acquiring wealth, which it depicts as senseless, using humorous imagery in v. 5. If the Q is followed in v. 5a there is a striking word-play which is lost in the EVV: 'If you let your eyes fly to it, it is gone . . . flying like an eagle.' Although wealth can be the reward of wise behaviour, the truly wise know when to desist from pursuing it for its own sake (v. 4b). The imagery of wealth flying away like a bird is found in *Amenemope,* but there it refers to riches gained by theft: 'they made themselves wings like geese, and flew away to the sky.'[211]

23:6-8 Saying 8

Like saying 6, this is about dining. In both cases there is advice to resist the attractions of seemingly good food (v. 3a, 6b). This saying is about a meal offered by a

209. XXVII.16-17, *COS* 1:122.
210. XXIII.13-20, *COS* 1:121.
211. X.4-5, *COS* 1:118.

stingy person. He seems to be a generous host, but this is a sham (v. 7bc). Verse 7a is unclear. The ESV gives a fairly literal translation of the MT: 'for he is like one who is inwardly calculating'. The REB's 'for they will stick in your throat like a hair' re-points the verb שָׁעַר/*šāʿar* ('he calculates') as שֵׂעָר/*śēʿar* ('hair', the LXX rendering) and takes בְּנַפְשׁוֹ/*bĕnapšô* ('in his soul', hence 'inwardly') in its alternative sense 'in his throat'. This fits with the reference to vomiting in v. 8, which is probably to be taken figuratively: 'the guest will afterwards regret and be revolted by the whole incident'.[212] The imagery of vomiting appears in *Amenemope*, but in a different context: 'Do not covet a poor man's goods, nor hunger for his bread; a poor man's goods are a block in the throat, it makes the gullet vomit.'[213]

23:9 Saying 9

The ESV's 'Do not speak in the hearing of a fool' is a rather over-literal translation of a Hebrew idiom which means, 'Do not speak to a fool' (NIV). The reason for the admonition is not simply that he is deaf to wise advice (17:10) but that he despises it — and so presumably the person who gives it. The sentiment is similar to Jesus' saying in Matt. 7:6.

23:10-11 Saying 10

Verse 10a repeats 22:28a (see the comment there) but applies the admonition specifically to the land of orphans. Like widows (15:25b) they were among those who were most vulnerable to exploitation. The unnamed 'redeemer' in v. 11 is clearly Yahweh. In the OT laws the 'redeemer' (גֹּאֵל/*gōʾēl*) was a close relative who had the duty to buy back family property when poverty compelled someone to sell it (Lev. 25:25-34), but their responsibilities might have been wider than this. Orphans might lack such close human relatives, so Yahweh will take up their cause.

23:12 Saying 11

The close similarities with *Amenemope* come to an end. A new sub-section, centred on the father-son relationship, begins with v. 12, which is similar in wording

212. Whybray, *Proverbs*, 334.
213. XIV.5-8, *COS* 1.118

and theme to 22:17 and the introductions to the lessons in chs 1–9. It is a general admonition to seek instruction in wisdom. It is linked to vv. 13-14 by the word מוּסָר/*mûṣār* which means both 'instruction' (v. 12) and 'discipline' (v. 13).

23:13-14 Saying 12

This saying is similar to other proverbs about disciplining children (e.g. 22:15). In the light of v. 14 the meaning of v. 13b is not that the child will survive a beating but that the discipline will save him from death, presumably the premature or shameful death that awaits the wicked.

A very similar saying occurs in *Ahiqar*: 'spare not your son from the rod; otherwise can you save him [from wickedness]? If I beat you, my son, you will not die; but if I leave you alone, [you will not live].'[214]

23:15-18 Saying 13

This saying has the instruction form of an introduction (vv. 15-16), a command (v. 17) and a motive (v. 18). The introduction provides a motivation in its appeal to the child's desire to make its parent happy (cf. v. 25). The lack of a verb in v. 17b leads the EVV to construe it in different ways. The ESV and NRSV supply the verb 'continue'. The NIV carries over the verb from the first colon but with a change of nuance from 'envy' to 'be zealous'. The REB also takes 'fear' to stand for 'those who fear' to give a stricter parallel with 'sinners' in v. 17a. The main thrust of the command is clear: do not be led astray by envy of those sinners who seem to be successful. The motivation is an assurance of the blessing that awaits the righteous. The use of 'a future and a hope' in Jeremiah's letter to the exiles about life in Babylon (Jer. 29:11) indicates that v. 18 refers to 'a life well lived in the here and now and celebrated by an honourable death which is not foreshortened or marked by adversity'.[215]

23:19-21 Saying 14

This saying is another instruction with an introduction (v. 19), command (v. 20) and motivation (v. 21). It follows on from saying 13 by specifying some of the

214. Lines 81-82, *OTP* 2:498.
215. Murphy, *Proverbs*, 176.

sinners the son might envy. Both sayings deal with the problem that peer pressure creates for young people.

Verse 19 picks up 'the way' imagery that is so prominent in chs. 1–9. Drunkenness and gluttony appear together in the law about the rebellious son in Deut. 21:18-21. The motivation is avoidance of poverty. This might be the result of excessive spending on food and drink, but v. 21 highlights the torpor that follows over-indulgence in them, a motif that echoes what is said of the sluggard (6:9-11).

23:22-25 Saying 15

This saying is an instruction which expands on the implicit appeal of vv. 15-16 by explicitly making the (good) child's desire to please its parents a motivation for heeding their teaching (cf. 10:1; 15:20; 17:25; 29:3). The references to them having given the child life which frame the saying (vv. 22a, 25b) make an implied appeal to a sense of indebtedness and gratitude. The introduction (v. 22) is reminiscent of 1:8 and 6:20. The command to value wisdom highly (v. 23) echoes 4:5, 7; 16:16. This saying expresses the importance the sages placed on the family as a place for instruction and the value they put on harmonious family relationships.

23:26-28 Saying 16

This saying returns to the subject of the 'adulteress' or 'foreign woman' (ESV footnote) of chs. 1–9 (see on 2:16-19) and is almost a summary of ch. 7.

Given the meaning of 'heart' in Hebrew (see on 4:23) v. 26a is an appeal for obedience, not love, as the second colon shows by picking up the metaphor of 'the way'. In v. 26b the EVV follow the Q (תִּצֹּרְנָה/*tiṣṣōrnâ;* 'watch, guard') rather than the K (תִּרְצֶנָה/*tirṣenâ;* 'delight in'). In v. 27 the prostitute/adulteress is depicted as a dangerous trap (cf. 22:14) using imagery with sexual connotations. In v. 28 the imagery changes to that of a predator. The meaning of v. 28a is that she encourages men to be unfaithful.

The REB takes vv. 27-28 to refer to two different types of women, with the prostitute being like the robber and the adulteress being 'unfaithful with man after man'. This requires taking the masculine active participle בּוֹגְדִים/*bôgĕdîm* ('treacherous, unfaithful') as a collective noun meaning '(act of) treachery/unfaithfulness'. This seems a rather forced reading of these verses.

23:29-35 Saying 17

This saying has a form unique in Proverbs. The introduction is a riddle (v. 29) followed by the answer (v. 30). This is followed by an admonition (v. 31) and an extended motive (vv. 32-35) which consists of a vivid portrait of the state of a drunkard. The meaning of the word translated 'top of a mast' in v. 34b is unclear, but the verse clearly depicts the disoriented state of a storm-tossed mariner. In v. 35a the EVV add the phrase 'you will say' from the LXX in order to make clear that the verse reports the drunkard's words.

On their own the six questions in the riddle highlight some negative effects of drunkenness. Verse 31 tells the alcoholic (v. 30) to steer well clear of wine, not even to look at it 'when it gives its eye in the cup' (v. 31b, literal translation) — when it is like the enticing look of a woman. It is pleasant to drink (v. 31c) but the after-effects are graphically depicted as disastrous (vv. 32-35): it can be as lethal as the bite of a poisonous snake; it causes hallucinations; it disorients; it dulls pain in a dangerous way. Worst of all, it takes control of the addict's life. He cannot wait to get over his hangover and start another drinking bout.

As Whybray[216] says, this piece 'is written in a jocular, not to say, burlesque style'. Its purpose is clear: it warns against the dangers of alcohol addiction.

24:1-2 Saying 18

This saying begins a new sub-section on wisdom and various forms of wickedness or folly. It parallels 23:17-18 and 24:19-20 but whereas they have a motivation clause about the future of the good or evil person, it describes the nature of the evil person. Maybe there is an implied warning: 'avoid them or you will become like them', or the implication may be that people like this are bound to have a bad end.

24:3-4 Saying 19

Since Proverbs promises that wisdom will bring material prosperity (e.g. 8:18, 21; 15:6) this saying can clearly be understood on that level. However, 'house' may refer to more than the physical building, to the household. Since wisdom also leads to harmonious personal relationships, the saying can be understood metaphorically on that level too. There may also be an intentional echo of the statement about Yahweh's creative work in 3:19.

216. Whybray, *Proverbs,* 340.

24:5-6 Saying 20

The text of v. 5 is problematic. The ESV and NIV make reasonable sense of the MT: wisdom and knowledge give a person strength. The NRSV and REB follow the LXX, Syr and Targ, which essentially say, 'A wise man is mightier than a strong man, and a man of knowledge than one who has strength.' Arguably, v. 6 follows on better from the MT reading since it does not contain a comparison but stresses the value of wisdom and counsel if victory is to be gained in war (cf. 20:18; 21:22). As a whole, the saying asserts that both wisdom and strength are needed to wage war successfully. It is possible to apply this to conflicts met in everyday life.

24:7-9 Sayings 21, 22 and 23

These sayings are about the drawbacks of folly. The words 'fool/folly' link vv. 7 and 9 and vv. 8 and 9 are linked by the words 'schemer' and 'scheming/devising' (see ESV footnote).

Verse 7 asserts that because the fool lacks any wisdom, he has nothing sensible to contribute in the public discussions (including legal cases) that took place in the open space near the city gates. Perhaps frustrated by this, some fools make their own plots and plans that are to the detriment of the community and gain a reputation as schemers (v. 8). Indeed, it leads to them being ostracised (v. 9). Most EVV translate v. 9a as 'the schemes of folly are sin'. The word for 'sin' (חַטָּאת/*ḥaṭṭā't*) basically means 'to miss the mark', hence the REB's 'the intrigues of the foolish misfire'. However, the labelling of their plans as 'evil' in v. 8a and the use of the term 'abomination' (usually used of what offends God, see on 3:32) in v. 9b seem to require the stronger meaning, 'sin'.

24:10 Saying 24

Scholars differ over whether or not this is an independent saying. Since vv. 11-12 have the form of an admonition followed by a motive, and v. 10 does make sense on its own, it can be treated independently (NIV). The Hebrew contains a pun between 'adversity' (צָרָה/*ṣārâ*) and 'small' (צַר/*ṣar*) that is lost in the EVV. It implies that 'the day of adversity' is a time when someone is hemmed in by difficult circumstances.

If taken closely with what follows, v. 10 has an accusatory tone (NRSV).

On its own it is a general observation 'that a man does not know what reserves of stamina he possesses, until he has to live through a situation in which severe demands are made on him'.[217]

24:11-12 Saying 25

This refers to one example of 'the day of adversity' of v. 10. The details of the situation are unclear but the overall message is fairly clear. People are facing death — perhaps because they are victims of injustice or because they are acting unwisely. Action should be taken to save them. It is no good making false excuses for inactivity. God knows our inner thoughts and motivations and will act and judge accordingly. Cowardice when called upon to help those in desperate need is reprehensible, and those who refuse to help others cannot expect God to help them when in need.

24:13-14 Saying 26

This saying begins a new sub-section, framed by sayings addressed to 'my son'. It is followed by four sayings which are all similar in form, a double admonition followed by a motive, and deal with the theme of the righteous and the wicked.

The son is urged to acquire wisdom by drawing an analogy with eating honey. Just as honey is both pleasant and beneficial (cf. 16:24), so is wisdom. The benefit of wisdom is that is brings a person a future, something to hope for (see the comment on 23:18 which is almost identical to v. 14bc). In Hebrew the analogy is supported by the fact that the word for 'soul' (נֶפֶשׁ/*nepeš*) also means 'appetite'.

24:15-16 Saying 27

This has echoes of 1:10-19. It is a warning against getting involved in criminal attacks on the homes of the righteous. The reason given is that the righteous will always recover ('seven times' indicates completeness) but the wicked will be overcome by calamity. By implication the saying is a word of encouragement to the righteous. They will experience some hard knocks in life, and sometimes fall under them, but they have the endurance to get up again. In

217. McKane, *Proverbs*, 400.

this sense the proverb is an illustration of the future and the hope that wisdom imparts (v. 14).

24:17-18 Saying 28

Verse 17 is linked to v. 16 by repetition of 'to fall' and 'to stumble'. 'Lest' at the beginning of v. 18 in the ESV does not convey clearly the sense of the Hebrew idiom used; the 'or (else)' of the other EVV is better.

Many commentators see the high moral tone of v. 17 let down by the motive in v. 18, which seems to endorse desiring God's wrath to fall on one's enemies. First, it should be said that in some circumstances such a desire might in fact be a desire that God should deal with a serious injustice. The applicability of a proverb depends on the circumstances. Second, the saying as a whole can be seen as warning against an attitude of self-righteous superiority which is only a step away from wanting to take vengeance, which is God's prerogative (20:22).

24:19-20 Saying 29

This is the third in this section of Proverbs to counsel against envying the wicked (see 23:17-18; 24:1-2). This time the motive is the reverse of 23:18 and a repeat of 13:9b (cf. 20:20). Psalm 73 can be seen as a commentary on this proverb as the psalmist describes his journey from envying the wicked, to discerning 'their end', to finding security in his relationship with God.

24:21-22 Saying 30

Only the opening colon is clear. Although the Judean king was regarded as Yahweh's representative and vice-regent it is unusual in its bracketing together of Yahweh and the king. The MT text of v. 21b reads, 'Do not associate with those who change/differ.' The ESV takes this to mean those who do not fear Yahweh and the king, while the NIV takes it to mean 'rebels'. On the basis of an Arabic cognate[218] the REB reads שׁוֹנִים/*šônîm* not as 'those who change' but as 'noblemen'. The NRSV follows the LXX: 'and do not disobey either of them' (i.e. Yahweh or the king). The grammar of v. 22 is difficult, and the versions construe it to fit their reading of v. 21b. The REB makes it a warning that the

218. Driver, 'Problems in the Hebrew Text', 189.

nobles will bring disaster on themselves, presumably by their court intrigues. In the other versions it is a warning that both Yahweh and the king will punish those who disobey them.

Proverbs 24:23-34

24:23a Marker

This marks the beginning of a short new section of Proverbs with six sayings. It has a structure: sayings 1 and 4 are on legal topics, sayings 2 and 5 deal with speech, and sayings 3 and 6 concern work.

24:23b-25 False Judges

Partiality in judging is condemned in Deut. 1:17; 16:19-20. It would usually be the result of bribery. Here both a negative and a positive motive are given for judges acting impartially. Those who do not are cursed by the people and those who do are blessed. The implication is that God supplies the 'good blessing'. A curse is a form of prayer to God to punish the evildoer, and in 17:15 the judge who acquits the wicked is abhorred by Yahweh.

24:26 Good Speech

This is about truth-telling in general, not just in court. The exact meaning of the metaphor used is uncertain, but Longman[219] probably gives the basic meaning: 'Kissing and truth-telling are two positive and pleasurable acts one can perform or receive from lips. Telling the truth is a kind act.' Fox[220] puts it more succinctly, 'The most genuine sign of affection is telling someone the truth.'

24:27 Good Work

This proverb is a command without a motive because it is an implicit appeal to common sense, though its counterpart (vv. 30-34) could be taken as the motive.

219. Longman, *Proverbs,* 442.
220. Fox, *Proverbs 10–31,* 771.

Whether taken literally or figuratively its message is clear: 'don't undertake anything hastily without due preparation.'[221]

24:28 False Witnesses

This is another proverb against perjury. See the comments on 12:17; 14:5, 25.

24:29 Bad Speech

This prohibition of revenge lacks a motive, but 20:22 makes clear that vengeance is God's prerogative, and v. 29b echoes what is said of God in v. 12d.

24:30-34 Laziness

Here is another piece of satire at the expense of the sluggard (see on 22:13). It is a didactic story which moves from introduction (v. 30) to observation (v. 31) followed by reflection (v. 32) resulting in the moral (vv. 33-34). This may give some insight into the teaching methods of the sages in Israel. The moral is nearly identical to 6:10-11 (see the comment there). Overall there is a clear warning against laziness because it leads to poverty.

Proverbs 25

25:1 Heading

This heading, marking a new section in Proverbs, is the only clue to the dating of the present form of the book. See in the introduction on 'Authorship and Date' and 'The Structure of the Book of Proverbs.'

Bryce[222] argues that 25:2-27 is a 'small wisdom book,' and Van Leeuwen[223] describes it as a 'proverb poem.' Van Leeuwen builds on, and improves, Bryce's work, and his detailed analysis[224] informs what follows.

221. Whybray, *Proverbs*, 354.
222. Bryce, 'Another "Wisdom Book"', 148.
223. Van Leeuwen, *Context and Meaning*, 61.
224. Van Leeuwen, *Context and Meaning*, 57-86.

25:2-3 A Clear Hierarchy of God-King-Subjects

Although both God and the king are to be honoured, God comes first. The two verses are linked by the keywords 'kings' and '(un)search(able)'. It is unclear whether the same 'things' are meant in the two cola of v. 2. Given the superiority of God it is likely that they are not. Verse 2b refers to the king's knowledge of his kingdom, his people, and what is going on, so that he can rule effectively. Just as God is inscrutable to his creatures, so the king's thoughts and intentions are inscrutable to his subjects (v. 3).

25:4-5 Searching out Wickedness

Searching out wickedness and removing it is one important kingly function. It is characteristic of this chapter that a metaphor precedes what it refers to (the EVV sometimes reverse the order). This produces suspense and expectation. Clifford[225] sums up this saying well: 'If you remove scum you get pure silver; if you remove scoundrels from the king's court you get a stable dynasty in that a just dynasty assures divine protection.'

Van Leeuwen[226] sees vv. 2-5 as introducing a series of admonitions and sayings about social hierarchy and social conflict and its resolution.

25:6-7ab Warnings against Pride

These are common in Proverbs, and this saying gives a specific example which illustrates 18:12 (see comment there). The context is the jockeying for position and power that goes on among courtiers but it has wider applicability, as Jesus' advice in Lk. 14:7-11 shows, advice that may be based on these verses.

25:7c-10 Two Admonitions about Legal Disputes between Peers

The first (vv. 7c-8) warns against drawing hasty conclusions on the basis of what one sees without further investigation. It may lead to a false accusation which, when disproved, brings shame on the accuser. Verse 7c echoes legal language (Deut. 21:7), and most EVV take v. 8 to refer to legal proceedings.

225. Clifford, *Proverbs*, 223.

226. Van Leeuwen, *Context and Meaning*, 23.

However, following Sym, Toy[227] re-points לָרִב/*lārīb* (to court) as לָרֹב/*lārōb* (to the crowd), which leads to the REB translation of v. 8a, 'be in no hurry to tell everyone', and makes the issue one of scandal-mongering. This seems less likely in context.

The second admonition (vv. 9-10) advises settling a dispute with a neighbour privately out of court. Once again the motive is that letting others know of your grievance might lead to you getting a reputation as a scandal-monger.

Amenemope also advises caution about hasty accusations:[228] 'Do not shout "crime" against a man, When the cause of (his) flight is hidden. Whether you hear something good or evil,/Do it outside where it is not heard.'

Jesus' advice in Matt. 18:15 is similar to v. 9.

25:11-14 Four Sayings about Words

Although the EVV make all of them similes, in the MT only v. 13 is a simile, and the others are metaphors. They form two pairs according to the kind of imagery used and their content.

Despite uncertainties in the details of v. 11, the overall message is clear. A proverb is of value only if used in the right context. When that happens it is like a beautiful ornament put in a setting which shows it off to the best effect. The point of v. 12 is that a proverb is of no value unless there is a willing hearer. To such a person it is like a beautiful piece of jewellery.

In the ancient Near East messengers were essential. They not only conveyed information, they transacted business on behalf of their sender. A trustworthy messenger was a great boon, as v. 13 makes clear. Its imagery has caused debate. Some see it a purely a piece of imagination. Others, noting that actual snow would have drawbacks at harvest time (cf. 26:1), suggest it refers to drinks cooled by compacted snow or ice brought down from the mountains in insulated jute bags and stored in caves or 'ice houses' for use in summer. Only the wealthy could afford such luxury.

By contrast with the reliable messenger of v. 13, v. 14 speaks of an unreliable person who makes empty promises. It is an implicit warning not to give favour or services on the basis of promises alone.

227. Toy, *Proverbs*, 462.

228. XI.6-9, *COS* 1:118.

25:15 The Power of Patience and Kindness

The paradox of the second colon is striking. The verse includes both themes of this chapter: social hierarchy and resolving social conflicts. With its reference to a ruler it forms an *inclusio* with vv. 2-3, closing a sub-section of the chapter.

25:16-20 Inappropriate Behaviours Which Might Cause Conflict

Verses 16-17 go together as the similarities in their second cola show. Honey is a good thing (cf. 24:13), but you can have too much of a good thing. This general truth is applied to visiting neighbours in v. 17. The sages constantly urge moderation as a virtue (cf. v. 28 and see on 17:27).

The theme of the damage that perjury does appears again in v. 18. Here it is likened to three dangerous weapons. For further comment on this theme, see on 24:28.

We rely on our body parts to support us in various ways, and when one of them fails it causes us pain and distress, and may incapacitate us. The same is true of people on whom we rely (v. 19). This saying acts as a warning to choose trusted companions carefully. The meaning of רֹעָה/*rōʿâ,* which describes the tooth, is uncertain. It may be a variant form of a participle meaning 'breaking', hence 'decaying' in the REB. The other EVV emend it to רָעָה/*rāʿâ,* 'bad.'

The only clear thing about v. 20 is the kind of inappropriate behaviour to which it refers. The comparisons are problematic. The meaning of the word which the ESV and NIV translate as 'soda' (with Sym, Vulg, Syr, Targ) is uncertain. The NRSV and REB follow the LXX in translating it as 'wound', which gives a better comparison for the purpose of the proverb: the pain produced by putting vinegar on a wound. The alternative, to take it as a reference to two incompatible things (vinegar, an acid, attacks soda, an alkali), is less obvious and striking. The NRSV also follows the LXX in omitting the clause about the garment and follows the LXX, Syr and Targ by adding the couplet, 'Like a moth in clothing or a worm in wood, sorrow gnaws at the human heart.'

25:21-22 Kindness towards Enemies

At the least, restraint is commended in 14:29; 19:11; 20:22; 24:17, 29. Verse 21 goes beyond these in its advocacy of compassion for a personal enemy who is in need. It is in the spirit of Exod. 23:4-5 and Lev. 19:17-18. A similar sentiment is expressed in *Amenemope:* 'steer, we will ferry the wicked,/We do not act like his kind;/Lift him up, give him your hand,/Leave him <in> the hands of the god;/Fill his belly with bread of your own,/That he be sated and weep.'[229]

No satisfactory explanation has been given for v. 22a. Some see reference to an Egyptian penitential ritual, though there is no evidence outside this verse that it was known in Israel. Others see it as a metaphor for a feeling of burning shame, perhaps evidenced by a red face. The Apostle Paul quotes this passage in Rom. 12:20 to discourage taking revenge on enemies.

25:23-24 Speech Which Provokes Conflict

Verse 23 is problematic since it is the wind from the west, not the north, which brings rain in Palestine. The REB follows the possibility that the verb in v. 23a means 'holds back' here rather than 'gives birth'. It then reverses the subject and object in v. 23b, 'so an angry glance holds back slander'. This is a rather contrived interpretation.[230] The fact that the word for 'north' (צָפוֹן/*ṣāpôn*) has the same consonants as the verb 'to hide' and that 'a backbiting tongue' is literally 'a hidden tongue' leads to two possible solutions. One is that the reader is expected to note an implied pun, 'hidden/north wind'/'hidden tongue' and not get hung up on the climatic realities. The other is to emend the word 'north' to the participle צָפוּן/*ṣāpûn* so that it does mean 'hidden/mysterious'.

Verse 24 is a virtual repeat of 21:9 (see the comment there).

25:25-26 Water Images

Water images, one positive, one negative, link these sayings. Verse 25 is similar to v. 13, but now it is the message, not the messenger, that is the source of refreshment (cf. 15:30). The REB is right to take the word translated 'soul' in the other EVV (נֶפֶשׁ/*nepeš*) to have the alternative meaning 'throat' here.

The issue in v. 26 is the meaning of the second colon. The verb here means 'to totter, slip', and most EVV translate it as 'gives way', which might imply a moral lapse by the righteous. The NJPSV translates it as 'fallen', meaning that the righteous have suffered at the hands of the wicked, but not necessarily implying a moral failure. In either case there is a contrast to 12:3b where the same verb is used to assert that 'the righteous will never be moved'. Here is another case of the sages recognising that the ideal does not always work out in the complexities

229. V.1-6, *COS* 1:117.

230. McKane, *Proverbs*, 583 comments that it 'can hardly be right'.

of life. When such a thing happens it is not right, not the way things should be. It is like a polluted water source.

25:27 Do Not Have Too Much of a Good Thing

This is similar to the message of v. 16. In fact v. 27a is a shorter reprise of v. 16a. For this reason Van Leeuwen[231] sees it as an *inclusio* closing the second subsection of the chapter. The mention of 'glory' in v. 27b forms an *inclusio* with v. 2, and closes the whole 'proverb poem'.

A literal translation of the MT v. 27b is: 'and the searching out of their honour is honour' or possibly; 'nor is the . . .' if the negative is carried over from the first colon. The differences in the EVV show the difficulty of making sense of this: 'nor is it glorious to seek one's own glory' (ESV, cf. NJPSV, NIV); 'or to seek honour on top of honour' (NRSV); 'and the quest for glory is onerous' (REB).

25:28 The Call for Self-Control

This verse reinforces the call for moderation in v. 27. In Hebrew the man in v. 28a is described as 'without restraint over his spirit'. In its use of 'spirit' the verse has close links with 14:29; 16:32 and 17:27 — all proverbs which urge the virtue of self-restraint (see on 17:27).

Proverbs 26

26:1-12 The Hermeneutics of Wisdom

This is the title Van Leeuwen[232] gives to this 'proverb poem'. Most commentators regard these verses as a distinct cluster of proverbs because the catchword 'fool' occurs in all of them except v. 2, and in vv. 13-16 there is a clear change of subject to 'the sluggard'. Van Leeuwen shows that there is a deeper cohesiveness than simply the catchword. Most obviously there are repeated phrases in vv. 7b, 9b and in vv. 5b, 12a, and the idea of honouring a fool is repeated in vv. 1 and 8. There are other, less obvious, links between these verses, such as the frequent use of words beginning with the Hebrew consonant *kaph,* which is the consonant at the start of the word for 'fool' (כְּסִיל/*kĕsîl*).

231. Van Leeuwen, *Context and Meaning,* 23.
232. Van Leeuwen, *Context and Meaning,* 99-106.

It is a carefully structured unit. It begins with an 'introduction' which consists of three sayings (vv. 1-3). In each of them a figurative comment using two images precedes the topic. The unifying theme (made explicit in v. 1) is the issue of 'what is fitting'. In v. 1 something good (honour) is given to someone bad (a fool), in v. 2 something bad (a curse) is given to someone good (an innocent person), and in v. 3 something bad (a rod) is given to someone bad (a fool). The reason for the apparent anomaly of v. 2 not containing the word 'fool' is because the pattern of good thing–bad person, bad thing–good person and bad thing–bad person did not allow this.

The next two verses (vv. 4-5) are the only admonitions in this section. This suggests that they may be the heart of the poem. The point of v. 3 is that a fool, like a dumb animal, cannot be reasoned with, and therefore it is fitting to beat sense into him. The admonition in v. 4 follows on naturally from this — don't make a fool of yourself by trying to reason with a fool! As a result the admonition in v. 5 comes as a shocking surprise. It seems to contradict the previous one. The point being made in a stark way is that wisdom itself is a matter of 'fittingness', and this is not simply a matter of the mechanical application of proverbs.

Verses 6-11 present a number of 'unfitting' actions in a series of sayings in which, as in vv. 1-3, an image precedes the topic. The topic is alternately an action that is unfitting in relation to fools (vv. 6, 8, 10) and an unfitting action committed by fools (vv. 7, 9, 11). The repetition in vv. 7 and 9 marks these sayings out as particularly significant.

Finally, the poem closes with a direct question which prompts the reader to think about its meaning. It is linked conceptually and verbally with the core verses, vv. 4-5. They warned the reader not to become like the fool (v. 4) and said that the fool was in danger of 'becoming wise in his own eyes' (v. 5). Now the reader is told that those who are 'wise in their own eyes' are worse than fools. This is because they do not recognise their own limits, or the limitations of all human wisdom. The contradiction of vv. 4-5 is intended to promote awareness of these limits and the humility that should go with it.

So, the meaning of this poem is that one *sine qua non* of wisdom is a sense of fittingness. Without this the use of proverbs will be ineffectual (v. 7) or even dangerous (v. 9). Those lacking this sense of fittingness are fools. The other *sine qua non* is a recognition of the limits of human wisdom, which means recognising that sometimes we will be left wondering just what is 'fitting' as we face two apparently contradictory possible course of action (vv. 4 and 5). Those lacking this sense of the limits of human wisdom are worse than fools. In the wider context of the Book of Proverbs, the recognition of these limits should lead the reader to trust in the LORD and not in their own wisdom (3:5-6).

The phrase 'and drinks violence' (v. 6b) is unusual (but cf. 4:17) and probably refers to experiencing the evil consequences of one's act. The REB's 'and displays the stump' depends on an improbable emendation.[233] The point of the simile in v. 8a is unclear, but may mean that it is folly to tie a stone into a sling so that it cannot be ejected. The exact meaning of v. 9a is also unclear. The ESV translation, in which the thorn enters the hand of the drunkard, gives the meaning that fools harm themselves by their (mis)use of proverbs. Other EVV picture a thorn bush in the drunkard's hand, implying that the harm is done to others (cf. 12:18). There are problems in the text of v. 10, but the overall meaning is clear: fools do harm by using proverbs indiscriminately and so should not be hired to do any task.

26:13-16 The Sluggard

This is the third cluster of proverbs about the sluggard. Like the others its tone is satirical but unlike them it has no narrative (see on 6:6-11; 24:30-34). It is linked to vv. 1-12 by the echo of v. 12a in v. 16a.

Verse 13 is a less vivid variant of 22:13 (see comment there). It uses two different words for lion, and the NJPSV and NIV are right to see intensification between the cola: 'cub/lion' (v. 13a), 'lion/fierce lion' (v. 13b). Verse 14 is a vivid and humorous picture of movement without progress. Verse 15 is a close variant of 19:24 (see comment there). The deepest problem with the sluggard is identified in v. 16. He believes his own excuses and is not open to criticism or advice from others.

Van Leeuwen[234] notes that basic to this cluster is the continuity of place:

> Having made his excuse not to go out of the house (v. 13), the sluggard doesn't even get out of bed (v. 14). He turns on his bed like a door, but won't even open the door — for fear of a cat. Verses 15 and 16 find him still at home, stuck to his table and feeling complacently wise.

26:17-19 Controversy

Van Leeuwen[235] sees another 'proverb poem' in vv. 17-28 and these verses as introducing its two themes: controversy and the 'verbal wounder'.

233. McKane, *Proverbs*, 597, thinks the emendation improbable and the resulting interpretation far-fetched.

234. Van Leeuwen, *Context and Meaning*, 110.

235. Van Leeuwen, *Context and Meaning*, 119-22.

The NIV and NJPSV follow the punctuation of the MT in v. 17 and make the person who gets involved in the quarrel the passer-by. In the other EVV it is the dog that is passing by. The MT expresses the point of the proverb more strongly: it is asking for trouble to get involved in someone else's quarrel. In the MT the man 'is enraged' (מִתְעַבֵּר/*mitʿabbēr*) at the other's quarrel. The EVV follow the Syr and Vulg and emend to מִתְעָרֵב/*mitʿārēb* 'meddle in'.

Verses 18-19 form one saying. The imagery of v. 18 is similar to 25:18, but in this case the behaviour to which it applies, although also deceptive words, seems to be stupid or thoughtless rather than malicious. Nonetheless, even if it does not cause physical harm, it will probably be fatal to the relationship.

26:20-22 Instigators of Controversy

Two proverbs about the 'whisperer' (ESV, NRSV) or malicious 'gossip' (NIV, cf. REB) frame one about the 'quarrelsome man'. Verse 21 is linked to v. 20 by the imagery of wood and fire as well as the idea of quarrelling. Fire is an apposite image for heated controversy and fuel of various kinds for the words of the whisperer or quarrelsome person. Verse 22 is a repetition of 18:8 (see comment there).

All three proverbs are simply statements, leaving the readers to draw their own morals from them. The first two give implicit advice to avoid people who cause controversy, and the third implicitly warns against listening to malicious gossip.

26:23-26 The Source of Controversy

This often lies in the human psyche, and people are good at hiding it. Therefore the wise need the insight to see through the façade to what is really going on inside a person so that they are not fooled by outward appearances and protestations.

In v. 23a the NJPSV ('base silver') follows the MT 'silver dross' (כֶּסֶף סִיגִים/*kesep sîgîm*). The reference is to the lead monoxide left over from the process of purifying silver which was used to give earthenware a silvery glaze. The other EVV emend this to כְּסַפְסָגִים/*kĕsapsāgîm*, an otherwise unknown Hebrew word which is taken to mean 'glaze' by appeal to Ugaritic and Hittite cognates, which has now been shown to be baseless.[236] The MT has 'burning lips' in v. 23b ('fer-

236. Waltke, *Proverbs 15–31*, 341-42, n. 42.

vent' in ESV, NIV). The reading 'smooth' in NRSV (cf. 'glib', REB) unnecessarily follows the LXX. Verses 24-26 give a portrait of someone motivated by secret hatred. He hypocritically displays a gracious demeanour but is inwardly 'totally abominable' — 'seven' indicating completeness (on 'abominable' see on 3:32). Verse 26 promises that his wickedness will be publicly exposed, though how this will happen is not explained. The 'assembly' may refer to a judicial setting.

26:27-28 Consequences

Verse 26 introduced the idea that the wicked will eventually suffer the consequences of their wickedness, an underlying theme of Proverbs. For this reason Van Leeuwen[237] includes it with these verses to form the conclusion of the 'proverb poem'. Verse 27 is a classic statement of the 'act-consequence' theme. Like all proverbs it should be understood to express a norm or ideal rather than a 'law'. It is unclear whose 'ruin' is meant in v. 28b, but its context suggests that it is the ruin of the liar/flatterer.

Proverbs 27

27:1-2 Don't Boast!

This is the common theme of these two admonitions, which are linked by the use of the root הלל/*hll* ('boast', 'praise'). They both call for a combination of humility and realism. Verse 1 warns against presumption about future achievements; the reason given is a reminder about human limitations. The implication is that the future is in God's hands (cf. 16:1, 3, 9). No reason is given for the advice in v. 2, but it is a matter of common experience that people find self-boasting obnoxious and that assessment of one's strengths and achievements by someone who can be relatively objective has considerable value. The ultimate objective assessor is Yahweh (16:2; 21:2).

27:3-4 Anger

Anger links these two sayings, though there is an intensification of emotion from 'provocation/vexation' through 'anger/wrath' to 'jealousy'. The sayings also

237. Van Leeuwen, *Context and Meaning,* 121.

have a common form as negative 'better than' sayings. The annoyance caused by a fool is harder to bear than the weight of a stone or of a bag of sand (v. 3). Jealousy, anger at a perceived threat to a valued possession, is a more damaging emotion than ordinary anger or wrath. These observations are implicit warnings, the first to avoid associating with fools and the second either to avoid provoking jealousy, or to control it in oneself (cf. 14:30).

27:5-10 Friendship

Verses 5 and 6 are linked by the root אהב/*'hb* ('love', 'friend'). Verse 7 is linked to v. 9 by 'sweet(ness)', and v. 9 to v. 10 by 'friend'. The idea of being away from home links vv. 8 and 10c. Verses 5-7 are all paradoxes.

In Proverbs growth in wisdom requires openness to correction. It follows that a true friend will offer such correction (v. 5a) even if it is painful (v. 6a). This, of course, assumes that it is constructive criticism. To hold back from such criticism is to hide true love (v. 5b). The word usually translated 'profuse' in v. 6b is of uncertain meaning. The LXX reads 'voluntary' and the Vulg 'deceptive' (cf. REB 'perfidious').

Honey is something good of which it is possible to have too much (see on 25:16, 27). Taken on its own v. 7 seems to mean 'circumstances make things relative'.[238] In context it prepares the way for what v. 10 says about friends and family, and one can point to 25:17 as an example of v. 7a applied to friendship. Verse 8 speaks of the loneliness and vulnerability of someone who is forced to leave home (נָדַד/*nādad* often means 'retreat, flee'), for whatever reason. Like v. 7, it prepares for v. 10.

The MT of v. 9 reads literally, 'and/but the sweetness of his friend from the counsel of soul'. The ESV ('and the sweetness of a friend comes from his earnest counsel', cf. NIV) tries to make sense of this. This is probably preferable to following the quite different reading of the LXX, 'but the soul is torn by trouble', as do the NRSV and REB, since the context seems to require a proverb on friendship.

Although v. 10 seems to be a collection of three disparate sayings, Clifford[239] sees a coherent message: 'Cultivate old family friends and neighbours; do not automatically count on kin for help in time of trouble, for neighbours and friends are ready at hand'. This assumes that the 'brother' in v. 10b is at some distance, as in v. 10c.

238. Murphy, *Proverbs*, 207.

239. Clifford, *Proverbs*, 238.

27:11 Family, Solidarity and Pride

Verse 11a echoes 23:15 (cf. 23:25) and adds the dimension of how the parent is regarded in the community. Proverbs 17:6b reminds the child that their parents' status in the community reflects back on them.

27:12-13 Prudence

Prudence is commended in v. 12, and v. 13 gives an example of imprudent behaviour — giving security for a stranger. Verse 12 is a virtual repeat of 22:3 (see the comment there). Verse 13 is a repeat of 20:16 (see the comment there) except that in the second colon it refers to 'a foreign woman' instead of 'foreigners'. This may be the original reading, alluding back to the 'foreign woman' of chs. 1–9 who is an adulteress (see on 2:16), or it could be a scribal adaptation to chs. 1–9. The NRSV and REB follow the Vulg and 20:16 in emending the word here to 'foreigners.'

27:14 Unneighbourly Behaviour

There is some debate about the exact meaning of this proverb. It might be an example of the importance of a word fitting the occasion (cf. 25:11-12, 20). On this occasion the greeting is given both at the wrong time and in the wrong manner. Alternatively, if the emphasis is on the loudness of the greeting, the point may be that it is insincere, done for show (cf. v. 6b). At the end of the verse the MT reads, 'it will be counted as a curse to him'. The 'him' may refer to the person greeted (as the EVV seem to understand it), who regards the blessing as a curse, or it may mean that the intended blessing will return as a curse on the greeter — the agent of this presumably being God.

27:15-16 The Quarrelsome Wife

The wife of 19:13b; 21:9, 19; and 25:24 reappears (see comment there). In fact v. 15 seems to be an expansion of 19:13b. Verse 16 is linked to v. 15 by the singular, feminine object suffix on the initial verb. That verb (צָפַן/*ṣāpan*) normally means 'to hide' but here the EVV translate it as 'to restrain'. In the MT the second colon is literally, 'and oil meets/calls his right hand'. In order to get a parallel with the first colon the EVV take this to mean something like, 'or to grasp oil in one's right hand' (ESV), making the point of the verse the uncontrollability of the woman.

27:17 One Cannot Become Wise by Oneself

This is how Clifford[240] sums up the meaning of this proverb. The second colon is literally, 'and a man sharpens the face of his friend'. There is an implicit pun here since the edge of a metal tool or weapon is called its 'face' in Hebrew (Eccles. 10:10). It is not clear if it has a specific referent here. The NRSV and REB take it to refer to a person's 'wits'. One way in which friends 'sharpen' each other has been indicated in vv. 5-6.

27:18 Faithful Service Gets Its Reward

This proverb uses an agricultural analogy to make its point. Such faithful service requires both diligence and patience, both highly regarded virtues in Proverbs.

27:19 An Enigmatic Saying

This verbless sentence says, 'Like water the face to the face, so the heart of a man to the man.' There is general agreement that the first colon is referring to water acting like a mirror, so that people recognise themselves in the water. The second colon might therefore be expected to say something about recognising one's character. The issue is whether the second 'man' in it is the same as the first. Is it saying that by looking into your own inner self you come to understand yourself (ESV, NIV), or that observing another person enables you to understand yourself (NRSV, REB)? The catchword linking back to v. 17 ('man', 'face') favour the second interpretation in this context, as does the general theme of friendship.

27:20 The Insatiability of Human Desires

This is represented by the eyes (cf. Eccles. 2:10) and is compared to the insatiability of Sheol and Abaddon. Here this pair (cf. 15:11) is a personification of death, perhaps as a monster with a huge mouth and voracious appetite (cf. Isa.

240. Clifford, *Proverbs*, 239.

5:14a), which is never satisfied because there is always room for more people to die. So, pursuit of any particular desire as an ultimate end is pointless (Eccles. 5:10). That is why the sages constantly counsel moderation as a virtue (e.g. 25:16).

27:21-22 Refining and Testing

Verse 21a repeats 17:3a (see comment there) but in this case the assayer is not the LORD but other people.

The meaning of v. 21b is a little ambiguous, perhaps deliberately. It could mean that how a person responds to praise is a test of character or that a person's character is shown by the amount and nature of praise they get from others.

The vivid agricultural metaphor of v. 22 makes the point that fools are beyond refining. This is one of several proverbs about their intractability (e.g. 17:10, 16; 26:11).

27:23-27 Sustainable Living

This poem has been understood in several ways. The key issue is the interpretation of v. 24, which is the basis for the admonition in v. 23, and on which vv. 25-27 expand.

Verse 24 clearly states that stored up wealth will not last forever. It is a diminishing resource. Some see in this a polemic against 'money quickly made in trade and commerce' because 'it is dissipated with equal rapidity'.[241] However, as Longman[242] comments, this could apply as readily to a farmer who has 'money in the bank'. One might think of the 'rich fool' of Jesus' parable (Lk. 12:13-21). The emphasis is more on relying on sustainable resources rather than on hoarded wealth. Trade and commerce can be pursued in sustainable ways. The mention of 'a crown' leads Van Leeuwen[243] to see the poem as 'an oblique address to the king or ruler as metaphorical "shepherd" of the people'. Reference to the crown may be evidence of the provenance of the poem in the court.[244] However, this does not require his metaphorical interpretation. The reference could be to aspirations to social status and a warning that such status

241. McKane, *Proverbs,* 618.
242. Longman, *Proverbs,* 483.
243. Van Leeuwen, *Proverbs,* 233.
244. Waltke, *Proverbs 15–31,* 390.

is no more reliable than hoarded wealth. Overall, it seems most satisfactory to take the poem as advocating diligent reliance on sustainable resources as the basis for a stable way of life — a message that is applicable to societies with various different economic bases.

Proverbs 28

Malchow[245] argued that chs. 28–29 form 'a manual for future monarchs' partly because of the number of references to rulers in these chapters, and partly because of the content: the themes of the righteous and the wicked and the rich and poor are fairly prominent. Nearly a third of the references to rulers in chs. 10–29 occur in these chapters, but that on its own does not settle the issue. There are about as many references to rulers in ch. 20 (four) as in each of these chapters (28, three; 29, five) but no one has suggested that that chapter is addressed to rulers. Nor is it clear that the content of these chapters is more applicable to rulers than to other people.

More convincing is Malchow's argument that these chapters have been carefully structured. They begin and end with proverbs about the righteous and the wicked (28:1; 29:27), and three proverbs with similar wording occur at key points: (28:12; 29:2, 16). He sees the proverbs in each of the resulting four sections as being linked by theme and assonance, though accepting that the thematic link is weak in the fourth section.

28:1-11 The Law and Treatment of the Poor

Although elsewhere in Proverbs תּוֹרָה/*tôrâ* seems to refer to the instruction given by a parent or sage, most commentators and EVV (not the NJPSV) think that in this section v. 9 points to it meaning the Mosaic Law and so translate it as 'law' rather than 'instruction/teaching'.

Verse 1 sets out a major theme of chs. 28–29: the different behaviours of the wicked and the righteous. Presumably the fear of the wicked arises from a guilty conscience. The phrase 'flee when no one pursues' occurs in the covenant curses in Lev. 26:17, 36.

The meaning of v. 2a is fairly clear in the MT. 'The many leaders may point to the fragmentation of a previously united land or perhaps to a succession of

245. Malchow, 'A Manual', 238-45.

leaders as they violently jockey for power.'[246] Verse 2b is unclear: 'By an intelligent man knowing thus he will prolong.' Most EVV takes this to mean that an intelligent/wise person/ruler will prolong the stability of a land. The LXX renders the whole verse differently: 'Through the sins of the godless, quarrels arise, but a clever man quells them.' The REB is based on this.

Some scholars find the idea of the poor oppressing the poor unlikely and so emend the first word for 'poor' in v. 3a (רָשׁ/*rāš*) to רֹאשׁ/*rō'š* 'chief, ruler'. However, none of the ancient versions supports this, and it is not difficult to imagine circumstances in which one poor person might oppress another. The disastrous effects of this are compared to torrential rain which washes away the crops. Verses 4-5 may describe the kind of person who would oppress a fellow pauper, those who forsake the law and who therefore do not understand the concept of justice. Those who keep the law are followers of Yahweh, and they understand what justice is all about. It is better to be like these latter people and be poor than to be rich and live a crooked life (v. 6). Again, a 'better than' proverb shows that the sages were aware that life does not always work out as it should. In an ideal world those who are righteous, not the crooked, would be rich.

Contrasting 'a companion of gluttons' with a wise son (v. 7) may seem strange, but as noted in discussion of 23:20, this is probably because in Deut. 21:18-21 gluttony is one of the vices of the rebellious son.

Verses 8-11 refer to different kinds of wickedness, with the first and last verses referring to the poor. Lending at interest (v. 8a) is forbidden in the OT law (Exod. 22:25 [Heb. 24]; Lev. 25:36; Deut. 23:19 [Heb. 20]), which has lending to those in distress in view because this would drive them further into poverty. How the ill-gotten wealth will be redistributed to the poor is not explained in v. 8b, which is a specific application of 13:22b. Generosity to the poor is commended in 19:17.

There is no doubt that in v. 9 the person to whom the prayer is an abomination is Yahweh (on this see on 6:16). Those who turn a deaf ear to his law will find that he is deaf to their prayers.

Verse 10 is a clear statement of the principle of retribution (cf. 26:27). Those who are tempted to lead the righteous to do evil are warned that they themselves will suffer the consequences of that evil. The addition of the third colon makes the proverb also a word to the righteous, encouraging them to avoid being led astray.

Those who are self-deluded about their wisdom are worse than fools (26:12). Wealth is one of the things that can lead to such self-delusion. As Longman[247]

246. Longman, *Proverbs,* 487.

247. Longman, *Proverbs,* 491.

comments, 'Wealth can sometimes cloud the mind so that the rich think they have more resources than they do. It can breed conceit and a feeling of self-reliance.' Someone with understanding, even if poor, can see through the delusion. This verse is one example of the principle enunciated in v. 6.

28:12-28 A Rogues' Gallery

Verses 12 and 28 form an *inclusio* for this section, with v. 12b and v. 28a being virtually identical. All the verses between them mention types of wicked people.

Verse 12 contrasts the social situation in communities under the control of the righteous and the wicked. When the righteous rule, the whole community benefits and flourishes. If the wicked come to power, people 'keep a low profile' to avoid becoming the target of unjust actions, and some literally have to hide to escape persecution.

How the 'dissembler' who hides his sins will fail to prosper is not made clear in v. 13a. One answer is given in Ps. 32:3-4, which describes the inner anguish caused by an uneasy conscience. Psalm 32:1-5 provides a good commentary on the whole of this proverb. The mercy granted to the person who confesses and turns from their sin could come from other people but most probably Yahweh is assumed to be its source. Many scholars think that Yahweh is also the assumed object of the 'fear' in v. 14a. The NRSV gives a fairly literal translation of the MT, 'Happy is the one who is never without fear.' The ESV and NIV take 'fear' to be a shorthand for 'the fear of the LORD' (cf. 14:16), though the verbal root used here (פחד/*pḥd*) is not the one normally used in the phrase (ירא/*yr'*). The REB takes the verb in its weaker sense of 'being cautious': 'Happy are those who are scrupulous in conduct.' The contrast in v. 14b with someone who 'hardens his heart' favours the ESV/NIV translation. In Hebrew the idiom does not refer to lack of compassion, but to 'stubbornness'. This often means a refusal to listen to Yahweh (e.g. Exod. 7:3-4; Ps. 95:7-8).

Verses 15-16 illustrate v. 12b by giving examples of the 'wicked' and the 'oppressive ruler'. The wicked ruler is compared to the two most dangerous predatory animals known in Palestine in OT times. The message of v. 16 is summed up well by Clifford:[248] 'The antithesis here is lack and abundance. Where there is lack of intelligence there is abundant violence: where there is lack of unjustly acquired wealth there is abundant life.'

The Hebrew of v. 17 is difficult. There is general agreement that the first colon refers to a 'murderer' oppressed by a guilty conscience. A literal transla-

248. Clifford, *Proverbs*, 246.

tion of the second colon is 'he will flee to a pit. Do not support him/hold him back'. The REB takes the pit literally and paraphrases: '(he) will jump into a well to escape arrest'. The other EVV take the reference to be to 'the pit', that is, death, hence the ESV, 'he will be a fugitive until death'.

Verses 18-20 each contrasts a good and bad way of behaving. The person who has integrity is contrasted with one who is 'perverse' (v. 18). The former will be 'delivered', presumably from trouble by God. The latter will meet disaster. The NRSV and REB follow the Syr and emend בְּאֶחָת/*bĕ'eḥāt* ('suddenly') to בְּשָׁחַת/*bĕšāḥat* ('pit'). Verse 19 is a close variant of 12:11 (see comment there), the difference being the explicit warning of poverty for the 'time-waster'. The 'get rich quick merchant' is regarded negatively in Proverbs (13:11; 20:21), probably because he usually employs dishonesty or injustice — as implied by the warning of punishment in v. 20b. 'Faithful' in v. 20a could mean 'honest' or 'diligent'.

The greed which motivates 'the partial person' is condemned in v. 21. On partiality in a legal context see the comment on 24:23b-25. Here the context is not so limited.

'The miser' (v. 22) is one kind of person attracted by 'get rich quick' schemes (v. 20). In Hebrew the idiom for 'miserly' is 'bad of eye' and there may be a play on this in the statement that misers cannot see poverty coming to them.

Verse 23 is similar to other proverbs which assert the value of an honest rebuke (e.g. 19:25; 25:12; 275-6). Here the key word is 'afterwards'. At the time it is given, a rebuke may not be appreciated, but eventually it will be. 'The flatterer's' words, on the other hand, soon lose their value.

'The robber of parents' (v. 24) breaks the commandment to honour one's parents (Exod. 20:12). The act is compounded by denying its criminality, perhaps because it is seen as appropriating one's inheritance (cf. 20:21). It is strongly condemned as the act of a 'destroyer' (the REB interprets this as 'murderer'). Clifford[249] comments, 'The children have no more right to their parents' property while they are living than a brigand from outside the family'.

'Greedy people's' desire for more results in conflict with others (v. 25a). Paradoxically, those who calmly trust in the LORD will be enriched (v. 25b). This is similar to Jesus' teaching in Matt. 6:25-33. In contrast to v. 25b, v. 26a speaks of the 'fool' who is too arrogant recognise the limitations of his own understanding. Those who are wise recognise this and so are 'delivered' (ESV), or 'kept safe' (NIV), from situations which would spell disaster for the fool (v. 26b).

Verse 27b condemns those who are 'wilfully blind to the poor' (cf. 21:13, about those who are wilfully deaf to them). Generosity to the poor is com-

249. Clifford, *Proverbs*, 247.

mended in 19:17 (see comment there) where it is said that Yahweh will reward it. This is implied in v. 27a. The curses of v. 27b may come from the poor, but no doubt it is implied that Yahweh will enforce them

Verse 28 depicts the reversal of an unjust social situation. It forms an *inclusio* with v. 12 (see the comment there), and v. 28a is a virtual repetition of v. 12b.

Proverbs 29

Several verses repeat the themes of previous sayings, sometimes in identical words. Hatton[250] argues that this chapter 'functions as a sort of conclusion to the debates of the book, revisiting and encapsulating them. However, this does not mean that the chapter contains a final word, a considered evaluative judgement on the book's complex debates'.

29:1 Stubbornness

Stubbornness in the face of rebuke is a fatal character flaw (12:1; 13:13-14; 15:10, 31-32). Verse 1b repeats 6:15b, which applies to various kinds of wicked people. It is significant that this warning against unteachability comes at what is the structural mid-point of chs. 28–29.

29:2-16 The Effects of Wickedness

This section reflects on the effects of wickedness particularly on the community.[251] There is a chiastic *inclusio* in that the content of vv. 2, 3, 4 matches that of vv. 14, 15, 16. Verse 2 echoes 28:12, 28 (see the comments there).

That 'prostitution' leads to poverty is the warning of v. 3. The first colon echoes 10:1; 15:20; 17:21 (see comments there). There is an implicit contrast in the two cola between wisdom and folly. In chs. 5–7 yielding to the seduction of the prostitute/adulteress is the act of a fool, which leads to loss of wealth and health (5:10-11). Here the wealth squandered may be the family inheritance.

That 'extortion' (REB) ruins a country seems to be the message of v. 4b, though the meaning the word תְּרוּמוֹת/*tĕrûmôt* is unclear. Elsewhere it refers to

250. Hatton, *Contradiction*, 68.
251. Malchow, 'A Manual', 242.

religious offerings, but here seems to mean either bribes (ESV, NIV) or heavy taxes (NRSV). Verse 4a echoes other proverbs about the effects of righteous rule (16:12; 20:28; 25:5).

'Flattery' is harmful (v. 5) because, unlike genuine encouragement, it is not based on truth. The second colon is ambiguous, though most commentators take it to refer to the neighbour's feet (NRSV, REB), sometimes appealing to 28:23 for support. Others think that the juxtaposition with v. 6 shows that the flatterer's feet are meant. The ambiguity may be intentional.[252]

'Transgression' is self-defeating. Verse 6a is a statement of the principle of retribution. The idea of a snare links it with v. 5b. The general force of the comparison in v. 6b is clear: the righteous can enjoy life free of the troubles that beset evil people. The REB follows a few Hebrew mss which have יָרוּץ/*yārûṣ* ('runs') for יָרוּן/*yārûn* ('sings') and reads, 'but the doer of good will live and flourish'. The other EVV follow the MT, which makes good sense.

'Disregard of the poor', and particularly their legal rights, is the form of wickedness dealt with in v. 7. The word דִּין/*dîn* ('right') has a legal connotation. The righteous 'know' these rights not just in the abstract, but are concerned about them (cf. 12:10), implying that they ensure that the poor get their due in court. Verse 7b is literally, 'the wicked do not understand knowledge'. The EVV rightly take this to mean that they do not share the righteous' concern for the poor.

'Scoffers' (see on 1:22) cause social unrest by their inflammatory language. Longman[253] comments that scoffers 'are those who would take a bad situation and intensify it into a riot. On the other hand, the wise are coolheaded. In a bad situation, they would calm tempers for the good of the community.'

'Foolishness' produces and prolongs irrational argument (v. 8). The verb used for 'argue' (נִשְׁפָּט/*nišpāṭ*) may indicate that this is a legal dispute (NRSV, REB). Although most EVV make the fool the subject of v. 9b, this is not clear in the Hebrew. It could refer to the reaction of the wise person, though this is unlikely. This proverb gives a basis for 26:4.

'Murderers' often kill those who are innocent (v. 10a). The meaning of v. 10b is unclear, 'and the righteous seek his life'. In the OT the idiom 'to seek the life of' normally means 'to kill'. The ESV, NIV and NRSV are based on the reading 'as for righteous, they seek his life', which is syntactically awkward. The NJPSV and REB prefer to take the idiom in a positive sense: 'but the upright righteous see to their (the blameless people's) interest'. Both Longman[254] and

252. So Murphy, *Proverbs*, 221.
253. Longman, *Proverbs*, 503.
254. Longman, *Proverbs*, 504.

Waltke[255] point to the OT laws on murder and take v. 10b to refer to the righteous seeking the punishment of murderers. However, in Proverbs it is usually Yahweh, not the righteous, who brings retribution on the wicked.

'Fools' lack self control (v. 11a) and the reference is probably to anger ('his spirit'). As elsewhere in Proverbs the wise are marked by their self-control and coolness (14:29; 17:27; 19:11). Verse 11b can be understood in three ways. The NIV (cf. NRSV) takes it to mean that the wise control their own anger, but it could refer to the wise calming the anger of the fool (NJPSV; cf. REB). Finally it could refer to the wise calming the emotions aroused by the fool's anger in others.[256]

'Moral laxity' (v. 12 refers specifically to lying) in a ruler leads to corruption in his court (cf. 25:5). 'Leaders are responsible for the quality of their staff'.[257]

'Oppression of the poor' is implicitly condemned in v. 13, which is a variant of 22:2 (see comment there). In Ps. 13:3 [Heb. 4] to 'light up' the eyes is the opposite of allowing to die, so here 'gives light to' (ESV) means 'gives life to'. Verse 14 is a positive counterpart to v. 13, encouraging just treatment of the poor because this will give stability to the king's rule. This verse gives a specific instance of the general principal enunciated in v. 4a (see comment there).

'An undisciplined child' brings disgrace on the parents (v. 15). This is the only proverb to mention the mother alone. The reason may be that she was responsible for the child's earliest education, or it may be a sign that this proverb is a deliberate structural counterpart of v. 3. The need to discipline children is a theme in Proverbs (see on 23:13-14).

Verse 16 gives the assurance that the wicked, and their harmful effect on society, will not last forever. The righteous will see their end. This verse is a variant of 28:12, 28; 29:2 (see the comments there).

29:17-27 Miscellaneous Proverbs

Malchow[258] admits that 'the content of vv. 17-26 has looser internal connections than the previous groups' in chs. 28–29. However, he points to word links between the verses and a frame of proverbs contrasting the righteous and the wicked (vv. 16, 27), which suggests that this is a distinct group.

'Child discipline'. Verse 17 has echoes of vv. 3, 15. The child who brings

255. Waltke, *Proverbs 15–31*, 438.
256. Longman, *Proverbs*, 504.
257. Clifford, *Proverbs*, 252.
258. Malchow, 'Manual', 243.

parents peace and delight is one who is wise (v. 3a), and this comes through discipline (v. 15a). The peace and delight contrasts with the shame of v. 15b. Verse 17b is literally: 'and give you choice foods in your throat'. Clifford[259] thinks this refers to care for elderly parents, but it is usually taken more generally to mean 'and bring you the delights you desire' (REB).

'Lack of restraint' is the concern of v. 18a, but its cause is unclear because of debate about the meaning of חָזוֹן/*ḥāzôn* ('vision'). One issue is whether or not it means 'prophetic vision' as it does elsewhere in the OT. Some take the occurrence of תּוֹרָה/*tôrâ* ('law, instruction') in v. 18b to mean that in this proverb there is a reference to prophetic vision and Mosaic Law as sources of guidance (ESV, NIV, NRSV). Because this would be a unique reference to prophecy in Proverbs others prefer to see here a reference to the 'vision' of life provided by the 'instruction' of the sages. An alternative[260] adopts the emendation חַזָּן/*ḥazzān* and appeals to cognate languages for the meaning 'leader, authority', as in the REB: 'With no one in authority'. The REB also reads the word for 'blessed is he' as 'he keeps them straight'. Whichever interpretation is accepted, the proverb makes the point that even when there is confusion at the corporate level, the individual can find personal guidance and blessing from the law/instruction.

'The disciplining of servants' requires more than words (v. 19). This is not due to lack of intelligence (v. 19b) but, apparently, a lack of motivation. The implication is that physical punishment is needed. This is the view of the Egyptian *Papyrus Insinger*: 'If the stick is far from the master, the servant does not listen to him.'[261]

'Haste in word or deed' (דָּבָר/*dābār* can mean either) is seen as bad in Proverbs (19:2). Speech or action should be preceded by reflection and thought (14:15-16; 15:28; 20:25; 21:5). Unconsidered speech is a mark of the fool (10:14; 12:16, 23; 15:2). Verse 20b is a repeat of 26:12b.

'The disciplining of servants', like that of children (22:6), should begin early otherwise there will be trouble for the master — this seems to be the meaning of v. 21. However, the final word of the proverb (מָנוֹן/*mānôn*) occurs only here and its meaning is unknown. The EVV make various guesses: 'heir' (ESV), 'grief' (NIV), 'bad' (NRSV, NJPSV), 'ungrateful' (REB). The ancient versions are of no help.

'Anger' is seen as a destructive emotion in Proverbs (27:24), which advocates a restrained expression of emotions (17:27). Verse 22a is a close variant of

259. Clifford, *Proverbs*, 253.
260. Driver, 'Misreadings', 235.
261. 14:11. *AEL* 3:196.

15:18 (see comment there) but here it is followed by a synonymous colon. The angry person not only causes quarrels among others, he commits offences (social or criminal) which get him into trouble. 'Anger hurts oneself and others.'[262]

'Pride and humility' are the subject of several proverbs. Verse 23a is similar to 11:2a; 16:18; 18:12a; and v. 23b to 15:33b; 18:12b (see comment on 11:2). The key difference between the proud and the humble is their teachability. The humble are ready to learn from advice and from their mistakes, and thereby they gain wisdom and esteem in their community. The proud are not and so are doomed to repeat their errors and end up in disgrace.

'Partners in crime' risk their own lives. The meaning of this proverb, especially v. 24b, is made clear by the law in Lev. 5:1 (which contains the expression 'hears the curse'). People are called upon to give witness to a crime on pain of coming under a curse if they do not. The accomplice who fails to testify will face divine retribution.

'Two kinds of fear' are contrasted in v. 25. Verse 25a is ambiguous. It may refer to fear of other people. People who are constantly anxious about what others think of them, or might do to them, face the snare of letting what others dictate override obedience to Yahweh's law. Alternatively v. 25a may refer to a person who is fearful for any kind of reason. In this case the snare is that their fears, not Yahweh's law, may dictate their behaviour. Since God's law charts the only safe way through life, and since Yahweh protects the righteous, the safest way through life is trust in the Lord.

'Rulers are not God'. Verse 26 has a close connection with v. 25 in its human/divine contrast. There can be a wrong 'fear' of rulers. Rulers ought to dispense justice, but at best their understanding and powers are limited. Only Yahweh can dispense it fairly and definitively.

'The contrasting values of the righteous and the wicked' are expressed in v. 27 by identifying what each group finds 'an abomination' (on this term see on 3:32). The righteous hate injustice. The wicked hate the 'straight path' which lies within the boundaries set by the fear of the Lord. This is a fitting end to chs 28–29.

Proverbs 30

'The "words of Agur" passage is easily the most difficult section of the book of Proverbs to translate and understand' says Longman.[263] Scholars differ over how

262. Clifford, *Proverbs*, 255.
263. Longman, *Proverbs*, 517.

much of this chapter should be attributed to Agur.[264] That the LXX separates 30:1-14 from 30:15-33 (see 'Texts and Versions' in the introduction) is seen by many commentators as evidence that these were originally separate units. However, the Greek division may be a secondary development.[265] It is, though, early evidence that this chapter does not form an indisputable single literary unit.

30:1-9 The Words of Agur

Franklyn[266] and Moore[267] have argued cogently that these verses are a coherent, orthodox confession of faith by a humble man aware that he is approaching death. Agur's identity is unclear. He and his father are mentioned only here in biblical and extra-biblical texts, and the names are probably non-Israelite.[268] The Midrash on Proverbs tries to make the names epithets for Solomon, but later Jewish scholars rejected this.[269] Scholars differ over whether הַמַּשָּׂא/*hammaśśā'* (v. 1a) should be read as 'the oracle' or be slightly emended to read 'from Massa' (מִמַּשָּׂא/*mimmaśśā'*, REB). An Arabian tribe called Massa is mentioned in Gen. 25:14 and 1 Chron. 1:30, as well as in Assyrian sources[270] beginning in the late eighth century. In the OT 'the people of the east' are renowned for their wisdom (1 Kgs. 4:30). The main argument for the emendation is that 'the oracle' seems redundant in view of the next phrase, but this is not a very strong point.

The phrase נְאֻם הַגֶּבֶר/*nĕ'ūm haggeber* ('oracle of/thus says the man') occurs in connection with the oracles of Balaam (Num. 24:3, 15) and an oracle of David (2 Sam. 23:1) which is presented as his 'last words'. In each case it clearly relates to a divinely inspired utterance. The meaning of what follows it in 30:1b is widely disputed. The main, but by no means only, translations are:

1. 'to Ithiel, to Ithiel and to Ucal' (NIV, NJPSV).
2. 'I am not God; I am not God, that I should prevail' (NAB).

264. McKane, *Proverbs,* 643 suggests his words may consist of vv. 1b-3, and certainly do not go beyond v. 4; Franklyn, 'Sayings of Agur', argues for vv. 1-9, as does Fox, *Proverbs 10–31,* 850-51; Murphy, *Proverbs,* 227, favours attributing vv. 1-14 to Agur; Waltke, *Proverbs 1–15,* 26-27, attributes the whole chapter to him.

265. See: Tov, 'Recensional Differences', 53-56; Cook, *Septuagint of Proverbs,* 304-7; Washington, *Wealth and Poverty,* 126-27.

266. Franklyn, 'Sayings of Agur'.

267. Moore, 'Home for the Alien'.

268. Whybray, *Proverbs,* 407.

269. Cohen, *Proverbs,* 200.

270. Kitchen, 'Proverbs and Wisdom Books', 101.

3. 'I am weary, O God; I am weary O God, and worn out' (ESV, cf. REB).
4. 'I am weary, O God, I am weary O God. How can I prevail?' (NRSV).

Although the name Ithiel occurs in Neh. 11:7, most commentators do not think that (1) is a likely rendering. The others are the result of re-dividing and re-pointing the MT. Rendering (2) is less likely than the others since it re-points the text as Aramaic. The difference between (3) and (4) is in the verbal root taken to lie behind the final word in the MT. Rendering (3) gains some support from the LXX (καὶ παύομαι, *kai pauomai,* 'and I cease').

The word for 'stupid' in v. 2a (בַּעַר/*ba'ar*) is a strong one, meaning a person 'who does not have the rationality that differentiates men from animals'.[271] The psalmist uses it of himself in Ps. 73:22 when questioning the wisdom and justice of God because of the prosperity of the wicked. Here Agur goes on to declare his lack of wisdom and knowledge of 'the Holy One', that is, God (the NRSV 'the holy ones' is a literal translation of the MT, but the plural is a plural of excellence[272] as in 9:10). The language of vv. 2-3 is probably hyperbolic,[273] expressing the self-effacement of an elderly person wearied with life and perhaps frustrated or perplexed by some of his experiences.

The questions in v. 4 can be compared with other passages where questions are used to expose the limits of human wisdom and the inaccessibility of divine wisdom. The best known is the divine speech in Job 38–39, where the questions expose Job's ignorance and display God's wisdom and power. The rhetorical questions in Isa. 40:12-14 point out that God cannot be compared to any human being. Van Leeuwen[274] has shown that behind the first question in v. 4 there is 'a widespread and very ancient topos of heavenly ascent and descent' and that its main purpose is 'to reaffirm the great gulf that separates humans from the divine realm and the prerogatives of the deity'. The first and the fourth questions refer to the vertical and horizontal limits of the cosmos, and the two in between refer to major natural forces. The implied answer to the rhetorical questions is, 'No human, only God.' Franklyn[275] pointed out the similarity between the 'creation-hymn' fragments in Amos 4:13; 5:8; 9:6 and Prov. 30:4. These make statements about things which the Creator did/does and end with the asservation, 'The LORD is his name.' This is an indication of the answer expected to the fifth, composite, question — Yahweh. The second part of the question is surprising, because people are usually defined by their parents

271. *NIDOTTE* 1:691.

272. Joüon §136d. See also Fox, *Proverbs 10–31,* 855.

273. Longman, *Proverbs,* 521; Van Leeuwen, *Proverbs,* 252.

274. Van Leeuwen, 'Background to Proverbs 30:4aα', 121.

275. Franklyn, 'Sayings of Agur', 247.

not their children. Longman[276] suggests that the form of the question 'makes sense by making clear that the questioner is asking about human beings in the previous questions'. Alternatively, Franklyn[277] follows the LXX in emending 'son' to 'sons' and takes it to refer to the heavenly council. He also points out that the question in Job 38:5a ends with 'surely you know!' and that in v. 7 Job is asked about the 'sons of God', though they are not named.

Verses 1b-4 are often seen as expressing scepticism, a view that, as Van Leeuwen[278] notes, 'is somehow appealing in our culturally uncertain times'. However, as Franklyn[279] shows, it is more plausible to read these verses as a vivid expression of the sense of the limitations of human knowledge that is to be found elsewhere in Proverbs. Fox[280] suggests that 'knowledge of the Holy One' in v. 3b is 'probably esoteric knowledge of divine mysteries' and not the kind of wisdom taught in Proverbs. There is therefore no ground for seeing vv. 5-6 as an 'orthodox response' to what has gone before.[281] Rather, in these verses, 'Agur dramatically states that only God can give him heavenly knowledge, and that knowledge is contained in reliable words from God.'[282] Verse 5 is a slight variant of 2 Sam. 22:31//Ps. 18:30 [Heb. 31]. It is notable that in Deut. 31:11-12 Moses makes the point that God's Law is readily available; no one needs to ascend to heaven to get it. Because this word is reliable humans must not add anything to it (v. 6a echoes Deut. 4:2a; 12:32 [Heb. 13:1]), pretending that they have true wisdom independently of God.

Verses 7-9 are the only prayer in the Book of Proverbs. It is a fitting conclusion to Agur's words, expressing his dependence upon God, even for his daily bread. The idea of balance and moderation that it expresses is a theme which recurs in Proverbs (see on 25:16). In the prayer Agur utters the personal name of God, Yahweh. Like the psalmist in Ps. 73, he has moved from a position of doubt and uncertainty to a sense of a personal relationship with Yahweh. This resonates with the motto of Proverbs that 'the fear of the LORD is the beginning of wisdom' (9:10a).

Moore[283] sees in the Words of Agur, with their allusions to the last words of Moses in Deuteronomy and of David in 2 Samuel, a linking of the wisdom tradition to Israel's two major covenant traditions — the Sinai and Davidic cov-

276. Longman, *Proverbs*, 523.
277. Franklyn, 'Sayings of Agur', 247.
278. Van Leeuwen, *Proverbs*, 256.
279. Franklyn, 'Sayings of Agur', 239-48.
280. Fox, *Proverbs 10–31*, 861.
281. McKane, *Proverbs*, 647-49; Perdue, *Proverbs*, 259.
282. Clifford, *Proverbs*, 262.
283. Moore, 'Home for the Alien', 104.

enants — and to the traditions of the Torah and the prophets. Fox[284] suggests that the 'Words of Agur' were included in Proverbs by an editor who 'believed that a cautionary comment was called for, after Proverbs' incessant glorification of wisdom, and he approved of Agur's exaltation of the Torah.' This may make a valid point, but probably over-emphasises it.

30:10 The Fair Treatment of Slaves

This is enjoined in Hebrew law (e.g. Deut. 23:15-16), which recognises their vulnerable position. Verse 10 is linked to vv. 11-14 by the catch word 'curse' and by being a warning about unacceptable behaviour.

30:11-14 Bad People Who Behave Unacceptably

These sayings are linked by their common opening. The kinds of behaviour listed are all condemned elsewhere in Proverbs.

'Rebellious children' who flout the fifth commandment (Exod. 20:12) are the subject of 19:26; 20:20; 30:17.

'Self-righteousness' which blinds a person to their own failings is condemned in 16:2; 20:9.

'Arrogance' is closely related to self-righteousness. As well as blinding a people to their failings it makes them unteachable (26:12). Such people are among those who are 'an abomination to the LORD' (6:17; 16:5).

'Rapacity' of various kinds is condemned in 1:10-19; 22:22.

30:15a Rapacity

Although עֲלוּקָה/*'ălûqâ* occurs only here in the OT there is little doubt that it means 'leech.'[285] The two 'daughters' are probably the suckers at each end of its body. One is used to attach itself to its victim; and the other to suck its blood until the leech is bloated. The saying is simply an observation, but in context is a warning to beware of a certain type of person. Its theme links the list in vv. 10-14 with the numerical proverb that follows in vv. 15b-16. Its use of 'two' forms a sequence with the 'three . . . four' of v. 15b.

284. Fox, *Proverbs 10–31*, 862.

285. Waltke, *Proverbs 15–31*, 487, n. 168.

30:15b-16 Four Insatiable Things

This is the first of a series of five numerical proverbs, interspersed with two that are not (vv. 17, 20). On the form of numerical proverbs see 'Numerical Saying' in the Introduction. The origin of this type of proverb may be an interest in observing and classifying natural phenomena and human behaviour but, as Aitken[286] comments, 'The sages' interest in nature is primarily for the light it can shed on human life and behaviour and for the lessons it can teach. The sayings, however, never press their lesson, but leave it to the reader to ponder and tease out.'

The insatiability of Sheol is mentioned in 27:20 (see the comment there). The insatiability of the barren womb presumably refers to the deep desire of barren women for children (e.g. Gen. 30:1; 1 Sam. 1:10-11), a desire that was fuelled by the importance of a married women producing children in the social and economic situation of ancient Israel. Sheol (death) and the womb (birth) are paired opposites. The same is true of water and fire, which can extinguish each other. The background to what is said about the land is the climatic conditions of Palestine, with its very dry summer and heavy dependence on the seasonal rains. Fire is insatiable because it continues to burn as long as it is fed fuel.

The moral of this proverb may be the need to recognise that there are some situations in which no matter how much is given, it will never be enough.[287]

30:17 Warning to Children Who Abuse or Disobey Their Parents

The warning is that nature will hit back at such unnatural behaviour. The sages stress the importance of children honouring parents (see on 20:20). Paying heed to parental instruction is a major route to wisdom (1:8; 6:20).

The word translated 'obedience' (לִיקֲּהַת/*lîqqăhat*) is generally taken as an anomalous form[288] of a word that occurs elsewhere only in Gen. 49:10. The LXX, Syr and Targ, however, have 'old age', a translation defended by Thomas[289] and followed by the REB.

The proverb may be included here because the word translated 'vultures' is the same word that is translated as 'eagle' in v. 19.

286. Aitken, *Proverbs,* 232.

287. Longman, *Proverbs,* 529.

288. Fox, *Proverbs 10–31,* 870; GKC §20h n. 2.

289. Thomas, 'Note', 154-55.

30:18-19 Four Wonderful Things

What the sage finds 'too wonderful' is the 'way' or 'manner' in which the four things move. Scholars differ over the exact cause of wonder. One reason for uncertainty is what is meant by the final line. Does it refer simply to sexual attraction, or to the act of sexual intercourse? Van Leeuwen[290] favours the latter, arguing that the preposition (ב/*b*) should be translated 'in' in the final line as it is in the preceding three. Some[291] scholars stress that the movements leave no external trace that they have occurred. Others that the movement has no visible cause — the eagle seems unsupported in the air, the serpent has no legs, the ship is propelled by the wind, the cause of sexual attraction is intangible.[292] However the saying is understood in detail, its main point is that there is much in the world that is beyond full human comprehension. As Murphy[293] says, 'In view of the not uncommon charge that the sages were simplistic in their observations and teachings, this openness to wonder and the contemplation of one of the deepest mysteries in human relationship is not to be forgotten.'

The word עַלְמָה/*'almâ* in the final line does not necessarily mean 'virgin' (ESV). It can be used of any young woman capable of child-bearing.[294]

30:20 A Wrong Way

This saying is linked to the previous one by the catchword 'way' and the theme of sexuality. It is one of many warnings against adultery in Proverbs. Whereas in 7:1-23 the emphasis is on the cunning of the adulteress, here it is on her nonchalance. Eating as imagery for sexual intercourse is also found in 9:17.

30:21-23 A World Upside Down

Van Leeuwen[295] has shown that behind this saying lies a topos, wide-spread in the ancient Near East, that depicts a chaotic, upside down world. This gives a

290. Van Leeuwen, *Proverbs,* 254.

291. Perdue, *Proverbs,* 263-64; cf. Wis. 5:9-11.

292. Clifford, *Proverbs,* 266.

293. Murphy, *Proverbs,* 235.

294. *NIDOTTE* 3:415-19.

295. Van Leeuwen, 'Proverbs 30:21-23', 601-608. The examples he gives are mainly Egyptian. To them one can add the Akkadian examples of the Marduk and Shulgi prophecies: Foster, *Before the Muses,* 357-59, 388-91.

serious edge to the saying's humorous satire. The ancients saw the cosmos as a unity. Chaos or harmony in one aspect of it affected the whole. Things which upset the social order threatened the overall stability of the cosmos. Hence the language of v. 21 is not purely hyperbolic.

The use of 'when . . .' indicates that the saying is about the behaviour of four kinds of people, two men and two women, who unexpectedly rise to positions of power or influence. The behaviour implied is probably overbearing arrogance.[296]

The male examples echo 19:10. The sages would assume that a slave would not have the ability or experience to rule. In addition he might well want to settle old scores by lording it over those who had lorded it over him. In the light of 19:10a the sufficiency of food in v. 22b is probably an example of luxurious living. The sages considered that only the diligent (10:4; 28:19) and wise (23:19-21) deserve luxury. For the fool to enjoy it threatens the proper moral order.

The 'unloved' (literally 'hated') women in v. 23a may be an unattractive person who belatedly and unexpectedly finds a husband.[297] It seems more likely that it refers to the second wife in a polygamous situation (e.g. Deut. 21:15-17) who comes to lord over the household as Peninnah did (1 Sam. 1).[298] Verse 23b is reminiscent of the conflict between Hagar and Sarah (Gen. 16; 21).

A significant aspect of this saying is that it implicitly recognises that life does not always follow the pattern that the sages' teaching presents as the norm.

30:24-28 Four Wise Creatures

Those demonstrate the 'life-skills' which are the essence of wisdom. The ants are successful in finding the food they need (cf. 6:6-8), the rock badgers find secure homes, the locusts are well-organised in a way that makes them relentless foragers, and the lizard is welcome in palaces, where it keeps down insects. The moral for the reader is clear: wisdom is more important than size or strength.

30:29-31 Four Stately Creatures

The identity of the second creature is uncertain. The Hebrew has 'girt of loins', presumably at the time a well-known epithet for some creature. The ancient

296. Whybray, *Proverbs*, 417; Perdue, *Proverbs*, 265.
297. Whybray, *Proverbs*, 418.
298. Van Leeuwen, *Proverbs*, 255.

versions take it as the cock. In the final line the meaning of אַלְקוּם/*'alqûm* is unknown. Possible emendations lead to the readings 'a king against whom there is no revolt' or 'a king whose army is with him'. The latter seems to fit the context better. The point seems to be that all these 'kingly' creatures are marked by a strength and confidence that is expressed in their demeanour.

30:32-33 A Call for Humility and Restraint

This saying is an admonition to stop self-promotion and intrigue (both forms of foolishness) because such behaviour provokes anger, which leads to strife. In Hebrew v. 33 contains some humorous puns which get lost in translation: the word for 'curds' is similar to a word for 'wrath', and the word for 'anger' is the dual form of the word for 'nose'.

Proverbs 31

The LXX separates 31:1-9 from 31:10-32 (see 'Texts and Versions' in the introduction), and most scholars see the two sections as separate compositions. The verbal and thematic links between the two poems noted by Lichtenstein[299] might explain the juxtaposing of the two poems without demanding common authorship. The overall unifying chiasm proposed by Hurowitz[300] is too unbalanced to be convincing,[301] and his 'chiastic chain of terms'[302] lacks conviction because of its dependence on word pairs.

31:1-9 The Words of King Lemuel

Since no Israelite or Judean king bore this name, Lemuel is clearly a foreigner, a conclusion supported by the appearance of Aramaisms in v. 2 (בַּר/*bar* for 'son') and v. 3 (מְלָכִין/*mĕlākîn* for 'kings'). Here there is a stronger case than in 30:1 for taking מַשָּׂא/*maśśâ'* to mean 'an oracle'. It lacks the definite article and is not followed by a parallel phrase. The oracle actually comes from Lemuel's mother.[303]

299. Lichtenstein, 'Chiasm and Symmetry', 202-203.

300. Hurowitz, 'Seventh Pillar', 215-16.

301. So Longman, *Proverbs*, 537.

302. Hurowitz, 'Seventh Pillar', 214-15.

303. On the role of the Queen Mother see Andreasen, 'Role of the Queen Mother'; Spanier, 'Queen Mother'.

It might well be instruction given to him at the time when he succeeded to the throne. 'Royal instructions' are known from Egypt[304] and Mesopotamia[305] but these do not come from the Queen Mother. Although the mother's teaching is mentioned in 1:8 and 6:20, only here in Proverbs does she herself speak. The exact force of מָה/*mâ* (normally, 'what?') here is debated. The NIV takes it as a simple exclamation, 'O'. It can mean 'No' (NJPSV, NRSV) in rhetorical questions expecting a negative answer[306] but that doesn't quite fit here. The speaker is Lemuel's birth mother (v. 2b), and v. 2c may indicate that his birth was an answer to prayer (REB, cf. 1 Sam. 1:11, 28).

Her first admonition is a warning against unrestrained sexual gratification. The harmful effect of this on the moral sensibility of a king is seen in David's adultery with Bathsheba (2 Sam. 11–12), and its effect on a king's loyalty to Yahweh is seen in the influence of Solomon's harem (1 Kgs. 11:1-8). A king's harem can also be a centre of court intrigue, including plots to seize the throne on behalf of a particular son — which is probably the point of v. 3b.

The second admonition is a warning against drunkenness. There is no more reason for taking it as enjoining total abstinence than for taking v. 3 as enjoining celibacy. Some see vv. 6-7 as cynical in tone[307] but they are better taken as sarcastic. Drinking to excess to forget your problems may be defensible to some degree for the poor who lack the power to solve their problems, but is indefensible for a king who has a duty to use his power to solve their problems for them (cf. Ps. 72:1-4, 12-14).

The two themes of this 'instruction' have appeared earlier in Proverbs (sexual restraint: 5:1-23; 6:20-35; 7:1-27; drunkenness: 20:1; 23:19-21, 29-35).

31:10-31 The Valiant Woman

This poem is an alphabetic acrostic. The initial consonant of each verse follows the order of the letters of the Hebrew alphabet. The acrostic form may be an aid to memory. It may also be intended to convey a sense of completeness, of covering a topic (notionally) from A to Z. Wolters[308] argues that the poem has the three-fold form typical of a hymn: an introduction in which the subject of praise is introduced (31:10-12); the body in which the subject's praiseworthy

304. *Instruction for King Merikare, COS* 1:61-66; *Instruction of King Amenemhet, COS* 1:61-66.

305. *Advice to a Prince, BWL* 110-15.

306. Joüon §144h.

307. Whybray, *Proverbs*, 424.

308. Wolters, *Song*, 4-8.

attributes and deeds are described (31:13-27); the conclusion, which includes an exhortation to join in praise of the subject (31:13-27). However, rather than being a liturgical hymn, it fits into the tradition of Hebrew heroic poetry.[309] In v. 10 the woman is described as אֵשֶׁת חַיִל/*'ēšet ḥayil,* and there is an *inclusio* in v. 29 in the phrase עָשׂוּ חָיִל/*'āśû ḥayil,* which elsewhere regularly means 'to do valiantly' in a military context. Hence his designation of the woman in v. 10 as 'a valiant woman'. *Ḥayil* occurs also in v. 3, where it is usually translated as 'strength'. It is notable that the woman's strength (using different words) is mentioned in vv. 17, 25. A number of other words and phrases in the poem have military connotations. For example, the word usually translated 'gain' in v. 11b normally means 'spoil, plunder'. Failure to recognise the use of heroic terms of a woman engaged in the 'battle of life' has led to the proposal that it be translated 'children' (REB) on the basis of an Arabic cognate.[310] Like other heroic poems it concentrates on what the woman does rather than the feelings or appearance of the hero.

The acrostic structure limits the possibilities for the use of poetic devices and thematic structure. Lichtenstein[311] notes the 'double frame' created by the use of 'valiant' (vv. 10, 29) and 'husband' (vv. 11, 28) and also the chiasm in vv. 19-20:

> *Her hands she stretches out* to the doubling spindle,[312]
> and *her hands* grasp the spindle.
> *Her hand* she spreads out to the poor,
> and *her hands she stretches out* to the needy.

This comes at the centre of the description of the woman in vv. 10-29. No one has proposed a convincing thematic structure for the poem, though after the chiasm, which links the woman's industry with generosity to the needy, there is more emphasis on her moral qualities.[313]

The rhetorical question in verse 10a makes clear that the woman described is a rarity, hard to find,[314] as v. 29 confirms. She works hard and with diligence (vv. 13b, 15a, 17, 18b, 27) to ensure that her household is well-fed (vv. 14-15) and well-clothed (v. 21, a re-pointing of the MT suggested by the LXX and Vulg changes 'scarlet' to 'double [thickness]', but Fox[315] rejects this). She produces material (vv. 13, 19) for the garments she makes (vv. 21-22), some of

309. Wolters, *Song,* 9-12.
310. McKane, *Proverbs,* 666-67.
311. Lichtenstein, 'Chiasm and Symmetry' 205-207.
312. Following Wolters' proposal for the meaning of *kîšôr; Song,* 42-56.
313. McCreesh, 'Wisdom as Wife', 36.
314. McCreesh, 'Wisdom as Wife', 36-37.
315. Fox, *Proverbs 10–31,* 896.

which she sells (v. 24). From the profits of her business ventures (v. 18a) she establishes a vineyard (v. 16). She is generous to the poor (v. 20) and a wise and gracious teacher (v. 26). Her husband trusts the running of the household to her (v. 11, note that 'heart' in Hebrew means something like 'mind' in English — see on 4:23), and she supports and enhances his standing and role in the community (vv. 12, 23). He and her sons praise her all-surpassing qualities as a valiant woman (vv. 28-29). It is not clear whether vv. 30-31 is part of their praise or a comment by the poet. Verse 30 does not condemn charm and beauty (5:19 commends them in 'the wife of your youth') but points out that they can be deceptive and ephemeral and that the most important quality a person can have is being one 'who fears the LORD'. The opening verb of v. 31 may come from a root meaning 'to recite' rather than a more common root meaning 'to give' (hence the REB 'praise her'). Wolters[316] argues that the song 'constitutes a critique of the literature in praise of women which was prevalent in the ancient Near East'. This was preoccupied with the physical charms of women from an erotic perspective. This song glorifies 'good works which for all their earthliness are rooted in the fear of the LORD'. He also thinks that there is a polemic against the Greek over-intellectual ideal of 'wisdom', basing this on taking צוֹפִיָּה/*ṣôpîyâ* as bilingual pun on the Greek word for 'wisdom' (σοφία, *sophia*).[317]

In a survey of the interpretation of this song up to 1600 Wolters[318] argues that from the earliest records up to the Protestant Reformation the song 'was overwhelmingly understood in allegorical terms. Since then, it has usually been interpreted "literally" as the portrait of an exemplary woman'. The woman was taken variously to represent the Torah, the human soul, wisdom or the Church. Despite the rise of literal interpretations, allegorical or symbolic ones did not disappear. In the last few decades scholars have tended to move away from adopting a simple either/or position. Thus although Waltke[319] emphasises that 'the valiant wife belongs to the historical, not the allegorical, realm', though incarnating wisdom ideals, and McCreesh[320] sees the woman as primarily a symbolic figure, a 'masterful portrait of Wisdom', many scholars adopt more nuanced positions. For example, Clifford[321] proposes that the song 'is a portrait of an ideal wife (of a great house) and, on a metaphorical level, a portrait of Woman Wisdom and what she accomplishes for those who come to her house

316. Wolters, *Song*, 13.
317. Wolters, *Song*, 30-41, but his arguments for this are considered weak by Fox, *Proverbs 10–31*, 897.
318. Wolters, *Song*, 60.
319. Waltke, *Proverbs 15–31*, 518.
320. McCreesh, Wisdom as Wife', 46.
321. Clifford, *Proverbs*, 274.

as disciples and friends'. What is said of the woman in 31:10b is very similar to what is said of Woman Wisdom in 3:15a and 8:11a, and what is said in 31:21b has echoes of 3:15b and 8:11b. In 9:1-11 Woman Wisdom builds a house (cf. 24:3-4) and invites people in to dine with her. The Song depicts a woman imbued with the essence of wisdom (31:30b) managing a house supremely well. It does seem that the song provides a closing frame for the Book of Proverbs, which relates back to the figure of Woman Wisdom in chs 1–9. As Yoder[322] puts it, the woman of the song 'is arguably a composite image of real women. She embodies no *one woman,* but rather the desired attributes and activities of *many.*' At the same time she is a portrait of Woman Wisdom because she incarnates the attributes of wisdom presented in Proverbs.

Feminist scholars bring fresh perspectives to interpretation of the song. Some regard it with an ambivalence such as that expressed by Brenner[323] with regard to the woman:

> she lives to advance male interests and male-well-being. In so doing, however, she ultimately subverts the male order by becoming its focal point and essential requisite. . . . The price for her implicit victory is explicit complicity in the system. . . . Thus male dominance is preserved while being overcome.

Many feminists choose to emphasise the positive portrait of the woman in the song, her business acumen, strength, wisdom and independence. Camp,[324] for example, argues that she completely overshadows her husband and that 'the female image in Prov. 31 defines not only the home itself but also indicates the proper identity and character of the public domain as well, namely one that finds its bearing in home and family life'. She sees the portrait of the woman as balancing that of Woman Wisdom in chs. 1–9 and regards these two female figures as providing the editorial frame and hermeneutical key to Proverbs.[325] Schroer[326] builds on this, arguing that the figure of personified Wisdom found in the editorial frame 'is the completely unpolemical attempt to put, instead and alongside of the masculine image of God, a feminine one, which connects the God of Israel with the experience and the life especially of women in Israel'. She sees no challenge here to Israelite monotheism.

322. Yoder, 'Woman of Substance', 446. She limits the image to women of the Persian period, but does not establish that it could not be equally valid for other periods of Judean history.

323. Brenner, 'Proverbs 1–9: An F voice?' 129.

324. Camp, *Wisdom and the Feminine,* 92.

325. Camp, *Wisdom and the Feminine,* 186-91.

326. Schroer, *Wisdom Has Built,* 42.

Some feminists argue that the song has been, and is, an empowering text for women. Valler[327] argues that this has been the case in Jewish tradition because the image of the woman 'highlights the actuality of a liberal conception of woman and womanhood among the sages'. Although the picture is domestic, it has enabled people to conceive of women acting beyond that sphere. Masenya sees the woman of the song as an ideal to be emulated by Northern Sotho women in Africa today, saying,[328] 'though the text does have oppressive elements, it also contains liberative or life-giving elements'. She is positive about the picture it gives of family life embracing a husband, wife and children.

Feminist ambivalence towards this text is understandable since, like the rest of Proverbs, it is written to appeal to a young male audience. Perhaps, though, Brenner does not do justice to its subversive nature. Van Leeuwen[329] comments: 'if Israelite males, like men throughout history, were sinfully prone to demean women as "the weaker sex," the praise of woman here is designed to alter errant male perceptions of women'. It is unfair to say as Carmody[330] does, that in v. 30 the author insinuates a fear of beauty. He simply puts physical attractiveness into a wider context, using typical Semitic hyperbole. It would be just as unfair to say that the author of 5:18-19 insinuates sexual abuse because it encourages the enjoyment of erotic pleasure in a marital context. It is not too difficult to imagine the song transposed into one addressed to women about a Valiant Man who incarnates the attributes of wisdom presented in Proverbs.[331] Psalm 112 provides a possible template, being an acrostic hymn about a man who fears the LORD. Significantly it does not major on 'macho' male qualities but moral and spiritual qualities similar to those described in the song of the Valiant Woman. As noted early on in this commentary (see comment on 1:8) readers who want to apply the message of Proverbs to their lives and situations today have to face the hermeneutical task of 'cultural transposition' of the message. This involves imagining themselves in the place of the original addressee(s) in order to understand what the message of the book is and then considering how it might apply to their situation today in a different historical and cultural setting.

327. Valler, 'Who Is *'ēšet Ḥayil?*', 96-97.

328. Masenya, 'Proverbs 31:10-31', 63.

329. Van Leeuwen, *Proverbs*, 264.

330. Carmody, *Biblical Woman*, 783.

331. Similar to Bellis's transposition of Prov. 7: 'Gender and Motives'.

Theological Horizons of Proverbs

Acts and Consequences in Proverbs

There are calendars for sale which provide a proverb for each day. However, using Proverbs as a guide to Christian living has its problems. There is a pastoral problem. It seems to say that there is a straightforward relationship between acts and their consequences. Good deeds lead to success and prosperity, evil deeds result in calamity and ruin.

> No trouble befalls the righteous,
> but the wicked are filled with calamity. (12:21)

If only life were as simple as this tidy dogmatism asserts! Strict adherence to it can lead to pastoral problems.

What about that faithful, committed Christian who suddenly faces calamity: redundancy, loss of income and consequent repossession of their home, or serious, maybe terminal, illness, or some family tragedy? Does it prove that they were not righteous after all? I've known people who have been driven into spiritual, if not clinical, depression by such thoughts. How many Christian parents flagellate themselves with Prov. 22:6?

> Train up a child in the way he should go;
> even when he is old he will not depart from it.

They have done what they thought was their best but their adult children are not believers, or even church-goers. How does one handle such pastoral situation? Is Proverbs right, or does it claim too much? Or are we misusing it?

This pastoral problem obviously has a theological dimension. In some accounts of the history of Israelite religion it is asserted that the cut-and dried, optimistic worldview of Proverbs was commonplace among the Hebrew sages. However, it could not stand up to the realities of life and came under attack from dissident voices among the sages. The evidence of this is to be found in the books of Job and Qoheleth, or Ecclesiastes as it is known in the English Bible.[1]

However, it seems to be a bit of an anomaly that two out of the three 'wisdom books' in the Hebrew Bible have been considered 'dissident' voices or 'protest literature'. After all, they form the majority of the extant Hebrew wisdom literature! Moreover, if they are so strongly at odds with the Book of Proverbs, why is it that the latter survived and found a place in the Hebrew canon of scripture? Maybe matters are not as cut-and-dried as has often been claimed.

The fact is that until the last half of the twentieth century the wisdom literature of the Hebrew Bible was largely neglected by OT scholars, especially the Book of Proverbs. The idea that it presented a rather simplistic worldview is one reason for this. Another reason was that the absence from the wisdom books of any significant references to Israel's history, cult and covenant relationship to her God made them problematic because scholars could not readily integrate them into their accounts of Israelite religion or OT theology.[2] Some went so far as to describe these books as 'a foreign body' within the Hebrew canon.

For various reasons the situation began to change a few decades ago, and scholars have begun to re-evaluate their understanding of these books. Here we will concentrate on the issue of the act-consequence relationship in the 'sentence literature' of the Book of Proverbs, which is basically Prov 10–29.

The Egyptian Connection

Before looking at the Book of Proverbs itself, we need to take account of its link with the wider 'international wisdom' of the ancient Near East. In 1923 E. W. Budge[3] published the Egyptian 'wisdom' text which came to be known as *The Instruction of Amenemope.*[4] There was immediate recognition that it

1. See for example: von Rad, *Wisdom in Israel,* 233.

2. Evidence of this is the small place that the wisdom literature has in the two major OT theologies of the twentieth century (Eichrodt, *Theology of the Old Testament;* von Rad, *Old Testament Theology*) and in the recent history of Israelite religion by Albertz, *A History of Israelite Religion in the Old Testament Period.*

3. Budge, *Facsimiles of Egyptian Hieratic Papyri,* Plates I-XIV. The text is British Museum Papyrus 10474.

4. For a modern English translation see: Lichtheim, 'Instruction of Amenemope', *COS* 1:115-22.

had a close relationship to a section of the Book of Proverbs: 22:17–24:22. The nature of the relationship has been a matter of some debate ever since but need not concern us here.[5] What is of relevance for our purpose is the assumption, which became widespread, that the Egyptian concept of Maʿat strongly influenced the Hebrew sages.[6] Maʿat was a central concept in Egyptian ethics and religion. There is no single English (or Hebrew) word by which to translate it. It is the force which creates and sustains 'justice and truth' — a single notion in Egyptian, not two separate notions. Various scholars came to hold that the idea of an underlying cosmic order was central to 'wisdom thought' in the ancient Near East and that this was taken over by the Israelite sages. This concept, it was argued, underlies Prov. 10–29. In addition, the hypothesis was put forward that the figure of personified Wisdom in Prov. 8 is based on Maʿat, perceived as a goddess in Egypt.[7]

In 1995 M. V. Fox[8] published an important paper which attacked this position. His attack was three-pronged.

1. He argued that while Maʿat can be seen as in some sense as a 'world order', it was not 'an automaton maintaining justice/truth by impersonal processes', which is how T scholars have sometimes presented it.
2. Secondly, the concept of Maʿat was so inextricably bound up with Egyptian religion and society that it could not be transferred into an Israelite context without becoming a 'denatured concept' very different from its origin.
3. Finally, the claimed parallels between the concept of Maʿat and wisdom in Proverbs are limited or non-existent.

There seems to be a growing recognition that Fox has made a good case, and that it requires a re-examination of what kind of worldview does underlie Prov. 10–29.

A different line of criticism has come from a change in the consensus among Egyptologists on the nature of Maʿat.[9] They now argue that there was shift over time from a belief in the *principle of Maʿat* as the dominant factor to an emphasis on the *will and power of the god.* From the 18th Dynasty onward there is a shift in Egyptian wisdom literature from the conventional view of

5. See the section 'Proverbs 22:17–24:22 and *The Instruction of Amenemope*' in the introduction.

6. H. Gese, *Lehre und Wirklicheit,* was seminal in promoting this view.

7. Kayatz, *Studien zu Proverbien 1–9.*

8. Fox, 'World Order and Maʿat'.

9. Boström, *God of the Sages,* 95-96.

Maʿat towards an emphasis on human piety and the free will of the god. *The Instruction of Amenemope* is singled out as a prime example of the new emphasis. This is significant since it predates the rise of the monarchy in Israel, and therefore the development of any Israelite wisdom literature. Many OT scholars seem unaware of this change in the consensus among Egyptologists.

The Act-Consequence Nexus

In 1955 K. Koch[10] published an influential paper in which he argued that there is in the Book of Proverbs, and elsewhere on the OT, the assumption of an act-consequence nexus. It is assumed that wicked actions will inevitably result in disastrous consequences and that good actions will result in blessing. In support of this he quoted a number of proverbs. The following are some of the more notable ones:

> Whoever digs a pit will fall into it,
> and whoever rolls a stone, it will come back on him. (26:27)
>
> Whoever misleads the upright into an evil way will fall into his own pit,
> but the blameless will inherit good. (28:10)
>
> Whoever walks in integrity will be safe,
> but he who is crooked in his ways will suddenly fall. (28:18)
>
> The righteousness of the blameless keeps his way straight,
> but the wicked falls by his wickedness. (11:5)
>
> The righteousness of the upright delivers them,
> but the treacherous are trapped by their desire. (11:6)

Koch argues strongly that what is being presented in such proverbs is the inevitable outcome of the actions themselves and not the result of God stepping in to administer punishments and rewards. His main reason for saying this is that, in his view, there is no hint of any 'judicial process' whereby God weighs up the actions according to an established norm and administers the appropriate punishment or reward.

10. Koch, 'Gibt es ein Vergeltungsdogma im Alten Testament'. An abridged English version has been published as Koch, 'Is There a Doctrine of Retribution in the Old Testament?'

To defend his case Koch has to deal with some proverbs which seem to speak of Yahweh administering rewards or punishments. For example:

> If your enemy is hungry, give him food to eat,
> and if he is thirsty, give him water to drink,
> for you will heap burning coals on his head,
> and the LORD will reward you. (25:21-22)

Here Koch questions the usual translation of the Hebrew word יְשַׁלֶּם *(yĕšallem)* as 'reward'. He points out that, since it comes from a root שׁלם *(šlm)*, meaning 'undamaged, complete', and is a *piel* form, a more natural translation would be 'make complete'. So, he argues,[11] what is being said is that Yahweh 'completes' the person's action by *'facilitating the completion of something which previous human action has already set in motion'.*

> Does not he who watches over your soul know it,
> and will he not repay man according to his works? (24:12b)

Here the key word is the one translated 'repay', הֵשִׁיב *(hēšîb)*. This is a *hiphil* form from the root שׁוּב *(šûb)*, meaning 'to turn back'. Koch translates it as 'turn (the effects of) the action back towards' the person who does it:

> The good obtain favour from the LORD,
> but a man of evil devices he condemns. (12:2)

In this case the word translated 'condemns' is a *hiphil* form of the root רשׁע *(rš')*, meaning 'to be(come) guilty'. Koch argues that the sense here is 'to treat someone as guilty'. The person's behaviour leads to the natural consequence of being treated as guilty by Yahweh.

Koch's conclusion, then, is that the Hebrew sages held to the conviction that Yahweh does not intervene directly, but maintains the act-consequence nexus and, where necessary, ensures that it is 'completed'.

Some scholars[12] have disagreed with Koch's conclusion, arguing that the distinction between an impersonal 'nexus' and the personal action of Yahweh would not have made sense in ancient Hebrew thought, which regarded the activity of Yahweh as all-pervasive in human affairs. Others have questioned

11. Koch, 'Is There a Doctrine of Retribution?', 61, his italics.

12. For example: Skladny, *Die älteten Spruchsammlungen in Israel;* Gammie, 'Theology of Retribution in the Book of Deuteronomy'; Murphy, *Proverbs,* 264-69.

whether the sages behind Proverbs really did assume that there is a more-or-less mechanical act-consequence nexus at work. It is the latter issue that we will consider.

The Act-Consequence Nexus Reconsidered

The first point to be made is that it is not appropriate to talk of an 'act-consequence nexus' with regard to the Book of Proverbs.[13] This is because the emphasis in Proverbs is not really on concrete, individual acts and their consequences. Rather, what concerns the sages is the long-term character of a person or a group of people.[14] This can be seen in the fact that one of the prominent metaphors in the book is that of 'the two ways'. People are faced with the choice of following either the way of life/light or that of death/darkness:

> But the path of the righteous is like a dawning light,
> which shines brighter and brighter until full day.
> The way of the wicked is like deep darkness;
> They do not know what they are stumbling over. (4:18-19)
>
> The man of integrity walks securely,
> but he who takes crooked paths will be found out. (10:9)

Another indication of the concern with character and not just individual acts is the frequent contrasts that are made between antithetical pairs such as: the righteous and the wicked; the wise and the foolish; the diligent and the lazy. It would be better therefore to talk in terms of a 'character-consequence nexus'. At the very least this loosens the link between individual acts and their consequences.

Second, it is important to recognise the limitations that are inherent in the proverb as a form of literature. What is a proverb? Answers to that question will probably vary somewhat from culture to culture. However, if we restrict ourselves to the 'sentence literature' in the Hebrew Bible, most scholars would agree that these sentences have the following characteristics. They

13. What follows builds on the work of three scholars in particular: Van Leeuwen, 'Wealth and Poverty'; Waltke, 'Does Proverbs Promise Too Much?'; Hatton, *Contradiction in the Book of Proverbs.*

14. Skladny, for certain sections of Proverbs, prefers the term 'Haltung-Schicksal-Zusammenhang' (attitude-fate-connection), *Die älteten Spruchsammlungen in Israel,* 8; Waltke, *Proverbs 1–15,* 72, argues for the terminology of 'character-consequence relationship'. See also the section 'The Formation of Character' in 'The Spirituality of Proverbs' below.

- are brief;
- are grounded in experience;
- often arise from careful observation of life and the world;
- are expressed in a memorable form;
- claim to present a valuable insight.

On this basis a Hebrew proverb might be defined as 'a realistic reflection on life crystallized in a brief, memorable sentence'. What this implies is that often a particular proverb will have arisen out of a particular experience or observation, and its meaning will relate to that original context. However, once it passes into general circulation, and perhaps even more so when it is collected into a written anthology, that context is lost. The hearer or reader has to intuit or imagine an appropriate context. Alternatively, with some imagination, the proverb can be applied to contexts other than the original one. So,

> The horse is prepared for the day of battle,
> but the victory belongs to the LORD. (21:31)

can be applied to situations other than military conflict. In any given difficult situation preparations cannot guarantee success. The outcome is in the LORD's hands.

The importance of context is one reason why, in any language or culture, seemingly contradictory proverbs arise. Two well-known cases in English are the following pairs:

> Too many cooks spoil the broth.
> Many hands make light work.

> Look before you leap.
> He who hesitates is lost.

The classic case in Hebrew is Prov. 26:4-5:

> Do not answer a fool according to his folly,
> lest you become like him yourself.
> Answer a fool according to his folly,
> lest he be wise in his own eyes.

Here we are faced with the choice between the risk of getting dragged down to a fool's level by getting into a debate with one, or the danger of the damage that might result from letting a fool continue in his or her self-delusion. Discernment is needed to know when to remain silent and when to speak. There are other, less stark, cases of apparent contradiction in Proverbs, but some are lost in the usual English translation. An example is Prov. 17:17-18:

> A friend loves at all times,
> and a brother is born for adversity.
> One who lacks sense gives a pledge
> and puts up security in the presence of his neighbour/friend.

In fact 'friend' and 'neighbour' in these two proverbs translate the same Hebrew word (רֵעַ/*rēaʿ*). It should probably be translated 'friend' in both cases. What the two proverbs are saying when taken together is that there are friends whom you can trust with your life, but there are others you cannot trust with your money. A wise person has to discern which kind of friend is which, and act accordingly!

The fact that the sages created or collected such 'contradictory' proverbs shows that they were well aware of the complexities of real life. Also, the fact that the compiler of the book sometimes deliberately put them together suggests that the reader is being warned against any mechanical application of proverbs.

One reason why the proverbs seem to assume the working out of an impersonal act-consequence nexus is the fact that in the sentences the consequences clause, especially if it describes a negative consequence, tends to be formulated in the passive and/or without the specification of any agent or course of events. Boström[15] argues that the passive formulation and the lack of specificity are used because they leave open the process whereby the consequence might come about. The sages were aware that this might happen in a variety of ways and by a variety of agents. A clear example of this is seen in the different reasons given as warnings against adultery. In 6:29 the consequence is unspecific:

> So is he who sleeps with his neighbour's wife;
> anyone who touches her will not go unpunished.

However, in other places specific consequences are cited: death (2:18), poverty (5:10), disgrace (5:14), the revenge of the wronged husband (6:34). These specific consequences are expressed in the instruction form of literature, which

15. Boström, *God of the Sages,* 116, 126, 135.

is more expansive in expression than the brief sentences. So, the impression of an impersonal nexus may be an artefact of the brevity of the sentence literature genre.

Contradiction in the Book of Proverbs

Hatton has critiqued Koch's thesis via a detailed study of Prov. 10–13.[16] He chose this section of Proverbs because Koch regarded a cluster of 13 verses in Prov. 11 (1, 3-6, 17-21, 27, 30-31) as providing clear support for his thesis. Hatton's critique is exemplified by his discussion of the opening verses of Prov. 10. He argues[17] that, 'In fact, two causal phenomena can be identified in Proverbs 10 and elsewhere in the book — one divine, the other human. These resist easy harmonization; often sayings that speak of these different mechanisms are placed together in a way that highlights possible tensions between them.'

Proverbs 10:2 asserts that there is a moral order in the world:

> Treasures gained by wickedness do not profit,
> but righteousness delivers from death.

This can be understood in the light of Koch's thesis, but nothing explicit is said about the connection between act and consequence. In the following verse Yahweh appears to act directly to protect the righteous and thwart the wicked:

> The LORD does not allow the righteous go hungry,
> but he thwarts the craving of the wicked. (10:3)

The following two verses, however, seem to attribute prosperity directly to human activity, in particular, diligence:

> A slack hand causes poverty.
> but the hand of the diligent makes rich. (10:4)
>
> He who gathers in summer is a prudent son,
> but he who sleeps in harvest is a son who brings shame. (10:5)

16. Hatton has pointed out that Koch's thesis is often misunderstood by English-speaking scholars because of the way his work has been translated into English. See Hatton, 'Cautionary Tale'.

17. Hatton, *Contradiction in the Book of Proverbs*, 85.

The first half of the next verse adds a further complexity,

> Blessings are on the head of the righteous,
> but the mouth of the wicked conceals violence. (10:6)

Are the blessings from Yahweh or are they bestowed on the righteous from their fellow citizens?

If the opening verses of Prov. 10 are read with the *a priori* assumption that Koch's thesis is correct, the tensions in these verses might be missed. It is significant that in his analysis of these verses McKane[18] does recognise the tension. He classes vv. 4 and 5 as 'Class A' sayings, originating from an old, secular wisdom. Verses 3 and 6 he classes as 'class C' sayings which rework the old wisdom in the direction of Yahwistic piety (on his classification see the section 'God and Proverbs' below).

Hatton[19] argues for a much earlier recognition of the tension: 'The extent of the tensions in the Hebrew becomes more apparent precisely because in the LXX's Greek they have been reduced and eliminated.' Any possible ambiguity is removed from v. 6.[20]

> LXX The blessing of the Lord upon the head of the righteous,
> but untimely grief fills the mouth of the ungodly. (10:6)

In v. 4a the possibility that the poor might be the authors of their own misfortune is removed, together with the antithesis between slack and diligent hands:

> LXX Poverty brings a man low,
> but the hands of the manly enrich. (10:4)

The change in v. 5 is even more striking:

> LXX A wise son is saved from heat,
> but a lawless son is blighted by the wind at harvest. (10:5)

The use of the passive, Hatton suggests, is an invitation to see divine agency here. This is supported by the use of the rare word ἀνεμόφθορος (*anemophthoros,* 'wind-blasted') in the second half of the proverb. This rare word is

18. McKane, *Proverbs,* 417-23.
19. Hatton, *Contradiction in the Book of Proverbs,* 86.
20. The translation is that given by Hatton.

used nine times in the LXX, always with reference to divine action. Most notably it is used in Deut. 28:22 in one of the curses that God threatens to visit on his people if they fail to keep the covenant laws. Hatton notes that the translator's departure from the Hebrew in these verses contrasts with his closeness to it in the surrounding verses. At the end of his study of Prov. 10 he says[21] 'Proverbs 10, in the Hebrew, does not contain one harmonious account of divine agency but encourages different accounts to clash. The Greek version of these verses, on the other hand, translates in such a way as to remove contradictions to produce a much blander and more pious version.'

After a detailed study of Prov. 10–13, including the verses used by Koch to support his thesis, Hatton says.[22]

> One negative conclusion is that verses offering unambiguous support for Koch's thesis are far from numerous; indeed, in the section surveyed, they are few and far between. . . . Moreover, the many sayings that give voice to a confidence that good and evil deeds receive some sort of appropriate reward — whatever is the precise mechanism — are contradicted by other voices. Some sayings confront the majority opinion with a minority report that insists that good things can happen to bad people. Others throw doubt on the possibility of seeing any clear connection between acts and their consequences, given that people deceive others about their true condition.

The 'Better-Than' Proverbs

There is one distinct form of proverb that occurs several times in the Book of Proverbs which clearly recognises the complexity of life and, in particular, that a simple character-consequence nexus does not always hold. These are the 'better-than' sayings. A few of them simply say that 'A is better than B', for example:

> How much better to get wisdom than gold!
> To get understanding is to be chosen rather than silver. (16:16)

This proverb implies that becoming wise does not always lead to prosperity. Indeed it suggests that sometimes one has to choose wisdom rather than financial

21. Hatton, *Contradiction in the Book of Proverbs,* 98.
22. Hatton, *Contradiction in the Book of Proverbs,* 115-16.

gain. Most of the 'better-than' proverbs are more complex than this. They have the form 'A with B is better than C with D':

> Better is a dinner of herbs where love is
> than a fattened ox but hatred with it. (15:17)
>
> Better is a little with righteousness
> than great revenues with injustice. (16:8)
>
> It is better to be humble of spirit with the poor
> than to divide the spoil with the proud. (16:19)

These proverbs clearly imply that the righteous do not always prosper (they may have 'a little' or even be poor) and the wicked sometimes do (they may 'divide the spoil' or even have 'great revenues').

The 'better-than' proverbs which speak of wealth and poverty (15:16, 17; 16:8, 19; 17:1; 19:1; 28:6) feature in Sandoval's[23] assessment of the act-consequence theme in Proverbs. He says,[24]

> Indeed although the act-consequence rhetoric of many wealth and poverty proverbs may suggest to some that the book promotes a simple retributive moral worldview where the righteous are rewarded with wealth and the wicked with poverty, other proverbs which do not employ cause and effect rhetoric call this view into question.

The 'better-than' proverbs do not promise any reward or punishment but use the language of wealth and poverty to assert the over-riding value of certain virtues, such as the fear of the LORD, righteousness, integrity, love and peace. Sandoval also points out that there are proverbs which commend certain types of social justice which do not express the acts-consequence approach.[25] These concern the use of accurate weights and measures (11:1; 16:11; 20:10, 23), proverbs about kindness to the poor (14:31; 22:22; 29:7) and the role of rulers with regard to social justice (28:15; 30:14; 31:8-9). They promote a concrete economic ethic as a 'good' in its own right without the support of the act-consequence nexus. Sandoval[26] concludes that 'These two sets of proverbs that do not employ a

23. Sandoval, *Wealth and Poverty*, 128-34.

24. Sandoval, *Wealth and Poverty*, 208.

25. Sandoval, *Wealth and Poverty*, 142-54.

26. Sandoval, *Wealth and Poverty*, 208. For a fuller discussion of Sandoval's work see the section 'Wealth and Poverty in Proverbs' below.

cause and effect rhetoric call into question any claim that Proverbs promotes a retributive moral view of the world in some simple or straightforward manner.'

Other 'Awkward' Proverbs

There are a significant number of proverbs that assert or imply that sometimes the wicked prosper and the innocent suffer:

> A gracious woman gets honour,
> but violent men get riches. (11:16)
>
> The fallow ground of the poor would yield much food,
> but it is swept away through injustice. (13:23)
>
> The poor utter entreaties,
> but the rich reply roughly. (18:23)

It is, perhaps, worth making the point here that Hebrew proverbs are sometimes simply observations on the way things are. This does not mean that the sages accept that this is how they should be. For this reason it is important to put these kinds of proverbs alongside those which do make an explicit evaluation of a certain pattern of behaviour. For example, on its own Prov. 17:8 might seem to be commending bribery:

> A bribe is like a magic stone in the eyes of the one who gives it;
> everywhere he turns he prospers.

However, two other proverbs about bribes show that this is not so:

> The wicked accepts a bribe in secret
> to pervert the ways of justice. (17:23)
>
> Whoever is greedy for unjust gain troubles his own household,
> but he who hates bribes will live. (15:27)

These proverbs, taken together, recognise that bribery sometimes succeeds, but brand the practice as wicked.

A small group of proverbs about what is not fitting/becoming also implies a recognition that the character-consequence nexus does not always work out, otherwise there would be no need to brand these situations as 'not fitting'; for example:

> It is not fitting for a fool to live in luxury,
> much less for a slave to rule over princes. (19:10)
>
> Eloquent speech is not becoming to a fool;
> still less is false speech to a prince. (17:7)

Even more extreme is a 'number proverb' which recognises that sometimes things go seriously wrong:

> Under three things the earth trembles;
> under four it cannot bear up:
> a slave when he becomes king,
> and a fool when he is filled with food;
> a despised wife when she rules,
> and a maidservant when she displaces her mistress. (30:21-23)

The third 'thing' here is translated 'a despised wife when she rules' following Van Leeuwen.[27] The reference is probably to the situation in polygamous marriages where there is competition between the wives (cf. Rachel/Leah, Hannah/Penninah). This proverb is about situations in which the social order gets turned upside down and something akin to chaos follows. The sages are realistic enough to acknowledge that it does happen, contrary to what the character-consequence nexus might lead one to expect.

Finally, there are a few proverbs which recognise that there are uncertainties and incalculables in life which limit human knowledge. For example:

> Do not boast about tomorrow
> for you do not know what a day will bring. (27:1)
>
> There is a way that is straight before a man
> yet its end is the ways of death. (14:12)

Although 14:12 (which is repeated in 16:25) could be a reference to the 'two ways' doctrine, as Whybray comments,[28] 'there is no suggestion here of making a

27. Van Leeuwen, 'Proverbs 30:21-23, 608-609.
28. Whybray, *Proverbs*, 215.

choice between good and evil or between wisdom and folly. The proverb simply states that life contains hidden snares'. What might seem a straightforward way to a desired (even good) goal may contain hidden, even fatal, dangers which humans cannot perceive in advance. Murphy[29] also thinks that this proverb shows that 'The sages were aware of incalculables in human existence.' The recognition of these uncertainties probably lies behind the sages' exhortations to humility as a mark of wisdom:

> When pride comes, then comes disgrace,
> but wisdom is with the humble. (11:2)

Given this evidence that the sages realised the limitations of the character-consequence nexus, why is it that so many of the proverbs do seem to presuppose it? Two kinds of considerations have a bearing on this.

Pragmatic Considerations

The fact is that the character-consequence nexus is often a good approximation to what happens. If this were not the case, proverbs would not have the place they do in most cultures. Also, human life would be far more chaotic than it is. In general humans do tend to 'reap what they sow', though it may be that as societies get more complex this is less easy to see. To the extent that the proverbs sum up what has been experienced or observed *usually to be the case,* they are a valuable guide to how to live. Things go wrong when people take them to be saying what *inevitably must be the case.* The fact that they can be misused is no reason to reject them.

Another pragmatic consideration in maintaining the character-consequence nexus is related to the overall purpose of the Book of Proverbs. It clearly has an educational purpose. Scholars debate the possible contexts in which that education took place, but that need not concern us. Education in 'life-skills', as in anything else, has to begin with what is *generally the case.* Only once this has been established and understood can the teacher move on to the qualifications and 'hard cases'. Rather than being seen as a 'protest' against the simplistic approach of Proverbs, Job and Qoheleth might be seen as providing the next stage in 'life-skills' education. To some degree Proverbs prepares the attentive reader for this next stage. As a result of his study of contradictions in Proverbs Hatton concludes,[30]

29. Murphy, *Proverbs,* 105.
30. Hatton, *Contradiction in the Book of Proverbs,* 170.

> our enquiry, limited as it has been, has established that Proverbs is a truly dialogic text in which voices that express genuine conflict are allowed to address the reader. In fact, all three wisdom books — Job, Qohelet and Proverbs — are dialogic texts that examine issues which are too complex and profound to admit of easy determinacy.

The difference between Proverbs and these other books is more one of degree than of kind.

Theological Considerations

There is plenty of evidence in the Book of Proverbs that the sages did not regard the character-consequence nexus as rooted in an impersonal 'order'. As Sandoval[31] puts it, in Proverbs the act-consequence nexus 'is not a mechanistic order through which one can infallibly predict outcomes. Rather it is a symbolic construction of the world within which the values and virtues of the sages make sense.' He sees[32] this symbolic worldview as rooted in a commitment to the fundamental value of righteousness and the ability of the virtues of wisdom to lead to human flourishing. This worldview is not based on empirical evidence but on the conviction expressed in Prov. 8:22-31 that this is the fundamental structure of the created world. Sandoval, however, cannot explain how it was that the sages could cope with the events which did not conform to this worldview beyond saying that they would tend to screen them out as not significant. I suggest that his understanding of their worldview does not go deep enough. It was not ultimately rooted in the structure of the world. Rather, it is rooted in the character and will of Yahweh.

Evidence of this is seen in the so-called abomination sayings. Most of these contrast something that is an 'abomination to the LORD' with what 'delights' him; for example:

> Those of a crooked heart are an abomination to the LORD,
> but those of blameless ways are his delight. (11:20)

This rooting of the nexus in the character and will of Yahweh is why

> The fear of the LORD is instruction in wisdom. (15:33)

31. Sandoval, *Wealth and Poverty*, 94, n. 48.
32. Sandoval, *Wealth and Poverty*, 61-66.

However, it is also why there are limits to the human understanding of how the nexus works out in real life. As the sages expressed it,

> Many are the plans in the mind of a man,
> but the purpose of the LORD that will stand. (19:21)

It is important to notice that this saying forms one of those seemingly contradictory pairs with the one that precedes it, which urges the reader to prepare for the future by listening to sound advice.

> Listen to advice and accept instruction,
> that you may become wise in the future. (19:20)

Clearly the second proverb is intended as a reminder that the sovereign purpose of God may override what seems to be best in terms of human wisdom. That purpose is not always readily accessible to humans, not even to the sages:

> It is the glory of God to conceal a matter,
> but the glory of kings is to search a matter out. (25:2)

As Perdue[33] comments, 'While the sages trusted in the goodness of their creator, they recognized that their understanding of God was quite limited.' That is why, in the end, the sages accept that

> No wisdom, no understanding, no counsel
> can avail before the LORD. (21:30)

In the Book of Proverbs, as elsewhere in the Hebrew Bible, there is an unresolved tension between human freedom and responsibility and divine sovereignty. The earnestness, and at times urgency, with which the sages urge people to follow the paths of wisdom, righteousness, honesty and diligence, rather than give way to folly, wickedness, lying, laziness and so on, makes sense only if the destiny of humans lies to some extent in their own hands. Yet, as we have seen, there is also the recognition of the overarching sovereignty of God which puts limits upon human understanding and actions. Perhaps the point of balance is expressed in the following proverb:

> Commit your work to the LORD,
> and your plans will be established. (16:3)

33. Perdue, 'Cosmology and the Social Order', 463.

So, one theological consideration behind maintaining the character-consequence nexus is that there is a moral order in the world, which is upheld by God. However, the sages accept that the connections between character and consequence which are summed up in their proverbs are not to be applied mechanistically, or to be considered as inevitable, because human understanding of life is limited, and, in particular, humans cannot fully understand the purposes of God.

Another theological consideration comes out in what have been called the 'future-oriented proverbs'. For example:

> Whoever mocks the poor insults his Maker;
> he who is glad at calamity will not go unpunished. (17:5)
>
> Whoever is generous to the poor lends to the LORD,
> and he will repay him fully. (19:17)
>
> Whoever closes his ear to the cry of the poor
> will himself call out and not be answered. (21:13)
>
> A faithful man will abound in blessings,
> but whoever hastens to be rich will not go unpunished. (28:20)

In these proverbs there is an implied 'distance' between behaviour and consequence. There seems to be a recognition that wrongs and inequities may exist for some time before they meet with their due consequence. Redress will come at some unspecified point in the future.

Of course death puts a limit on how long redress can be delayed. It is not clear how the sages dealt with this issue. One reason for this is that when death and/or Sheol are mentioned it is not always clear whether the reference is to death as an *event* at the end of life or to death as a spiritual *power* which can afflict people during their lives. For example:

> The path of life leads upward for the prudent,
> that he may turn away from Sheol beneath. (15:24)

This proverb could be read as referring to the destiny of the prudent beyond death. However, it can be seen as doing no more than expressing graphically the 'two ways' contrast that is a feature of the Book of Proverbs when dealing with the experience of the righteous and the wicked in this life. A parallel to this would be Moses saying to the Israelites that in offering them the covenant he is offering a choice between 'life and good' and 'death and evil' (Deut. 30:15). The context shows that 'life' means entering the Promised Land and prospering and multiplying in it. The opposite of this is considered a 'living death'.

There are problems in translating the Hebrew of the second part of Prov. 11:7, but the point of the proverb seems to be that death makes nonsense of the plans of the wicked to amass wealth because affluence cannot save you from death and you cannot take your wealth with you when you die:

> When the wicked dies, his hope will perish,
> and the expectation of wealth perishes too.

Proverbs 11:21 asserts that there is a difference in destiny beyond death for the wicked and the righteous, but it rests in the experience of their offspring:

> Be assured an evil person will not go unpunished,
> but the offspring of the righteous will be delivered.

The great majority of scholars agree that, 'life after death lies beyond the horizon of Proverbs'.[34] However, there are a few proverbs in which some scholars have seen a reference to life beyond death. Proverbs 15:24, discussed above, is one of them. Another is,

> The path of righteousness is life,
> and in its pathway is no death. (12:28)

Unfortunately there are textual, lexicographic and grammatical problems with the second half of the verse in Hebrew, which mean that other readings of it are possible, for example,

REB	The way of the righteous leads to life, But there is a well-worn path to death.
GNB	Righteousness is the road to life; wickedness is the road to death.

The REB reading is a result of revocalising one Hebrew word. The GNB basically follows the LXX as a way round the problems of the MT. Both of these readings makes the proverb another statement of the 'two ways' concept.

Also problematic is,

34. Kidner, *Proverbs*, 56.

> The wicked is overthrown by his evildoing,
> but the righteous finds refuge in his death. (14:32)

Because the second half is rather enigmatic some translations (e.g. the NRSV) follow the LXX and replace 'his death' by 'his integrity'. This requires the transposition of two consonants in one Hebrew word, but it does produce a balanced antithesis. Taken as it stands the MT could be read as indicating a hope of life beyond death. Alternatively, it could be a rather cryptic way of saying that the righteous will experience God's protection even to the very end of life. This understanding of the proverb would bring it in line with two other significant sayings:

> Let not your heart envy sinners,
> but continue in the fear of the Lord all the day.
> Surely there is a future,
> And your hope will not be cut off. (23:17-18)

> Do not get angry because of evildoers,
> and do not be envious of the wicked,
> for the evil man has no future;
> the lamp of the wicked will be put out. (24:19-20)

Here the Hebrew word translated 'future', אַחֲרִית *('aḥărît)* means 'an end'. It could have an eschatological sense, but here the general sense 'future' is probably correct. If so, these sayings are a particular case of the 'future-oriented proverbs' and express the sages' faith that 'in the end' Yahweh will ensure that both the righteous and the wicked will experience what they deserve. Of course, the fact that this is not always experienced in this life eventually led the Hebrews to the intuition that there must be life, and judgement, beyond death.

Conclusion

In the light of this discussion of the evidence in Prov. 10-29 it seems reasonable to conclude that the sages were well aware that the character-consequence nexus was only a 'rule of thumb' with regard to developing life-skills, with many exceptions. The tensions in the book make this clear to attentive readers. The sages saw it as pragmatically useful as a teaching 'model' at the early stages of learning life-skills. Moreover, it was theologically justified because it was rooted in the character and purposes of Yahweh. This provided some explanation of why it was only a 'rule of thumb'. Humans should not expect to understand

Yahweh's purposes fully. However, it also provided grounds for the expectation that 'in the end', whenever that might be, the righteous would be vindicated and the wicked punished — because Yahweh is the upholder of righteousness.

Characters in Proverbs

The Wise

The most frequently mentioned attribute of the wise in Proverbs is that they are teachable. About 40 percent of the sayings which explicitly mention the wise refer to this in one way or another. The Book of Proverbs was written on the assumption that the wise would pay heed to its teaching and grow in learning (1:5). It is a characteristic of the wise that they accept instruction and so grow wiser (9:9; 13:1; 21:11). They store up knowledge (10:14). The wise are willing to take advice (12:15; 19:20) and humble enough to accept reproof and learn from it (9:8; 17:10).

The process of acquiring wisdom is not easy or comfortable. It involves 'instruction' or 'training' (מוּסָר/*mûsār,* 1:2a, 3a). Fox[35] says that this term conveys the idea of teaching people how to avoid moral faults and that it refers to 'correction, whether by verbal rebuke or physical punishment'. In Proverbs it is often linked with 'reproof/correction' (תּוֹכַחַת/*tôkaḥat,* 1:23; 3:11; 5:12; 6:23; 10:17; 12:1; 13:18; 15:5, 10, 32). This is a noun, as Kidner[36] notes, 'whose derivation emphasizes verbal rather than physical persuasion: an appeal to reason and conscience'. The process indicated by the combination of these two terms can be described as 'discipline'.

The second most mentioned attribute is their use of words. By their speech they spread knowledge to those ready to receive it (13:20; 15:2, 7) and so their teaching becomes a 'fountain of life' to their community (13:14). Where it is needed, their words bring healing (12:18). Their speech is of great value because of the knowledge it conveys (20:15). They choose their words carefully so that their words are judicious and persuasive (16:23). Instead of inflaming situations, they know how to calm them down (29:8; 15:1). An aspect of being judicious in speech is knowing when to stay silent. By staying silent in the right situation even a fool can seem to be wise (17:28)! The wise person, therefore, exercises restraint in speech (10:14, 19; 12:23).

Two words from the same root express another attribute of the wise per-

35. Fox, *Proverbs 1–9,* 34.
36. Kidner, *Proverbs,* 36.

son 'wise-dealing', 'good sense' or 'prudence' (שֶׂכֶל/*śekel*, מַשְׂכִּיל/*maśkîl*). Fox[37] says of *śekel* that, when it denotes a form of wisdom, it is 'discernment or prudence, the ability to understand practical matters and interpersonal relations and make beneficial decisions.' In Proverbs it is a quality which results in a person having a good standing in their community (3:4; 12:8; 13:15). The *maśkîl* is a person whose prudence or good sense, illustrated by the son who works hard in summer (10:5), leads to success of various kinds: royal favour (14:35), prosperity (16:20), the slave who gains advancement over the son (17:2). A prudent wife is God's gift to her husband (19:14). The prudent know how to be restrained in their speech (10:19) and their reactions (19:11).

An attribute that is closely linked with wisdom is 'understanding' (תְּבוּנָה/*tĕbûnâ*, 2:2, 6; 3:13; 19; 5:1; 8:1; 24:3). Its importance is seen in the fact that both Woman Wisdom (8:1) and the Creator (3:19) possess it. Fox[38] defines it as 'the pragmatic, applied aspect of thought, operating in the realm of *action;* it aims at efficacy and accomplishment'. It therefore refers to competence. Perhaps because they are secure in their competence, those with 'understanding' show self restraint (11:12; 14:29; 17:27; 18:2) and are able to draw out other people's thoughts (20:5). They enjoy behaving wisely (10:23) and do what is right (15:21). The contrast with 'folly' in 15:21a suggests that 'walking straight' in 15:21b means 'doing the sensible thing'.

A word that is used in parallel with 'understanding' in Prov. 2:3 is 'insight' (בִּינָה/*bînâ*). It, too, is something which Woman Wisdom possesses (8:14), and it is used in parallel with 'wisdom' (4:5, 7; 7:4; 9:10; 16:16). Having it is a mark of maturity in wisdom (9:6). True 'insight' derives from 'knowledge of the Holy One' (2:3-5; 9:6), and the father warns his son against relying on his own insight (3:5) rather than on the Lord. According to Fox[39] *bînâ* 'designates the faculty of intellectual discernment and interpretation' and 'is similar to the modern concept of intelligence, except for the modern assumption that intelligence is innate.' *Bînâ* is certainly something which the sages urge readers of Proverbs to make every effort to acquire (2:3-5; 4:7; 16:16).

The term עָרְמָה *('ormâ)* and its cognate verb and adjective have a negative sense in the Hebrew Bible outside Proverbs: 'crafty' or 'cunning' (e.g. Gen. 3:1). In Proverbs it denotes 'prudence'. It is the quality Woman Wisdom has (8:12) and urges people to learn (8:5). To have it is a mark of growth from being 'simple' towards being wise (1:4; 8:5). In Prov. 1:4 it is put in parallel with מְזִמָּה *(mĕzimmâ),* another word which can have a negative meaning, even in Prov-

37. Fox, *Proverbs 1–9*, 36.
38. Fox, *Proverbs 1–9*, 37.
39. Fox, *Proverbs 1–9*, 30.

erbs. It can refer to 'scheming' in the sense of planning evil (12:2; 14:17; 24:8). However, in other contexts it denotes a positive quality which enables people to avoid being led astray: 'discretion' or 'prudence' (2:11; 3:21; 5:2). It, too, is an attribute of Woman Wisdom (8:12).

Much of what characterises wise people can be summed up by saying that they possess 'knowledge' (דַּעַת/*da'at*). This is something which fools hate (1:22, 29) but which the wise love (12:1), seek out (18:15) and store up (10:14). Its use in parallel with several of the terms discussed above shows that this 'knowledge' is not purely intellectual information and understanding. As Kidner[40] says, it implies 'not so much an informed mind as a knowing of truth and indeed of God Himself (2:5; 3:6)'.

Whatever one concludes about the origins of wisdom in ancient Israel,[41] in the Book of Proverbs as we have it the wise person is a godly person. 'The fear of the LORD ' and 'knowledge of God' are essential characteristics of being wise (1:7; 2:5; 9:10; 15:33). Those who are wise live trusting in the LORD and not simply in their own abilities (3:5-8). This means living a life which is not merely pragmatic but which has a moral dimension (3:7; 1:3). Brown[42] argues that the list of moral virtues in Prov. 1:3b is put in the middle of the purpose statement of Proverbs because it expresses the goal for the use of the surrounding virtues and skills.

This discussion of terms used in connection with 'the wise' in Proverbs is not exhaustive.[43] It does, however, show that being 'wise' requires a considerable spectrum of overlapping attributes and abilities: teachability, acceptance of discipline, careful use of speech, prudence, discretion, good sense, understanding of things in a practical sense, insight, intelligence, a grasp of the truth of things, moral sense, godliness. This coheres with what was said in the 'Introduction', that wisdom is about the ability to cope with life. It also shows that training in wisdom is about the formation of character. What is striking is the picture it implies of the godly person as someone who in not simply, or even primarily, concerned with the obviously 'religious' aspect of life but who is concerned with coping in the right way with the whole of life. D. J. Estes[44] sums up his survey of the different terms used in Proverbs 1–9 by saying, 'The aggregate sense of these terms is that education endeavours to develop in the learner the competence necessary to function independently as a godly person in Yahweh's world.'

What might this have to say about Christian living today? In that gaining

40. Kidner, *Proverbs*, 37.

41. See the section 'Proverbs: Secular or Religious?' below.

42. Brown, *Character in Crisis*, 25.

43. See Fox, 'Words for Wisdom'.

44. Estes, *Hear, My Son*, 86.

wisdom requires teachability and discipline, it challenges us to think about what sometimes goes under the title of 'discipling' in churches today. Is it concerned with producing good church members or with godly living in society at large? Is it about developing skills or about the formation of godly people? Estes' discussion of teaching and learning in Prov. 1–9 provides a lot of valuable material that those involved with 'discipling' in churches would do well to ponder and apply.

The Righteous

There are about the same number of sayings in Proverbs that refer explicitly to 'the righteous' as there are that refer explicitly to 'the wise'. Since being wise involves 'the fear of the LORD ' and 'knowledge of God' (1:7; 2:5; 9:10; 15:33) it might be assumed that the terms 'the righteous' and the 'the wise' should be synonymous, interchangeable. However, on the basis of a careful semantic study of Prov. 10, Heim[45] argues that this is not the case. Rather than being synonymous, the terms are co-referential. This means that the terms do not have the same *sense* but that they do apply to the same *referent.* To adapt an example given by Cotterell and Turner,[46] in 2012 in the UK it was possible for someone reporting an event to say both 'the Leader of the Conservative Party was present' and 'the Prime Minister was present'. This is not because the terms 'the Leader of the Conservative Party' and 'the Prime Minister' are interchangeable but because they both refer to the same person. The ideal in Proverbs is clearly that a person should be both wise and righteous, but the two terms are not simply interchangeable. The explicit overlap between them is surprisingly limited.

One characteristic that is shared by both the wise and the righteous is their careful use of words. Indeed, it is said of both that their speech is 'a fountain of life' (10:11; 13:14). In fact a deeper connection lies behind this shared attribute. The fear of the LORD is the beginning of wisdom (9:10) and is also 'a fountain of life' (14:27). In addition, the speech of the righteous expresses wisdom (10:31) which is itself said to be 'a fountain of life' (16:22). This can be related to what is said in Prov. 10:21a. Here the verb that is used implies the metaphor of shepherding, and so the idea of the words of the righteous nourishing many people is appropriate. One way they do this is by giving good advice (12:26). The righteous take time to ponder before they speak (15:28). What they say is appropriate to the situation (10:32). There is a moral quality to

45. Heim, *Like Grapes of Gold Set in Silver,* 77-103.

46. Cotterell and Turner, *Linguistics and Biblical Interpretation,* 160-61.

what they say because they abhor falsehood (13:5). All this makes the words of the righteous very valuable, like choice silver (10:20).

The righteous are marked by justice (12:5), generosity (21:26) and compassion towards both animals and people (12:10; 29:7). Not surprisingly, they have a high reputation in their community (11:10; 28:12; 29:2).

Proverbs asserts that the righteous will get their just reward (10:28; 11:23; 14:14), and this includes prosperity (13:21, 25; 15:6) and life (10:16; 11:28, 30; 12:12). It is a constant theme in Proverbs that, in contrast to the wicked, the righteous are kept secure in times of trouble (10:25, 30; 11:8, 21; 12:3, 7; 13:9; 14:32; 29:16). This security is explicitly linked with their trust in the LORD, expressed through the imagery of taking refuge in a strong tower (18:10). The LORD's care for the righteous is made explicit in two other proverbs (10:3; 15:29). The relationship between God and the righteous is discussed in more detail in the section 'God and Proverbs' below.

The Simple

One of the purposes of Proverbs is 'to teach prudence (עָרְמָה/*'ormâ*) to the simple' (1:4). In Proverbs the simple person (פֶּתִי/*petî*) appears as someone who is naive and gullible, willing to believe anything (14:15), and so is easily led and misled. Such people need to develop prudence and understanding. Being 'simple' is not in itself a hopeless state since the simple can learn to be wise both by heeding the instruction of the sages and by learning from what happens to those who lack wisdom, like the 'scoffer' (19:25; 21:11). It is a dangerous state, however, since simple-mindedness easily leads to folly. This seems to be the meaning of Prov. 14:18 if one follows the MT reading that the simple 'inherit' folly. Also the simple tend not to recognise danger, and suffer as a result (22:3; 27:12). A classic example of this is the story in Prov. 7 of the simple youth who becomes prey to the seductress (7:7). In Proverbs both personified Wisdom and personified Folly are depicted appealing to the simple to dine at their houses (9:4, 16). The question is whether or not the simple are so enamoured with their current state that they will not heed or accept the offer of Wisdom, unaware of the danger that not doing so could be fatal (1:32). The contrast between the two halves of Prov. 14:18 indicates that a basic weakness of the simple is a lack of knowledge. As Kidner[47] puts it, the problem is that 'one does not stay still: a man who is emptyheaded will end up wrongheaded'.

In three sayings the simple are linked with those who 'lack mind' (חֲסַר-לֵב/

47. Kidner, *Proverbs*, 39.

ḥăsar-lēb, 7:7; 9:4, 16). As Fox[48] points out, in this and similar phrases *lēb* refers to the human cognitive faculties and so is better translated as 'mind' than by the more literal sense of 'heart', giving the meaning 'lacking mind' or 'senseless'. In more colloquial English terms it can be expressed as 'empty-headed'. The truly empty-headed person follows worthless pursuits (12:11), makes risky financial pledges (17:18) and is lazy (24:30). Both the adulterer (6:32) and the oppressive ruler (28:16) are said to be empty-headed people. Not surprisingly, those who are empty-headed are said to be in need of correction or disciplining (10:13).

Clearly, being truly empty-headed is a step on the slippery slope from being simple to being a fool, and what is said about it acts as a warning to the simple not to start out on that slope but to heed the teaching of the sages and set off on the upward path to wisdom. It is also a challenge to Christian pastors to look out for, and take responsibility for, those in their community who are 'simple' and to give them the teaching and mentoring they need to enable them to progress towards wisdom.

The Fool

There are two main Hebrew words that are translated as 'fool' in Proverbs. The more common one is כְּסִיל *(kĕsîl),* which occurs 49 times. The other word is אֱוִיל *(ʾĕwîl),* which occurs 19 times. The closeness of these two terms in meaning is shown by the fact that the word that is used for the 'folly' that characterises both of them is אִוֶּלֶת (*ʾiwwelet,* putting reference to *kĕsîl* first: 14:24; 16:22), which comes from the same root as *ʾĕwîl.* Fox[49] defines the meaning of this term as, 'moral corruption from the standpoint of its impact on judgment and reason' and goes on to distinguish the two terms for 'fool' by saying, 'If the *ʾĕwîl* is obtuse by virtue of his moral perversion, the *kĕsîl* is, or probably will become, morally perverse by reason of his obtuseness.'

The vices of both types of fool are, naturally, largely the opposite of the virtues of the wise. Both, of course, lack wisdom (14:33; 1:7) and reject the correction and discipline that are essential to growth in wisdom (17:10; 15:5). Their folly is so ingrained in them that it has become part of their very nature (26:11; 27:22). As a result they always think they are right and do not listen to others (28:26; 12:15). This is an attitude which in anyone, not only incorrigible fools, can have fatal consequences (14:12; 16:25). They lack self-control, as is shown by them being hot-tempered (19:11; 12:16). They are without honour (3:35; 20:3)

48. Fox, *Proverbs 1–9,* 39-40.
49. Fox, *Proverbs 1–9,* 40-41.

and deserve punishment for their folly (18:6; 14:3, assuming the emendation adopted by most EVV).

No doubt because there are more sayings about the *kĕsîl* we are given a more detailed picture of this kind of fool. This is particularly true with regard to wisdom and understanding. The *kĕsîl* wants to acquire wisdom in a relatively quick and easy way, by paying for it (17:16). As Aitken[50] notes, this is a sardonic comment making the point that the fool 'is just wasting his money, for he does not have the resolve to apply his mind to learning but expects it to be handed to him on a plate.' Should he find someone willing to teach him, he learns nothing because he is inattentive, not concentrating on what is being taught (17:24). He is not open to the kind of correction that is part of the learning process (17:10, 12). The fact is that he thinks he knows it all anyway (28:26) and so is not interested in fresh understanding but only in expressing his already established opinions (18:2). For this reason what little learning he does take in and use is either ineffectual (26:7) or harmful (26:9) in its outcome. He readily takes in folly and just as readily pours it out (15:14, 2). As a result the sages' advice is to avoid the company of the *kĕsîl* (13:20; 14:7) and not to give them any responsibility (26:6).[51]

The *ʾĕwîl,* too, thinks that he is right and ignores advice (12:15). Rather than listen to wise teaching he pours out this self-opinionated folly, with disastrous effect (10:8). However, the root of his foolishness is expressed in more explicit moral and spiritual terms. He despises the instruction given by his father (15:5) and, indeed, wisdom and instruction in general (1:7). The implication of Prov. 1:7 is that this attitude is related to the *ʾĕwîl* not having 'the fear of the Lord'. There is debate about the meaning of Prov. 14:9a but it is generally taken to mean that the *ʾĕwîl* makes light of sin. It is not surprising that the ways of the *ʾĕwîl* lead to disaster (10:8, 14, 21).

When faced with unattractive character portraits such as that of the fool it is all too easy for readers to refuse to see in the picture a portrait of themselves. This may be a dangerous piece of self-deception. Also, there are proverbs that remind us that all of us can exhibit one or more of the vices of the fool, possibly with disastrous results:

> Do you see a man who is wise in his own eyes?
> There is more hope for a fool than for him. (26:12)

50. Aitken, *Proverbs,* 96.

51. On the apparently contradictory advice about the treatment of fools in 26:4-5, see the comments on these verses in the Commentary and in the section 'The Act-Consequence Nexus' in 'Acts and Consequences in Proverbs' above.

Do you see a man who is quick to speak?
There is more hope for a fool than for him. (29:20)

The Scoffer

The 'scoffer' or 'mocker' (לֵץ/*lēṣ*), like the 'sluggard', is one of the most frequently mentioned of a group on minor characters in Proverbs. Proverbs 21:24 makes clear the essential characteristic of the scoffer: arrogant pride. For this reason the scoffer is contrasted with the humble (3:34). Although spoken of in parallel with the fools and the simple (1:22) the essence of the scoffer's problem is not lack of mental capacity but his mental attitude. He is full of conceit and utterly self-opinionated. This is shown in his refusal to accept any kind of correction. Those who do try to correct a scoffer are met with abuse and even hatred (9:7-8). The only value to be gained from disciplining or punishing a scoffer is the lesson that the simple might learn from observing how scoffers deserve to be treated (19:25; 21:11).

Since humility and openness to correction are essential to growth in wisdom it is not surprising that when the scoffer seeks wisdom he does so in vain (14:6). As Fox[52] notes, this saying about the scoffer can be understood in two ways. It may mean that when a scoffer finds himself in a difficult situation and needs wisdom to cope with it successfully he will not have the inner resources to be able to do so. His opinions of which he is so proud will not meet his needs. The other possibility is that, should a scoffer decide that some learning would be useful, perhaps because of the prestige and power it would bring, he will not be able to acquire it because he does not have the teachability to gain it. For example, he will not go to the wise to learn from them because he is not willing to accept their rebukes (15:12).

The scoffer does not simply harm himself by his arrogant attitude. His disdain for other people's opinions and patronising attitude towards them, probably expressed in cynical and barbed comments, provokes quarrels and abuse and causes trouble in the community (22:10; 29:8). Although it does not explicitly refer to him, what Prov. 13:10 says about insolence leading to strife would apply to the scoffer. It is not surprising that scoffers bring down condemnation on themselves and may be repudiated by their community (19:29; 24:8-9). McKane[53] explains why.

52. Fox, *Proverbs 10–31*, 574.
53. McKane, *Proverbs*, 399.

> No man earns more universal detestation or deserves it more than he who wears a perpetual sneer, who is himself incapable of deep loyalty and reverence and who supposes that it is his mission in life to promote the corrosion of the values by which individuals and society live.

However, the worst thing of all is that they are scoffed at by God (3:34).

The scoffer is the epitome of one of the worst traits of the fool, a smug belief that his own ideas and opinions are better than those of anyone else. This attitude of mind is a pitfall into which we can all stumble from time to time, sometimes with serious results. The sages provide us with the best antidote to it:

> Do not be wise in your own eyes;
> fear the LORD and turn away from evil. (3:7)

The Sluggard

The 'sluggard', or 'lazy person' (עָצֵל/*ʿāṣēl*), like the scoffer, is one of the most frequently mentioned minor characters in the Book of Proverbs. The references to him show that the sages in ancient Israel had a sense of humour. He is depicted as a figure of tragi-comedy, a butt for their satirical wit.

A collection of sayings in Prov. 26:13-16 provides a comic portrait of the sluggard. When he wakes up in the morning he is reluctant to leave his bed. He is 'hinged' to it and, like a well-oiled door, he turns over and back again, without going anywhere. Noises in the street outside his house give him an excuse for not getting up and going out because he convinces himself that there is a lion in the street (an excuse repeated in 22:13, with the addition of 'I shall be killed'). When he does get up and sits down to a meal he stretches out his hand to get the food but is too tired to bring it back to his mouth (so also 19:24). Like other types of fools there is a certain self-satisfied smugness about the sluggard. He believes his own excuses for not doing things, thinking that they show that he is wiser than other people, like those who risk being mauled by a lion in the street.

In Prov. 24:30-34 the sage uses the consequences of the sluggard's behaviour to provide a moral lesson for his reader. Because the sluggard is too indolent to take care of his land it is overgrown with weeds, which would choke any useful crop that had been planted there. The stone wall has fallen into disrepair, allowing animals access to any of the crop that might have succeeded in growing. Fox[54] makes the point that the meaning of v. 32 is not that the sage

54. Fox, *Proverbs 10–31*, 774.

learned any new lesson from what he saw. Rather it reinforced what he already knew. This was that indulging in any sleep or rest beyond what was necessary is the road to poverty. Poverty is depicted as a highwayman or armed brigand waiting to pounce on the unwary traveller in the road of life.

Proverbs 20:4 is obviously closely related to 24:30-34. It spells out what lies behind the sluggard's neglect of his land and crops. He is too stupid (24:30) to realise that action needs to be taken at the right time to prepare for the future.

In Prov. 6:6-11 the sage tries to get some sense into the sluggard. He urges the sluggard to observe the behaviour of the ant and to learn from it. The ant is self-motivated and diligent. It doesn't need to have someone standing over it making it get on with its work. Unlike the sluggard of 20:4 it does take action at the right time to prepare for the future. The time during which appropriate action must be taken is limited, and the sage upbraids the sluggard for letting it slip away bit by bit because of his indolence. He is heading for poverty.

These vignettes illustrate various characteristics of the sluggard:

1. He is unwilling to take the decisive step to start anything. There is always time for 'a little sleep, a little slumber' before getting on with anything meaningful. As a result, moment by moment, opportunities to do what is needed slip away.
2. He is good at making up excuses for his inaction, and at convincing himself that they are valid when others can see that they are preposterous.
3. He will not finish things, not even his meal! For this reason the sages warn against ever giving a sluggard a job to do; that is a recipe for irritation and frustration (10:26), or worse (18:9, though this does not explicitly mention the sluggard, it is about those who are lazy at work).
4. The sluggard himself suffers from the frustration of unsatisfied desires (13:4; 21:25-26, see the commentary on these two verses). In addition he finds himself helplessly hemmed in by the tangled mess of his affairs (15:19) and so unable to do what he may want to do.

Aitken's[55] comments on these proverbs about the sluggard are worth noting.

> Clearly the sages enjoyed poking fun and pouring ridicule on this lazy fellow. They saved some of their best humour and liveliest imagery for him, As we read their proverbs we are meant to smile. We are also meant to recall when *we* got out of our beds this morning and how *we* spent our time today!

55. Aitken, *Proverbs,* 118.

The Wicked

The type of person most frequently mentioned in Proverbs is 'the wicked' (רָשָׁע/*rāšāʿ*). Most of the sayings that refer to them explicitly contrast them with 'the righteous'. One might expect that 'the wicked' would be synonymous with 'the fool' in Proverbs. However, on the basis of a careful semantic study of Prov. 10, Heim[56] argues that this is not the case. Rather than being synonymous, the terms are co-referential. This means that the terms do not have the same *sense* but that they do apply to the same *referent.*

The general picture given of the wicked is, of course, a black one. They desire evil (21:10) and regard those who behave uprightly with loathing (29:27). They act shamefully (13:5) but use bravado to cover up their evil intent (21:29). Traits that are characteristic of the wicked are arrogance (21:4), a lack of mercy towards both people (29:7) and animals (12:10), and a violent rejection of any attempt to rebuke them (9:7). They ignore the moral law (28:4) and pervert the judicial process by accepting bribes (17:23) and giving worthless evidence (19:28).

Their use of words is mentioned specifically in a number of sayings. It is, as one might expect, perverse (10:32). Their advice is therefore treacherous, comparable to a deadly ambush for those who take it (12:5-6) because it leads people astray (12:26). It can bring disaster to a whole community (11:11).

The possible communal impact of the wicked is recognised in a number of proverbs which refer to rulers. The wise ruler will seek to remove the influence of the wicked form his realm (20:26). As Fox[57] says, this proverb 'may refer to forensic judgment or to the banishment of all evildoers — from his court and from his land.' If the reference is to forensic judgement, the saying parallels Prov. 20:8. The need to remove the influence of the wicked from the royal court so that the king's rule might be marked by righteousness is underlined in Prov. 25:4-5, using the imagery of removing dross from silver. Proverbs 29:12 warns of influence going the other way. A ruler who entertains lies will corrupt his own officials. This will have wider effects (29:12). The people then become the prey of their ruler (28:15; 29:2), and the best they can do is 'keep their heads down' (28:12, 28) while they wait for the downfall of the wicked, which will be greeted with jubilation (11:10).

Over a third of the proverbs about the wicked concern their life-experience and its outcome. The basic message is that the righteous prosper in life while the

56. Heim, *Like Grapes of Gold Set in Silver,* 77-103. See the reference to this study in the section 'The Righteous' above.

57. Fox, *Proverbs 10–31,* 676.

wicked suffer. It is, however, recognised that it may not always look like that. People may be tempted to envy them and follow their way (24:19; 4:14). The wicked may gain wealth, which they invest in more wickedness (10:16) but this is not reliable wealth (11:18); it will lead to trouble (11:8; 12:21; 15:6). They will find themselves in want (13:25), and their house, probably meaning 'household', destroyed (14:11; 21:12). Unlike the righteous, they will not survive the storms of life (2:21-22; 3:25; 10:25; 12:7; 21:18, see the commentary on this verse; 24:15-16). Therefore, others should not envy them or follow their way (24:19-20; 4:14, 19). The disasters that befall the wicked are, in fact, the consequence of their own wickedness (5:22; 11:5, 31; 14:32; 21:7). In the end their hopes and desires will be left unfulfilled (10:28; 11:7, 23). Instead what they feared might happen, will overtake them (10:24). That fear leads them to live in constant anxiety and take unnecessary precautions (28:1). The implication of these two proverbs is that the wicked do have an underlying sense of guilt.

Perhaps surprisingly there are only a handful of proverbs which explicitly express God's attitude towards the wicked. The wicked are among those who do not fear the LORD (10:27). They and their household live under his curse (3:33). Perhaps this is why the sages say that he made the wicked for the day of trouble (16:4). God is far from them and does not heed their prayers, as he does those of the righteous (15:29). He thwarts the fulfilment of their desires (10:3). Both their sacrifices and their way of life are an abomination to him (15:8-9; 21:27). Anyone who seeks to justify the wicked suffers the same condemnation.

The Two Ways

The apparently black and white picture given of the life-experience of the wicked and the righteous in Proverbs may seem idealistic, if not unrealistic. However, to understand this picture properly it is necessary to take proper account of the genre of the Book of Proverbs and its purpose. Bricker[58] argues that there are at least four factors which lie behind this black and white presentation of life.

1. The constraints of Hebrew poetry. Its use of parallelism, especially the antithetic parallelism that is common in the sayings about the righteous and the wicked in Proverbs, and its terseness, results in a tendency to express things in a black and white way.
2. The nature of a Hebrew proverb. These are concise summary statements expressed in poetry. Most proverbs contain only six to eight words in

58. Bricker, 'Doctrine of the "Two Ways" in Proverbs'.

Hebrew. This leaves no room for shades of grey or mention of exceptions. Also, any one proverb can deal with only a small aspect of life and should not be treated as a generalisation. In a culture where the use of proverbs was far more widespread than it is in Western cultures today, this would, no doubt, have been recognised instinctively. It is not the case that a soft answer always turns away wrath but this does happen more often than not. For that reason it is worth expressing the balance of experience in a proverb (15:1). So, the original students of Proverbs would probably not take the statements about the life-experience of the righteous and the wicked as anything more than expressions of what generally happens.

3. The use of the metaphor of 'the two ways' as a teaching aid. Habel[59] argues that this is the basic symbol used in Prov. 1–9. However, it also pervades the rest of the book. The reader is frequently presented with the choice to follow the way of the wise or the fool, the righteous or the wicked. Proverbs 4:10-19 is a classic presentation of this theme.
4. The didactic purpose of the book. Bricker[60] says, 'If the ancient Israelite teacher's purpose was to see students succeed in life, then drawing clear lines between good and bad choices would have been of utmost importance. The choices offered are deliberately set out to impress on the youthful audience the possible dangers of taking the wrong path.' Successful living is a complicated business and when teaching 'the simple' one has to begin with clear-cut choices and then, as their life-skills increase, one can move on to consider the exceptions and the 'grey' situations, as Qoheleth does in Ecclesiastes. In Proverbs itself the existence of 'contradictory' proverbs shows an awareness of the complexity of life.[61]

All these are valid points and suggest that the sages who coined and compiled the proverbs did not believe, or intend to convey, the idea that life is as black and white as a superficial reading of the book might seem to imply. Nor would their students have concluded that. The teaching of the book gave them a basis for approaching life-choices with some sense of the likely consequences of their decisions. As time went on they could developed a more nuanced approach. For a full discussion of some of the issues touched on here, see the section on 'Acts and Consequences in Proverbs' above.

In their teaching about 'the two ways' in life the Israelite sages foreshad-

59. Habel, 'Symbolism of Wisdom, 133.

60. Bricker, 'Doctrine of the "Two Ways" in Proverbs', 515.

61. For a detailed discussion of this see Hatton, *Contradiction in the Book of Proverbs.*

owed the choice between the two roads that Jesus sets out in the Sermon on the Mount: 'Enter by the narrow gate. For the gate is wide and the way is easy that leads to destruction, and those who find it are many. For the gate is narrow and the way is hard that leads to life, and those who find it are few' (Matt. 7:13-14, ESV).

Family, Friends and Neighbours in Proverbs

Family

Proverbs assumes that the basis of the family is the union of one man with one woman. This is the picture of the family given in the only two extended descriptions of it in the book (5:15-20; 31:10-31). Also, there is no reference in the proverbs to the discords that might arise from polygamy, the kind of tensions described in some of the stories about the patriarchs. Proverbs is written from a male point of view, a father instructing his son(s). As noted elsewhere in this commentary, everyone reading the Bible today has to do some 'cultural transposition' of its message if it is to be applied today. For female readers this includes the need for gender transposition.

The husband-wife relationship is presented as a fully personal one, both of lovers ('be intoxicated always in her love', 5:19b, ESV) and companions (2:17, 'the companion of her youth') which involves trust (31:11) and appreciation (31:28). Proverbs 2:17b probably speaks of marriage as a covenant relationship made before God (see the commentary on this verse). Although the father's voice is the dominant one in Proverbs, it is made clear that both parents have a role in the teaching of the children:

> My son, keep the commandment of your father,
> and do not reject the teaching of your mother. (6:20)

Proverbs 29:15 may also refer to the mother's role in disciplining children:

> Rod and reproof yield wisdom,
> but a youth unrestrained brings shame to his mother.

See also 1:8-9 and 31:1. Proverbs 14:1a states the important role of the wise wife in establishing a home (see the commentary on this verse). For a full discussion of 31:10-22 see the section 'The Strong/Valiant Woman' below. There it is argued that the Strong Woman is a picture of a human person, not of any one woman but a composite picture based on the different roles played by Judean women. At the same time she incarnates characteristics of personified Wisdom. Therefore this is not a picture of *the* ideal wife, but it does show the kind of things which the sages could envisage women doing, at least in the upper strata of society. The fact that her husband is not depicted as doing any gainful work is, no doubt, an artefact of the poem, especially the depiction of the woman as to some degree an incarnation of Wisdom. He could well be running his business, or his side of the family business, while she ran hers.

A good wife is seen as a gift from the LORD:

> House and wealth are an inheritance from fathers,
> but a prudent wife is from the LORD. (19:14)

> He who finds a wife finds a good thing
> and obtains favour from the LORD. (18:22)

In the commentary it is argued that the point of 12:4 is the importance of making a wise choice when seeking a marriage partner.

> An excellent wife is the crown of her husband,
> but like rot in his bones is a shameful one.

The imagery used in v. 4a may allude to the crowns worn by bride and groom in the wedding ceremony of the time. The antithesis in v. 4b does not define in what way a wife might 'bring shame' to her husband. The only two domestic troubles (apart from troublesome children) mentioned in Proverbs are nagging (19:13; 27:15) and infidelity (by either partner: 2:16-17; 5:18-20). In the section 'The Strange/Foreign Woman' below it is pointed out that warnings against adultery such as those found in Proverbs are common in ancient Near Eastern wisdom literature. This is because of the importance placed on strong families as the basis of a stable society.

Parents and Children

Since part of the aim of Proverbs is 'to give knowledge and discretion to the young' (1:4b) it is not surprising that there are numerous exhortations to the son(s) to listen to their parents' teaching (1:8; 4:1; 6:20; 13:1; 15:5; 23:22). The need for discipline in the training of children is a common theme in Proverbs. The first colon of 22:15 is often taken to imply that there is an innate folly in children but Van Leeuwen[62] may be right in suggesting that the proverb should be taken as an implicit conditional sentence:

> If folly is bound up in the heart of a youth,
> the rod of discipline will drive it far from him.

The sages mention a number of ways in which children may prove wayward: idleness (10:5b), scoffing at teaching (13:1b), despising parents (15:20), being violent towards parents (19:26), cursing parents (20:20; 30:11), robbing parents (28:24), profligacy (29:3), mocking parents (30:17). In any case, the earlier a child is given good training, the better:

> Whoever spares the rod hates his son,
> but whoever loves him disciplines him early on. (13:24)

> Train a youth in the way he should go;
> even in old age, he will not turn from it. (22:6)

Children who respond positively to discipline and training and grow up as wise people bring joy and gladness to their parents (10:1; 15:20; 23:24-25; 29:3). Of course, as some of these proverbs also say, foolish children bring them sorrow:

> A wise son makes a glad father,
> but a foolish son is a sorrow to his mother. (10:1)

Proverbs' references to 'the rod' (above and 23:13; 29:15) may seem harsh, but as Kidner[63] comments: 'The book tacitly condemns the martinet by its own reasonable approach, its affectionate earnestness, and its assumption that the old find their natural crown, and the young their proper pride, in each other (17:6).'

> The crown of old men is grandchildren,
> and the glory of children is their fathers.

The matter of the appropriate way to administer discipline is another one that needs cultural transposition.

The sages recognise that as well as disciplining their children, parents have

62. Van Leeuwen, *Proverbs*, 199.
63. Kidner, *Proverbs*, 51.

a responsibility to set them a good example by modelling righteous behaviour (20:7, see the commentary on this verse in its context).

Brothers

There are very few proverbs about brothers, and the Hebrew term for brother can refer to cousins and other more distant relatives. The basic assumption is that they will come into their own in difficult times:

> A friend loves at all times,
> and a brother is born for adversity. (17:17)

However, they do not always live up to this assumption:

> All the brothers of the poor man hate him;
> how much more do his friends desert him! (19:7)

This is a case where 'brothers' probably refers to relatives in general. Proverbs 18:19 is probably a warning against the intractability of family feuds:

> A brother offended is stronger than a city,
> and disputes are like the bars of a castle.

Someone who sows discord among brothers is an abomination to the LORD (6:19).

There is some uncertainty about the meaning of 27:10b (see the commentary on this verse):

> Do not forsake your friend and the friend of your father,
> and do not enter the house of your brother on the day of your misfortune.
> Better is a near neighbour than a distant brother. (27:10)

It may be that it is to be understood in the light of v. 10c: turn for help to a nearby friend rather than going to a distant relative. Alternatively, as Fox[64] suggests, its point may be 'to encourage us to cherish friendship. Brotherhood is mentioned as a point of comparison. The brother is still the benchmark for fidelity because "A brother is born for sorrow" (17:17b).'

64. Fox, *Proverbs 10–31*, 808.

Friends and Neighbours

The Hebrew word רֵעַ *(rēaʿ)* can mean both 'friend' and 'neighbour'. The meaning has to be decided in the light of the context. As Longman[65] puts it, 'The translation "friend" indicates emotional attachment, while "neighbour" fits those contexts where spatial intimacy is meant.' Sometimes, especially in the limited context of a proverb, the meaning is ambiguous.

Neighbours. The sages were aware of 'the neighbour from hell'. The son is exhorted not to be one of these:

> Do not plot evil against your neighbour
> who lives trustingly beside you. (3:29)

They are aware that some people can be the target of merciless harassment from a neighbour (21:10). The problem may be slander (11:9), which may lead to perjury in court (24:28; 25:18). Sometimes, though, the neighbour's behaviour may be stupid or thoughtless rather than malicious (26:18-19). However, it will probably be fatal to the relationship nonetheless. Another form of thoughtlessness is warned against in 25:17:

> Let your foot be seldom in your neighbour's house,
> lest he has his fill of you and hate you.

Noisy neighbours can be a problem too:

> Whoever blesses his neighbour with a loud voice early in the morning,
> will be counted as cursing. (27:14)

A good neighbour is someone who seeks to create and promote harmony in the community. He knows that there are times when remaining silent is wiser than criticism (11:12) and will seek to settle disputes by negotiation with his neighbours rather than reverting to the courts (25:7c-10). When he is able to help others he will do so promptly:

> Do not tell your neighbour, 'Go, but come back again,
> and tomorrow I will give', although you can do it now. (3:28)

This has particular application in help given to the poor (14:20-21). However,

65. Longman, *Proverbs*, 555.

this does not mean being a 'soft touch' and getting involved in unwise transactions (6:1-5, see the commentary on these verses).

Friends. The sages give implicit warnings against 'fair weather friends', particularly those who attach themselves to people with wealth (14:20; 18:24a; 19:4, 6). Therefore true friends need to be cultivated, not neglected (27:10a). Making and keeping friends is the subject of 17:9:

> One who covers an offence seeks love,
> but one who repeats a matter divides close friends.

Friendship will not grow where there is unwillingness to overlook the occasional failings and faults of the other person. If those failings and faults are gossiped about to others, it will destroy the friendship.

In contrast to mere 'fair weather friends' a true friend is faithful, constant. 'A friend loves at all times' (17:17a). Indeed there are some friends that are more reliable than close family: 'a friend who sticks closer than a brother' (18:24b). Discussion with a friend can be encouraging and uplifting (27:9, see the commentary on this verse) but good friendship also involves the healthy debate which sharpens ideas and wits:

> Iron is sharpened by iron,
> and a man sharpens the face of his friend. (27:17)

True friends do not use flattery, which can be dangerously misleading for the recipient (29:5). Instead, they are prepared to say things that are true but may initially be hurtful (27:5-6).

> Better an open rebuke
> than a love that is hidden. (27:5)

> Faithful are the wounds of a friend,
> profuse are the kisses of an enemy. (27:6)

Hopefully they will later be thanked for it (28:23), and the friendship deepened.

Reflection

In Western societies today there are people advertising themselves as 'life-coaches' who offer mentoring in 'life-skills', the very thing with which the sages of ancient Israel were concerned. The mentors in Proverbs are parents (1:8; 6:20), primarily the father, and so the parents are important 'life-coaches'. There are strong echoes of Deut. 6:6-8 and 11:18-19 in Prov. 6:21-22. Regarding the parents' teaching the father says,

> Bind them over your heart always,
> tie them around your neck. (6:21)
>
> Wherever you walk it will lead you,
> when you lie down it will guard you,
> and when you wake up it will talk with you. (6:22)

Compare this with:

> And these words that I command you today shall be on your heart. You shall teach them diligently to your children, and shall talk of them when you sit in your house, and when you walk by the way, and when you lie down, and when you rise. (Deut. 6:6-7)

These echoes show that the parents in Proverbs are depicted as seeking to fulfil their responsibility to teach God's law to their child. It is therefore appropriate that what is said of the parents' teaching in 6:23, 'for the commandment is a lamp and the teaching a light', echoes what Ps. 119:105 says of God's word, 'Your word is a lamp to my feet and a light to my path'. It is a clear theme throughout the Bible that when parents accept and fulfil this responsibility to bring their children up 'in the training and instruction of the Lord' (Eph. 6:4), the family forms a firm basis for a stable society. In a world in which there is increasing evidence of, and concern about, dysfunctional families, there is a particular need for godly parents to rise to the challenge of building functional families. To do this they must give godly life-coaching to their children.

Of course, as the sages were aware, children have to play a part in creating a functional family too. In applying the message of Proverbs it must be recognised that it is not saying that all children should listen unquestioningly to what their parents say and obey it blindly. The parents in Proverbs are an ideal couple. They are wise, godly parents. To the extent that real parents are wise and godly they deserve to be listened to, but all real parents are fallible to some degree and therefore open to having their teaching and advice questioned. However, this should be done in way that is consonant with the command to honour parents (Deut. 5:16; Eph. 6:1-3). Some of the behaviour of children which the sages present as reprehensible (see above) is similar to reports today about 'elder abuse', which is a growing concern is societies with an aging population.

We are not all parents, but are all children. We are not all married but are all family members. So, we all can play our part in creating functional families.

God and Proverbs

Proverbs: Secular or Religious?

The Problem

The writers of OT theologies have found it difficult to incorporate the wisdom literature in general, and Proverbs in particular, into their theologies. One of the reasons for this is expressed by Wright,[66] 'In any attempt to outline a discussion of Biblical faith it is the wisdom literature which offers the chief difficulty because it does not fit into the type of faith exhibited in the historical and prophetic literatures.' Wright, like many other OT scholars, saw Hebrew theology as centring on Yahweh's acts in history and the interpretation of, and response to, these acts. One of the characteristics of the wisdom literature in the Hebrew canon is a lack of reference to Israel's historical traditions, including the fundamental ones of the exodus from Egypt and the covenant-making at Sinai. In addition, whereas theology based on historical traditions naturally leads to an emphasis on Yahweh's relationship with the nation, the emphasis in the wisdom literature is on the individual. Wright[67] concluded that the material in the Book of Proverbs in particular, 'remains near the pagan source of wisdom in which society and the Divine work in history played no real role'.

The second quotation from Wright highlights a common assumption that wisdom in Israel was not 'home-grown' but was appropriated from the international 'pool' of wisdom in the ancient Near East to which the literatures of Egypt and Mesopotamia bear witness. As a result, Eichrodt[68] held that wisdom in Israel 'has a strongly secular favour, and is only loosely connected with religious faith'. This wisdom was mainly concerned with the skill in practical matters which is the basis for success in daily life. In Eichrodt's view[69] this

66. Wright, *God Who Acts,* 103.
67. Wright, *God Who Acts,* 104.
68. Eichrodt, *Theology of the Old Testament,* 2:81.
69. Eichrodt, *Theology of the Old Testament,* 2:82.

'unprejudiced borrowing of foreign wisdom' was only gradually integrated into Hebrew Yahwism.

The Religious Reinterpretation of Proverbs

A few scholars have questioned whether that integration ever really happened. Most notably, Preuss[70] argued that the teaching of Prov. 10–29 is entirely in accord with that of international wisdom and, despite appearances, is alien to the faith of Israel. Although the name Yahweh is used and there are admonitions to fear Yahweh and trust Yahweh, the characterisation of Yahweh as the guarantor of the moral order and the assumption of the principle of retribution puts him on a level with the gods mentioned in other ancient Near Eastern wisdom literature. His argument has not convinced many. As Whybray has said,[71] 'His extreme position leaves it unclear how the retention of Proverbs as Jewish scripture is to be accounted for and why its authors gave their god the name of the God of Israel'.

A more mainstream approach is that of McKane. He divided the sentence literature into three classes:[72]

- Class A sayings which are 'set in the framework of old wisdom and . . . concerned with the education of the individual for a successful and harmonious life'.
- Class B sayings in which 'the centre of concern is the community rather than the individual'. These mainly describe the harmful effects of antisocial behaviour.
- Class C sayings which 'are identified by the presence of God-language or by other items of vocabulary expressive of a moralism which derives from Yahwistic piety'.

According to McKane,[73] 'the class C material is best explained as a Yahwistic reinterpretation of an older, empirical, mundane wisdom represented by the class A material'. This Yahwistic reinterpretation is also to be seen in Prov. 1–9. McKane often found it difficult to decide whether or not to put a particular saying in class B.

70. Preuss, 'Gottesbild der ältesten Weisheit Israels'.
71. Whybray, *Book of Proverbs*, 127.
72. McKane, *Proverbs*, 11.
73. McKane, *Proverbs*, 17.

Whybray[74] questioned the value of distinguishing class B sayings, based on a sociological criterion rather than the moral and religious criteria used to distinguish between classes A and C. In his view the class B sayings should be distributed between the other two classes. He went on to argue that if the class C sayings do represent a Yahwistic reinterpretation of the class A material, one would not expect them to appear randomly scattered among the class A sayings in the Book of Proverbs. Rather,[75] 'if there was a deliberate reinterpretation of older sayings it is surely more likely that this would be carried out in a more systematic way, with the C-sayings placed where they would be most relevant and effective.' Whybray went on to investigate the occurrence of sayings which use the name Yahweh in Prov. 10:1–22:16. They comprise 55 out of the 375 sayings in this section. He found a number of instances in which a Yahweh saying modifies another, so forming a linked pair, and some in which two or more Yahweh sayings enclose two or three other proverbs to form a small cluster. In particular he argued that a quite large cluster, 15:33–16:15, which consists almost entirely of Yahweh sayings and 'royal sayings', had been deliberately positioned at the exact centre of Prov. 10:1–22:16 to form its 'theological core'. They are about Yahweh and his relationship to the king who represented Yahweh on earth.

The Problem Reconsidered

One reason why wisdom has been regarded as an alien element in the faith of Israel is the assumption of a close link between Israelite wisdom and Egyptian wisdom, with the consequent understanding of wisdom in terms of Egyptian concepts, especially that of *ma'at*. Fox[76] has shown the weakness of the parallels that have been drawn between Egyptian and Israelite wisdom thought.

Another, and to some extent connected, reason for regarding wisdom as alien to Yahwism is the view that in the Book of Proverbs there is an underlying assumption of a strict act-consequence nexus. Recently this too has been strongly challenged.[77]

Murphy has argued that the perceived problem of integrating wisdom with Yahwism is the result of a methodological error. It arises because it is assumed that God's revelation in history is to be given priority. He says,[78]

74. Whybray, 'Yahweh-Sayings', 156-57.

75. Whybray, 'Yahweh-Sayings', 157.

76. Fox, 'World Order and Ma'at', 37-48. See the discussion of this in the section 'The Egyptian Connection' in 'Acts and Consequences in Proverbs' above.

77. See the section 'Acts and Consequences in Proverbs' above.

78. Murphy, *Tree of Life*, 124.

> This view is biased. Rather, one should look directly at the wisdom experience (which is also historical!) that the worshiper of the Lord actually had. What is the religious dimension of this wisdom experience? It is an appropriation of the lessons that one can draw from day-to-day living, from the realm of personal intercourse and the surprises of creation. The dialogue between the Israelite and the environment was also a dialogue with the God who was worshiped in Israel as creator and redeemer.

Instead of taking only one perspective as determinative for Israelite thought, both ought to be taken into account as aspects of a single worldview. He quotes with approval some words of Plöger:[79]

> Would it not be astonishing if an Israel that meets us primarily as the people of its God, Yahweh, in the Old Testament, would have pursued questions about life style with a conscious exclusion of Yahweh? Even in the old wisdom period Yahweh will have certainly been known to sapiential thought, to the consideration of the expert sages, even though they will not always have used the name so readily.

Murphy also refers to the study of the ethical aspects of Prov. 10:1–22:17 and 25:1–29:27 by Delkurt.[80] He found no contradiction between wisdom ideals and the rest of the OT. This suggests that the early sages were aware of the religious premises underlying Yahwism. Delkurt also argued that it is not surprising that wisdom is silent about the *Heilsgeschichte,* since it deals with the individual's everyday experience of life and not with the cult and its traditions.

Hatton[81] argues that there is another methodological error in McKane's approach. To demonstrate this he concentrates on McKane's discussion of proverbs about bribery. Commenting on the differences in attitude displayed in these sayings McKane[82] says, 'If this is not evidence of reinterpretation, it is at least irreconcilable with the view that all of the material in Proverbs can be accommodated within a single theological structure or unitary ethos.' Later in his commentary[83] he is less cautious, suggesting that the existence of the differences 'is an aspect of the reinterpretation of old wisdom which involved

79. Murphy, 'Wisdom and Yahwism Revisited'. The quote on p. 198 is from Plöger, *Sprüche Salomos (Proverbia),* xxxv.

80. Delkurt, *Ethische Einsichten in der alttestamentlichen Spruchweisheit,* 143-61.

81. Hatton, *Contradiction in the Book of Proverbs,* 137-48.

82. McKane, *Proverbs,* 18.

83. McKane, *Proverbs,* 512.

the superseding of hard-headed, pragmatic attitudes by a stringent Yahwistic ethic in which righteousness and wickedness were sharply differentiated.'

Following a detailed study of the proverbs about bribery Hatton concludes that the different attitudes they express on the topic are more complex than McKane recognises. They do not fit easily into the two categories of 'pragmatic' and 'Yahwistic ethical'. He accepts that, as McKane said, they cannot 'be accommodated within a single theological structure or unitary ethos.' However, Hatton contends, the attempt to explain this by a diachronic theory of development, as McKane attempts to do, is not successful. Instead Hatton[84] concludes that,

> An understanding that the contradictions about bribery were incorporated within a deliberate synchronic compositional process enables a more precise understanding of the sayings on this topic in the book. Here, as elsewhere, Proverbs eschewed a monologic unitary ethos and attempted to promote a dialogue between elements of wisdom which saw bribes as useful and others that believed them to be ineffective.

While not denying that one source of Israelite wisdom is international wisdom, there has been increasing recognition that it does also have a 'home-grown' element in the wisdom formulated and transmitted in the family and the tribe.[85] This wisdom would have developed within the context of a Yahwistic worldview.

McKane's argument that his class C sentences represent a Yahwistic reinterpretation of an earlier mundane wisdom rests to a large extent on his claim that a number of terms which have positive connotations in mundane wisdom are given a pejorative sense in Yahwistic wisdom.[86] Wilson[87] has reassessed the evidence on which McKane based his claim and has argued that it is not convincing. For example, McKane argues that in mundane wisdom מְזִמָּה *(mĕzimmâ)* has the positive sense 'discretion' (Prov. 8:12b, where it occurs in the plural form מְזִמּוֹת/*mĕzimmôt*). However, in Yahwistic wisdom it is used in the pejorative sense 'deviousness, evil scheming'. It has this sense in Prov. 12:2.

> A good man obtains favour from the Lord,
> but a man of evil devices *(mᵉzimmôṯ)* he condemns.

84. Hatton, *Contradiction in the Book of Proverbs,* 148.
85. Crenshaw, 'Three Main Contexts of Israelite Learning'; Westermann, *Roots of Wisdom.*
86. McKane, *Proverbs,* 17.
87. Wilson, 'Sacred or Profane?'

He therefore argues that Prov. 24:8 is an example of Yahwistic reinterpretation since it uses the term in a pejorative sense, despite the absence of any explicit 'God-language' in the proverb:

> Whoever plans to do evil
> will be called a schemer *(mĕzimmôt).*

Wilson contends[88] that here McKane's argument is becoming circular, especially since this verse is closely linked to the following one, which uses the language of mundane wisdom,

> The devising (זִמַּת/*zimmat*) of folly is sin,
> and the scoffer is an abomination to mankind.

Morever, Wilson points out, McKane accepts that in Prov. 14:17b (one of his class A sentences) the meaning of *mĕzimmôt* is ambiguous, as the renderings of the EVV show:

> A man of quick temper acts foolishly,
> but a man of discretion is patient. (RSV)

> A man of quick temper acts foolishly,
> and a man of evil devices is hated. (ESV)

It should be noted that the ESV follows the MT, whereas in order to give the second colon a positive sense the RSV translators had to emend the text. Wilson argues that Prov. 14:17b suggests the possibility that in mundane wisdom *mĕzimmâ* had both positive and negative connotations. He also points out that in the Hebrew Bible in general the word usually has a negative sense when referring to human intentions (e.g. Job 21:27; Pss. 10:2; 37:7) and a positive sense when referring to Yahweh's intentions (e.g. Job 42:2; Jer. 23:20). Therefore it does not always have a pejorative meaning in Yahwistic piety. It is also worth noting, as Clifford[89] comments, that the three times when the word is used pejoratively in Proverbs is in the phrase אִישׁ מְזִמּוֹת *('îš mĕzimmôt).* This suggests the possibility that the negative use of the word is the result of use of a particular idiom rather than any theological reinterpretation.

88. Wilson, 'Sacred or Profane?', 321.
89. Clifford, *Proverbs*, 146.

McKane also argues[90] that Prov. 14:27 is a Yahwistic reinterpretation of Prov. 13:14:

> The teaching of the wise is a fountain of life,
> that one may turn away from the snares of death. (13:14)
>
> The fear of the LORD is a fountain of life,
> that one may turn away from the snares of death. (14:27)

Wilson, however, argues[91] that if McKane's understanding is right, it is hard to explain why Prov. 13:14 was retained and not simply replaced. He suggests that both proverbs are included because they were seen to complement each other. 'The teaching of the wise, far from being reinterpreted, is encompassed by and oriented toward the fear of the Lord.'

In Wilson's view there is no clear evidence of a sacred-profane polarity in Israel's proverbial wisdom. He agrees with Crenshaw[92] that

> The truth residing within this attempt to isolate secular wisdom is that a definite editing of earlier sayings has taken place, one in which deeply felt religious sentiments were consciously allowed to interpret older texts. However, this editing process must surely have found a kindred base upon which to work. It follows that wisdom contained a religious element from the beginning.

Conclusion

Wilson concludes that[93] 'The problem with wisdom is not whether wisdom is in part secular, but whether the theology of wisdom contradicts or complements and supplements other dimensions of Hebrew theology'. In his view it does complement and supplement the revelation of Yahweh in the Torah and the prophets because,[94]

> If there was a theological innovation in Israel's wisdom thinking, it was the recognition of an additional dimension of divine revelation. That Yah-

90. McKane, *Proverbs*, 18.
91. Wilson, 'Sacred or Profane?', 323.
92. Crenshaw, *Old Testament Wisdom*, 77.
93. Wilson, 'Sacred or Profane?', 328.
94. Wilson, 'Sacred or Profane?', 330.

weh could speak through the world of experience as well as through the mouths of his prophets was wisdom's distinctive contribution to Hebrew theology.

God in Proverbs

God is referred to directly in ninety-four verses in the Book of Proverbs.[95] God is also referred to anaphorically in Prov. 2:2-8; 3:6, 20, 34; 8:26-31 (represented in English translation as he/him/his). In Prov. 23:11 God is referred to as 'their Redeemer' and in Prov. 24:12 as 'he who weighs the heart' and 'he who keeps watch over your soul'. There is debate over whether 'the righteous one' in 21:12 refers to God. This means that nearly 12 per cent of the book's 915 verses refer to God.

Nearly all the references to God use the divine tetragrammaton ('Yahweh'), the name by which God was known as the one who was in covenant relationship with Israel. The general term אֱלֹהִים (*'ĕlōhîm,* 'god') is used twice with clear reference to Yahweh (2:5; 3:4), and on two other occasions (25:2; 30:9). The singular form אֱלוֹהַּ *('ĕlôah)* is used in Prov. 30:5. The uses in Prov. 30:5, 9 are in a section attributed to a non-Israelite source.

Monotheism

There is an implicit monotheism in Proverbs. No gods other than Yahweh are mentioned. The consistent use of 'Yahweh' to designate God makes it clear that only the God of Israel is in mind in the book. Here there is a contrast with the wisdom literature of Egypt and Mesopotamia, in which the deity is usually referred to by a generic term instead of a proper name. This is not because of any monotheistic tendency. As Boström argues,[96]

> The reason for the use of the generic term for the deity which is so common in wisdom texts, is rather that the specification intentionally is left open to the reader and to the situation. These generic designations of god functioned in a way parallel to a blank space in a liturgical text which is to be filled in with the appropriate expression by the supplicant.

95. Boström, *God of the Sage,* 33. He gives the following breakdown of occurrences: 21 times in Prov. 1–9; 57 in 10:1–22:16; 5 in 22:17–24:34; 7 in chs 25–29; and 4 in chs 30–31.

96. Boström, *God of the Sages,* 44-45.

It was the polytheistic context in Egypt and Mesopotamia which required the use of a generic term rather than a specific divine name.

Yahweh as Creator

Yahweh is spoken of as Creator of the world in Prov. 3:19-20 and 8:22-31. The assumption in these poetic passages is that Yahweh is the sole, sovereign Creator. Their purpose, however, is not to exalt the Creator but, rather, to enhance the status of wisdom. Proverbs 3:19-20 makes the point that it was by wisdom that Yahweh created (v. 19) and sustains (v. 20) the world. The main point of Prov. 8:22-31 is that Woman Wisdom is transcendent, being before and above all creatures. Because she was brought into existence before the creation of the world, her presence (in whatever role) at, and delight in, the creation of the world means that she has a relative omniscience that gives authority to her teaching.[97] God's challenge to Job,[98] 'Where were you when I laid the foundations of the earth?' was meant to emphasise Job's lack of knowledge and understanding. Wisdom could respond to it by saying, 'I was there beside the Creator'.

There is no mention of the creation of the world in the sentence literature. Instead the emphasis is on Yahweh as the Creator of human beings (14:31; 16:4; 17:5; 20:12; 22:2; 29:13; with a slightly different emphasis in 16:11). Proverbs 14:31; 17:5; 22:2; and 29:13 state that Yahweh created the poor person as well as the rich and powerful and that the poor therefore must be given dignity and treated fairly. Yahweh's creation of everything (and implied sovereignty over all) is the basis for a warning of punishment to the wicked (16:4). The meaning of Prov. 20:12 is not immediately clear, but most commentators[99] take it to mean that since Yahweh has created the ear and the eye they should be used to gain wisdom. The theme of Prov. 16:11 is not so much creation, but the Creator's concern with the ethics of the market-place. This is expressed by saying that the weights used in buying and selling are 'his work'. Boström summarises the function of the theme of Yahweh's creation of humans in these sentences by saying,[100] 'Creation functions as the philosophical basis for social ethics.'

97. See the discussion of this point by Waltke, *Proverbs 1–15*, 79.

98. Job 38:4.

99. See the discussion in Whybray, *Proverbs*, 293-94.

100. Boström, *God of the Sages*, 60.

Yahweh's Transcendence

The understanding of Yahweh as the sole Creator leads naturally to the idea of his transcendence. To say he is transcendent is to assert that[101] 'he is not bound in either his nature or his scope of activity by any spatial and/or temporal limitation'. There are a number of ways in which Yahweh's transcendence is expressed in the Book of Proverbs besides the theme of Yahweh as Creator.[102]

First there is the fact that anthropomorphisms are almost completely lacking in Proverbs. Then there is the fact that in Proverbs Yahweh never addresses humans directly. This might not be expected in the sentence literature, but there is no reason why it should not happen in the instruction genre. Instead, in Prov. 1–9 it is personified Wisdom who speaks to people as Yahweh's representative. In these two ways a distance is kept between Yahweh and human beings. To this can be added the fact that Yahweh's ways are incomprehensible to humans (20:24; 25:2).

In Proverbs it is clear that Yahweh is the supreme Judge and guarantor of justice in the world. This is a role that only a transcendent God could fulfil since it requires detailed knowledge and understanding of each individual and each specific situation. There are proverbs which assert that Yahweh knows everything that happens (5:21; 15:3; 24:12) and that he even knows a person's innermost thoughts (15:11; 24:11-12) and motives (16:2).

Yahweh's Immanence

In Proverbs, Yahweh's transcendence means that he is not limited by anything in the world. It does not mean that he is not active and involved in the world. There are a number of proverbs which depict Yahweh as a God who relates personally to individuals and is concerned about, and active in, the world.

It is a characteristic of Yahweh in the Law[103] and the Prophets[104] that he is the defender of the widow, the orphan and the alien sojourner. In Proverbs Yahweh is said to be the defender of the 'poor' in general (19:17; 22:22-23), with the widow (15:25) and the orphan (23:10-11) being mentioned specifically. Yahweh's wider concern for social justice is expressed in some sentences. One issue

101. Waltke, *Proverbs 1–15*, 70.
102. Boström, *God of the Sages*, 142-92.
103. Exod. 22:22-24; Deut. 10:17-18.
104. Isa. 1:23; Ezek. 22:7; Mal. 3:5.

that is referred to several times is that of accurate measures (11:1; 16:11; 20:10, 23). Again, there is a parallel with the Law[105] and the Prophets.[106]

Yahweh's Relationship with the Righteous

Yahweh is said to have a special relationship with those who are 'righteous'. Boström[107] argues that in Proverbs the term 'righteous' (which occurs about 60 times) always denotes both correct behaviour (as taught by the sages) and obedience to Yahweh. The 'righteous' are those who live rightly because they are obedient both to Yahweh and to the teaching of the sages. The righteous person is described in a number of ways, the most prominent being one 'who fears Yahweh'.[108] There are a number of sayings which depict Yahweh as the protector of the righteous (2:5-8; 18:10; 29:25) and as the one who grants them success and well-being (3:5-10, 33-34; 10:3; 16:20; 28:25).

Yahweh's relationship with the righteous is sometimes expressed in intimate terms. They are treated as his 'confidants', those who belong to his סוֹד *(sōd),* his circle of trusted intimates (3:32). This is the language of friendship. Yahweh is also said to 'love' the righteous (15:9). This love is compared to that of a father for his son in whom he delights (3:11-12). The human response to this should be to 'trust' Yahweh completely and live in a way which 'acknowledges' (or 'knows') him (3:5-6), using a verb which implies a relationship with the person 'known'.[109] In 2:5 and 9:10 knowing God is put in parallel with 'the fear of the Yahweh'. As discussed in the commentary[110] there is no reason to assume that in Proverbs this concept has become purely moral in content and lost the connotation of religious awe and love and devotion to Yahweh which it has elsewhere in the Hebrew Bible. Proverbs is not concerned simply to inculcate a pattern of prudential moral living. It makes clear that what is needed is *godly* living, a pattern of life which flows from living in a loving and trustful relationship with Yahweh.

Kidner[111] rightly comments that Proverbs' function 'is to put godliness into working clothes; to name business and society as spheres in which we are to acquit ourselves with credit to our Lord'. This is an expression of the intimacy

105. Lev. 19:36; Deut. 25:13-16, note the phrase 'abomination to the LORD'; cf. Prov. 11:1.

106. Amos 8:5.

107. Boström, *God of the Sages,* 213-25.

108. Both the 'righteous' and those who 'fear Yahweh' are contrasted with 'the wicked'; e.g. 10:27-28.

109. See the comment on 'know' under 1:1-7.

110. See under 1:1-7.

111. Kidner, *Proverbs,* 35.

of the relationship with Yahweh. It is not limited to the obviously 'religious' aspects of life. It pervades the whole of life.

The Personification of Wisdom in Proverbs

There has been a great deal of debate about the nature and origin of the personification of Wisdom as a woman in Prov. 1:20-33; 8:1-36; 9:1-6. Some scholars have argued that in Prov. 8:22-36 Wisdom is not a 'personification' but a 'hypostasis'. A major problem with this debate is, as Murphy[112] points out, that 'there is no agreement on the meaning of these relatively abstract words as they apply to wisdom.' Ringgren's study is still one of the most comprehensive presentations of the view that Wisdom is a hypostasis, 'a concrete being, self-existent beside God'[113] in Prov. 8. However, he does not provide a clear case for his view[114] that in Prov. 1:20-33; 8:1-21; and 9:1-6 Wisdom is presented in terms of 'allegories or poetic personifications' while asserting that in Prov. 8:22-31 she is a true hypostasis of Yahweh's attribute of wisdom. It is also questionable whether the concept of 'hypostasis' would have been meaningful or conceivable in ancient Israel given the normative monolatry of Israelite religion. Personification, the personalizing of impersonal things or abstract concepts, however, is well-attested in the Hebrew Bible and other ancient Near Eastern literature.

A variety of foreign deities and mythological figures have been proposed as the prototypes for the figure of personified wisdom found in Proverbs. Others have suggested more down-to-earth sources.

The Egyptian Goddess Maʿat

Maʿat was the Egyptian goddess of truth/justice (which were a single concept in Egyptian thought). Kayatz[115] argued that Maʿat was the prototype for the personified figure of Wisdom in Prov. 8. In support of this she listed several features that they had in common.

- The mutual love formula ('I love him who loves me' and variants).
- The self-predication formula ('I am X . . .').

112. Murphy, 'Personification', 222.
113. Ringgren, *Word and Wisdom*, 104.
114. Ringgren, *Word and Wisdom*, 99.
115. Kayatz, *Studien zu Proverbien 1–9*.

- Wisdom's existence before creation.
- Wisdom as a child of God playing before him.
- Wisdom's service in giving life and protection.
- Wisdom as the effective power behind kings.
- Wisdom's offering of life in one hand and riches and honour in the other.
- The exhortation to wear wisdom as a neck ornament.

Fox[116] questions the relevance of these 'parallels'. None of these features are exclusive to Maʿat. All have parallels in various proclamations of gods and kings, and not only in Egypt. Moreover, there is no recorded speech by Maʿat and, while there are examples of 'playing' in Egyptian iconography, there is no known example of Maʿat herself shown playing before a god. Although the concept of *maʿat* was deeply embedded in Egyptian religion and was a foundation principle of its society, as a goddess Maʿat was never popular or well-known. Unlike some other Egyptian deities, she never became well-known outside Egypt either. Fox thinks it unlikely that the scattered references to Maʿat in Egyptian texts could have provided ancient sages, Egyptian or Israelite, with a figure that would make a credible prototype for the figure of Wisdom in Proverbs.

Kayatz drew a parallel between Wisdom offering life in her right hand and riches and honour in her left hand (Prov. 3:16) and Maʿat being depicted with the *ankh* (a symbol of life) in one hand and a sceptre in the other. However, Camp[117] argues that it was the prerogative of most ancient deities, and indeed of kings, to bestow life and wealth. She also raises something which is a problem for all suggestions that a goddess figure lies behind the personification of Wisdom in Proverbs. This is the fact that, as recognised by Kayatz, the figure of personified Wisdom in Prov. 1:20-33 does not look at all like a goddess but more like an Israelite prophet. Kayatz was forced to separate the two figures, arguing that in Prov. 1 Wisdom is only a 'poetic personification' but that Wisdom in Prov. 8 is a case of 'hypostatizaton'. Apart from the unsatisfactory nature of this expedient of separating the two figures, attempts to define what is meant by an 'hypostasis' have not led to any consensus. In any case, it is doubtful whether ancient Israelite sages would have recognised the difference between 'literary personification' and 'hypostatization'. As von Rad[118] commented, 'Even if one feels obliged to speak of a hypostasis, this does not absolve one from answering the question of how Israel actually conceived of such a hypostasis.'

116. Fox, 'World Order and Maʿat', 37-48.
117. Camp, *Wisdom and the Feminine*, 29-34.
118. von Rad, *Wisdom in Israel*, 144.

Sinnott[119] makes some other points in a critique of Kayatz's proposal. She notes that, although Maʿat is personified in some Egyptian literature, Maʿat is never personified in Egyptian wisdom literature. Kayatz drew attention to the exhortation to keep 'sound wisdom and discretion' as an 'adornment for your neck' (3:22). A similar exhortation is made about parental teaching (1:9; 6:21) and 'steadfast love and faithfulness' (3:3). She noted that the Egyptian judge who called himself 'the priest of Maʿat' wore a chain around his neck with a symbol of Maʿat attached to it. Sinnott makes the point that the two neck adornments have very different purposes. For the Egyptian judge it is a mark of rank and authority. In Proverbs the purpose of the neck-wear is to make sure that the wearer does not forget the teaching or the practice of the virtue mentioned. Also, the wearing of neck ornaments was not unique to Egypt but was common in many cultures. In fact, as Sinnott notes, Day[120] has argued with regard to this neck adornment imagery that a better claim can be made for it being a free adaptation of Deut. 11:18. Here Moses exhorts his hearers to 'lay up these words of mine in your heart and in your soul (נֶפֶשׁ/*nepeš*)'. He points out that *nepeš* can be taken to mean 'neck' as seems to be the case in the parallelism of Prov. 3:22 and that there is a close parallelism between Deut. 11:18-19 and Prov. 6:21-22.

With regard to the motif of Wisdom offering life in Proverbs, Sinnott observes that in Egyptian literature allusions to 'life' usually occur in writings about death, especially in rituals and cults concerned with death and achieving life beyond death. There is no reflection of this kind of context in Proverbs.

The Goddess Isis

In Hellenistic times Isis became the most popular goddess in the Near East and the Aegean. She was regarded as the giver of the first laws and principles. Because she was consummately wise, she was given the epithet Sophia (Wisdom). Her virtues and powers were proclaimed in 'aretalogies' (hymns in praise of gods). Although these had their origins in Egyptian texts and traditions they were mostly written in Greek. The following lines[121] from the great aretalogy from Cyme have some similarities with Prov. 8.

(3a) I, Isis, am the ruler of all lands,
(3b) and I was educated by Hermes . . .

119. Sinnott, *Personification*, 38-41.
120. Day, 'Foreign Semitic Influence', 68.
121. Fox, *Proverbs 1–9*, 336-37.

(4) I set down laws for men and legislated that which none can alter.
(5) I am the eldest daughter of Kronos.
(16) I have made justice powerful . . .
(28) I have made justice more powerful than gold and silver.

Knox[122] first noted some similarities between Isis and Wisdom in Prov. 8:1-31. He suggested that this text was composed as an 'orthodox' response to the attractions of Isis worship. A major problem with this suggestion is that the Hellenistic Isis religion began to spread widely only in the late third century BC, which is too late for it to have had an influence on even the latest redaction of the Book of Proverbs. What is more, it is the aretalogies which provide the basis for suggesting any link between Isis and Wisdom, and these are not attested before the first century BC.

A Canaanite Goddess

Albright[123] suggested that behind the figure of Wisdom in Proverbs lies a Canaanite goddess of wisdom. She might have been a hypostatisation of an attribute of the Canaanite high god El. There are references to El's wisdom in the texts from Ugarit. Albright later[124] supported this suggestion by arguing that there are numerous 'Canaanitisms' in Prov. 8 and 9. This includes the unusual form of the Hebrew word 'wisdom' in 9:1 (חָכְמוֹת/*ḥokmôt,* also in 1:20). Albright also appeals to a passage in the Aramaic *Words of Ahiqar* in which wisdom seems to be personified, if the damaged text has been correctly restored.

Whybray[125] has criticised Albright's arguments in some detail. He shows that there are many fewer 'Canaanitisms' in Prov. 8 and 9 than Albright claimed. In particular, the case for *ḥokmôt* being a Canaanite feminine singular form is not conclusive, and other credible explanations have been given for it. The passages about El's wisdom in the Ugaritic texts show that El, who was wise, could confer wisdom on others, but do not show that wisdom was regarded as a personal being distinct from El. The probable personification of wisdom in *The Words of Ahiqar,* a sixth-century Aramaic text, which probably originated in Mesopotamia, provides no evidence of such personification in Canaanite thought. Moreover, there is no known Canaanite goddess of wisdom, nor has

122. Knox, 'Divine Wisdom'.
123. Albright, 'Goddess of Life and Wisdom'.
124. Albright, 'Some Canaanite-Phoenician Sources'.
125. Whybray, *Wisdom in Proverbs,* 83-87.

any Canaanite wisdom literature survived. Albright simply assumed these existed.

Also, as Fox[126] points out, personified Wisdom in Proverbs shows none of the characteristics of the Canaanite goddesses about which something is known. In particular, she is not sexually aggressive or desirable, nor does she represent the realm of fertility and vegetation.

An Israelite Goddess

Lang[127] developed a variant version of Albright's thesis. He argues that the origin of the figure of personified Wisdom in Proverbs is an Israelite goddess who was worshipped in the pre-exilic era. She was a daughter of Yahweh. It may be that Athirat was her mother, but Lang thinks it more likely that she was a 'motherless deity' like the Greek Athena and the Egyptian Thoth. With the rise of the 'Yahweh-alone' party, especially in the late pre-exilic period, the worship of other deities was suppressed. In the post-exilic era it was possible for the orthodox sages to take over poems that were originally about this goddess and apply them to a personification of Yahweh's wisdom.

There is virtually no evidence to support Lang's thesis. The deities mentioned in the OT as worshipped by polytheistic Israelites were members of the Canaanite pantheon. As already noted, there is no evidence for a Canaanite goddess of wisdom, let alone a specifically Israelite one. The only evidence that Lang puts forward to support the idea that polytheistic texts lie behind the poems about Wisdom in Prov. 1–9 is the use of the plural קְדֹשִׁים (*qĕdōšîm*, holy ones) in Prov. 9:10. This is usually taken to be a 'plural of majesty' or 'plural of abstraction', so that the verse is translated,

> The fear of the Lord is the beginning of wisdom,
> and the knowledge of the Holy One is insight.

Lang suggests that here the name Yahweh has replaced an original reference to 'the gods'. In support of this he argues that restoring this reference and the plural sense of 'the holy ones' gives a perfectly balanced couplet. He also suggests that Yahweh may have replaced a reference to El in 8:22. The weakness in all this is that he builds his hypothesis on what are no more than conjectures.

126. Fox, *Proverbs 1–9*, 335.
127. Lang, *Wisdom and the Book of Proverbs.*

The Babylonian ummānu

Clifford[128] argues that the personified figure of Wisdom in Proverbs is derived from the pre- and post-flood sages of Babylonian mythology who were the bringers of culture to the human race.[129] According to a passage from the *Babyloniaca* of Berossus (third century BC), preserved by Eusebius of Caesarea in his *Chronicle*, an awesome being named Oannes came out of the sea to the Babylonians at a time when they lived an animal-like existence. He taught them language, intellectual skills and a civilised way of life. In addition he wrote about creation and politics. This story is illuminated by a document from Uruk which was published by van Dijk in 1962. This is a list of seven pre-flood and seven post-flood kings. Each pre-flood king has an associated *apkallu* and each post-flood king an associated *ummānu*. The *apkallu* are divine beings, and the first is called U'an, which is very probably the origin of the name Oannes. The post-flood kings are historical rulers, and the *ummānu* are human sages, some of whom have the names of known authors. The last of them, from the reign of Esarhaddon, is identified as 'Aba'enlildari, whom the Arameans call Ahiqar'. This identification, Clifford argues, shows that the Babylonian tradition of the 'culture bringers' was known in Syria-Palestine. He suggests that this mythology is the general background for personified Wisdom in Proverbs.

In support of his case Clifford argues that the Hebrew word אָמוֹן *('āmôn)* in Prov. 8:30a, the meaning of which has been much debated, should be vocalised as *'ommān* and recognised as a loanword from the Akkadian *ummānu*. Wisdom would then be understood as saying, 'I was at his side as a (heavenly) sage', that is, as a heavenly figure who mediates to humans the knowledge they need in order to live as their Creator intends they should.

Clifford's suggestion provides a plausible background for Prov. 8:22-31. It does not, however, provide much illumination for the other aspects of personified Wisdom presented in this poem and the others in Prov. 1–9.

A Literary Creation

Personification is a literary device which is found in many cultures. Sinnott[130] notes that in the Hebrew Bible its use is not confined to portrayals of Wisdom.

128. Clifford, *Proverbs*, 23-28.

129. Greenfield, 'Seven Pillars of Wisdom', suggests that the *apkallu* mythology lies behind the 'seven pillars' of Prov. 9:1.

130. Sinnott, *Personification*, 19.

Human actions are sometimes attributed to abstract qualities and inanimate entities, for example: 'Steadfast love and faithfulness meet; righteousness and peace kiss each other' (Ps. 85:10 [Heb. 11]); 'Wine is a mocker, strong drink a brawler' (Prov. 20:1). However, in the case of Wisdom the personification is developed to a far greater extent than elsewhere in the Bible. Sinnott[131] sees this as a literary creation in which 'Wisdom as a personified figure gives bodily form to an abstraction, with its attendant physical imagery, and links the senses with the understanding. The wisdom authors use this convention to convey to their audiences abstract knowledge in an attractive form.' Sinnott sees personification as inseparable from symbolism. A symbol is something which points beyond itself.[132] By means of personification the Wisdom of God is presented 'symbolically rather than anthropomorphically or metaphysically'. It points to a God who communicates with all creation and with humans in particular.[133]

Sinnott argues that the creation of the figure of personified Wisdom was a response to the fall of Jerusalem in 587 BC and the subsequent exile of many Israelites in Babylon. She gives four arguments to support this view.[134]

1. The Israelites' understanding of how Yahweh acted for them before the fall of Jerusalem did not enable them to address effectively the resulting crisis.
2. Similarities between Prov. 1–9 and the Priestly account in Genesis suggest an exilic or post-exilic dating for these chapters.
3. Wisdom's appearances in unnamed public places suggests either places of no significance or places in foreign territory.
4. Wisdom's speeches use motifs and styles found in the exilic prophets.

The strength of these arguments is debatable. It is clear that the crisis of the exile did raise important theological questions. Sinnott does not discuss how these are dealt with in the prophetic corpus. Ezekiel's vision of the glory of Yahweh by the Chebar canal gives assurance that the presence of Yahweh is not tied to the temple in Jerusalem but can be experienced even in exile. His oracle about Yahweh giving the people 'a new heart and a new spirit' (Ezek. 36:22-38) promises a new covenant relationship, as does Jeremiah in Jer. 31:31-34. In Isa. 40–55 there is the promise of a 'new exodus'. What evidence is there that this response to the crisis was considered inadequate and that some other response

131. Sinnott, *Personification,* 21.
132. Sinnott, *Personification,* 22.
133. Sinnott, *Personification,* 24, see also 175.
134. Sinnott, *Personification,* 33.

was needed? It is not impossible that the sages felt a need to make a response to the crisis of the exile, but nothing in Proverbs in general, or Prov. 1–9 in particular, gives any clear hint of this as a pressing issue for the sages. Indeed, nothing in Prov. 1–9 hints at any kind of social breakdown. On the contrary, as Fox[135] says, 'The Personification poems breathe an atmosphere of social and ideological security. They do not do this polemically, as an antidote to decay and uncertainty, but as something taken for granted.'

Sinnott has very little to say about the similarities between the Priestly material in Genesis and Prov. 1–9.[136] She suggests that the idea of humans being created in the 'image' and 'likeness' of God may have been 'the theological point of departure for personified Wisdom' but does not expand on this suggestion. Nothing in Proverbs gives it any clear support. She notes that Gen. 1:1–2:3 is theocentric whereas Gen. 2:5-25 is anthropomorphic. Again, there is no discussion of the relevance of this to the personification of Wisdom. It is arguable that the personification of the Wisdom of God is closer to the anthropomorphism of Gen. 2–3 than the transcendence of God in Gen. 1.

The only explicit reference to the Genesis creation accounts in Prov. 1–9 is, as Sinnott notes, in Prov. 3:18, where it is said of wisdom 'She is a tree of life to those who lay hold of her'. This, of course, does not refer to the Priestly material but to what is widely regarded as the older, pre-exilic, 'J' material.

In a book which lacks any geographical or historical references the fact that Wisdom appears in unnamed places does not seem at all strange or in need of explanation. It seems a natural reflection of the universal nature of the wisdom tradition.

Sinnott lists[137] a number of 'prophetic echoes' in Prov. 1:20-33. However, a number of the references she gives come from oracles that are widely held to be pre-exilic (Hos. 5:6; 8:5; 11:2; Mic. 3:4; Isa. 1:15; Hab. 2:6). This undermines her claim that Wisdom's speeches reflect motifs and styles particularly linked with the exilic period.

With regard to echoes of the prophets in Wisdom's speeches in general Fox[138] suggests that this is not the result of any direct influence of prophetic usages on these speeches. Rather it is because prophets sometimes take on the role of a teacher. Teachers, like the parent in Proverbs, sometimes have to warn, threaten and verbally chastise their hearers, and also insist on their authority. He concludes that, 'At most, prophetic usages provide a few pigments for Wis-

135. Fox, *Proverbs 1–9*, 342.
136. Sinnott, *Personification*, 6.
137. Sinnott, *Personification*, 69-70.
138. Fox, *Proverbs 1–9*, 334.

dom's portrait.' While seeing some prophetic characteristics in Wisdom, her use of reproof and threat and her claim to authority, McKane[139] notes that she does not speak like a prophet. Commenting on Wisdom's speech in 1:22-33 he says, 'Her vocabulary is that of the wisdom teacher, not that of the prophet, and there are still traces of the Instruction in this piece.'

It may be the case that personified Wisdom in Prov. 1–9 is a literary creation, but Sinnott has not made a convincing case for the crisis of the exile being the cause for this act of creation.

Israelite Women

In Proverbs Wisdom is personified as a woman. No doubt one reason for this is that in Hebrew the noun for wisdom (חָכְמָה/*ḥokmâ*) is feminine in grammatical gender, as are some of the other important nouns which are used in parallel with it, e.g. בִּינָה (*bînâ*, 'understanding'), עָרְמָה (*'ormâ*, 'prudence'). Camp[140] has argued that the figure of personified Wisdom in Prov. 1–9 is a literary creation based on several roles that were actually fulfilled by Israelite women.

The status of women in ancient Israel was largely related to their fulfilment of the roles of wife and mother. They didn't have any explicitly legitimated authority in the public sphere. However, they seemed to have had a rather high status in the domestic realm, where they could exercise both authority and power. With regard to Proverbs Camp[141] points out that 'where mother imagery occurs, the connotation is neither biological nor theological but rather educational'. In a number of places the mother is depicted as having an authority equal to that of the father in passing on wisdom as their teaching roles are mentioned in parallel (1:8; 6:20; 10:1; 15:20; 23:22-25). Particularly striking is the instruction given to King Lemuel by his mother (31:1-9), which has no parallel in the Egyptian instructions. No mother imagery is applied to personified Wisdom in Proverbs, and there is only passing mention of her children in the poem about the 'woman of worth' (31:28). It seems that the sages didn't consider such imagery as necessary for these female figures to have authority either in the home or the public sphere. 'In this sense', says Camp,[142] 'the woman is imaged in this book as a virtual equal of the man'. She argues that personified Wisdom and the 'woman of worth' provide literary models for women idealised as creative,

139. McKane, *Proverbs*, 276.

140. Camp, *Wisdom and the Feminine*. See especially pp. 79-147.

141. Camp, *Wisdom and the Feminine*, 81-82.

142. Camp, *Wisdom and the Feminine*, 82.

authoritative individuals who are not defined primarily by their role in human reproduction. It is the teaching role of the mother that contributes implicitly to the figure of personified Wisdom.

On the basis of examining depictions of women in narratives in the OT, Camp argues that there are two main recurrent images of the wife in ancient Israel. The first is the picture of the wife as the manager of the household. This is idealised in Prov. 31:10-31. The OT narratives suggest that when a woman did this job well it gave her some authority. The second image is that of the wife as a counsellor who could influence her husband in the areas where he had decision-making authority. The narratives in which this image is found cover a range of dates and depict women of different social status in a range of different situations. This leads Camp[143] to agree with Otwell that it seems 'likely that the motif of the wise wife reflected a commonplace reality in ancient Israelite culture'.

Camp notes that all the female figures in the Book of Proverbs give advice of some sort, whether it is good advice or bad. They are all evaluated on the basis of their advice rather than on the basis of child-bearing. The position of the husband of the 'woman of worth' among the elders of land who sit in the city gate arises from her abilities and activities in the home. The home is 'her house' (31:21, 27), defined by the way she manages it. Her works sing her praises in the gates (31:31). Through her influence on her husband she influences the way the land is governed (31:23). Camp[144] argues that if the 'woman of worth' is a 'crystallized vision of the finer qualities of a real woman' which represents 'a universal type of wisdom' then it is possible that 'Israel's appropriation of personified Wisdom too, was influenced by features of their experience and perception of the counsellor-wife, perhaps mediated through such literary images as the woman of worth, Abigail, and others.'

The language of human love is pervasive in Prov. 1–9. Camp notes similarities between the love language of these chapters and in the Song of Songs. In both 'seeking and finding' is a prominent motif. The image of a strong, independent woman seeking her lover which is present in the Song of Songs is also found in Egyptian love poetry. There is no need to appeal to parallels in texts about goddesses to put it in an ancient Near Eastern cultural and literary setting. In Proverbs Wisdom goes out seeking for those who will love her in a way similar to the woman in the Song of Songs, and brings them to her house (8:34; cf. Song 8:2). However, whereas in the Song of Songs it is primarily the

143. Camp, *Wisdom and the Feminine,* 87. The quote is from Otwell, *And Sarah Laughed,* 108.

144. Camp, *Wisdom and the Feminine,* 93.

woman who 'seeks and finds' (but note Song 8:13), in Proverbs it is the man who is exhorted to seek and find Wisdom (8:17, 36). The depiction of Wisdom as the beloved is clear in Prov. 4:6-9; 7:4 and, to a lesser extent, in Prov. 8:17. It has been argued that the imagery of jewels and precious metals that is used to express the value of Wisdom in Prov. 3:14-15 and 8:19 implies a royal setting for the figure of Wisdom. However, this kind of imagery is found in Song 5:11, 14-15 and in ancient Near Eastern love poetry in general.

One of the genres of ancient Near Eastern love poetry is self-description. It is used by the woman in the Song of Songs to justify or defend herself (1:5-6; 8:8-10) or to provoke the admiration and active response of her lover (2:1-2). The self-description of Wisdom in Prov. 8:6-21 makes no reference to physical beauty, but it does serve the same function as the self-descriptions in Song of Songs — to justify the speaker and to motivate the hearer to respond to her. It is clear that self-presentation by deities or rulers is not the only possible ancient Near Eastern context in which to seek the origins of that motif as an aspect of the personification of Wisdom in Prov. 1–9. Camp[145] concludes that, 'In their experience of the poetry of human love, then, the Israelite readers found at least one way to appropriate the assertive words of Wisdom in Prov. 8.'

Camp[146] argues that the two stories of the wise women of Tekoa (2 Sam. 14) and of Abel (2 Sam. 20) provide evidence of 'a non-regular but recurrent leadership role for women in pre-monarchic Israel.' She suggests that it is probable that this continued in some form under the monarchy and that the 'great woman' of Shunem (2 Kgs. 4:8-10; 8:1-6) may provide evidence of this. The wise woman of Abel clearly has a leadership role. Both women make effective use of proverbial language to influence their audience. In the stories they represent the values of justice, well-being, life and 'the heritage of Yahweh.' These are covenant values, but also values upheld by Wisdom (2:20-22; 8:18-21, 32-36; 22:22-23; 23:10-11). To a considerable extent their stories exemplify Prov. 25:15:

> With patience a ruler may be persuaded,
> and a soft tongue will break a bone.

While accepting that there is not enough evidence to speak of any 'literary dependence' of personified Wisdom on these 'wise women' stories, Camp thinks that they do provide a cultural context for Israel's theological appropriation of a female figure for personified Wisdom who makes the claims of Prov. 8:14-16.

A recurrent motif in stories in the OT which include women is the way in

145. Camp, *Wisdom and the Feminine,* 103.

146. Camp, *Wisdom and the Feminine,* 120.

which they use indirect means to achieve their goals. Of course, their exclusion from the established hierarchies of authority and power in their society made this necessary. Tamar and Ruth use their sexuality in asserting the rights of the under-privileged. Their stories also involve appeal for justice in the city gates. Rebekah and Esther use the preparation of meals to achieve their ends. Because the notion of indirection is an essential characteristic of proverbs Camp[147] suggests that 'female imagery can be seen to be extraordinarily apt for the figurative presentation of wisdom.'

Camp also draws attention to two examples of women authenticating a written tradition. The prophet Huldah authenticated the newly found book of the law (2 Kgs. 22:11-20). Esther authenticated the written edict regarding the observance of the Feast of Purim (Esth. 9:32). The fact that women could have this role in Israel provides a context in which the female personified figure of Wisdom could both represent and authenticate the written wisdom tradition as she does in Proverbs.

Not all Camp's arguments are of equal weight, but she does build a strong case for the view that the roles which women played in ancient Israel provide the primary context in which the creation of the literary figure of personified Wisdom is understandable. The suggestion that Wisdom is a personification which incorporates relevant roles that women fulfilled in Israel is at least as plausible as any of the other suggestions and avoids the more-or-less unsupported hypotheses that some of them require.

Camp argues that personified figure of Wisdom in Proverbs has more than a literary function. It is[148] 'an *authoritative religious symbol,* whose function it is to mediate between lived experience and a particular world view.' She goes on to argue that this is best understood in the post-exilic context when in the Judean worldview, Yahweh seemed increasingly distant. The figure of personified Wisdom then functioned as a mediator between God and humanity.

In particular, Camp[149] argues that with the end of the monarchy the 'father's house' emerged as 'the source of community-wide decision-making authority and as a social structure providing a definitive symbol for Israel's collective identity'. With the home defining the character and identity of society, the woman plays an important role in defining society, since she defines the character and identity of the home. This is the picture given regarding the 'woman of worth' in Prov. 31:10-31. Female Wisdom both reflects this and legitimates female authority. Also, during the monarchic period the king had been

147. Camp, *Wisdom and the Feminine,* 140.
148. Camp, *Wisdom and the Feminine,* 228 (her italics).
149. Camp, *Wisdom and the Feminine,* 261.

the most important mediating figure between God and the people, mediating his blessing and his revelation to the covenant people.[150] Wisdom was able to fill the gap left by the absence of the king. Some of the female characteristics discussed above made personified female Wisdom a viable mediator figure in the context of post-exilic Judah.

This proposal for the historical and social setting of the literary creation of the figure of personified Wisdom is a possible one. However, it is vulnerable to the criticism from Fox quoted above with regard to Sinnot's somewhat similar proposal. The poems about personified Wisdom do not seem to reflect, or be directed towards, a situation of social and ideological uncertainty. Camp thinks that the social importance of the family that she proposes for the post-exilic Judah is a something of a return to the situation before the rise of the monarchy. It is possible that she over-estimates the effect of the monarchy on the role of the family in Israelite society. Indeed, the ability of family structure to survive the experience of the collapse of Judah and the exile may be a testimony to its role and strength under the monarchy. In that case the figure of personified female Wisdom could have been a literary creation of the pre-exilic era.

The Personification of Wisdom: Conclusion

Personification is quite a common literary technique, especially in poetry. In the Hebrew Bible cities and countries are often referred to as if they are persons. Abstract concepts such as faithfulness, justice, love, peace, righteousness, truth and uprightness are all personified (Ps. 85:10 [Heb. 11]; Isa. 59:14). In the Egyptian tale[151] 'Truth and Falsehood', truth and falsehood are personified as two brothers in an extended allegory.

There is one place in ancient Near Eastern literature outside Proverbs where wisdom may be personified, in Aramaic *Ahiqar*[152] lines 94b-95, but the text is uncertain and its interpretation depends on how it is reconstructed. Fox[153] accepts the personification here, while Murphy[154] does not. On the basis of a fresh reconstruction of the fragmentary text of *Ahiqar* which separates line 94 from line 95 Bledsoe[155] concludes, 'in light of the new data and a fresh assess-

150. Camp, *Wisdom and the Feminine*, 282.

151. Lichtheim, *AEL* 2:211-14.

152. Lindenberger, *Aramaic Proverbs of Ahiqar*, 68-69; 'Ahiqar', 499.

153. Fox, *Proverbs 1–9*, 332-33.

154. Murphy, *Proverbs*, 279.

155. Bledsoe, 'Can *Ahiqar* Tell Us Anything about Personified Wisdom?', 137.

ment of the material, it seems evident that the Aramaic book of *Ahiqar* cannot tell us about personified Wisdom'.

Fox[156] points out that 'inchoate personification' of wisdom is to be found a number of times in Proverbs; 'Various metaphors speak about wisdom as if she were a woman without cohering into a consistent woman figure or governing the development of the passage as a whole.' This, he suggests, 'shows that the full-fledged personification of wisdom is an organic literary development in the Book of Proverbs'.

It is very probable that the feminine gender of the noun 'wisdom' in Hebrew led to the personification of Wisdom as a woman. This would have been helped by the reality of 'wise women' in Israel and the fact that in Israelite society women fulfilled various roles that could appropriately be assigned to Wisdom. As a literary construct personified Wisdom is able to combine different roles that might never be expected to be found together in any one human person. In Prov. 8 in particular some of the claims of Wisdom transcend the purely human and here there may well be incorporated elements from concepts to do with deities and the mythological 'culture bringers'. The personification of Wisdom also brings a sense of unity to the concept of 'wisdom'. As the prologue to Proverbs (1:1-7) shows, there are various components to the wisdom taught by the sages, but wisdom is presented as a single entity in the figure of personified Wisdom. Another important result of the personification of Wisdom, noted above in discussing Sinnott's work, is that it enables the presentation of abstract knowledge in an attractive, even sensual, way.

Both Sinnott and Camp see the figure of personified Wisdom as having the nature of a 'symbol'. For Sinnott this means that Wisdom points beyond herself to a God who communicates with humans. Camp's understanding of a 'religious symbol' is more complex and leads her to suggest that Wisdom played a mediating role, offering people blessings and knowledge from God. Both suggestions provide helpful, valid insights into the role of personified Wisdom in Proverbs.

However, talk of Wisdom as a 'symbol' may obscure what seems to be an important aspect of the personification of Wisdom in Proverbs. This is the use of the language of love and commitment to Wisdom, and probably of marriage in 4:5-9 (see the commentary on these verses). This presents Wisdom as more than a 'mediator' between God and humans. Rather, through Wisdom humans can come into a personal relationship with God.

There are three other female figures in Prov. 1–9: the 'strange/foreign woman', 'Folly' and the 'wife of one's youth'. There is also the 'woman of worth' or

156. Fox, *Proverbs 1–9*, 331-32.

strong/valiant woman' who appears in the poem which concludes the book. The personification of Wisdom needs to be considered in relation to these figures.

The Strange/Foreign Woman

This figure appears in four passages in Prov. 1–9: 2:16-19; 5:1-23; 6:20-35; 7:1-27. The picture of her becomes clearer as the reader progresses through the passages, and in the fourth one she is not just described but speaks. The two Hebrew words which are used of her, זָרָה (*zārâ*, 'strange') and נָכְרִיָּה (*nokriyyâ*, 'foreign') occur in parallel in 2:16, 5:20 and 7:5. The discussion of these terms in the commentary on 2:12-19 gives the grounds for concluding that she is 'strange' and 'foreign' because she in 'off limits', 'beyond the pale' both morally and socially since she is someone else's wife.

Taking the four passages together it is possible to compile a picture of this woman. She is married and is being unfaithful to her husband (2:17; 6:26, 29; 7:19-20). In 7:10 she is said to be 'guarded of heart', which modern EVV tend to take in the sense 'wily, crafty'. This indicates secretiveness, hiding her motives. The point could be that she is hiding things from her husband, or from her victim. She is described as physically attractive in a general way in 6:25, but the two things about her that are mentioned most often are her lips and her feet. Her most prominent characteristic is her 'smooth words', her seductive speech[157] (2:16; 5:3; 6:24; 7:21). Her feet wander (5:5-6) and will not stay at home (7:11). They lead to death and Sheol (5:5). The references to her 'lips' and 'feet' have sexual connotations. Lips are used not only for speaking but also for kissing (7:13). Lips that 'drip honey' (5:5) are also mentioned in an erotic context in Song 4:11. In Hebrew 'feet' can be a euphemism for the sexual organs.

Commentators and translators differ in their understanding of the two words that are used to describe her in 7:11a: הֹמִיָּה *(hōmiyyâ)* and סֹרָרֶת *(sōrāret)*. Some translate these as 'loud and defiant' (NIV), others as 'flighty and inconstant' (REB). The verb הָמָה *(hāmâ)*, of which *hōmiyyâ* is the feminine *qal* participle, can mean both 'to be boisterous' and 'to be in commotion'. The latter sense, with its implication of 'being unstable', lies behind the translation 'flighty'. It is arguable that this sense fits the context here but the same word is used of Folly in 9:13 where the meaning 'loud, boisterous' seems more appropriate. The participle *sōrāret* normally means 'stubborn, rebellious'. The REB translation, and the NRSV 'wayward', is based on the fact that the Akkadian cognate[158]

157. Aletti, 'Séduction et parole'.

158. Driver, 'Problems in "Proverbs"', 141-42.

sarāru can mean 'to be unstable'. Either 'defiant' (of her husband's authority) or 'wayward' could fit with v. 11b, but the description of the woman's behaviour as 'bold' or 'brazen' in v. 13 might favour the former sense.

Several suggestions have been made as to the possible origin of this figure, some of which have implications for the understanding of the personification of Wisdom. One of these is Boström's[159] view that the Strange Woman is a foreign resident who is a devotee of Aphrodite-Astarte who seeks to lure young men into fertility rituals which involve sacred prostitution and the 'sacred marriage' ritual at the new moon. In Boström's view the personification of Wisdom was a conscious attempt to provide an attractive figure in opposition to the pagan goddess worshipped by the Strange Woman. Boström's proposal about the Strange Woman has been discussed and critiqued in the commentary on 7:6-23.

Clifford[160] suggests that the figure of the Strange Woman is derived from a goddess and her behaviour which is found in a type-scene that occurs in epic literature. In this a goddess deceitfully offers a young hero love or marriage, something which will transform his life. The hero realises the deceitfulness of the offer and refuses it. While there is some similarity to the scenario in Prov. 7, there are notable differences. What is offered the young man is not marriage, but a 'one night stand'. He does not refuse it, but accepts it. The woman does not claim that 'life' is on offer, only pleasure.

Blenkinsopp[161] and Washington[162] have argued that the background to the figure of the Strange Woman is the issue of marriage to foreign women in post-exilic Judah, an issue with which Ezra (Ezra 9–10) and Nehemiah (Neh. 13:23-27) contended and which is also mentioned in Malachi (Mal. 2:10-16). This was an issue which had social, economic and religious dimensions. The Strange Woman, it is suggested, was a literary creation intended to give a warning against such marriages. The figure of personified Wisdom was then conceived as a counter-part to the Strange Woman. A major weakness with this approach is that the warnings against the Strange Woman are clearly warnings against adultery, not against marriage with a non-Israelite.

Given the setting of the lessons in Prov. 1–9 as teaching from a parent, usually the father, to a son, the most obvious background for understanding the figure of the Strange Woman is the age-old temptation to adultery. This might be considered a too mundane issue to warrant the repeated severe warnings against the allure of the Strange Woman. Such a view would, however, fail to

159. Boström, *Proverbiastudien,* 103-55.
160. Clifford, *Proverbs,* 27.
161. Blenkinsopp, 'Social Context'.
162. Washington, 'Strange Woman'.

understand the significance of adultery in ancient Israel. In a discussion of the socio-theological reason for the commandment against adultery in the Decalogue, Wright[163] has argued that, although the land was the primary symbol of the covenant relationship between Yahweh and Israel, it was the family that provided the primary tangible locus of realisation of that relationship. Therefore Israel's existence as a covenant community in the land depended on the stability of the family not only for socio-economic reasons but also for theological reasons. Adultery was regarded as totally unacceptable because it was a threat to the stability of the family, and therefore to the whole social order of the covenant community. It was an evil to be removed by applying the death penalty to both the man and the woman involved (Deut. 22:22).

Warnings against adultery are, in fact, fairly common and widespread in ancient Near Eastern wisdom literature. Longman[164] quotes an example from the Sumerian *Instruction of Shuruppak,* which was later translated into Akkadian. McKane[165] quotes examples from Egyptian and Babylonian literature, as well as from *Ahiqar.* At the end of a study of the figure of the Strange Woman in the light of Egyptian wisdom literature, Shupak[166] comments, 'the act of adultery has throughout history threatened the family setting and warnings against it were common in the literature of the Ancient Near East.' He concludes,[167]

> Comparison with the Egyptian material reinforces the view that the image of the Strange Woman in Proverbs and the opposing Wife of one's Youth, belong to the realistic stratum of the Hebrew teacher's instruction. His counsels are designed to guide the maturing youth along his path of life.

Personified Wisdom and the Strange Woman seem to be deliberately presented as rivals for the attention of the young men to whom the lessons are addressed. Both seek to influence their audience primarily by their use of speech. However, while Wisdom does this openly in the public places of the city (1:20-21; 8:1-3) the Strange Woman does it somewhat secretly in the streets at night (7:10-21). Both have houses in which they prepare entertainment, of a contrasting nature, for their guests (9:1-6; 7:16-20). In 7:4 Wisdom is spoken of in terms appropriate for a good wife while the Strange Woman is compared to a prostitute (7:10) and is clearly an unfaithful wife (2:17; 7:18-20). Both can be embraced (3:18; 4:8; 5:20) but while contact with Wisdom brings life (3:16-18,

163. Wright, 'Israelite Household', 102.

164. Longman, *Proverbs,* 50.

165. McKane, *Proverbs,* 94 (Egyptian), 339-40 (Babylonian), 312 *(Ahiqar).*

166. Shupak, 'Female Imagery', 321.

167. Shupak, 'Female Imagery', 322-23.

21-22; 8:35) the Strange Woman is a *femme fatale* who brings death (2:18-19; 5:3-5; 7:22-27). If one concludes in the light of Prov. 8 that the figure of personified wisdom is intended to represent and validate the wisdom tradition (see the section 'Wisdom and Creation' below), then it would seem that the figure of the Strange Woman has been deliberately drawn with some contrasting characteristics in order to make clear that adultery is an act of serious 'unwisdom', of folly.

The Wife of Your Youth

This figure is clearly an antithesis to the Strange Woman. This is clear in the lesson in which the description of her (5:15-19) is preceded (5:3-14) and followed by warnings against the Strange Woman (5:20-23). The fact that she is called 'the wife of your youth' clearly contrasts with the description of the Strange Woman as one who 'forsakes the companion of her youth' (2:17). The contrasting of these two figures does strongly suggest that the origin of the figure of the Strange Woman is in the real life situation of the temptation to adultery and that the purpose of the warnings against her is to protect the stability of the family, and through it, that of society as a whole. Further, see the commentary on 5:15-20.

The Woman Folly

This personified figure appears only in Prov. 9:13-18. In the commentary on this section it was noted that Woman Folly shares some characteristics with the Strange Woman. She is noisy (7:11), lacking in knowledge (5:6); she invites men to secret meals (7:15-20), and consorting with her leads to death and Sheol (2:18; 5:5; 7:27). However, as Murphy[168] says, 'She stands for more than sexual misconduct.' She has a demonic and destructive aspect. She is the true antithesis to personified Wisdom, as the placing of the two vignettes together in ch. 9 clearly indicates. As Fox[169] puts it, 'Lady Folly is a literary personification with no mythological roots. . . . The motive for the creation of this personification is rhetorical, to create a symmetry between wisdom and folly.' Both women call out to the 'simple' in almost identical words. The change in order from bread/wine (v. 4) to water/bread (v. 17) forms a chiasm which links the two speeches

168. Murphy, *Proverbs,* 282.
169. Fox, *Proverbs 1–9,* 300.

together. The outcome of accepting the two invitations could not be more different, life (v. 6) and death (v. 18). For more detail see the commentary on ch. 9.

In the commentary we noted the views of Longman and Perdue which suggest that the choice between Wisdom and Folly is a metaphor for the choice between Yahweh and the pagan gods, the choice implied by the motto of 1:7a that is repeated in 9:10a, 'The fear of Yahweh is the beginning of knowledge/wisdom', and that emphasises the seriousness of the constant call to 'get wisdom' above all else.

The Strong/Valiant Woman

As noted in the commentary on Prov. 31:10-31, although most commentators have recognised that on the surface the passage describes an actual human woman, many have found the 'message' of the passage in an allegorical reading of it. Fox[170] argues that an intentional allegory always has something that disturbs the surface reading and acts as a cue to the reader that an allegory is intended. For example, in Jotham's fable (Judg. 9:8-15) trees talk. Some have seen that cue in what they regard as the unattainable 'ideal' picture of the wife in Prov. 31:10-31. However, it is the nature of 'ideals' that they appear somewhat superhuman. Moreover, as noted in the commentary, v. 10 indicates that what is presented is something rare, but not impossible to find, as v. 29 confirms. Therefore one does not have to resort to allegory in order to get a message out of the passage. Others seem to think that a picture of a human role model, however 'ideal', is too mundane as a meaning for the passage and so there must be a more 'spiritual' meaning. This is the same attitude that has produced allegorical readings of the Song of Songs. However, Proverbs is full of human role models, both negative and positive. Yoder[171] has shown that the Strong Woman 'is arguably a composite of real women. She embodies no *one woman*, but rather the desired attributes and activities of *many*.'

Although intended to be seen as a human person, the Strong Woman does share characteristics with personified Wisdom. Both are said to be more precious than jewels (31:10; 8:11) and both bring wealth (31:11; 8:18, 21). Each is depicted as mistress of a household (31:15, 21, 27; 9:1) with maidservants (31:15; 9:3). Both provide food (31:14; 9:5) and produce 'fruit' (31:16, 31; 8:19). They both

170. Fox, *Proverbs 10–13*, 909-11.

171. Yoder, 'Woman of Substance', 446 (italics in original). She uses evidence from the Persian period, but does not establish that it could not be equally valid for other periods of Judean history.

give wise instruction (31:26; 8:6-11). Each has honour (31:25, 28-31; 8:18) and strength (31:17, 25; 8:14). The works of the Strong Woman praise her in the city gates, and Wisdom takes her stand and declares her worth in the gates (8:3). This does not mean that the two figures are to be identified with one another. Rather, while Woman Wisdom *personifies* wisdom, the Strong Woman *typifies*[172] wisdom by *incarnating* some of its characteristics. The Strong Woman can be seen as a filling out of the picture of 'the wife of your youth' (5:18-19) and is the strict antithesis of the Strange Woman, who incarnates some characteristics of Folly.

Camp is one of a number of recent scholars who see Prov. 31:10-31 as providing an intentional 'bracketing' of the Book of Proverbs with the figure of the Strong Woman (or 'woman of worth' as she denotes her) resonating with that of personified Wisdom in Prov. 1–9. She argues[173] that this 'bracketing' provides an 'interpretive framework' for the body of the book (Prov. 10–30). Her argument is based on correlations between Wisdom and the Strong Woman, such as those noted above, and also 'an interweaving of the beginning, middle and end of the book by virtue of a web of subsidiary images connected both with the female imagery and with wisdom.'[174] Some of the examples she gives to establish the existence of this 'web' seem rather contrived and the 'web' itself rather diffuse. If it were an intentional construction, one would have expected it to be more obvious. However, although Camp may overstate the case for an 'interpretive framework', Prov. 31:10-31 does seem to provide an intentional and fitting ending for the book by presenting a picture of a woman who in considerable measure incarnates characteristics of personified Wisdom and provides a concrete example of how the teachings of Wisdom can be applied in real life and the real benefits they bring.

That the Strong Woman is a picture of a human person, even if an exceptional one, based on the roles played by Judean women and at the same time incarnates characteristics of personified Wisdom strengthens the case that personified Wisdom is a literary creation based on the roles played by such women.

Proverbs and Women

In the commentary on 5:1-23 and 31:10-31 there is some discussion of the gender issues raised by the way women are depicted in Proverbs. This is an appropriate

172. Fox, *Proverbs 10–31*, 911.

173. Camp, *Wisdom and the Feminine*, 179-208.

174. Camp, *Wisdom and the Feminine*, 207.

point to take the discussion further by considering some general issues that have been raised by feminist scholars.

Brenner and van Dijk-Hemmes[175] argue that the speaker in parts of Prov. 1–9 is not the father, as traditionally assumed, but a female (F) voice. While this might be considered a positive factor from a feminist point of view, it is not as far as Brenner is concerned. She[176] considers that this F voice has internalised male (M) patriarchal values. With regard to Prov. 7 she says, 'It appears that we read here not just complicity with androcentric values, not simply voiced conformity, but also overzealousness in protecting those values' and that F self-interest is silenced through identification with M interest. She sees the F voice adopting M ideology by recommending 'control over female sexuality'. However, another feminist scholar, Bellis, sees things differently. She sees the voice which urges the son to avoid the Strange Woman as countering the 'infamous double standard' which tolerated a certain degree of male promiscuity in Israelite society. So, she says[177] that this voice 'is not necessarily any more an internalized androcentric one than the voice of twentieth-century feminists who challenge the remnants of the same double standard today'. The difference is that the teacher in Proverbs seeks to undercut the double standard by limiting male sexual freedom whereas some modern feminists wish to increase female sexual freedom. Either approach could lead to a 'more egalitarian ethic'. She notes that, contrary to what Brenner and some other writers assert, the teacher does not try to control *female* sexuality but *male* sexuality. Indeed she argues[178] that in the context of ancient Israelite society, it was more in the women's self-interest for men to be monogamous than it was in the men's. It is also worth noting that, despite what some feminist writers[179] suggest, the father, if he is indeed the 'voice' in Prov. 1–9, does not have any problem with female sexuality in itself, as his advice about enjoying sexual relations with 'the wife of your youth' in 5:15-19 shows.

The figure of the Strange Woman is, understandably, offensive to many modern readers of both genders today. Yee[180] says, 'The personification in a woman's form of all that is evil and destructive is, indeed, a disturbing one.' Camp, however, seems to find some mitigation in considering the literary factors at work here. She argues[181] that the figure is not a stereotype of a real per-

175. Brenner and van Dijk-Hemmes, *On Gendering Texts*, 57-62, 117-26. See the critique of their arguments by Fox, *Proverbs 1–9*, 258.

176. Brenner, 'Proverbs 1–9', 125-26.

177. Bellis, 'Gender and Motives', 82.

178. Bellis, 'Gender and Motives', 83-86.

179. For example, Newsom, 'Woman and the Discourse', 153.

180. Yee, 'I Have Perfumed My Bed', 66.

181. Camp, *Wisdom and the Feminine*, 116-17.

son or class of persons but an imaginative construct formulated as a contrast to Woman Wisdom and suggests a need to recognise the 'wisdom tradition's predilection for organizing and patterning perceptions in antithetical terms, especially its moral judgments of good and evil, and for depicting these judgments in vivid and memorable vignettes'.

Two other things can be said in response to Yee's comment. The first follows from Camp's point, namely that in Proverbs all that is good and life-giving is personified in a woman's form, Wisdom. True, there are similarities in the way both women make their appeal to 'the simple', but this does not depict a problem in being a woman, but in being an untutored man who lacks insight. Second, most of those who have written about the Strange Woman have taken the warnings about her as more or less isolated texts. They have not recognised that she has a male counterpart, or counterparts, different kinds of evil men. The first lesson in Prov. 1–9 is a quite lengthy warning against such male 'sinners' who seek to use enticing speech to lead the son into the way that will lead to death (1:8-19). There are resonances here with what is said later in the warnings against the Strange Woman. The first passage about the Strange Woman is preceded by an admonition to seek wisdom because this will provide deliverance from evil men, who are described in quite vivid terms (2:12-15), as well as from the Strange Woman (2:16-22). The use of the verb 'delivered' in vv. 12 and 16 links the male and female portraits. A warning against 'the wicked' (4:14-19) comes shortly before the second warning about the Strange Woman (5:1-23). Another warning against 'a wicked man' (6:12-15) closely precedes the warning against the 'evil woman' in 6:24-35. These evil male characters give the lie to Yee's comment that the Strange Woman personifies 'all that is evil and destructive' because they tempt the son in areas that she does not. In 1:11-14 they offer the chance to play the role of Sheol rather than becoming its victim, to be the oppressor rather than the oppressed, and they offer wealth of the kind that Wisdom offers later on. Money, sex and power are often linked as the three great motivations to doing evil. The Strange Woman only plays on one of these. The male 'sinners' play on the other two. Weeks's comment[182] that 'What they offer is more tempting, but they offer it less temptingly' than the Strange Woman is a subjective judgement with which not all might agree. It all depends on what someone finds most alluring.

Some feminist interpreters[183] see in Proverbs an expression of a patriarchal mentality in which woman is the quintessential 'Other'. Fox[184] rightly

182. Weeks, *Instruction and Imagery*, 146.

183. For example, Maier, 'Conflicting Attractions'; Camp, 'What's So Strange'.

184. Fox, *Proverbs 1–9*, 259 (his italics).

rejects this as a mind-set that is foreign to Proverbs in which 'there is indeed an essential Other: evildoers (and some kinds of fool) of both sexes. . . . *This* Other is beyond influence and redemption, possessing an inverted and incorrigibly perverse set of values. Women are not the "other" in such a radical sense.'

In the commentary on Prov. 31:10-31 it is noted that some feminist scholars regard the Strong Woman as someone who lives to advance male interests. In large part this is based on v. 23, which implies that her activities contribute to her husband's status in the community. However, it doesn't follow that it depends on that alone. He might have had his own responsibilities in the fields, in a workshop or in some other kind of business. The poem is silent about his activities because it is not about him, or even aiming to give a rounded view of family life, it is about the wife and mother. It is true that this woman does work for others, but it is not to advance male interests, rather to advance the interests of her family. If that is something that is of primary importance to her, then she is advancing her own interests. As noted in the commentary, some feminist scholars regard this poem as an empowering text for women. Valler[185] argues this in the case of Jewish tradition, and Masenya[186] does so with regard to Northern Sotho women in Africa today.

More than once in the commentary the point has been made that readers who want to apply the message of Proverbs (or indeed any part of the Bible) to their lives and situations today have to face the hermeneutic task of 'cultural transposition' of the message. This involves imagining themselves in the place of the original addressee(s) in order to understand what the message of the text is and then considering how it might apply to their situation today in a different historical and cultural setting. The poem about the Strong Woman presents men with the challenge of asking what it would mean to be a Strong Man today who incarnates the characteristics of wisdom presented in Proverbs. Psalm 112, an acrostic poem about a man who fears Yahweh, provides a possible template for doing such a cultural transposition. The warnings about the Strange Woman present women with an undoubtedly more difficult task of cultural transposition. One feminist scholar, Bellis,[187] provides an example of how this might be done in 'A Letter to My Daughters'.

As a feminist, Schroer finds some positive features in Proverbs. She[188] sees its idea of a just order that embraces the social and cosmic sphere as providing

185. Valler, 'Who Is *'ešet Ḥayil*', 96-97.
186. Masenya, 'Proverbs 31:10-31', 63.
187. Bellis, 'Gender and Motives', 90-91.
188. Schroer, *Wisdom Has Built*, 6.

'an extraordinarily provocative impulse for feminist theology that would begin with the necessity of a world-encompassing justice and from there develop a theology of relationship, an eco-feminist theology, and so on.' In response to those who suggest that personified Wisdom serves as a figure to bind women into a patriarchal system, she[189] points out the significance of the fact that Wisdom never appears as a motherly figure, the crucial role for women from a patriarchal perspective. Schroer thinks Wisdom provides a constructive image for women, able to promote change. As part of this, the figure of Wisdom as a counsellor[190] provides a non-androcentric image for women. Like Longman,[191] but for different reasons, Schroer[192] sees personified Wisdom as in some sense a representation of Yahweh, and therefore providing a helpful feminine image of God.

In concluding this discussion of some gender issues arising from feminist studies of Proverbs, it is important to note that although male language is the predominant language used of God in the Bible, the God of the Bible is beyond gender, neither male nor female. The Decalogue forbids the making of any images of God, and in Ezek. 16:17 male images of God are condemned. At the same time human beings, both female and male, are made in the image of God (Gen. 1:27). They have the same nature (Gen. 2:22-24) and are co-equals (Gen 2:18). The sexual aspect of being human is therefore somehow rooted in the Creator God. The female metaphor of personified Wisdom who is closely associated with God and in some sense represents God provides a helpful balance to the tendency to think of God in male terms.

The Spirituality of Proverbs

The term 'spirituality' is a word that has come to have a wide range of meanings in postmodern Western use. It is therefore helpful to have a definition of it to indicate the sense in which it is being used. Here it will be used in the fairly classical sense which McGrath[193] gives as a basic definition of 'spirituality': 'Spirituality concerns the quest for a fulfilled and authentic religious life, involving the bringing together of the ideas distinctive of that religion and the whole experience of living on the basis of and within the scope of that religion.' He

189. Schroer, *Wisdom Has Built,* 41-42 (note).

190. Schroer, *Wisdom Has Built,* 63-65.

191. Longman, *Proverbs,* 222.

192. Schroer, *Wisdom Has Built,* 26-41. The exegesis of Prov. 8:22-31 in this commentary undermines some of her reasons.

193. McGrath, *Christian Spirituality,* 2.

sums this up by saying: 'Spirituality is the outworking in real life of a person's religious faith — what a person *does* with what they believe.'

The Book of Proverbs is all about how to cope with the demands of everyday real life. One possible way to approach understanding the spirituality of the book in the form in which we now have it is to take as a starting point the so-called Yahweh proverbs, those proverbs which explicitly mention Yahweh. Fifteen of these[194] are about 'the fear of Yahweh'.

The Fear of Yahweh

Proverbs 1:7 is often referred to as the 'motto' of the Book of Proverbs. It forms an *inclusio* with 9:10 so that the concept of 'the fear of Yahweh' frames chs. 1–9. It probably forms an *inclusio* with 31:30 so that the concept frames the whole book. Also, it may be significant that 15:33a, which is very similar to 1:7, comes near the middle[195] of the book. What follows expands on the comments made in the commentary on 1:7.

The phrase 'the fear of Yahweh' occurs more often in Proverbs than in any other biblical book, but the concept of 'the fear of Yahweh' is found throughout the Hebrew Bible. There is general agreement that it has its origins in the response of awesome fear that people experience in the presence of the Numinous, such as that described in Exod. 14:31; 19:16; 20:18-21. It does, however, undergo development in different ways within the Hebrew Bible. In Deuteronomy and the Deuteronomistic literature the emphasis is on a loyalty and love for Yahweh as the God of the covenant which is expressed in obedience to his commandments.

> And now, Israel, what does the LORD your God require of you, but to fear the LORD your God, to walk in all his ways, to love him, to serve the LORD your God with all your heart and with all your soul, and to keep the commandments and statutes of the LORD which I am commanding you today for your good? (Deut. 10:12-13, ESV)

In the Holiness Code in Leviticus there is appeal to the fear of Yahweh as a motivation for moral behaviour, especially towards other people and in situations where it might not be easy to bring the law to bear (Lev. 19:14, 32; 25:17, 36, 43).

194. Prov. 1:7; 3:7; 8:13; 9:10; 10:27; 14:4, 26, 27; 15:16, 33; 16:6; 19:23; 22:4; 23:17-18; 24:21-22. Note also 1:29; 2:5; 31:30.

195. The Masoretes mark 16:17 as the middle of the book based on the number of verses.

It is this ethical aspect of the fear of Yahweh that predominates in Proverbs, as expressed in 8:13a: 'The fear of Yahweh is hatred of evil' (see also 3:7; 16:6).

There is, however, no reason to assume that in Proverbs the concept has lost the connotations of religious awe or of love and loyalty to Yahweh. Fox[196] sees an element of dread implied in 14:27 where the fear of Yahweh is put in parallel with 'the snares of death', and also in 24:21-22 where fear of the LORD is linked with fear of the king because both can bring ruin to those who do not fear them. He suggests that the appeal to the fear of Yahweh as motivation for moral behaviour, especially where legal sanctions do not exist or are hard to enforce, also implies an element of real fear — fear that Yahweh will punish the wrongdoer in some way.

In 2:5 the fear of Yahweh stands in parallel with 'the knowledge of God' which implies a personal relationship with God (see the commentary on 2:5). According to 14:26 this is a relationship which brings confidence and trust in Yahweh (see also 29:25). It also gives hope for the future (23:17-18). As well as leading to moral behaviour, the fear of Yahweh leads to 'life', variously presented as a long life (10:27), escape from the 'snares of death' (14:27) and a fulfilled life (19:23; 22:4). This does not, however, necessarily mean an easy life (15:16). The nature of the relationship with Yahweh envisaged by the sages is expressed in 3:5-6:

> Trust in Yahweh with all your heart,
> and do not lean on your own understanding.
> In all your ways know him,
> and he will make your ways straight.

Here 'know' is the same verb as used in 2:5 and clearly means something like 'acknowledge' or 'live in dependence on'. Van Leeuwen[197] sums up the meaning of the fear of Yahweh in Proverbs as '*religion* in the comprehensive sense of life in its entirety devoted to God's service. Here *all* activities are undertaken in the light of God's presence and purposes in the world.' The relevance of this to our opening definition of spirituality is obvious.

The fear of Yahweh is the 'beginning' of knowledge/wisdom. The parallel between 1:7a and 9:10a shows (see the commentary on these verses) that the primary sense here is 'first in time'. The fear of Yahweh precedes the acquisition of wisdom. However, this does not mean that the fear of Yahweh is an initial stage that can be left behind, but that it is the necessary precondition for gaining

196. Fox, *Proverbs 1–9*, 70.
197. Van Leeuwen, *Proverbs*, 33.

wisdom. That this is so is supported by 15:33: 'The fear of Yahweh is instruction in wisdom, and before honour, humility.' It is clear here (as in 18:12) that humility is the precondition for honour, not the first stage towards it. Also, the fact that the fear of Yahweh is said to be 'instruction in wisdom' indicates that what is involved is a process, not just an initial stage.

It is clear that in Proverbs a correct attitude and relationship to Yahweh, 'the fear of Yahweh', is the precondition for attaining true 'wisdom'. The sages were aware that people sought wisdom in other ways than through a proper relationship to Yahweh. In particular there are warnings against 'being wise in your own eyes' (3:7; 26:12) because this is sheer folly. Humans need to recognise and understand their place in the world. People are totally dependent on Yahweh, who created the world and them, and sustains both. To be able to cope successfully with life in this world requires wisdom from the Creator.[198] This comes from living in a right relationship to him.

'The thesis that all human knowledge comes back to the question of commitment to God is a statement of penetrating perspicacity' says von Rad,[199] and he goes on to tease out what this implies:

> One becomes competent and expert as far as the orders of life are concerned only if one begins from knowledge about God. To this extent, Israel attributes to the fear of God, to belief in God, a highly important function in respect of human knowledge. She was, in all seriousness, of the opinion that effective knowledge about God is the only thing that puts a man into a right relationship with the objects of his perception, that it enables him to ask questions more pertinent, to take stock of relationships more effectively and generally to have a better awareness of circumstances.

The statement 'The fear of Yahweh is the beginning of wisdom' was, as von Rad notes, 'Israel's most special possession'. Fox[200] points out that the importance that Israelite wisdom gives to 'the fear of Yahweh' is not paralleled in the ancient Near East. In Egyptian and Mesopotamian wisdom 'the fear of God' is just one virtue among many. It does not have the fundamental role that it has in Israelite wisdom. It may be that one reason for this is the original rooting of the concept of 'the fear of Yahweh' in Israel's covenantal relationship with God. This is obvious in Deuteronomy and the Deuteronomistic literature. It is not explicit in Proverbs but may still be there in the background. If so, the concept

198. See the section 'Wisdom and Creation' below.

199. Von Rad, *Wisdom in Israel*, 67-68.

200. Fox, *Proverbs 1–9*, 71.

is not purely individualistic but has a communal aspect. Those who genuinely 'fear Yahweh' contribute to the health of the whole community.

An Abomination to Yahweh

The phrase 'an abomination to Yahweh' occurs in 11 proverbs[201] and also in a number proverb which lists seven things which are an abomination to Yahweh (6:16-19). The noun תּוֹעֵבָה *(tô'ēbâ)* 'denotes the persons, things, or practices that offend one's ritual or moral order. . . . The abominable or repugnant nature is determined by a person's character, values or culture.'[202] The subjective nature of the response of 'abomination' is indicated by 29:27:

> An unjust person is an abomination to the righteous,
> but one whose way is straight is an abomination to the wicked.

Outside of Proverbs the phrase 'an abomination to Yahweh' occurs most frequently in Deuteronomy (16×). The noun 'abomination' occurs most frequently in Ezekiel (43×). In these two books the term refers primarily to alien cult objects and to deviant sexual practices, which may have been associated with alien cults. The use of the phrase and noun in Proverbs is quite different.

Some of the things that are 'an abomination to Yahweh' are very general: 'the way of the wicked' (15:9), 'the thoughts of the wicked' (15:26), 'those of a crooked heart' (11:20). Somewhat more specific are 'the devious person' (3:32), 'lying lips' (12:22), 'all who are arrogant of heart' (16:5). Specific acts that are mentioned are hypocritical worship (12:22), perversion of justice in court (17:15) and corrupt commercial practices (11:1; 20:10, 23). The list of seven things which are 'an abomination to Yahweh' refers to the misuse of body parts for evil (eyes, tongue, hands, heart, feet) and concludes with 'one who sows discord among brothers'. In 11:1, 20; 12:22 those things or people that are the antithesis of 'an abomination to Yahweh' are said to be 'his delight'.

There are eight proverbs[203] which refer to certain things or people as 'an abomination' without mention of Yahweh. They cover very similar ground to those that refer to Yahweh: 'the scoffer' (24:9), 'an unjust person' (29:7), doing evil (16:12), wicked words (8:7), hypocritical worship (21:27; 28:9). This indicates that there is considerable overlap between things which evoke a response of

201. Prov. 3:31-32; 11:1, 20; 12:22; 15:8, 9, 26; 16:5; 17:15; 20:10, 23.

202. *NIDOTTE* 4:314.

203. Prov. 8:7; 13:19; 16:12; 21:27; 24:9; 26:24-25; 28:9; 29:27.

outrage and abhorrence in humans and those that do so in Yahweh. This, of course, is not surprising with regard to those people who 'fear Yahweh' but with the exception of 8:7, where Wisdom is speaking, and 29:27, which refers to 'the righteous', there is no indication that the reaction of such people is specifically meant. Indeed, 24:9 says that the scoffer is an abomination to people in general.

Clements[204] argues that the lack of any clear distinction between what is said to be an 'abomination' in general and what is 'an abomination to Yahweh', most obvious in 21:27 and 15:8, suggests that 'The very idea of abomination has taken on a kind of absolute quality that implies that such actions are contrary to the very order of life and creation as a whole.' He also notes[205] that in these proverbs in general, and in the number proverb in 6:16-19 in particular, 'Bad attitudes are condemned as much as bad actions, since the former lead to the latter.' Also, there is no explicit reference to retribution, or other prudential reasons, for not adopting these bad attitudes and actions. They seem to be condemned simply because they are wrong in themselves. They are recognised as such by the sense of outrage and abhorrence that they engender in most people. The bad attitudes and most of the bad actions mentioned in these proverbs could not be dealt with through the legal system. Therefore the sharp proverbs of reproof, using the strong condemnatory term 'abomination' seek to deal with them by means of moral education. Since there is no obvious difference in the kinds of attitudes and actions dealt with in the two forms of 'abomination' proverbs, Clements[206] suggests that the purpose of the addition of 'to Yahweh' to some of them is to add urgency and force to the warning they give.

Clements[207] sees two ethically significant features in these proverbs. First, they show 'a valuable concern to relate fundamental moral concepts to experienced social realities' by their appeal to the widespread sense of outrage and abhorrence evoked by certain attitudes and actions. Second,

> these sayings bind together the sense of an ultimate divine authority with the felt needs and responses of human beings acting in a context of social reality. As such, they mark a noteworthy step in the integration of ethical and social concepts, seeing in an educative principle a path to virtue.

It is clear that, like the concept of 'the fear of Yahweh', attitudes and actions being 'an abomination to Yahweh' is an expression of 'spirituality' in the sense

204. Clements, 'Abomination', 219.
205. Clements, 'Abomination', 222.
206. Clements, 'Abomination', 224.
207. Clements, 'Abomination', 225.

of the definition given above: 'the outworking in real life of a person's religious faith — what a person *does* with what they believe.' In this case, though, there is a more obvious communal dimension since the sense of outrage it expresses is part of the community's ethos.

The Formation of Character

Clements' suggestion quoted above that the concept of 'abomination' was seen by the sages as an educative principle that could be used to promote virtue does not apply only to one type of proverb but to the book as a whole. Brown[208] argues that the Hebrew wisdom literature in general, and the Book of Proverbs in particular, is concerned with the formation of character. He noted that traditionally character formation has been understood in terms of the cultivation of virtue. He says[209] that 'Virtue is a disposition, which denotes the pattern of choices an individual makes', and quotes two classical definitions of virtue:

> Aristotle defined virtue as 'a deliberated and permanent disposition, based on a standard applied to ourselves and defined by the reason displayed by the man of good sense'. Similarly, St. Thomas Aquinas described virtue as 'that which makes good he who has it and renders good his work'.

These definitions highlight certain aspects of virtue: it is both a disposition and a standard; it is based on reason and is the source of good conduct; since it leads to doing certain actions in particular situations it is not static but dynamic; it is not wholly inborn but must be cultivated.

The opening verses of Proverbs set out the purpose of the whole book. Proverbs 1:2-7 is, as Brown[210] puts it, 'thick with sapiential terms, whose density is matched only by its comprehensive scope'. These terms, which overlap to some degree in meaning, are discussed in detail in the commentary on 1:1-7. As von Rad[211] observes, 'By the cumulation of many terms the text seems to aim at something larger, something more comprehensive which could not be expressed satisfactorily by means of any one of the terms used.' Commenting on the significance of this list of terms for understanding the purpose of the book McKane[212] says, 'The educational process was more occupied with

208. Brown, *Character in Crisis,* especially 22-49.
209. Brown, *Character in Crisis,* 9.
210. Brown, *Character in Crisis,* 24.
211. Von Rad, *Wisdom in Israel,* 13.
212. McKane, *Proverbs,* 265.

developing mature intellectual attitudes than with morality. . . . It did not educate men to change the existing world into something better, but to make their way successfully in the world as it was.' In saying this he undervalues the significance of the moral virtues listed in v. 3b (righteousness, justice and equity), about which he says very little. On the basis of the number of terms used, these distinctively moral virtues may seem to be outweighed by the other, more pragmatic, terms. However, Brown[213] argues that these moral virtues take the central place in what seems to be a carefully constructed chiasmus:

A Comprehensive, intellectual values: 2a
  B Literary expressions of wisdom: 2b
    C Instrumental virtue: 3a
      D Moral, communal virtues: 3b
    C′ Instrumental virtues: 4-5
  B′ Literary expressions of wisdom: 6
A′ Comprehensive, intellectual virtues: 7

He points out[214] that there is an underlying movement in this structure from the more general to the more specific. The 'words of insight' mentioned in v. 2b are specified in v. 6. The 'instruction' mentioned in v. 3a is detailed in vv. 4-5. From v. 4 onwards certain types of people are introduced so that the values introduced in vv. 2-3 are rooted in people in vv. 4-7. As well as having a particular centre, the structure moves to a specific climax in v. 7, 'the fear of Yahweh'. This deals with the very centre of a person's character, their relationship to God. So, this statement of the purpose of Proverbs indicates that it is about the formation of personal character in which certain moral virtues have a central place. Without this the intellectual values, instrumental virtues and literary skills listed will not be put to good use. The Book of Proverbs may not have much to say explicitly about changing the existing world into a better world, but the sages were concerned about changing people into better people. By the way they lived such people would change the world into a better place. This is particularly so because the moral virtues which are highlighted in v. 3b are ones that are essential for the maintenance and proper governance of a community. In fact these communal virtues are key in Israel's understanding of the nature of the covenant community. As various commentators[215] have

213. Brown, *Character in Crisis,* 25.

214. Brown, *Character in Crisis,* 28-29.

215. For example: Longman, *Proverbs,* 96; Murphy, *Proverbs,* 4; Van Leeuwen, *Proverbs,* 33.

noted, 'righteousness, justice and equity' are virtues that are promoted by both the Law and the Prophets.

Further evidence that character formation is an important aim in Proverbs is seen in the nature of Prov. 1–9. This consists primarily of parental instruction given by a father to his son. As Brown[216] points out, there is a pervasive element of reproof in this instruction, indicating a concern to correct and improve the character of the son. Even Yahweh's instruction is presented as being of this form (3:11-12):

> My son, do not despise Yahweh's instruction,
> and do not weary of his reproof,
> for Yahweh reproves the one he loves,
> as a father the son in whom he delights.

Wisdom, too, utters words of reproof. The term 'reproof' occurs three times in her speech in 1:22-33. In fact this speech goes beyond reproof to indictment of those who are of bad character, 'the simple ones' and 'the scoffers'. Coming after the first of the parental lessons addressed to an individual, Wisdom's speech complements it and extends the reproof into the realm of the community since she cries aloud in the streets, the market and the city gates and addresses people in the plural.

The community aspect of the father's instruction surfaces in various ways. The five prohibitions listed in 3:27-31 all deal with the maintenance of harmonious relationships within the community. This leads Brown[217] to comment that 'The prudent lifestyle is profiled *relationally,* beyond the perspective of the efficient and successful attainment of individual goals.' The list of seven things that are an abomination to Yahweh (6:16-19) contains things which would be disruptive of community and ends with 'one who sows discord among brothers'. The warnings against 'the strange woman' and adultery and the emphasis on marital faithfulness in chs 5, 6 and 7 arise from the importance of a stable family as the basis of a stable community. See further the discussion of this in the section 'The Strange/Foreign Woman' above.

The metaphor of 'the two ways' is widely recognised as an important motif in Proverbs. Habel[218] argues that 'the way' it is a primary symbol in Prov. 1–9 and acts as a 'nuclear symbol' which has a system of 'satellite symbols'. He argues that the metaphor of 'the two ways' is one of the primary 'polarities' in

216. Brown, *Character in Crisis,* 30-33.
217. Brown, *Character in Crisis,* 35.
218. Habel, 'Symbolism of Wisdom', 131-39.

Proverbs. It is set out with particular clarity in Prov. 4:10-19. Here the 'way of wisdom' is 'straight/upright' and free of the causes of 'stumbling'. It is 'the path of the righteous' and 'like a bright light'. By contrast the 'way of the wicked' is 'the way of evil' and is 'like heavy darkness' where people will 'stumble' and seek to cause others to do so too. Newsom[219] argues that the metaphor of 'the way/path/track' for customary behaviour has communal connotations: 'A path is a social product, made by many feet over a period of time.' In being urged to follow the 'way of the righteous' the son is not being asked to blaze a new path on his own but to join the path that the righteous have walked and are walking. The virtues of justice, righteousness and equity are markers of this path, which is the one that is best for a harmonious and healthy community.

In Prov. 1–9 the central virtues of justice, righteousness and equity remain at the level of generality. It is left to the reader to see how these virtues are given specific shape in the proverbs which make up the rest of the book. In a brief survey Brown gives examples of how they are expressed in both individual conduct and communal structure. He notes that sometimes the language of the proverbs is similar to that of the classical prophets. He concludes,[220] 'To summarize, productive and responsible citizenship within the community is of central concern to the editors who produced the Book of Proverbs. An armchair document full of philosophical musings on wisdom this book is not.'

Given this evidence of the sages' concern with the formation of the character of the individual within a harmonious and healthy society, it is clear that Proverbs is not simply a collection of pragmatic sayings about how to succeed in life. It is a handbook on the spirituality of Yahwistic religion. In its emphasis on character formation the Book of Proverbs stands as a challenge to the modern church. Even in the fairly rare cases where there is a coherent church 'education programme' or 'discipleship programme' it is often oriented primarily to the acquiring of skills rather than personal formation. However laudable and useful these skills (for example: biblical interpretation, creative worship, different ways of praying, how to share your faith with others) may be, the curriculum is like Prov. 1:2-7 with v. 3b and v. 7 missing. It needs to be embedded in a programme which encourages Christian character formation. In addition to Brown's book, that by Estes,[221] which examines teaching and learning in Prov. 1–9, might provide stimulus and help in thinking through what form such a programme might take.

219. Newsom, 'Woman and the Discourse', 147-48.

220. Brown, *Character in Crisis,* 47.

221. Estes, *Hear, My Son.*

Other Yahweh Proverbs

In addition to the proverbs about 'the fear of Yahweh' and the things that are 'an abomination to Yahweh', there are another 43 proverbs in chs 10–31 which explicitly mention Yahweh. These are fairly well scattered throughout the chapters except for a concentration of 'Yahweh proverbs' in 15:33–16:9. This block includes a 'fear of Yahweh' proverb (15:33), an 'abomination to Yahweh' proverb (16:5) and a proverb which does not mention Yahweh (16:8). Although most scholars see 15:33 as linked most closely with the verses which precede it, especially vv. 31-32 (see the commentary on 15:28-33), it is no doubt significant that it immediately precedes, and so introduces, a block of Yahweh proverbs. Whybray[222] sees 16:8 as 'a subsequent interpolation' into a group of Yahweh proverbs, though he accepts[223] that it makes sense in context, providing an example of a 'way' that 'pleases Yahweh' (v. 7a). Van Leeuwen[224] thinks that this verse 'properly belongs in its present context', not only for the reason Whybray gives, but because it is a 'near duplicate' of 15:16, a 'fear of Yahweh' proverb, and 'anticipates the frequent mention of justice or righteousness in vv. 10-13'.

Whybray[225] has argued that the Yahweh sayings were added to the collections in Prov. 10:1–22:16 and positioned in such a way as to reinterpret older 'secular' wisdom sayings. For a discussion and critique of this view see the section 'Proverbs: Secular or Religious?' above. Here we are concerned with the spirituality of the Book of Proverbs in its final form. It is no doubt significant that there is a highly 'theological' block of Yahweh proverbs more or less at the centre of the whole book. Whybray[226] rightly points out that this block of proverbs presents 'a picture of the character of Yahweh in his relation to the world and to man' and that it also serves 'to indicate the principles of conduct which Yahweh requires of men'. The following summary of the teaching of this block is a modification of that given by Whybray:

1. Yahweh is the creator of everything and has a purpose for it all (16:4).
2. Yahweh knows humans through-and-through, and they are entirely subject to, and dependent on, him (16:1a, 2, 3, 9).
3. Yahweh hates and punishes the arrogant, who do not accept his rule (16:4b, 5) but gives success and security to those who do accept it (16:3, 7).

222. Whybray, 'Yahweh-Sayings', 158.
223. Whybray, *Proverbs*, 242.
224. Van Leeuwen, *Proverbs*, 159.
225. Whybray, 'Yahweh-Sayings', 157-65.
226. Whybray, 'Yahweh-Sayings', 158.

4. Humans should base their lives on certain principles: they must recognise Yahweh's superior knowledge and power (16:1, 2, 3, 4, 9); they must submit to his instruction (15:33); they must fear Yahweh and commit themselves to him (15:33; 16:3, 6, 7, 9). The essential principle is summed up in 16:3: 'Commit what you do to Yahweh, and your plans will be established.'

It is interesting that this summary is similar to the 'worldview' which Estes derives from Prov. 1–9. By a 'worldview' he means,[227] 'not a full-blown philosophy of life, but the beliefs, attitudes and values that cause a person to see the world in a certain way.' He adds: 'It is crucial to realize that a worldview is not just a description of how one sees life as it actually is. It also provides a vision for seeing life as it ideally ought to be.' He argues[228] that the worldview of Prov. 1–9 can be summed up in four general propositions:

1. Creation: the universe is Yahweh's creation. For this reason there is a common ethical system which applies to all humans. Therefore, knowing the wisdom that was present at creation is crucial.
2. Order: Yahweh is sovereignly controlling the world. He has established and sustains an order in the world which derives from his righteous character. Wisdom is skill in living according to Yahweh's righteous order, folly is choosing not to. As a result of this order there is a general pattern of acts and consequences. So, living by Yahweh's righteous norms brings success in life.
3. Rationality: Yahweh's world is knowable, but also mysterious. Yahweh has endowed humans with the capacity to discover the order in his universe, at least in part. The search for wisdom involves careful observation of life through personal experience. The wisdom tradition gathered generalisations based on recurrent patterns discerned in these observations to form a traditional corpus of tested information. However, there is also recognition that some of life is inscrutable. Yahweh is free to act in ways beyond human understanding.
4. Fear of Yahweh: humans must reverence Yahweh in their lives. This follows from the fact that Yahweh created the universe and that everything in it, including humans, is dependent on him. He alone has total knowledge and control in the universe and so humans should commit themselves to him in trust even though they cannot fully understand his ways.

227. Estes, *Hear, My Son,* 19-20.
228. Estes, *Hear, My Son,* 19-39.

Most of the Yahweh proverbs in Prov. 10-31 can be subsumed readily under the four themes identified in 15:33–16:9. Those that cannot, fall into three groups.

1. Proverbs about false weights and balances: 11:1; 16:11; 20:10, 23. Three of these are 'abomination' proverbs which simply state what is unacceptable to Yahweh. The other (16:11) is simply a statement of (theological) fact. These could, perhaps, be subsumed under points 2 or 3.
2. Proverbs about wives: 18:22; 19:14. Both are ways of asserting the importance of marriage in Yahweh's purposes. These could, perhaps, be subsumed under point 3, as examples of God blessing those who accept his rule.
3. Proverbs about the inscrutability of Yahweh: 19:21; 20:24; 21:30. These fit into Estes's worldview summary. The inscrutability of Yahweh might be seen as implied in the stress on his superior knowledge and power in 16:1, 2, 3, 4, 9.

What this study of the Yahweh proverbs shows is that there is a coherent worldview which forms the basis for the spirituality expressed in the Book of Proverbs — how one should live a life committed to Yahweh in the world which he has created.

An Integrated Spirituality

The Book of Proverbs deals with mundane, down-to-earth situations such as farming, trade in the market-place, credit and debt, the law courts, the royal court, behaviour at meals, families, neighbours, friends. Topics that one might expect to appear in a handbook on spirituality appear in only a handful of proverbs: prayer (15:8, 29; 28:9), sacrifice (15:8; 17:1; 21:3, 27) and vows (20:25). Only fractionally over a tenth of the verses make explicit mention of Yahweh (87 out of 853). This has led some scholars to suggest that it is fundamentally a 'secular' book with only a veneer of Yahwistic piety (see the section 'Proverbs: Secular or Religious?' above). However, as von Rad[229] has commented,

> The modern exegete is always tempted to read into the old texts the tensions with which he is all too familiar between faith and thought, between reason and revelation. Accordingly, there has been a tendency to infer too much from the preponderance of worldly sentences over religious ones.

229. Von Rad, *Wisdom in Israel*, 61.

He, as well as others, has questioned whether the idea of a sacred-secular division would have made any sense to ancient Israelites, or their neighbours. For them there was only one world of experience. Whether or not that is true, this section has shown that in the Book of Proverbs as we have it there is a coherent and pervasive spirituality. The sages were very concerned with spirituality in the sense in which it is defined at the start of this section, the bringing together of the ideas distinctive of Yahwism and the whole experience of living on the basis of and within the scope of that religion. When they concentrate on the mundane experiences of life they are not ignoring Yahweh or commitment to him, they are assuming it. It is Yahweh's character and purposes which define what is 'wise' and 'righteous'. That is why 'the fear of Yahweh is the beginning of wisdom'.

Because of its worldview the spirituality of Proverbs is one which, to use our modern terms, thoroughly integrates the sacred and the secular. There is no dichotomy between them. As Estes[230] puts it, 'In proverbs the juxtaposition of the routine details of daily life with reminders of Yahweh's evaluation of those activities (*cf.* Pr. 3:27-35) reveals that all of life is regarded as a seamless fabric.' This has a lesson for us today. Sheriffs[231] points out that 'The dichotomies that plague Christian denominations and books on personal sanctification are not found in these maxims in Proverbs.' Such issues as drunkenness and sexual immorality which usually loom large in such books do find a place in Proverbs, but such issues as injustice, exploitation, oppression, dishonesty, lying, anger and arrogance are dealt with just as forcefully. It is a very integrated spirituality.

The spirituality of Proverbs is not only 'integrated' in the sense that it brings the whole sweep of life's experiences within the scope of what it means to live out 'the fear of Yahweh'. It also, and more fundamentally, seeks to produce integrated people. The sages are concerned with character formation. They want to produce better people who will produce a better world. The key to this is people whose 'being' is shaped by 'the fear Yahweh'. This will then determine their 'doing'. A person's inward commitment and their outward behaviour should be an integrated whole. This comes across clearly in the handful of proverbs that do refer to 'religious' observances. They condemn hypocritical religion in which the outward action is not a true reflection of the inward commitment.

> If one turns away his ear from hearing the law,
> then his prayer is an abomination. (28:9)

230. Estes, *Hear, My Son,* 25.
231. Sheriffs, *Friendship of the Lord,* 177.

> The sacrifice of the wicked is an abomination;
> how much more when he brings it with evil intent? (21:29)

This concern leads to an insistence that obedience to Yahweh in the sanctuary, by bringing sacrifices, means nothing unless it is matched by obedience in everyday life.

> To do righteousness and justice
> is more acceptable to Yahweh than sacrifice. (21:3)

The concern voiced here is expressed in similar fashion in the prophets (1 Sam. 15:22; Hos. 6:6).

Kidner[232] comments that the great majority of the influences which help to produce a godly character are what we would regard as natural rather than supernatural. He goes on to say,

> The Book of Proverbs reassures us that this, if it is true, is no reflection on the efficiency of God's grace; for the hard facts of life, which knock some of the nonsense out of us, are *God's* facts and his appointed school of character; they are not alternatives to His grace, but means of it; for everything *is* of grace, from the power to know to the power to obey.

He supports his final comment by reference to Prov. 20:2.

The Book of Proverbs ends with an example of someone who displays the integrated spirituality of the book — in the poem about the valiant woman (31:10-31). All her actions as she runs her house and her businesses and looks after her family are rooted in, and express, her fear of Yahweh.

Overcoming the Sacred-Secular Divide

In a discussion of the history of the interpretation of what he calls 'The Song of the Valiant Woman' (Prov. 31:10-31) Wolters[233] outlines four views about the relationship between 'nature' and 'grace' which he argues have influenced interpretation of this song. He gives them tags which make a play on Latin prepositions and relates them to particular Christian traditions.

232. Kidner, *Proverbs*, 35.
233. Wolters, *The Song*, 16.

1. *Gratia contra naturam:* Grace opposing nature. The Christian life is incompatible with the ordinary world and provides a radical alternative to it. This is a view strongly represented in the Anabaptist tradition.
2. *Gratia supra naturam:* Grace completing nature. These are understood in such a way that a 'spiritual', or 'supernatural', *ordo* (order) 'perfects' the 'natural' one. This is a classical Roman Catholic position.
3. *Gratia iuxta naturam.* Grace flanking nature. Nature and grace are two realms alongside each other without any intrinsic connection between them. This is often associated with Lutheranism.
4. *Gratia intra naturam.* Grace restoring nature. Nature and grace are not distinct realms. Grace means re-creation and renewal of perverted nature. This has been strong in the Calvinistic tradition.

Wolters shows how the first three views have all prompted interpretations of the song in ways which import a sacred-secular divide which undervalues the woman's 'secular' activities. This may be done by allegorising the whole song so that these activities are 'spiritualised' or by divorcing them from 'the fear of Yahweh' rather than seeing them as an expression of it.

In 1638 the English Puritan Thomas Cartwright,[234] interpreting the song in conscious opposition to current Anabaptist and Roman Catholic interpretations, commented that 'This passage must be given careful attention in order to establish us more firmly in the common duties of this life as duties pleasing to God.' In saying this Cartwright is following in the steps of the leading Protestant Reformers. In his work *To the Christian Nobility of the German Nation,* Luther[235] wrote,

> Therefore just as those who are now called 'spiritual', that is priests, bishops or popes, are neither different from other Christians nor superior to them, except that they are charged with the administration of the word of God and the sacrament, which is their work and office, so it is with the temporal authorities. They bear the sword and rod in their hand to punish the wicked and protect the good. A cobbler, a smith, a peasant — each has the work and office of his trade, and yet they are all alike consecrated priests and bishops. Further, everyone must benefit and serve every other by means of his own work and office so that in this way many kinds of work may be done for the bodily and spiritual welfare of the community, just as all members of the body serve one another [1 Cor. 12:14-26].

234. Quoted in Wolters, *Song,* 25.

235. Luther, *Luther's Works,* 44:130.

Here Luther clearly and deliberately breaks down the sacred-secular divide. Each and every Christian has a 'work and office' by which they should contribute to both the 'bodily and spiritual welfare' of the community. In terms of the value of their work no distinction is to be made between 'spiritual' workers such as 'priest, bishop, or pope' and 'secular' workers such as 'cobbler, smith, or peasant'. Calvin[236] makes the same point more succinctly when he writes: 'in following your proper calling, no work will be so mean and sordid as not to have splendour and value in the eyes of God'.

Although there have been those who have kept this aspect of reformation teaching alive down the centuries the fact is, for whatever reason (and it is possible to suggest several) the sacred-secular divide is widespread in churches of all traditions today. Greene[237] lists four questions which he sees as exposing symptoms of the divide today:

1. Why do 50 percent of Christians say that they have never heard a sermon on work? And why have they probably not asked for one?
2. Why do we pray for teenagers going on short-term missions overseas but not for their daily mission in their local schools?
3. Why are so few of our contemporary worship songs about the nitty-gritty of daily life and mission in the world?
4. Why do we believe that church-paid ministry and mission is a higher calling than any other?

He quotes[238] a comment by a teacher who was very aware of the effect of the sacred-secular divide in church: 'I spend an hour a week teaching in Sunday school and they haul me up to the front of the church to pray for me. The rest of the week I'm a full-time teacher and the church has never prayed for me. That says it all.'

How can the sacred-secular divide be overcome? There is no single, simple answer[239] but an integrated spirituality such as that found in Proverbs must be an essential part of it. It needs to be transposed into a fully Christian context if it is to impact churches today. This could be done by a re-assertion of the Reformers' doctrine of Christian vocation, Christian 'calling'. Wolters[240] notes the influence of Luther's doctrine of *Beruf* or vocation on Melanchthon's commentaries on the Song of the Valiant Woman. In them he speaks of her *vocatio*

236. Calvin, *Institutes,* 3.10.6.

237. Greene, *Great Divide,* 6.

238. Greene, *Great Divide,* 7.

239. The book by Greene and the resources associated with it provide practical suggestions for individuals, groups and churches. It is oriented towards the UK context.

240. Wolters, *Song,* 23.

and says that in the song 'the chief virtues and duties of her calling are listed'. Weber[241] recognised the importance of Luther's doctrine. It gave 'worldly' activity a religious significance. Each legitimate calling has the same worth to God. In his view, 'This moral justification of worldly activity was one of the most important results of the Reformation, and particularly of Luther's part in it.' He also argued that Calvinism played an important part in establishing this view of calling. As the quotation from Calvin's *Institutes* given above shows, he shared Luther's view of calling.

A Christian understanding of 'calling' which draws on the spirituality of Proverbs and reformation teaching can be set out briefly in the following way:

1. The Lordship of Christ over *all* of life. Through him everything was created and through his atoning sacrifice everything will be reconciled to him (Col. 1:15-20). Therefore he has authority over the whole of creation (Eph. 1:22-23; Phil. 2:9-11).
2. Jesus' work of redemption is not separate from, or a replacement of, the purpose of God in creating the world. It does, in fact, enable that purpose to be fulfilled. This is spelt out in the first two chapters of the letter to the Hebrews, which begin with the statement that the Son is 'the heir of all things' through whom God created the world (Heb. 1:2). The author's use of a quotation from Ps. 8:4-6 is particularly significant (Heb. 2:5-9). This is used to express the fact that God's purpose in creation that humans, who were made 'lower than the angels', should be 'crowned with glory and honour' and have sovereignty over the earth can at present be seen *not* to have been fulfilled. *But* we do see Jesus, who for a little while was 'made lower than the angels' when he became a human being, 'crowned with glory and honour because of the suffering of death'. So, Jesus' redemptive work enables humans to be restored to fulfil the purpose God had for them when he created the world. (See further on this in the section 'Creation and Salvation' below.)
3. Humans have been given stewardship over *all* of creation (Gen. 1:27-30), so all of it can be used in his service. In the light of Heb. 2, redeemed humans have a special responsibility, and the ability, to do this. The Apostle Paul makes this clear in his exhortations: 'So, whether you eat or drink, or whatever you do, do all to the glory of God' (1 Cor. 10:31); 'And whatever you do, in word or deed, do everything in the name of the Lord Jesus, giving thanks to God the Father through him' (Col. 3:17).
4. Through the Holy Spirit, Christ gives a gift to *each and every* person to use for the common good (1 Cor. 12:7; Eph. 4:7-8). It is an indication of

241. Weber, *Protestant Ethic*, 79-92 (81).

the influence of the sacred-secular divide that much Christian discussion of Paul's lists of gifts and gifted people in Rom. 12:3-8; 1 Cor. 12:8-11, 27-30; and Eph. 4:11 concentrates on those that appear more obviously supernatural (such as prophecy and 'various kinds of tongues') and has less to say about those which could be seen as more natural (such as those in Rom. 12:7-8; helping and administrating in 1 Cor. 12:28). Paul, of course, is writing to churches and focuses on gifts used in that context, but many of the gifts could be used in the general community. In any case, there is no reason to suppose that the lists are meant to be exhaustive.

5. *All* are accountable to God for what we do with our lives, the gifts he has given us and the resources of his creation (Matt. 25:31-46; 1 Cor. 3:10-15).
6. It is not God's purpose that this world, which is part of the inheritance of his Son (Col. 1:16; Heb. 1:2), should be destroyed and replaced.[242] Rather, it will be renewed, transformed, and the work which humans do for God in the present will play its part in contributing to this transformation. That is expressed in John's vision of the New Jerusalem in Rev. 21. Revelation 21:1 must be understood in the light of v. 5. The 'passing away' of the first heaven and earth is not a destruction of them but a renewal of them. John then sees that 'the kings of the earth will bring their glory into it' (v. 24) and that 'they will bring into it the glory and honour of the nations' (v. 26). This speaks of a continuity with the first creation to which human endeavour makes its contribution.

This worldview, as Wolters would call it, leads to a view of Christian vocation/calling which embraces the whole of life and human activity. What matters is not *what* you do but *whether* God has called you to do it. This could range from bus driver to bishop, craft-worker to clergyperson, politician to pastor, missionary to musician. If done in the service of the Lord Christ all are equal in value in the eyes of God. This removes any sacred-secular division.

Wealth and Poverty in Proverbs

The topic of wealth and poverty is more prominent in the Book of Proverbs than it is in any other book in the Hebrew Bible.[243] According to Whybray,[244]

242. On 2 Pet. 3:7-13, which is sometimes understood this way, see Lucas, 'New Testament Teaching', 207-209.

243. Washington, *Wealth and Poverty*, 1.

244. Whybray, *Wealth and Poverty*, 15.

158 of the 513 verses in Prov. 10:1–22:16 and 25–29, the 'sentence literature' in the book, refer to wealth, poverty and social status. Scholars are agreed that the book presents a rather complex discourse about wealth and poverty, the rich and the poor, but disagree over how far there is coherence in this discourse.

The Vocabulary of Wealth and Poverty

In the Hebrew Bible as a whole there is only one noun that is used to denote the rich person: עָשִׁיר/*'āšîr.* In all but one (18:11) of its nine occurrences in Proverbs it is used in contrast to a word meaning 'a poor person'. What is remarkable in Proverbs is that, as we shall see, a generally negative picture is portrayed by this word. There is not a single virtue attributed to the rich.

The cognate verb עָשַׁר/*'āšar* ('to be, become rich') is used five times in the *hiphil* ('to make rich', 10:4, 22; 21:17; 23:4; 28:20) and once as the *hithpael* participle ('one presenting himself as rich', 13:7). One other verb, דָּשֵׁן/*dāšēn* is used three times in the *pual* ('to be made fat, enriched', 11:25; 13:4; 28:25).

The cognate noun עֹשֶׁר/*'ōšer* is the second most common noun for 'riches' in Proverbs, used nine times. The most common is הוֹן/*hôn,* used 18 times (in 30:15-16 it seems to have the sense 'enough'). A handful of other nouns are used, each on only a few occasions.

In contrast to the single noun for 'rich person' in the Hebrew Bible there are several words to denote 'poor person'. The commonest in Proverbs are רָאשׁ/*rā'š* (15 times) and דַּל/*dal* (15 times). The other two most commonly used nouns are אֶבְיוֹן/*'ebyôn* (four times) and עָנִי/*'ānî* or עָנָו/*'ānāw* (eight times). The question as to whether these latter two words are two separate words, *'ānî* ('poor') and *'ānāw* ('humble'), or variants of a single word is of little significance in Proverbs, unlike in the Psalms.

Pleins[245] points out that the frequency of the use of these four nouns in Proverbs is the reverse of what is the case in the prophets and Psalms, where *dal* and *rā'š* are rarely used. He sees in this evidence that the sages have a value system that differs substantially from that of the prophets. This, however, is a precarious argument. Barr[246] has warned of the danger in semantics of 'illegitimate identity transfer', of assuming that the semantic meaning of a word can be simply transferred from one context to another. That the prophets didn't use particular words whereas the sages did doesn't necessarily mean

245. Pleins, 'Poverty in the Social World of the Wise', 63.
246. Barr, *Semantics,* 218.

that they saw the same difference of meaning in the various nouns and chose those which suited their different value systems. In fact Whybray[247] concludes from his study of the use of these different nouns in Proverbs that 'it appears probable that no significant distinction between the words for "poor" and "poverty" was intended by these speakers'. He goes on to comment that it is not clear why such an abundance of synonyms is used. Sandoval,[248] however, does note one significant pattern in usage. Most of the occurrences of *ʾebyôn* and *ʿānî*/*ʿānāw* are in indicative statements or admonitions in which these words are the grammatical objects that are acted on, not subjects that act. These are among the proverbs that he classifies as concerned with social justice. The noun *dal* also occasionally occurs in these kinds of statements. In the Prophets and Psalms *ʾebyôn* and *ʿānî*/*ʿānāw* are often paired or put in parallel. This is true of three of the four occurrences of *ʾebyôn* in Proverbs (30:14; 31:9, 20).

The most common noun for 'poverty' in Proverbs is מַחְסוֹר/*maḥsôr* (used eight times). The noun רִישׁ/*rêš*/*rîš* occurs five times and רֵאשׁ/*rēʾš* occurs twice.

The verb רוּשׁ/*rûš* meaning 'to be poor' occurs only once, in the *hithpolel* (13:7, 'to make oneself poor'). Verbs that are used with reference to poverty usually refer to specific kinds of poverty such as hunger and destitution.

The Prologue of Proverbs

The prologue of Proverbs (1:1-7) is a carefully structured chiasm which lists various intellectual and moral virtues. At the heart of it is the trio of communal or social virtues of 'righteousness, justice and equity'. The prologue sets out Proverbs' concern with the shaping of the character and way of life of its readers (see the section 'The Spirituality of Proverbs'). It presents the purpose of the book and the outcomes that careful study of it offers to the readers. In it there is no indication that it offers the attainment of material wealth. As we shall see, material prosperity does appear in Proverbs as an aspect of a good and flourishing life, but the point the prologue makes is that what you *are* is foundational to the good life. What you *have* is a secondary matter. The trio of social virtues at the heart of the prologue do, of course, have obvious relevance to the subject of wealth and poverty since the unequal distribution of material prosperity in a society is a social justice issue related to the unrighteous behaviour of some members of the society.

247. Whybray, *Wealth and Poverty*, 22.

248. Sandoval, *Discourse of Wealth and Poverty*, 142-43.

Sandoval[249] argues that sufficient attention has not been given to v. 6 as a 'hermeneutical cue' to the reading of the book. This verse lists four kinds of literature which readers of the book need to understand. The meaning of two of the terms used (מְלִיצָה/*mĕlîṣâ*, 'saying, parable, figure'; חִידֹת/*ḥîdōt*, 'riddle') is a matter of debate, and even the meaning of the word מָשָׁל (*māšāl*, 'proverb') in this context is questioned by some (see the discussion of v. 6 in the commentary). The fact is that Proverbs contains very little in the way of riddles or parables. However, Sandoval notes, a number of scholars have seen in this verse a more general statement that Proverbs contains some 'opaque speech' which requires thoughtful interpretation. Understanding it in depth requires some literary expertise. Noting that vv. 4-5 address both 'the young' and 'the wise', he says,[250] 'In sum, although much in Proverbs might be appropriate for the instruction of younger males, the prologue indicates as well that the book often requires — as a trope or figure does — a more sophisticated reading beneath the surface or literal meaning.'

In his view this is particularly relevant to the proverbs that deal with wealth and poverty. He argues that scholars tend to read them too literally, not paying attention to the way that many are used figuratively as part of the sages' rhetoric on this subject. How is the reader to know when a proverb should be read figuratively? Sometimes it is because a literal meaning does not make sense. An example is Sandoval's reading of Prov. 10:16:

> The wage of a righteous person leads to life;
> the produce of a wicked person to sin.

He says,[251] 'Any attempt to understand literally how a wage leads to life, and especially how produce leads to sin, ends, in Ricoeur's terms, in an absurdity. A literal understanding of the line is non-sensical.' The 'wage' and 'produce' of this proverb have to be read metaphorically as what a person gains from acting in a righteous or wicked manner. Proverbs 11:18 and 15:6 are other examples of proverbs which require a figurative reading. In other cases it is what Sandoval calls the 'literary and moral Gestalt' of the Book of Proverbs, of which the prologue is an indication, which requires that a proverb should not be read primarily in literal terms. This is particularly so for proverbs which promise well-being, or threaten the reverse. We will consider examples of this later.

249. Sandoval, *Discourse of Wealth and Poverty*, 49-55.
250. Sandoval, *Discourse of Wealth and Poverty*, 55.
251. Sandoval, *Discourse of Wealth and Poverty*, 158.

Proverbs 1–9

There is no mention of 'the poor' in Prov. 1–9. It is generally agreed that, given the context and the contrast with 'scorner/mockers', the word עֲנָיִים/*'ănāyîm* in 3:34 means 'humble'. Poverty is mentioned in 6:10-11, which introduces a theme that is repeated in Proverbs — laziness leads to poverty.

There is no mention of 'the rich' in Prov. 1–9 either, but wealth is a theme that runs through these chapters. Wealth and riches are something which Wisdom has and offers to those who find her:

> Length of days are in her right hand,
> and in her left are riches and honour. (3:16)
>
> Riches and honour are with me,
> lasting wealth and righteousness. (8:18)

However, there is an important command in 3:9-10:

> Honour the LORD with your riches
> and with the first fruits of your produce;
> then your barns will be filled with plenty,
> and your vats will overflow with new wine.

Here the enjoyment of wealth is subordinated to, and dependent on, honouring the LORD. Indeed, as noted in the commentary on 3:1-12, this is the third of three 'commands with motivation': 'trust in the LORD ' (v. 5), 'fear the LORD' (v. 7) and now 'honour the LORD'. Sandoval[252] argues that vv. 9-10 should not be taken too literally. In them the rhetoric of wealth is being used in a figurative way to motivate behaviour. The language of v. 10 is clearly hyperbolic. It is 'paradisiacal and utopian'. The same is true of the language of v. 8, which promises physical healing and health for those who 'fear the LORD' in terms which most commentators are less prone to take literally than they do the language of v. 10. In fact vv. 8 and 10 are expressing the ways in which 'trust in the LORD ' (v. 5), described in particular ways in vv. 7 and 9, leads to one's life-path being made 'straight' (v. 6). The whole unit is saying that commitment to the LORD leads to human flourishing, using hyperbolic language. For this reason vv. 8 and 10 are not to be taken as simple, literal promises, but as figures of speech used to motivate the reader to heed the commands. They do suggest that commitment

252. Sandoval, *Discourse of Wealth and Poverty*, 102-4.

to the Lord will lead to a healthier, more prosperous, life but the language used should not be taken literally.

It is significant that the first mention of wealth in Proverbs is put in the mouth of 'sinners' in the first lesson in the book (1:8-19). Here the prospect of gaining wealth quickly is used as an enticement to get the young man to join the sinners in their plot to ambush innocent people (v. 13, which includes the word הוֹן/*hôn*). As a result, it is made clear at the outset of the book that wealth is not an absolute good but is ambiguous in nature. Abiding by the social virtues of wisdom listed in 1:3b is more important than acquiring wealth. Both the motivation for acquiring it and the way it is acquired must accord with these virtues. The son is warned not to be 'greedy for unjust gain' (v. 19). This warning is supported by the picture of the sinners suffering the very fate that they had in mind for their victims (v. 18). This is a clear example of figurative language being used as (negative) motivation in relation to wealth and poverty. From this point on there is, as Sandoval[253] points out, 'a progression in Proverbs' use of the rhetoric of wealth' in this section of the book.

Proverbs 2:4-5. In the second lesson the father begins by using the same verb as that used by the sinners in 1:11 and in his warning in 1:18 (צָפַן/*ṣāpan*). Whereas in ch 1 it is used in the sense 'hideaway in ambush' the father now uses it to mean 'hideaway/store up' with reference to his commandments. He then uses wealth imagery to express the value of wisdom and so motivate the son's search for it. The son is urged to search for wisdom *as* he would search for silver and treasure. Wisdom, it is implied, is at least as valuable as such material wealth.

Proverbs 3:14-16. These verses are part of a poem in praise of wisdom in which wisdom is personified as a woman. They go beyond simply comparing the value of Wisdom and what she offers to the value of material wealth. They assert that Wisdom is *better than* silver and gold, *more precious than* jewels (on the nature of these jewels see the commentary on v. 15). In her left hand she holds riches (עֹשֶׁר/*ʿōšer*). There is no straightforward promise here that finding Wisdom will lead to material prosperity. The imagery of wealth is used to motivate the search for wisdom, and its use relativises the value and importance of material wealth. Verse 16 might be taken to imply that finding wisdom will lead to human flourishing in terms of health, wealth and status. However, the imagery here is part of the figure of speech of personified Wisdom and might be intended to point beyond material goods to the moral goods which lead to human flourishing.

Proverbs 4:5-9. See the commentary on v. 7 for a discussion of the textual

253. Sandoval, *Discourse of Wealth and Poverty*, 95.

and translational issues relating to that verse. In the commentary it is argued that in these verses, in which Wisdom is again personified as a woman, bridal imagery is being used. Wisdom is presented as a desirable bride whom the son should acquire at all costs. The use of the verb קָנָה/*qānâ* here is significant. It often means 'to acquire by purchase, buy' (see the discussion of this verb in the commentary on 8:22). However, in Ruth 4:5, 10 it is used of acquiring a wife, where it seems to have the sense of 'marry as part of a legally valid commercial transaction'.[254] This aspect of the verb's use makes it a particularly apposite one for the father to use in this lesson as he urges his sons to use all they have, if necessary, to acquire Wisdom as their bride. This goes beyond asserting that Wisdom is much more valuable than material wealth to taking the next logical step. Rather than holding on to such wealth, one should be willing *to dispose of it in order to acquire wisdom.* Once again, the language is being used figuratively, but clearly the ultimate good is wisdom, not wealth.

Proverbs 8:10-11. These verses are part of a speech in which personified Wisdom, not the father, speaks of her value. It is addressed not just to the son but to all humans (v. 4, 'the sons of man'). The opening of this admonition is quite stark in the Hebrew text, 'Take my instruction *not* silver', though the following clause with its 'rather than' indicates that this is not a call to totally eschew material wealth. What is being asserted here in strong terms is the very great value of Wisdom. The next verse reinforces this in its statement that not only is Wisdom better than jewels, it is better than anything one might desire. Nothing can be compared with it in value.

Proverbs 8:17-21. The phrase 'those who love me' in vv. 17, 21 acts as an *inclusio* for this section of Wisdom's speech in which she speaks of the benefits she bestows on those who love her and seek her diligently. Whereas the sinners in 1:13 offered 'precious wealth' to the son if he followed them, a wealth which the father suggested was illusory, Wisdom has 'enduring wealth' (v. 18). The word translated as 'enduring' (עָתֵק/*'ātēq*) occurs only here in the Hebrew Bible, and its meaning is uncertain. A few take it to mean something like 'increase' ('boundless', NEB), but most scholars[255] and translations take it to mean 'enduring'. This enduring wealth is coupled with צְדָקָה/*ṣĕdāqâ.* Many modern translations take this to mean 'prosperity' (NEB, NIV, NRSV) or 'success' (NJPS). Most commentators, however, take the word here in its more usual meaning of 'righteousness', which is the meaning it has in all its other 17 occurrences in Proverbs, including a few verses later in 8:20. Its use in 8:18, 20 is probably a deliberate echo of the mention of the 'righteousness' (using the cognate noun

254. Campbell, *Ruth,* 146-47.

255. See the brief discussion in Fox, *Proverbs 1–9,* 277-78.

צֶדֶק/*ṣedeq*) in 1:3b, where it is linked with 'justice'. These two cognate words have a high degree of overlap in meaning and can be used as synonyms.[256] Wisdom's 'enduring wealth and righteousness' seem to be a deliberate contrast with what is offered by the sinners. Verse 19 echoes 3:14 but the language now becomes hyperbolic. Wisdom's 'fruit' is not just better than gold and silver, but is better than 'fine gold' and 'choice silver'. Many scholars see in v. 21 a literal promise of material prosperity. Sandoval,[257] however, questions this. The passage is part of a larger figurative one in which Wisdom is personified and is speaking. Verse 19 introduces the agricultural metaphor of 'fruit', and v. 21 has a promise to fill 'storehouses' (it is the assumption that material wealth is in mind which leads to the translation 'treasuries'). He argues that the nature of the metaphor in vv. 19-21 suggests that what will fill the 'storehouses' is Wisdom's 'fruit', which is better than the finest material wealth, namely Wisdom's virtues, especially righteousness and justice. Taken as a whole, vv. 17-21 may indeed imply that those whom Wisdom loves will enjoy a measure of prosperity and status in life (v. 18) but the primary 'goods' on offer are wisdom's virtues, which are of incomparable value.

Conclusion. Some scholars[258] see the lack of mention of the poor, and especially the need to help them, as a deficiency in Prov. 1–9. This, however, fails to take sufficient account of the purpose of these chapters. There is general agreement that they are intended as an introduction to the whole book. As such their purpose is to present and commend a general framework for a life lived according to the wisdom virtues set out in the prologue. These include the social virtues of justice, righteousness and equity. Much of the content of the lessons is taken up with warnings against those temptations which would draw the son away from learning and following the way of wisdom. Apparently high on the list of such temptations are the indulgence in illicit sexual fulfilment and the seeking to 'get rich quick' by means of unjust gain. The one mention of poverty in these chapters comes in a warning against giving way to the temptation to laziness (6:6-11).

A clear attitude to wealth comes through in a careful reading of these chapters. Material wealth is a good which it is legitimate to seek and enjoy. It is a blessing which may well come to those who follow the way of wisdom. However, it is a secondary good and should not be sought for itself. The search for wisdom must be the top priority in seeking 'the good life'. Material wealth, like the other secondary goods mentioned in these chapters — such as sexual

256. *NIDOTTE* 3:746, 751.

257. Sandoval, *Discourse of Wealth and Poverty,* 99-101.

258. For example: Houston, *Contending for Justice,* 118; Whybray, *Wealth and Poverty,* 102.

fulfilment, physical health and social status — must be sought and enjoyed within the framework of the communal social virtues of justice, righteousness and equity, because those who do otherwise threaten the well-being of the community. If we are to take these chapters seriously as an introduction to the whole book we must take their attitude to wealth (their 'moral Gestalt' as Sandoval calls it) as a guide to understanding the proverbs on wealth and poverty in the rest of it (*i.e.* treat them as a 'hermeneutical key').

Scholars have had a tendency to treat the proverbs on wealth and poverty in different sections of Prov. 10–31 separately. This is partly because, faced with what seem to be 'tensions' or 'contradictions' between proverbs on this topic, they try to find an explanation for them in different postulated social settings for the different collections in Proverbs. There is some logic in this, though it is a somewhat subjective pursuit. At some point, however, an editor, or editors, brought these collections together and, unless we assume this was done in a fairly unthinking 'cut and paste' way, presumably these 'tensions' did not worry them. We need to consider why this is. We have treated Prov. 1–9 on its own because it does seem to have been composed as an introduction to the rest of the book. Maybe its view on material wealth will enable us to understand, or resolve, the tensions. Using its view in this way is a reasonable thing to do. In the introduction it was pointed out that proverbs have to be understood in a context and that one of the skills of 'the wise' is knowing the right context in which to use a proverb. The sage(s) who compiled the Book of Proverbs may have given us Prov. 1–9 as the context within which to read Prov. 10–31 as a whole.

Proverbs 10–31

Wealth and prosperity. As in Prov. 1–9 material prosperity is presented in these chapters as something good which those who live by the fear of the LORD and by wisdom can expect to enjoy as a gift from God:

> The blessing of the LORD brings riches,
> and no toil can add to it. (10:22)
>
> The crown of the wise is their riches,
> the folly of fools is folly. (14:24)
>
> The reward for humility and the fear of the LORD:
> riches and honour and life. (22:4)

See the comments on these verses in the commentary with regard to the translations given.

However, it is recognised that one's ultimate trust must be in God, not riches, since riches are an unreliable source of security:

> Whoever trusts in his riches will fall,
> but the righteous will flourish like foliage. (11:28)
>
> Wealth does not profit in the day of wrath,
> but righteousness delivers from death. (11:4)

As noted in the commentary, 'the day of wrath' here probably does not have an eschatological meaning but refers to any disaster that threatens death. A rather double-edged comment on the security provided by riches is given in 13:8:

> The ransom for a man's life, his riches
> but a poor man hears no threat.

In the commentary we have argued for the understanding of this as a statement that while the wealthy have the resources to get themselves out of certain kinds of trouble (perhaps kidnapping or blackmail are in mind) the poor person's lack of wealth means that they are not subject to such threats.

The sages are concerned with how wealth is acquired. One concern is the ill-treatment of the poor. This is probably what is in mind in 28:8:

> Whoever increases his wealth by interest and overcharging
> gathers it for him who is generous to the poor.

Lending at interest (v. 8a) is forbidden in OT law (Exod. 22:25 [Heb. 24]; Lev. 25:26; Deut. 23:19 [Heb. 20]), which is concerned about lending to those in distress because this would drive them further into poverty. How the ill-gotten wealth will be redistributed to the poor is not explained in v. 8b. Ill-treatment of the poor is the concern of 22:16. This proverb is difficult to translate and understand. See the comments in the commentary in favour of the way it is usually understood:

> Oppressing the poor to enrich oneself,
> giving to the rich, leads only to loss. (22:16)

The oppression of the poor might be through loans at excessive interest, as in 28:8, or tax-farming. The gifts to the rich are presumably attempts to gain favour with them. How these strategies to get rich will lead to poverty is not spelt out.

Another concern is attempts to 'get rich quick':

> Wealth gained hastily will dwindle,
> but one who gathers by hand will increase it. (13:11)

Presumably the concern is that those who are impatient to gain wealth will ignore the social virtues of righteousness, justice and equity in their 'get rich quick' schemes, the sinners of the father's first lesson being an example of this. The suspicion of hastily gained wealth is repeated in 20:21; 28:20, 22. The proper way to gain wealth is by hard work:

> A lazy hand causes poverty,
> but the hand of the diligent makes rich. (10:4)

> A lazy man will not roast his game,
> but the diligent man will get precious wealth. (12:27)

(See the comment on the translation of 12:27 in the commentary.) However, the diligent search for wealth should not be overdone because material wealth is ephemeral:

> Do not toil to acquire wealth,
> be discerning enough to desist.
> When your eyes fly to it, it is gone,
> for it will surely grow wings,
> like an eagle and fly heavenwards. (23:4-5)

This is a warning against a fixation on gaining wealth which makes wealth an ultimate good.

Proverbs 10:4 and 12:27 are warnings that laziness will lead to poverty. So will excessive indulgence in pleasures:

> A lover of pleasure will be a poor man,
> a lover of wine and oil will not be rich. (21:17)

See also the warning of 29:3b.

Most striking are the 'better-than' sayings which assert that commitment to God and moral virtue is more important that having material prosperity:

Better a little with fear of the LORD
than great wealth and trouble with it. (15:16)

Better is a little with righteousness
than great income with injustice. (16:8)

Getting wisdom is better than gold,
and getting understanding is to be preferred rather than silver. (16:16)

A variety of particular virtues appear in other 'better-than' proverbs as preferable to forms of material prosperity: love (15:17), humility (16:19), peaceability (17:1), a good reputation (22:1), integrity (28:6). These are virtues which would promote social justice and harmony, which we have suggested seems to be an important concern of the sages in Prov. 1–9. Scholars who hold that there is a strong act-consequence nexus in Proverbs find these 'better-than' proverbs anomalous or problematic. For discussion of this see the section 'Acts and Consequences in Proverbs' above.

The rich. Early on in this section we commented that the picture given of 'the rich person' in Proverbs is a negative one. The wealth of the rich gives them a sense of security.

The wealth of a rich man is a strong city,
the ruin of the poor their poverty. (10:15)

This can be taken as an observation on the fact that wealth can protect people from some of the vicissitudes of life. Proverbs 18:11 puts this reliance on wealth for security in a more critical light by suggesting that it might be an illusion:

The wealth of a rich man is a strong city
and like a high wall in his imagination.

Moreover, the juxtaposition of this proverb with the one that precedes it is presumably deliberate, as indicated by the catchword 'strong':

A strong tower is the name of the LORD,
into it runs the righteous man and is safe. (18:10)

The implied criticism seems clear. It is not wealth that provides true security but the LORD. This is the point that is made in 11:28, quoted earlier.

The rich are said to have confidence in their own wisdom, perhaps because they think their wealth proves their wisdom:

> A rich man is wise in his own eyes,
> but a poor man with understanding can see through him. (28:11)

The contrast with the poor man clearly makes a negative comment on this self-confidence. Moreover, in Proverbs in general someone who is wise in their own eyes is branded as a fool, or worse (28:26; 26:12).

The sages recognise that some people become rich through crooked ways or violence:

> Better is the poor man who walks in his integrity
> than with crooked ways, though rich. (28:6)

> A gracious woman gets honour,
> but violent men get rich. (11:16)

See the comment in the commentary on the meaning of 11:16.

The rich are said to lord it over the poor:

> The rich man rules over the poor,
> and the borrower is slave to the lender. (22:7)

It may be that 28:8 (see above) has a bearing on this proverb. The rich are also unsympathetic to the entreaties of the poor:

> The poor utter entreaties
> but the rich answer roughly. (18:23)

The implied negative comment on the rich here is strengthened by Prov. 21:13 and 28:27.

The rich do not lack friends:

> The poor man is hated even by his neighbour,
> but those who love the rich are many. (14:20)

> Wealth makes many friends,
> but a poor man is deserted by his friend. (19:4)

However, these friends of the rich may well have selfish motives (see the comment on this verse in the commentary):

> Many seek the favour of a generous man,
> and everyone is a friend to one who gives gifts. (19:6)

It is striking that not a single positive virtue is attributed to the rich. However, we have seen that wealth itself is not regarded as something evil in Proverbs but as something to be desired provided one's priorities and motives are right. This leads Whybray[259] to conclude that in Proverbs *'āšîr* may have a special connotation, suggesting 'that it refers not simply to persons who have achieved or inherited greater prosperity than others, but to a particular kind of person who represents the exact opposite of the truly indigent, and who is regarded by the speakers with hostility'. He goes on to make the point that there is no indication that the sages who compiled Proverbs envied the *'āšîr* or wished to attain the status and power which they had.

Poverty and the poor. The references to 'the poor' in Proverbs are not simply to those who live in a state of relative poverty. They seem to be to people living in a state of serious deprivation:

> A rich man's wealth is his strong city,
> the poverty of the poor is their ruin. (10:15)

Here the state of the poor is described as 'ruin' using a word that can refer to a ruined city (see the commentary on this verse). Even granted that there may be an element of hyperbole in the contrast used, a great gap is implied here between rich and poor. In his study of proverbs on poverty Whybray[260] concludes that 'the kind of poverty these proverbs depict is not simply straitened means but actual destitution, a lack of the basic means of sustaining life.'

Some proverbs warn that poverty will come as a result of laziness:

> A little sleep, a little slumber,
> a little folding of the hands to rest,
> and poverty will come upon you like a robber;
> and want like an armed man. (24:33-34)

This proverb repeats 6:10-11. See also 10:4, quoted above, and 14:23. There are

259. Whybray, *Wealth and Poverty,* 23.
260. Whybray, *Wealth and Poverty,* 32.

other proverbs which denounce laziness and speak disparagingly of those who are lazy, for example:

> Laziness casts in to a deep sleep,
> and an idle person will suffer hunger. (19:15)
>
> The desire of the lazy person kills him,
> because his hands refuse to work. (21:25)

For this reason some scholars conclude that the sages present a negative view of the poor. Pleins[261] says that 'the poor are considered a despised and lazy lot in the proverbial literature' and[262] 'the wise see poverty's origins in a lack of commitment to the labors at hand.' However, as Houston[263] comments, 'It is not a logical conclusion from the fact that laziness leads to poverty that poverty, wherever it exists, is caused by laziness.' He goes on to point out that in the whole of the sentence literature in Proverbs there is only one example (16:31) where a conduct is deduced from its result. So he concludes, 'Hence it is far from demonstrable that the point of the sayings warning of laziness leading to poverty is to hold up the actual poor as a horrid example of what laziness leads to.' All the warnings about the danger of laziness leading to poverty are addressed to the relatively well-off and are not intended to say anything about how the poor *as a class in society* originate. Sandoval[264] sums up the point of these sayings well when he says, 'their purpose is not to explain disparities in the distribution of wealth, but like the other sayings belonging to wisdom's virtues discourse, to recommend a virtue and to discourage a vice.' This is supported by the fact that there are also warnings about other forms of behaviour which are likely to lead to poverty:

> The plans of the diligent lead surely to abundance,
> but everyone who is hasty comes only to poverty. (21:5)
>
> Whoever loves pleasure will be a poor man;
> he who loves wine and oil will not be rich. (21:17)
>
> A lover of wisdom makes his father glad,
> but a companion of prostitutes squanders his wealth. (24:3)

261. Pleins, 'Poverty in the Social World of the Wise', 69.
262. Pleins, *Social Visions*, 469.
263. Houston, 'Role of the Poor', 233.
264. Sandoval, *Discourse of Wealth and Poverty*, 140.

> One who works his land will get plenty of bread,
> but one follows worthless pursuits will get plenty of poverty. (28:19)

No one has taken these as suggesting that 'get rich quick schemes', hedonism, consorting with prostitutes and wasting time and energy on pointless activities explain the origins of the poor as a class in society.

It is also worth noting, as Houston[265] does, that far from there being a 'veritable attack on the poor' in Proverbs, as Pleins asserts,[266] there are no condemnatory statements about the poor or how they have brought their poverty on themselves. On the contrary, the tone of many of the proverbs which speak of the poor seems to be 'either regretfully objective or positively sympathetic'.

Houston's comment runs against a fairly widespread consensus that tends to see many of the proverbs about the rich and the poor as 'neutral' observations about what was a social reality. Washington[267] points out that, in saying this, scholars often ignore the fact that seemingly 'ethically neutral' proverbs are often qualified by ethically evaluative proverbs in their immediate or close context. One of the examples he gives concerns the attitude some people have to poor neighbours:

> The poor is disliked even by his neighbour,
> but the rich has many friends. (14:20)
>
> Whoever despises his neighbour is a sinner,
> but blessed is he who is generous to the poor. (14:21)

It is clear that v. 21 provides a critical corrective to the previous proverb. The stark observation of Prov. 22:7 is immediately followed by two proverbs which qualify it by calling for the poor to be treated with justice and generosity (22:7-9):

> The rich rules over the poor,
> and the borrower is the slave of the lender.
> Whoever sows injustice will reap calamity,
> and the rod of their anger will fail.
> Those who are generous are blessed,
> for they share their bread with the poor.

265. Houston 'Role of the Poor', 234-35.
266. Pleins, *Social Visions*, 437.
267. Washington, *Wealth and Poverty*, 196-202.

In Washington's view, reading proverbs in their editorial context, rather than merely as isolated sayings, removes at least some of the tensions which scholars have seen among the sayings on wealth and poverty.

Justice and equity, to which generosity contributes, are two of the three social virtues of Prov. 1:3b which contribute to the 'moral Gestalt' of the book. Sandoval argues that the view that many of the proverbs about the rich and poor are 'neutral observations' cannot be sustained if one reads these proverbs within the context of the overall 'moral Gestalt' of the book. After a detailed study of Prov. 18:23 and 22:7 (which have been quoted above) he concludes[268] that although they

> may represent 'the way the world is', the book's social justice discourse, which has constituted the poor as a class of moral concern, provides a critical perspective for discerning what sort of observation each statement constitutes. They are an articulation of the fact that something 'is', but ought not to be; and in both verses, the instruction's particularly resonant images implicitly critiques the reality it observes.

We will now see what more can be gleaned about the 'moral Gestalt' of the book with regard to the poor and poverty.

Social causes of poverty. Pleins's claim[269] that 'in general the writers of Proverbs betray no awareness that the poor as a group are poor because they have been wronged by the ruling elite, as the prophets consistently proclaimed' is undermined by more than just the single exception he notes (28:15). There is recognition that there are those who oppress the poor in various ways (see above for comment on 22:16):

> Oppressing the poor to enrich oneself,
> giving to the rich, leads only to loss. (22:16)
>
> There are those whose teeth are swords,
> whose fangs are knives,
> to devour the poor from off the earth,
> the needy from among humankind. (30:14)

The reference to 'swords' and 'knives' in 30:14 may be a way of referring to those who have the power of punishment in society, and so to the political elite,

268. Sandoval, *Discourse of Wealth and Poverty*, 193.
269. Pleins, 'Poverty in the Social World of the Wise', 67.

and the reference to 'teeth' and 'fangs', indicating the use of words, could point to their abuse of the legal system. Such abuse of the legal system is explicitly condemned in Proverbs:

> Do not rob the poor because he is poor,
> or crush the afflicted at the gate,
> for the LORD will plead their cause
> and rob the life of those who rob them. (22:22-23)

We have suggested above that making loans to the poor at exorbitant interest is condemned in Prov. 22:7 and 28:8. These, and other practices, would be encompassed by the following proverb:

> The fallow ground of the poor would yield much food,
> but it is swept away through injustice. (13:23)

Pleins's exception is a statement that wicked rulers bring poverty on those whom they (mis)rule:

> Like a roaring lion or a charging bear
> is a wicked ruler over a poor people. (28:15)

While it is true to say that the sages in Proverbs do not provide any detailed analysis of why the poor as a class exist in society, it is wrong to say that they are unaware of, or uninterested in, at least some of the reasons why they exist. They recognise, and condemn, a variety of kinds of social injustice which cause poverty.

The treatment of the poor. Proverbs does not present any programme for the eradication of poverty. It does, however, insist that the poor should be treated in ways that would at least alleviate their poverty and might even result in more than that. This has a theological basis:

> Whoever oppresses a poor man insults his Maker,
> but he who is generous to the needy honours him. (14:31)

Perdue[270] thinks that it is 'remarkable that the saying in Proverbs 14:31 admonishes unqualified support for the poor, whoever they may be'. In Proverbs there is no hint of any distinction between 'deserving' and 'undeserving' poor

270. Perdue, *Wisdom and Creation*, 103.

when it comes to treatment of the poor. This is because, as we have argued in the section 'Wisdom and Creation', there is a clear and coherent theme which runs through the four proverbs which refer to God as the Creator of the poor (14:31; 17:5; 22:2; 29:13). It is that poor people share a common origin with rich people. Both were created by the same God. Therefore to oppress poor people is to insult God, while to recognise their status as fully fellow human beings is to honour God. As Whybray[271] comments, 'The theological implications of this thought are immense.' It implies, among other things, that everyone, the poor included, has a God-given right to the necessities of life. There is therefore a theological imperative to actualise social justice by moral behaviour that will enable the poor to have an equitable share of communal resources, which ultimately are God-given. That this is what the sages believed is expressed in proverbs which assert that God defends the poor (see 22:22-23 quoted above) and rewards those who care for them:

> Whoever is generous to the poor lends to the LORD,
> and he will repay him for his deed. (19:17)

> Whoever has a bountiful eye will be blessed,
> for he shares his bread with the poor. (22:9)

The following proverb probably implies that God will also repay those who are wilfully blind to the needs of the poor (see the comment on this verse in the commentary):

> Whoever gives to the poor will not want,
> but he who hides his eyes will get many a curse. (28:27)

Generosity to the poor is one of the virtues which characterises the 'valiant woman' in the acrostic poem at the end of Proverbs who incarnates the virtues of wisdom:

> She opens her hand to the poor,
> and reaches out her hands to the needy. (31:20)

Clearly generosity to the poor is assumed to be a normal part of life in a household whose members 'fear the LORD' as this woman does.

271. Whybray, *Proverbs*, 223.

Houston[272] finds a 'serious contradiction in the wisdom teachers' position' in the fact that in calling for generosity to the poor they are appealing to the rich, whom they characterise in other proverbs as treating the poor badly, even to the point of oppression. However, if one accepts Whybray's conclusion (see above) that 'the rich' in Proverbs are not the sum total of the wealthy, but only a reprehensible sub-set, then the 'contradiction' does not exist. In fact none of the appeals to be generous to the poor is addressed specifically to 'the rich', and there is no reason to think that only the very wealthy were being urged to be generous.

The sages insist that the poor are to be listened to when they call for help:

> Whoever closes his ear to the cry of the poor
> will himself call out and not be answered. (21:13)

This might apply particularly to their pleas for justice through the legal system. We've seen that they are to be given justice in the courts (22:22-23), but rulers are especially admonished to ensure that this is the case:

> If a king faithfully judges the poor,
> his throne will be established for ever. (29:14)

> Open your mouth, judge righteously,
> defend the rights of the poor and needy. (31:9)

The latter proverb is addressed to Lemuel, King of Massa.

In general, the sages assert that a righteous person should know, and the implication is uphold, the rights of the poor:

> A righteous man knows the rights of the poor;
> a wicked man does not understand knowledge. (29:7)

Proverbs 30:7-9. This passage stands out in Proverbs in two ways. It is the only prayer in the book and it expresses a desire not to be rich:

> Two things I ask of you;
> do not deny them to me before I die;
> remove falsehood and lying far from me;
> give me neither poverty nor riches;

272. Houston, 'Role of the Poor', 238.

> feed me with the food that I need,
> lest, being full, I deny you
> and say, 'Who is the LORD?'
> or lest, being poor, I steal,
> and blaspheme the name of my God.

Although in some ways, most notably in 30:8b, this prayer goes beyond what is expressed elsewhere in Proverbs, one can see why the sages who edited Proverbs included this prayer towards the end of the book. It makes clear the ultimate priority in life, a person's relationship with God. The hazards of wealth (well-recognised in other proverbs) and poverty (only previously alluded to in 6:30) are both clearly articulated. What is unique, but quite understandable in the light of the rest of Proverbs, is the firm preference for a 'middle way' between wealth and poverty.

Conclusion. Proverbs is sometimes criticised for lacking the radical approach to social justice found in the prophets and for not presenting a programme for the elimination of poverty but only for alleviating it. There is some justice in these criticisms, which is why Christians must pay attention to the whole canon of Scripture. However Proverbs should be given credit for what it does do. It does give considerable attention, more so than most other biblical books, to the issue of wealth and poverty in society. It does present it as an issue of social justice and gives a theological basis for this. While it does not present any programme for eliminating poverty what it makes clear is that the 'wise' and the righteous' cannot pass off responsibility for facing up to this issue of social justice to 'the government' but must take personal responsibility for responding to it in the various ways the sages outline.

An African Perspective

Kimilike[273] has asserted that 'the African view challenges the dominant position held by Western studies of the Book of Proverbs which appears to emphasise that the book upholds the *status quo* of the poor and rich in society.' He argues that the affluence of the 'Northern' societies in which these scholars live has influenced the way they understand the biblical proverbs and that reading them in an African context gives a different understanding.

The aim of his work is quite specific. It is to answer the question,[274] 'In

273. Kimilike, *Poverty in the Book of Proverbs,* 9.
274. Kimilike, *Poverty in the Book of Proverbs,* 9.

what way can the African view on poverty (derived from relevant African proverbs) enable Bible readers to make meaning of, or understand, OT proverbs on poverty in an attempt towards facilitating the empowerment of the poor in African Christian contexts.' Because the aim is so specific we will not survey his work as a whole, but look at a few selective examples of how his approach leads him to interpret some biblical proverbs.

Kimilike argues that proverbs must be understood in the context of the worldview of the society which produced them. He lists[275] three common components of the African worldview:

1. A unitive view of reality with no matter/spirit or profane/sacred divides.
2. A belief in the divine origin of the universe and the interconnectedness between God, humans and the cosmos.
3. A sense of community whereby a person's identity is defined in terms of belonging to a community.

He suggests that this worldview is close to that of ancient Israel.

Proverbs 13:7.[276] This proverb has puzzled Western commentators:

One pretends to be rich, yet has nothing,
another pretends to be poor but has great wealth.

In African culture boastfulness, self-glorification and pride are strongly discouraged and regarded as taboo because they are considered a danger to the well-being of the community. Pretending to be poor can be a way of limiting generosity when asked to help others. The proverb relates to the priority of generosity in a society where egalitarian principles engage everyone. It reinforces communal solidarity by warning against corrupting motives.

Proverbs 19:7.[277] This is one of a number of proverbs about the 'friendlessness' of the poor:

All a poor man's brothers hate him;
how much more do his friends go far from him.

African proverbs stress the importance of establishing the maximum number of social relationships for a person's welfare. This takes priority over material

275. Kimilike, *Poverty in the Book of Proverbs*, 166.
276. Kimilike, *Poverty in the Book of Proverbs*, 170-80.
277. Kimilike, *Poverty in the Book of Proverbs*, 188-96.

possessions. Taken with v. 6 this proverb is more about the *causes* of poverty than about its *consequences:*

> Many seek the favour of a generous man,
> and everyone is a friend to the man who gives gifts. (19:6)

It is a call to the hearers to promote strong social networks to rehabilitate the poor in society.

Proverbs 21:13.[278]

> Whoever closes his ear to the cry of the poor
> will himself call out and not be answered.

In an African context offering help in various ways, such as generosity, is a moral responsibility. To refuse the disadvantaged access to communal resources is detrimental to both the perpetrator and the victim. It brings estrangement into the community and this threatens its survival. The proverb warns against limiting the potential of solidarity to challenge poverty by the denial of social access to the community's resources.

Proverbs 22:2.[279] This can be compared with the African proverb 'We are all tools (of the same master); we were all made in the same smithy':

> The rich and the poor meet together;
> the LORD is the maker of them all.

In the communal nature of African society the egalitarian principle denies God's involvement in the stratification of society. God's creation is considered perfect. Wealth is intended to promote the social welfare of the whole community.

Kimilike's work shows the considerable influence of social context on the understanding of proverbs. It suggests that a dialogue between Western and African scholars could be fruitful in the study of biblical proverbs.

Conclusion

Until very recently there has been a widespread assumption in Western civilisation that the well-being of a nation depended primarily on material prosperity.

278. Kimilike, *Poverty in the Book of Proverbs,* 197-204.
279. Kimilike, *Poverty in the Book of Proverbs,* 281-87.

It was measured by such things as the average national wage and the Gross National Product (GNP). More recently, perhaps due the economic setbacks of recent years, there has been some interest in the wider concept of Gross National Happiness (GNH), a term originally coined by the King of Bhutan in 1972. Some progress has been made in finding ways of constructing a GNH Index for a community or country.[280] At a time when at least some people are questioning the priority of material wealth for human well-being the sages of ancient Israel have a relevant message with their relativising of material wealth and the primary place they give to the importance of the spiritual and moral aspects of wisdom for the well-being of communities and human flourishing in them. Christians need to consider how this can be brought into the current market-place of ideas.

Kimilike's work is a reminder that while these ideas are discussed, there is an urgent need, in the West as well as in Africa and elsewhere, to engage in the day-to-day battle against poverty. Proverbs exhorts individuals to play their part in this and gives some practical guidelines as to what this might involve.

Wisdom and Christology

The personification of Wisdom in Proverbs was taken up and developed in later Jewish wisdom literature. These developments influenced the way early Christian thinkers, from the NT writers onwards, expressed their beliefs about Jesus.

The Wisdom of Jesus ben Sirach

This is one of the books in the OT Apocrypha. Its author is identified in 50:27 as 'Jesus son of Eleazar son of Sirach of Jerusalem'. 'Sirach' is how the name is spelt in the Greek text, in Hebrew it is spelt 'Sira', and scholars use both forms.[281] In the Latin Vulg it is given the title 'Ecclesiasticus'. The book is only known in full in Greek translation. In the prologue of the Greek version the author's grandson says that after he had gone to Egypt in the thirty-eighth year of the reign of Euergetes he translated his grandfather's book from Hebrew into Greek.

280. On this see the website www.grossnationalhappiness.com/ maintained by the Centre of Bhutan Studies, whose website is www.bhutanstudies.org.bt.

281. The χ was added to the end of the name in Greek to indicate that it was an indeclinable foreign word. See Oesterley, *Introduction to the Apocrypha*, 223.

In the late nineteenth century portions of four different Hebrew mss of Ben Sirach were found in the Geniza (the storeroom for worn-out or discarded mss) in the Cairo Synagogue. Small fragments of the Hebrew version were found in Qumran Cave 2, and fragments of a Hebrew scroll of the book were found at Masada. Di Lella[282] estimates that about 68 per cent of the book is now known in Hebrew. Because there are two different recensions of both the Hebrew and the Greek text, 'The problems of ascertaining the original text of the book of Ecclesiasticus are difficult and complicated', as Metzger[283] puts it.

It is generally agreed that the king mentioned in the prologue is Ptolemy Physkon Euergetes II. This makes the date when Ben Sirach's grandson went to Egypt 132 BC. There is no hint that the author of the book was aware of the horrific persecution of the Jews by Antiochus IV Epiphanes (175-164 BC). In 50:1-21 there is a poem in praise of a high priest called Simon. It is generally agreed that this is Simeon II, who served as high priest from 219-196 BC. He is spoken of in a way that leads most scholars to conclude that the poem was written after Simeon's death. So, the consensus is that the book was composed and published between 196 BC and 175 BC. What Ben Sirach says about the work of the scribe in contrast to other occupations (38:24-25; 38:34b–39:11) strongly suggests that he himself was a man of leisure who studied the Torah and pursued wisdom in the biblical sense of that word. In the autobiographical piece at the end of the book he invites the uneducated to stay in his 'house of instruction', which indicates that he was also a teacher of wisdom.

Nickelsburg[284] comments that, 'In genre and contents the book can generally be compared to the Book of Proverbs, although it is about twice as long as its canonical counterpart. For fifty-one chapters Ben Sira expounds his views on right and wrong conduct.' Apart from chs. 44–50, which praise the ancestors of the Jews from Enoch to the high priest Simon, there is no obvious structure to the book as it deals with a variety of social and religious duties.

The introduction to the book (1:1-10) is about the origin of wisdom. It contains echoes of Prov. 8:22-31 and Job 28. All wisdom comes from God:[285]

> All wisdom is from the LORD,
> and with him it remains forever. (1:1)

Wisdom was created by God before anything else:

282. Skehan and Di Lella, *Ben Sira*, 53.
283. Metzger, *Introduction to the Apocrypha*, 79.
284. Nickelsburg, *Jewish Literature*, 55-56.
285. All quotations are taken from the NRSV.

> Wisdom was created before all other things,
> and prudent understanding from eternity. (1:4)

Only God fully comprehends wisdom and God gives wisdom as a gift to his creatures:

> It is he [the Lord] who created her;
> he saw her and took her measure;
> he poured her out upon all his works,
> upon all the living according to his gift;
> he lavished her upon those who love him. (1:9-10)

Here, as Di Lella[286] points out, there is a three-fold level of giving. Wisdom is poured out on the whole of creation, but especially on humans — which must include Gentiles. However, it is given in specially abundant measure on 'those who love him', that is the faithful Jews.

Di Lella[287] argues that the fundamental thesis of the book is that 'wisdom, which is identified with the Law, can be achieved only by one who fears God and keeps his commandments':

> The whole of wisdom is the fear of the Lord,
> and in all wisdom there is the fulfilment of the law. (19:20)

The identification of Wisdom with the Law is made clear in Sir 24. This begins with a poem in which personified Wisdom praises herself (24:1-23) and is followed by a poem which identifies Wisdom with the Law (24:23-29).

In the introduction to the self-praise (24:1-2) Wisdom is located in Divine Council. She then speaks of her origin in God:

> I came forth from the mouth of the Most High,
> and covered the earth like a mist. (24:3)

This evokes the creation story in Gen. 1 with its theme of God's creative word. Psalm 33:6 puts this creative word in parallel with 'the breath of his mouth'. The mention of a mist covering the earth evokes the 'moisture' (REB) or 'mist' (NIV footnote) which covers the whole surface of the ground in Gen. 2:6. Later on

286. Skehan and Di Lella, *Ben Sira*, 139.
287. Skehan and Di Lella, *Ben Sira*, 77.

Wisdom refers to God as 'my Creator' (24:8b) and says, 'Before the ages, in the beginning, he created me' (24:9a).

Wisdom then speaks of her activity in heaven and on earth. She begins by saying,

> I dwelt in the highest heavens,
> and my throne was in a pillar of cloud. (24:4)

This clearly states that Wisdom dwells with God. Clouds are a common feature of theophanies in the OT. It is hard, however, not to see in v. 4b a reference to the pillar of cloud which accompanied the Israelites through the desert. If this is so, then Wisdom is being presented as a mode of God's presence on earth. In what follows (24:5-7) Wisdom describes her knowledge of, and 'sway' over, all of creation. There are echoes here of Prov. 8:24-29. It ends with Wisdom seeking a 'resting place' on earth.

In the next section (24:8-12) Wisdom tells how 'my Creator chose the place for my tent' (24:8b), and commanded her to make her 'resting place' among the Israelites in Zion where,

> In the holy tent I ministered before him,
> and so I was established in Zion. (24:10)

This identifies Wisdom with the laws relating to the way God was to be worshiped in Israel. By comparing herself to various trees Wisdom then speaks of how she flourished in Israel (24:13-17), giving forth perfume and fruit.

In the final part of the poem Wisdom calls on people to come to her and to enjoy her fruits. Here there are echoes of Prov. 8:4-10, 32-36.

Ben Sirach then becomes the speaker and identifies Wisdom with the Law, with Torah:

> All this is the book of the covenant of the Most High God,
> the law that Moses commanded us as an inheritance for the congregations
> of Jacob. (24:23)

He goes on (24:25-29) to speak of the Law in terms of overflowing rivers as it brings wisdom, understanding, and instruction. He ends with a statement of the unfathomable nature of Wisdom:

> For her thoughts are more abundant than the sea,
> and her counsel deeper than the great abyss. (24:29)

The main development in Ben Sirach is the identification of personified Wisdom with the Torah. As Perdue[288] puts it,

> Ben Sira is suggesting that through performance of sacred liturgy and the teaching of the Torah and the wisdom tradition divine presence is realized in the life of the Temple community. Yet Ben Sira does not compromise divine transcendence, for he points to Wisdom's coming forth from the heavenly world, being the imaginative incarnation of the words that come from the mouth of God.

However, as we shall see, the important development from the point of view of Christology is the equating of Wisdom with the creative word of God, so that Wisdom clearly becomes an agent in the creation of the world.

Baruch

This OT apocryphal book opens with an introduction (1:1-14) which presents the book as written by Baruch, the scribe of the prophet Jeremiah, among the Judean exiles in Babylon five years after the fall of Jerusalem to the Babylonians. This dates it to 582/1 BC. The introduction is followed by a lengthy prayer (1:15–3:8). It begins as a prayer of confession of sin and then moves into a plea for divine mercy and restoration. Up to this point the book is written in prose. There then follow two sections in poetry. With the change in literary form there is also a change in the way in which God is addressed, from 'LORD' (representing the sacred name of the God of Israel, Yahweh) to 'God'. The first of these sections is a poem about Wisdom (3:9–4:4). The second is a series of messages of comfort, encouragement and hope, marked by the refrain 'take courage'.

The book is known only in Greek. However, some scholars[289] argue for some parts, or all of it, being originally composed in Hebrew. There are notes in the Syro-Hexaplar which refer to a Hebrew text of the book.[290] Nickelsburg[291] comments that, 'Baruch is a prime example of a book whose time of composition is difficult to date. There are no unambiguous historical allusions. The theme of Dispersion and Return fits any period after 587 B.C.E.' Moreover, the

288. Perdue, *Wisdom and Creation*, 287-88.
289. For example, Moore, *Additions*, 257-60.
290. Oesterley, *Introduction to the Apocrypha*, 265, n. 1.
291. Nickelsburg, *Jewish Literature*, 113.

apparently composite nature of the book opens up the possibility that different sections of it had their origins at different times. The poem about wisdom is generally taken to have been influenced by Sir. 24 in its identification of wisdom with the Torah. If that is the case, then it must be dated later than that book, but it is difficult to say anything more than that about its date.

The poem about Wisdom begins with the exhortation,[292]

> Hear the commandments of life, O Israel,
> give ear, and learn wisdom! (3:9)

This implies the identification of Wisdom with the Torah, 'the commandments of life'. The poem is then connected with what has gone before by a strophe (3:10-14) which begins with the question,

> Why is it, O Israel, why is it that you are in the land of your enemies,
> that you are growing old in a foreign country . . . ? (3:10ab)

The answer given is that it is because 'You have forsaken the fountain of wisdom' (3:12). The remedy for the present situation, therefore, is to 'Learn where there is wisdom' (3:14).

Three strophes follow which are strongly influenced by Job 28:12-28. They list those who have not found wisdom: Gentile rulers (3:15-19), Gentile sages (3:20-23) and the giants of old (3:24-28). Only God has found the way to Wisdom (3:29-35) and he has given her to Israel (3:36-37). The wording of 3:29-30 strongly echoes Deut 30:11-13, implying an identification of Wisdom with the Torah. This identification is made explicit in the final strophe (4:1-4), which begins,

> She is the book of the commandments of God,
> the law that endures forever.
> All who hold her fast will live,
> and those who forsake her will die. (4:1)

The poem is about Wisdom, who never speaks as she does in Proverbs and Sirach, and the personification of Wisdom does not really come to the fore until the final strophe.

Heim[293] notes a significant change in the way personified Wisdom is

292. All quotations are taken from the NRSV.
293. Heim, 'Personified Wisdom', 58-60.

spoken of in Baruch as compared to Sirach. In Sirach the feminine aspect is very evident and the search after Wisdom is spoken of in erotic terms. This is most evident in Sir. 14:20-27 where the seeker after Wisdom is spoken of as a lover pursuing the object of his desire 'like a hunter and lying in wait on her paths.' There is no such language in Bar. 3. As Heim puts it, in Sirach Wisdom is a woman who is 'hard to get'. In Baruch Wisdom is knowledge that was 'hard to get to' but is now found in the Torah.

The Book of Baruch became popular among Christians in the early centuries after Christ. The verses about Wisdom being given to Israel attracted the attention of the early church fathers:

> He [God] found the whole way to knowledge,
> and gave her to his servants Jacob
> and to Israel, whom he loved.
> Afterward she appeared on earth
> and lived with humankind. (3:36-37)

The following verse (4:1, quoted above) makes clear that the mode of Wisdom's appearing and dwelling on earth with humans was the Torah. However, as Metzger[294] puts it,

> In view of the notorious lack of exegetical discrimination displayed by many Fathers, it is not surprising that the natural meaning of these verses was abandoned for a mystical interpretation that saw here a witness to the doctrine of the Incarnation.

Some modern scholars[295] have suggested that this passage in Baruch might be an interpolation by an early Christian scribe. Even if this is so, as Metzger points out, the fathers who quoted it thought it an original part of the book.

The Wisdom of Solomon

This is another book in the OT Apocrypha. There is no reason to think that its original language was anything other than the Greek in which it is known. Winston[296] sums up the purpose of the book as follows:

294. Metzger, *Introduction to the Apocrypha*, 94.
295. Moore, *Additions*, 301.
296. Winston, *Wisdom of Solomon*, 63 (italics original).

> The author is primarily addressing his fellow Jews in an effort to encourage them to take pride in their traditional faith. He seeks to convince them that *their* way of life, rooted in the worship of the One true God, is of an incomparably higher order than that of their pagan neighbours, whose idolatrous polytheism has sunk them into the mire of immorality. Moreover, he attempts to justify their present suffering through the promise of immortality as a reward for their steadfast perseverance in the pursuit of righteousness.

The focus on the exodus and God's judgements on Egypt in chs. 10–19 suggests that the author was a Jew living in Egypt, probably in Alexandria. There are many parallels with the religious and philosophical thought of Philo of Alexandria.

Widely differing dates have been suggested for the book, but it is generally dated around the turn of the eras. References to 'the judges of the ends of the earth' (6:1)[297] and to rulers who live at a distance from those they rule (14:17) fit the Romans as rulers better than the Ptolemies. Egypt came under Roman rule in 47 BC. Some see a particular significance in the use of the word κράτησις (*kratēsis*, 'dominion') in 6:3. The date on which Augustus captured Alexandria in 30 BC is referred to in the papyri[298] as *tēs kaisaros kratēseōs*. Winston[299] has argued for a date in the reign of Caligula (AD 37-41). One reason for this is that he thinks that the threat to Judaism towards the end of his reign provides a suitable background for the apocalyptic passage in 6:16-23. Also, he notes that there are at least 35 words in the book which are not attested in literature before the first century AD. Grabbe[300] thinks that these, and other arguments which Winston uses, are consistent with any time in the early Empire and favours an earlier date in the reign of Augustus.

Most scholars see the book as falling into three sections:

Chs. 1–5	Book of Eschatology
Chs. 6–9	Book of Wisdom
Chs. 10–19	Book of History

There is some disagreement about the point of transition between the different sections. The first section deals with various aspects of the problem of reward and retribution. In the second section the author adopts the persona of Solomon, though without actually using his name, and describes his search for

297. All quotations are taken from the NRSV.
298. Winston, *Wisdom of Solomon*, 153.
299. Winston, *Wisdom of Solomon*, 20-25.
300. Grabbe, *Wisdom of Solomon*, 89-90.

Wisdom and extols her attributes. The final section begins with a description of Wisdom's role in history from Adam to Moses (ch. 10). It is then structured around a series of antitheses comparing punishments of Egypt related to the exodus and blessings to Israel in the wilderness period.

The figure of Wisdom appears primarily in chs. 6-10 but appears in other places as well. In the opening exhortation of the book (1:1-15) the 'rulers of the earth' are urged to seek the LORD 'with sincerity of heart' (1:1) because otherwise they will not receive wisdom:

> because wisdom will not enter a deceitful soul,
> or dwell in a body enslaved to sin.
> For a holy and disciplined spirit will flee from deceit,
> and will leave foolish thoughts behind,
> and will be ashamed at the approach of unrighteousness. (1:4-5)

Here v. 5 seems to be a description of Wisdom. So, Winston[301] translates the opening of the verse as, 'the holy spirit, that divine tutor, will fly from cunning stratagem'. Wisdom is then called 'a kindly spirit' (1:6) and is described further in the following verses:

> Because the spirit of the LORD has filled the world,
> and that which holds all things together knows what is said,
> therefore those who utter unrighteous things will not escape notice,
> and justice, when it punishes, will not pass them by. (1:7-8)

Wisdom is given an exalted status in this prologue to the book. She is depicted as a spiritual entity whose closeness to God is indicated by calling her 'the spirit of the LORD'. She is holy and is linked especially with righteousness and justice, two more key attributes of God in the OT. In v. 7 she is described as omnipresent, since she 'filled the world', and omniscient in the sense of knowing all that is said. She is also the power 'which holds all things together'. This gives her a key role in the maintenance of the created order.

Wisdom's role in the creation of the cosmos, which is rather unclear in Prov. 8:30, is made clear in Wis. 7:22a and 8:6, which no doubt allude to that verse:

> For wisdom, the fashioner of all things, taught me. (7:22a)

> And if understanding is effective,
> who more than she is fashioner of what exists? (8:6)

301. Winston, *Wisdom of Solomon*, 99.

Here Wisdom is presented as having an active role in the process of creation. Her continuing role in creation is stated in 8:1 in terms which echo 1:7:

> She reaches mightily from one end of the earth to the other,
> and she orders all things well. (8:1)

In a prayer for Wisdom (9:1-18), which makes clear that Wisdom can only be obtained as a gift from God, the writer, speaking as Solomon, describes Wisdom as 'she who knows your works and was present when you made the world' (9:9). Moreover, Wisdom is identified with the word of God in the creation story in Gen. 1:

> O God of my ancestors and Lord of mercy,
> who made all things by your word,
> and by your wisdom have formed humankind
> to have dominion over the creatures you have made. . . . (9:1-2)

Wisdom is given an exalted status in this prayer. She is referred to as 'the wisdom that sits by your throne' (9:4a) and Solomon pleads,

> Send her forth from the holy heavens,
> and from the throne of your glory send her,
> that she may labour at my side,
> and that I may learn what is pleasing to you. (9:10)

This exalted status is expressed more fully in a poem which describes the nature of Wisdom (7:22b–8:1). It begins by listing twenty-one characteristics of Wisdom as 'a spirit that is intelligent, holy'. Wisdom is then described in amazing language:

> For she is a breath of the power of God,
> and a pure emanation of the glory of the Almighty;
> therefore nothing defiled gains entrance into her.
> For she is a reflection of eternal light,
> a spotless mirror of the working of God,
> and an image of his goodness. (7:25-26)

Winston[302] comments,

302. Winston, *Wisdom of Solomon*, 184.

> Employing a fivefold succession of metaphors [exhalation, effluence, effulgence, mirror, image], the author states quite emphatically that Wisdom is an emanation from God's power, glory, light or goodness. This is very bold language indeed for someone who is writing within the biblical tradition.

Ben Sirach had identified Wisdom with the Torah. The author of the Wisdom of Solomon comes close to identifying Wisdom with God. Grabbe[303] says of these verses,

> This statement seems to fit the interpretation usually given that wisdom in the Wisdom of Solomon is a *hypostasis.* That is, she is both product of God and a manifestation of him. She represents him and she is him. Thus many statements about God are interchangeable with statements about Wisdom.

Crenshaw[304] is more cautious, questioning whether the language about Wisdom in this poem does move beyond metaphor to actual hypostasis. He points out that answering that question needs to take into account the author's subsequent characterisation of Wisdom as Solomon's bride (8:2). However one answers that question, the fact is that the elevated concept of Wisdom found in the Wisdom of Solomon prepared the way for later Christian discourse about Jesus and his relationship to God.

With regard to the bridal imagery which leads to wifely imagery in Wis. 8:2-21 Heim[305] makes the point that the *erotic* language of Sirach has now changed to *romantic* language. In response to the question of how Wisdom could acquire quasi-divine features in Second Temple Judaism he suggests that it was because, 'In the context of the Wisdom of Solomon in particular and within the wider cultural milieu of contemporary Judaism, the identity of personified wisdom as a *literary* creation that ultimately was to be identified with the "law" of God always remained transparent.'

Wisdom and Word

In both Sirach and the Wisdom of Solomon, Wisdom is identified with the creative word of God. This identification is significant for early christological thinking. To appreciate this it is necessary to consider briefly the writings of

303. Grabbe, *Wisdom of Solomon,* 78 (italics original).
304. Crenshaw, *Old Testament Wisdom,* 227, n. 37.
305. Heim, 'Personified Wisdom', 61.

Philo of Alexandria. Wisdom plays a part in his thought but the central concept in his philosophical and theological system is the Logos (λόγος, 'word').

Philo was a Jew who lived in Alexandria from about 20 BC to about AD 50. He was, at least in his own mind, a faithful Jew for whom the Jewish Scriptures had absolute authority. He was a scholar who wrote in Greek and was well acquainted with the ideas of Middle Platonism and Stoicism which were popular in his day. For centuries Greek scholars had employed allegorical exegesis to discover hidden meanings in the writings of Homer and Hesiod. Philo applied this approach to the Hebrew Scriptures, especially the Torah. This enabled him to interpret Jewish theology in terms of Hellenistic philosophy and also to claim that the best ideas of the Greek philosophers had been anticipated by Moses in the Jewish Scriptures.

There are many similarities of thought between the Wisdom of Solomon and Philo. Because of the uncertainty in dating the Wisdom of Solomon it is not possible to say whether one has influenced the other, or whether both are influenced by a common world of thought. Winston[306] provides quite an extensive list of ways in which thought about Wisdom in Philo and the Wisdom of Solomon are analogous. However, the primary personification or hypostasis in Philo is not Wisdom but the Logos. Unfortunately, as Sandmel[307] comments, 'At no time does Philo, in the abundance of what he has to say about the Logos, ever define Logos for us.'

For Philo there is one, utterly transcendent God, who is the Creator of all things:

> God is alone: a single being, not a combination . . . for whatever could be combined with God must be either superior to him, or inferior to him, or equal to him. But there is nothing equal to God, and nothing superior to him. . . . God is older than the world and is its Creator.[308]

In the context of Platonism this raised the problem of how God relates to the world and, indeed, how he could be its Creator, because, as Sandmel[309] explains,

> It is an axiom in Philo that matter is evil; he is unwilling to bring God into direct contact with matter. On the other hand, Logos is the device by which God can be affirmatively viewed as connected with the world. The actual divine contact with the world accordingly is ascribed to the Logos.

306. Winston, *Wisdom of Solomon,* 59-61.
307. Sandmel, *Philo,* 94.
308. Yonge, *Philo, Leg. All.* 2.2-3.
309. Sandmel, *Philo,* 94-95.

Philo could not accept the Platonic idea of a hierarchy of divine beings between the Supreme God and the material order. Instead he thought in terms of intermediary powers which seem to be, as Kelly[310] puts it, 'not so much distinct beings as God's operations considered in abstraction from himself'. The most important of these is the Logos, which is 'the most ancient and most universal of all things that are created'.[311] It is the Logos that was God's agent, or instrument, in the creation of the world. Using the analogy of someone planning and building a house or city, Philo[312] says,

> Now he by whom a thing originates is the cause; that from which a thing is made is the material; that by means of which it is made is the instrument . . . [with regard to] this world . . . you will find that God is the cause of it, by whom it was made. That the materials are the four elements, of which it is composed; that the instrument is the word of God, by means of which it was made.

Following the creation of the world the Logos has a continuing role as 'the helmsman and governor of the universe'.[313]

Philo speaks of the Logos as God's first-born son and the image of God,[314] but this personification should not be pressed too far since he also refers to the material world as God's younger son.[315] In a restricted sense, Philo can refer to the Logos as 'God'. God himself is unknowable. Humans can only know God through 'his word, which is the interpreter of his will. For that must be God to us imperfect beings, but the first mentioned, or true God, is so only to wise and perfect men.'[316]

Collins[317] sums up his understanding of the role of the Logos in Philo's thought as follows:

> The Logos was a metaphysical reality distinct from God, but still participated in the reality of God. It was the image and reflection of God, the model for the rest of creation, but it was also the power through which the universe was ordered and continued to be ordered . . . the Logos was the

310. Kelly, *Early Christian Doctrines*, 10.
311. Yonge, *Philo, Leg. All*, 3.175.
312. Yonge, *Philo, De Cherub.* 125-27.
313. Yonge, *Philo, De Cherub.* 36.
314. Yonge, *Philo, De Conf. Ling.* 97, 146-47.
315. Yonge, *Philo, Quod Deus*, 31.
316. Yonge, *Philo, Leg. All.* 3.207.
317. Collins, *Jewish Wisdom*, 202.

> guide of the human soul in its mystical ascent, in the process of becoming like God. . . . In all this, Philo's Logos is similar to Wisdom in the Wisdom of Solomon, although it is more elaborately conceived.

Sandmel[318] is more cautious about the nature of the Logos in Philo's thought:

> Does Philo regard the Logos as a reality, as a distinct entity having real existence, or is the Logos no more than an abstract construct, convenient to Philo's philosophy, but without true existence? Scholars have espoused both views for the reason that there is no decisive clarity in Philo's presentation.

The New Testament

Hebrews 1:1-4. There are at least three places in the NT where scholars see evidence of ideas about wisdom influencing what is said about Jesus. Perhaps the most obvious is in the opening verses of Hebrews. After referring to God's revelation in the past through the prophets the writer speaks of the revelation of God in Jesus:

> but in these days he has spoken to us by his Son, whom he appointed the heir of all things, through whom also he created the world. He is the radiance of the glory of God and the exact imprint of his nature, and he upholds the universe by his word of power. After making purification for sins, he sat down at the right hand of the Majesty on high. (Heb 1:2-3, ESV)

Scholars debate whether ἀπαύγασμα *(apaugasma)* at the beginning of v. 3 should be translated as 'radiance' or 'reflection' (NRSV) in this context, since both meanings are possible for this word. Most favour 'radiance'. This is the only time the word occurs in the NT. It occurs in Wis. 7:26 and often in Philo.

Although there is no explicit mention of Wisdom here, there seem to be many echoes of Wis. 7:25-26 in these verses. Several of the metaphors which Winston noted in those verses (see above) are found here: exhalation in the idea of the spoken word; effulgence or mirror, depending on the translation of ἀπαύγασμα; image, although the word used here is χαρακτήρ (*charaktēr,* 'imprint') rather than εἰκών (*eikōn,* 'image'). There are possible echoes of wider ideas about Wisdom in the references to the creation of the world, the upholding of the universe and sitting 'at the right hand of the Majesty on high' —

318. Sandmel, *Philo,* 98.

though this latter imagery may well be derived from Ps. 110:1, which is quoted explicitly in v. 13. Ellingworth[319] sees in Heb. 1:2-3 'an implicit reapplication to Christ of what had been written of the divine wisdom' in passages such as Prov. 8:22-31 and Wis. 7. Lane[320] also recognises the echoes of the Wisdom of Solomon, especially Wis. 7:21-27, in Heb. 1:2-3. Because of the similarity between what is said about Wisdom in the Wisdom of Solomon and in Philo, and between what Philo says about Wisdom and about the Logos, one cannot rule out Philonic influence in these verses. This is especially the case in view of the fact that scholars debate the wider influence of Philo's thought on the writer of this letter.

Referring to the whole of Heb. 1:1-4 Lane[321] says, 'the writer gave Christological precision to a cluster of ideas derived from Hellenistic Judaism. He boldly applied the categories of Wisdom to a historical figure, Jesus.' What motivated this bold move? It may have been the ascension of the resurrected Jesus, seen as prophesied in Ps. 110:1, because this put Jesus by the throne of God, the location of Wisdom in Hellenistic Jewish thought.

Colossians 1:15-20. This passage is a carefully constructed piece of poetry. Many commentators conclude that the writer of the letter has made use of a pre-existing hymn to Christ. Some argue that the hymn itself is a development of a pre-Christian hymn to wisdom, though there is considerable disagreement about what the form and content of that hymn might have been.

The hymn has two strophes (vv. 15-16 and vv. 18b-20) which are clearly linked by their opening phrases: 'He is . . . the firstborn . . .'. They each contain a 'whether . . . or . . .' clause and reference to 'in heaven, on earth'. The use of 'through him' in v. 20 echoes the same words in v. 16. The first strophe speaks of the supremacy of Christ over the 'old creation', the cosmos. The second strophe speaks of his supremacy over the 'new creation', the church. The two strophes are joined by a 'hinge' consisting of two statements, each beginning, 'He is . . .'

The first strophe contains a couple of particular rhetorical devices. The phrase 'in/for him were created' forms a clear *inclusio,* coming at the beginning and end of the verse. Also, the phrase 'in heaven and on earth, visible and invisible' has a chiastic structure (ab:ba) with 'visible' corresponding to 'on earth' and 'invisible' to 'in heaven':

> *He is* the image of the invisible God,
>   *the firstborn* of all creation.

319. Ellingworth, *Hebrews,* 99.
320. Lane, *Hebrews,* 12.
321. Lane, *Hebrews,* 19.

For *by him were created* all things
in heaven and on earth,
visible and invisible,
whether thrones or dominions
or rulers or authorities —
all things through him and *for him were created.*
And he is before all things, and in him all things hold together.
And he is the head of the body, the church.
He is the beginning,
the firstborn from the dead,
that in everything he might be supreme.
For in him all the fullness of God was pleased to dwell,
and through him to reconcile to himself all things,
making peace by the blood of his cross,
whether on earth
or in heaven.

Verses 15-17 echo many of the things that are said of wisdom in Proverbs and in later Jewish wisdom literature. Dunn[322] comments, 'As the sequence of parallels with motifs characteristically used of Jewish Wisdom in these verses will confirm, the writer here is taking over language used of divine Wisdom and reusing it to express the significance of Christ.' There is much debate about the translation of v. 19, of which a literal translation is: 'For in him it pleased all the fullness (πλήρωμα, *plērōma*) to dwell'. The noun 'fullness' is not found with this kind of theological and cosmological sense prior to this letter. Dunn[323] points to a partial background in the use of the cognate verb in Wis. 1:6-7, where Wisdom, called the Spirit of the LORD, is said to have 'filled the world', and also to references in Philo to God 'filling all things'. In the OT, of course, God is said to 'fill heaven and earth' (Jer. 23:24). The meaning of 'fullness' in Col. 1:19 is probably 'the fullness of God'. For a full discussion see the commentaries.[324]

Dunn[325] comments concerning v. 19, 'Here the thought reaches well beyond that of Wisdom or even God "dwelling in" a good or compassionate person . . . to grasp at the idea of the wholeness of divine immanence dwelling in Christ.' O'Brien[326] says of the hymn, 'It begins with a series of predicates and activities employed in the OT and Judaism of the personalized Wisdom of God

322. Dunn, *Colossians,* 89.
323. Dunn, *Colossians,* 100.
324. For example: Dunn, *Colossians,* 99-102; O'Brien, *Colossians,* 51-53.
325. Dunn, *Colossians,* 101.
326. O'Brien, *Colossians,* 61.

which are applied to the One who had been so ignominiously executed only a few years before.' What motivated this amazing development? The second strophe indicates that it was the death, resurrection, and presumably also the ascension, of Jesus.

John 1:1-18. The use and development of the concept of the Logos in the prologue to John's Gospel has no parallel elsewhere in the NT. Scholars have for a long time debated possible backgrounds to John's use of the concept: the creative and revelatory word of God in the OT; Jewish thought about personified Wisdom; Hellenistic philosophy, especially Stoicism; Philo's concept of the Logos; Jewish speculation about the Torah; Targumic use of the Aramaic word *memra* ('word') as an alternative to the word 'God'; early/proto-gnostic ideas. When considering possible backgrounds it is necessary to distinguish between two possibilities, as Brown[327] points out with specific reference to the suggested Hellenistic background. The first is that the content of the idea comes from a particular background. The second is that the content of the idea comes from elsewhere but that the term Logos was chosen to express it because of the connotations it had in some other background(s), so possibly gaining the attention of a wider public. Barrett,[328] for example, says, 'That John was familiar with the Old Testament and with Judaism seems clear; yet it is highly probable that in developing Sophia and Torah speculation he intentionally chose for employment those aspects of Jewish thought which had Hellenistic parallels.'

Some of the suggested backgrounds listed above have been the subject of much debate and have not found much support. The two about which there is a general consensus are the OT and Jewish wisdom thought. Lincoln,[329] for example, says, 'The origins of the prologue's use of "the Word" are in all probability to be found in earlier Jewish thought about both Wisdom and the Word of God.' In the OT God's word is the means by which he created the world (Gen. 1; Ps. 33:6). The revelatory word which God spoke to and through the prophets is presented in Isa. 55:8-11 as an agent that achieves God's purpose on earth. The word of God, in the form of the Torah, is spoken of as a source of light (Ps. 119:105, 130) and life (Deut. 32:46-47). Dodd[330] says, 'There are obvious and striking similarities between certain of the propositions of the Prologue and passages in the Wisdom literature.' He then gives a list of 11 phrases from the prologue for which he provides parallels from Prov. 1, 3, 8; Wis. 7, 8, 9; Sir. 24. He says that the list is not exhaustive but 'is sufficient to show that in composing

327. Brown, *John,* 519.
328. Barrett, *John,* 129.
329. Lincoln, *John,* 95.
330. Dodd, *Interpretation,* 274-75.

the Prologue the author's mind was moving along lines similar to those followed by Jewish writers of the "Wisdom" school'.

More controversial is the possible influence of Philo on the writer of the prologue. Dodd[331] provides a list of eight phrases from the prologue to which he finds some parallel in Philo's writings. However, Brown[332] finds this list much less impressive than the previous list of parallels with Jewish wisdom books. Both he and Lincoln[333] think that the similarities with Philo arise from John and Philo independently developing ideas from the Jewish wisdom literature. They also both suggest[334] that the choice to use Logos rather than Wisdom in the prologue may be due to two factors: that unlike 'wisdom', 'logos' is grammatically masculine in Greek and also because 'the word' was a term that had come to be identified with the good news about Jesus.

As is the case with Heb. 1:1-4 and Col. 1:15-20, what is said of the Logos in the prologue goes beyond the bounds of earlier thought about Wisdom. This is so in the opening verses. Whereas Wisdom was said to have been created before 'the beginning of the earth', before anything else (Prov. 8:22-24; Sir. 1:4), the Logos is not said to have been created but to have existed 'in the beginning'. Wisdom was thought of as sitting beside God's throne (Wis. 9:4) but the Logos is described as always having had an intimate relationship with God such that it can be said that 'the Logos was with God, and the Logos was God'.

When John says that 'the Logos dwelt among us' (v. 14) he uses a verb, σκηνόω *(skēnoō)*, that can mean 'to live in a tent'. It also sounds like the Hebrew verb שָׁכַן *(šākan)* 'to dwell', from which the noun (מִשְׁכָּן/*miškān*) used to refer to the 'tabernacle' in the wilderness is derived. These words are used in Exod. 25:8-9 of God 'dwelling' in Israel in the 'tabernacle'. So, the use of this verb in John 1:14 might remind readers of the passage in Sir. 24:8-12 in which the Creator chooses a place for Wisdom's 'tent' in Israel and she ministers before him in 'the holy tent'. However, John 1:14 says 'the Logos became flesh and dwelt (lived in a tent) among us'. This statement would be astounding to Jews because it would seem to breach the clear distinction between Creator and creature. It would be equally astounding to Hellenistic thinkers for whom the Logos belonged to the rational and spiritual realm which could only be reached by transcending material existence. Thus Sandmel[335] says, with reference to Philo's thought, 'The Logos never descends from the intelligible world into the sensible world; man must move into the intelligible world to encounter the Logos.'

331. Dodd, *Interpretation*, 276-77.

332. Brown, *John*, 521-22.

333. Brown, *John*, lvii-lviii; Lincoln, *John*, 95.

334. Brown, *John*, 523; Lincoln, *John*, 96-97.

335. Sandmel, *Philo*, 95.

If Jewish speculation about the Torah is somewhere in the background of John's thought, then in v. 17 he goes beyond that too. God's grace and truth, he claims, now come through Jesus, not the Torah. God's Word is to be found embodied in Jesus, not the Torah.

In John's prologue, as in the previous two passages, we see attributes and activities of personified Wisdom now applied to the historical person of Jesus of Nazareth. In doing this, however, these Christian writers find that they have to go beyond the bounds of Jewish thought about Wisdom in order to express their understanding of Jesus. What was it about Jesus that motivated this? John tells us that he wrote his Gospel to answer that question (20:30-31).

Jesus the Sage

Was there anything in the life and ministry of Jesus of Nazareth which provided a basis for talking about him in terms taken from the Jewish discourse about personified Wisdom? It is interesting that the Jewish historian Josephus, writing in his *Antiquities of the Jews* towards the end of the first century AD, described Jesus as 'a wise man (σοφὸς ἀνήρ, *sophos anēr*) . . . a doer of wonderful works, a teacher' (*Ant.* 18.3.3). What he meant by 'a wise man' is indicated by his application of this description to both Solomon (*Ant.* 8.2.7) and Daniel (*Ant.* 10.11.2).

Dunn[336] argues that when one looks at the evidence in the Synoptic Gospels, 'it becomes clear that whatever else Jesus was, he was indeed a teacher of wisdom'. He lists[337] some of this evidence:

1. The most frequent title for Jesus in the Synoptics is 'teacher'. It is used by both his disciples and critics.
2. Jesus' use of parables, ranging from vivid one-sentence images to longer stories.
3. Jesus' use of forms of sayings typical of wisdom teaching: short aphorisms, epigrams and brief exhortations. Bultmann, in his analysis of the Synoptic tradition, listed about 70 such sayings under the heading 'Jesus as the teacher of wisdom'.
4. Dunn is not convinced by those who argue that, because Jesus' teaching includes a radical social criticism, he is best identified with the itinerant Cynic teachers of his day. In Dunn's view, when the full range of Jesus'

336. Dunn, 'Jesus: Teacher of Wisdom', 82.
337. Dunn, 'Jesus: Teacher of Wisdom', 83-85.

teaching is taken into account, the closest parallels are with the Jewish wisdom tradition and the social criticism of the Hebrew prophets.

Dunn[338] goes on to consider whether there is evidence that Jesus thought of himself as more than a wisdom teacher, as Wisdom incarnate. He lists evidence that points in this direction:

1. Jesus claimed that blessings of 'the age to come', of the kingdom or reign of God, were already to be seen in what he was doing. This is most explicit in Jesus' claim that his exorcisms were carried out by 'the Spirit/finger of God' (Matt. 12:28/Luke 11:20), which implies that he saw a distinctive power at work in himself.
2. When John the Baptist asked whether he was the expected Messiah Jesus' answer points to the presence of the blessings of the age to come in his ministry (Matt. 11:5/Lk. 7:22) and then goes on to say that John was the greatest man ever born, but that even the least in the kingdom of heaven was greater than him (Matt. 11:11/Lk. 7:28). This implies that something new and greater is present in Jesus. This is expressed more clearly in the 'something more than' sayings in Matt. 12:41-42/Lk. 11:31-32. The comparison with Solomon implies that Jesus is more than simply a great teacher of wisdom like Solomon.
3. Jesus' distinctive use of the word 'Amen' to preface his teaching. Jeremias's argument that this attests to Jesus' sense that his words had a special significance still carries weight.
4. The same is true of Jeremias' argument about Jesus' use of 'the emphatic "I"', as in the phrase, 'But I say to you . . .'. It is particularly notable when Jesus uses it in interpreting Scripture. He asserts that he has a unique authority to do so.
5. Jesus claimed a final authority for his teaching in general. This is seen especially in his astonishing claim that his hearer's eternal destiny would depend on how they respond to him and his teaching (Mark 8:38).

Dunn regards this as convincing evidence that Jesus saw himself as 'God's spokesman and final emissary' and so as more than a wisdom teacher. He is hesitant about describing Jesus as 'Wisdom incarnate' because he thinks the distinction between 'inspiration' and 'incarnation' is hard to define. However, he concludes,[339] 'the Jesus who is remembered in the Synoptic tradition made

338. Dunn, 'Jesus: Teacher of Wisdom', 86-91.
339. Dunn, 'Jesus: Teacher of Wisdom', 92.

a claim, both implicitly and explicitly, which transcended that of his precursors and which in the event could only find satisfactory expression in the evaluation of this Jesus as "Wisdom incarnate"'.

Witherington[340] does not share Dunn's hesitation. He is sure that[341] 'Jesus saw himself as a sage, as one who embodied the very Wisdom of God, indeed even saw himself as God's Wisdom come in the flesh.' To support this conclusion he appeals to the following evidence:

1. In Matt. 11:16-19/Lk. 7:31-35 Jesus responds to the criticism that he is a glutton and drunkard who eats with tax-collectors and sinners by asserting that 'Yet wisdom is justified by her deeds' (he argues[342] that Matthew preserves the original form of the saying, Luke having changed 'deeds' to children to conform to 'children' in v. 32). Here Jesus identifies himself with Wisdom. Witherington sees the 'justification' as provided by Wisdom giving a feast for unlikely guests in Prov. 9:1-6 and meals being an occasion for teaching in antiquity. So in his feasting Jesus is acting out the part of Wisdom.
2. Sirach 24:6-11 depicts Wisdom as having nowhere to dwell on earth until God assigns her a place in Jerusalem. In the late wisdom poem in 1 Enoch 42, Wisdom is said to have been unable to find a permanent dwelling place on earth because of the iniquity of humans, and so she returned to dwell in heaven. Sirach 36:31b says, 'So, who will trust a man that has no nest, but lodges wherever night overtakes him?' Witherington sees these passages echoed in Jesus' saying about the Son of Man having nowhere to lay his head, unlike the birds which have nests (Matt. 8:20/Lk. 9:58). Sirach 24:11 adds poignancy to Jesus' lament over Jerusalem (Matt. 23:37-39/Lk. 13:34-35). The female imagery that Jesus uses of himself in this saying would be understandable if he saw himself as Wisdom incarnate, since personified Wisdom is female in the Jewish tradition.
3. Witherington agrees with de Jonge that the relationship between Jesus and the Father depicted in Lk. 10:21-22/Matt. 11:25-27 resembles the relationship of Wisdom to God as depicted in the Wisdom of Solomon.
4. The statement in Lk. 11:49 that the Wisdom of God will send out 'prophets and apostles' is somewhat ambiguous. Witherington argues[343] that the future tense, the mention of apostles and the fact that the accusation is

340. Witherington, *Jesus the Sage*. He provides a useful summary of his position in Witherington, *Jesus Quest*, 185-94.

341. Witherington, *Jesus Quest*, 187.

342. Witherington, *Jesus Quest*, 184.

343. Witherington, *Jesus Quest*, 183.

laid against 'this generation' (v. 50) favours a reference to Jesus' own emissaries. If so, Jesus is called 'the Wisdom of God'. He also argues that Jesus' exhortation to people to take his 'yoke' is a modification of Sir. 51:26-28, which speaks of Wisdom's yoke.

5. Jesus' teaching is marked by the kind of creation theology found in Proverbs. This is to be seen in such things as Jesus' references to nature in his teaching, his appeal to the God's purpose in creation when speaking about marriage, his enjoyment of feasting and his universalistic vision of Gentiles sitting with Jews in the banquet in the kingdom of God.
6. Jesus' social critique has something in common with the wisdom literature. Qoheleth in Ecclesiastes sees the world as being askew. Jesus shared the belief in the wisdom literature that there is a moral order with good deeds ultimately being rewarded and bad ones punished. A concern for righting wrongs in the long run is a feature of the wisdom literature, leading the Wisdom of Solomon to incorporate the idea of everlasting life to explain how God would achieve this.

Witherington does not claim that understanding Jesus as the sage who is the embodiment/incarnation of Wisdom is the *only* way to understand Jesus. He accepts that other ways of understanding Jesus are also needed, such as prophet, Messiah, Son of Man, healer. What he does argue[344] is that

> if we ask what heuristic category comes closest to explaining the most about who Jesus thought he was and what he said and did, what comes closest to explaining why early christological thinking about Jesus developed as it did, then we must come to grips with sages and Wisdom.

The evidence that he and Dunn present makes a good case for this claim.

Wisdom and Christology in Patristic Thought

Commenting on the prologue of John's Gospel, Lincoln[345] says,

> The questions John 1.1 provokes in the light of the rest of the prologue are those which later creedal and doctrinal formulations attempted to answer and contemporary Christology continues to explore . . . it might well be

344. Witherington, *Jesus Quest*, 185.
345. Lincoln, *John*, 98.

> claimed that most of the Christological affirmations of an ecumenical confession, such as the Nicene Creed, are already implicit in the prologue read within the Gospel as a whole.

From early on most Christian thinkers followed the identification of the Logos with Wisdom that is implied in John's prologue. However, a few took a different path.

Among the apologists Theophilus of Antioch (died *c.* AD 184) identified the Holy Spirit with Wisdom. This may have been prompted by Wis. 1:6-7 which speaks of Wisdom as a 'kindly spirit' and as 'the spirit of the Lord'. He understood Ps. 33:6 to refer to the involvement of both the Word and the Spirit ('breath/spirit of his mouth') in creation. He introduced the term 'triad' to speak of God, referring to the holy Triad as God, His Word and His Wisdom. He thought of God as having his Word and his Wisdom eternally in himself. They were generated and put forth for creation. This did not mean that they were separated from God. They remained in communion with God.[346] Irenaeus of Lyon (*ca.* AD 130-200) also thought of God as one and yet containing in himself from all eternity his Word and his Wisdom. God extrapolated or manifested these for the work of creation and redemption. He spoke of them as God's 'hands'. He made use of Prov. 3:19 and 8:22-31 as a basis for speaking of the role of the Holy Spirit in creation.[347] Hippolytus (died AD 235) affirmed an eternal plurality in the one God because God was never without his Word and his Wisdom. God engendered his Word to create the universe and his Wisdom to adorn it.[348] Following Hippolytus nothing more is heard of this line of thought for over a century.

The general consensus that equated personified Wisdom with the Logos and so with Christ, the Son of God, led to Prov. 8 having a significant place in the debates about Christology provoked by Arianism. In his study of Arius Williams[349] concludes that 'the passages on which the theological disagreements between Arius and Alexander first focused were: Psalm 45:7-9, Proverbs 8:22, Isaiah 1:2, and a number of unspecified New Testament texts'. The Arians thought of God as utterly transcendent, eternal and immutable. Such a God could not have direct contact with a mutable creation nor could he suffer to redeem a fallen creation. Therefore there had to be an intermediate being to fulfil the roles of creator and redeemer. This being could not share the substance

346. Kelly, *Early Christian Doctrines*, 102-104.
347. Kelly, *Early Christian Doctrines*, 104-106.
348. Kelly, *Early Christian Doctrines*, 111.
349. Williams, *Arius*, 109.

of God for two reasons. First, if he did he could not have the role of mediator. Second, for him to be generated or produced from the substance of God would require a change in the immutable God. Therefore, it seemed to the Arians, the Son had to be a creature, a being created from nothing. He existed before time existed because he created the world and time, but he had a beginning. Hence they coined the slogan, 'There was when he was not.' With particular reference to the work of redemption Hanson[350] says of the Arians,

> they only achieved their doctrine of incarnation at the expense of an account of the Christian doctrine of God which, in effect taught two unequal gods, a High God incapable of human experiences, and a lesser God who, so to speak, did his dirty work for him.

The Arians appealed to Prov. 8:22 to support their contention that the Son was a created being. In the commentary we note that the meaning of the second word of v. 22 (קָנָנִי/*qānānî*) has been a matter of dispute. In the LXX, the version of the Bible used by both sides in the Arian debates, it is translated as ἔκτισέν με *(ektisen me)* which the Arians insisted should be understood in its usual sense 'he created me'.[351] Almost the whole of the second book of Athanasius's *Orationes contra Arianos* is taken up with discussing Prov. 8:22ff. He argues that its terms apply to the incarnate Christ, not to the pre-existent Christ. Hanson[352] refers to 'the devious windings of his attempts to prove that the obvious is not true' and to his explanations of this text, and other passages, as 'sometimes ingenious but almost always unsound'. Athanasius was concerned to interpret the passage in accord with his conviction, derived from the whole of Scripture, that the Son of God cannot be created. As Hanson puts it, 'Athanasius' hermeneutical method was to keep the basic message, the *skopos,* of the Bible firmly in sight, and then to let individual texts look after themselves.' Interestingly, two participants in the Arian debates, Phoebadius of Agen and Gregory of Elvira, returned to the interpretation of Wisdom as the Holy Spirit. Gregory argued that the reference to 'creation' in Prov. 8:22 referred not to the nature of the Spirit but to the effect of its operation.[353]

The treatment of Prov. 8:22 in the debates about Arianism illustrates the problems that arise with 'proof-texting'. Both sides were primarily concerned to use the text to support their pre-conceived ideas. To put it in modern terms,

350. Hanson, *Search,* 122.
351. Hanson, *Search,* 559-60.
352. Hanson, *Search,* 434.
353. Hanson, *Search,* 521.

each side brought to the text their own horizon of understanding and sought to incorporate it into that horizon. Neither side attempted to understand the text within its own horizon first. To begin with there is the fact that the original text was written in Hebrew. This, at least, prompts the question of the appropriateness of the LXX's translation of קָנָנִי *(qānānî)* as 'he created me'. In the Vulg, for instance, it is translated as *possedit me,* 'he possessed me'. More fundamental, however, is the fact that both sides treated a poetic personification of a divine attribute as an ontological description of an actual being, Christ — whether pre-existent or incarnate. Hanson[354] comments, 'The key text, Prov. 8:22, for instance, was allowed by everybody to refer to Christ, whereas we today would hesitate to regard it as more than, on the most liberal interpretation, a possible faint foreshadowing of him.' Hanson[355] notes that the Arian debates did eventually lead all the pro-Nicene writers to recognise the analogous nature of all language used about God. They came to appreciate that since 'God is not as man' all language drawn from human experience only applies to God imperfectly. Images such as Son, Word and Wisdom should not be pressed when applied to God, and different images are needed to complement and modify each another. In human experience a father has to precede a son in time. This aspect of the image may not apply to God. The images of Word and Wisdom do not raise this issue because both word and wisdom can co-exist within a person before being expressed.

Creation and Salvation

It seems to have been the application of the attributes and activities of personified Wisdom, as understood within the Judaism of the time, to the risen and ascended Jesus that led the early Christians to see the pre-existent Christ as God's agent in creation. This is clearly seen in Col. 1:15-20 where the two strophes of the poem put the creation of all things 'through him' in the first strophe in parallel with the reconciliation of all things 'through him'. The poem itself does not give any explanation as to why reconciliation is necessary. It simply implies that following the creation of all things something happened to bring disruption, disorder and disharmony into the cosmos. The death of Jesus on the cross seen as a sacrifice, as indicated by the use of the word 'blood' in v. 20, has made the restoration of order and harmony possible. There has been much debate about the meaning of 'all things, whether on earth or in heaven' in this

354. Hanson, *Search,* 825.
355. Hanson, *Search,* 435-36.

verse.[356] The most obvious and satisfactory meaning in context is that expressed by Dunn[357] when he says,

> What is being claimed is quite simply and profoundly that the divine purpose in the act of reconciliation and peacemaking was to restore the harmony of the original creation, to bring into renewed oneness and wholeness 'all things', 'whether things on earth or things in the heavens'.

The poem, then, presents what Jesus achieved on the cross not as something to be understood as a 'free-standing' event but as the achievement of what God intended in the original creation of the cosmos through Christ. The poem does not say how the cross achieves this reconciliation and pacification. It would seem reasonable to assume that it at least involves the submission to Christ of the thrones, dominions, rulers and authorities mentioned in v. 16. That submission might be given voluntarily or it might have to be forced. It seems reasonable to let Col. 2:15, which also mentions rulers and authorities in the context of Jesus' death on the cross, throw some light on the poem. In itself it is a difficult verse to understand in detail (see the commentaries on it). However, there is general agreement that in this verse the writer is making use of the image of the Roman 'triumph' — the procession in which a successful Roman general was allowed to parade the captives and spoils of war which he had gained by the defeat of Rome's enemies through the streets of Rome. This suggests that not all will accept reconciliation and pacification by voluntary submission to Christ. However, by whatever means, God's original purpose for the creation will be achieved.

The connection between Christ's work in creation and salvation is less clear in John 1:1-18. However, it might not be pressing things too far to see such a connection implied in vv. 10-13. Verse 10a asserts that the world was made through him, but then vv. 10b-11 imply that something went wrong, because the world does not know him and is not willing to receive him. Here 'the world' in the author's mind seems to be the world of sentient beings, of humans. The achievement of the Logos is described in v. 12. He gave humans the right to become 'children of God'. There is general agreement that the opening of v. 1 deliberately echoes Gen. 1:1 as in the LXX. It may be that v. 12 echoes Gen. 1:26-27 with John transposing 'image of God' into 'child of God' in the light of the Father-Son imagery which pervades his Gospel. If so, we once again have the connection between creation and salvation. God's original purpose in creating human beings through the Logos is achieved through the incarnate Logos.

356. O'Brien, *Colossians,* 54-56, surveys six different views.

357. Dunn, *Colossians,* 104.

In the section 'Overcoming the Sacred-Secular Divide' above, attention is drawn briefly to the quotation of Ps. 8:4-6 in Heb. 2:6-8a. This deserves fuller discussion. Hebrews 1 emphasizes the deity of the Son. He shares and reveals the nature of God and is utterly superior to angels. He is the one through whom God created the world and he upholds everything by his powerful word (vv. 2-3). Hebrews 2 emphasizes that he shares the nature of humans, being 'made like his brothers in every respect' (v. 17). The centrepiece of these two chapters, which shows how they are linked, is the quotation from Ps. 8. This very clearly alludes to Gen. 1:26-28 and God's purpose in creating humans. God's purpose in creating humans in his own image was that they should rule over the world as his representatives, his vice-regents. However, says the writer, this is not what we see happening in reality (2:8b). Humans have forfeited their sovereignty over creation. As in Col. 1:15-20 and John 1:10-13 there is the clear implication that something has gone wrong and prevented the fulfilment of God's original purpose for the creation. But all is not lost. The writer of Hebrews declares, 'But we see him . . . namely Jesus' (2:9). Jesus, through his incarnation and death as a human being has regained for humans the sovereignty that God originally intended for them. God's purpose in creating the world has been put back on track.

This intimate connection between creation and salvation which arose out of the influence of thought about Wisdom on the understanding of the significance of Jesus and his incarnation and death, and so of the salvation he achieved for us, has great importance in the light of the ecological crisis which faces us in the twenty-first century. All too often Christians have thought that all that matters is the salvation of their (immaterial) 'soul' for an eternal existence in 'heaven' away from this world. The created (material) world is seen as a disposable container. This can lead to an attitude that is dismissive of ecological concerns. If God is going to dispose of this creation, why bother about what human exploitation is doing to it? There are one or two biblical passages (Rev. 21:1; 2 Pet. 3:7-13) which may seem to support the 'disposable container' view, but to read them this way is to misunderstand them and to go against the general tenor of Scripture.

Taken on its own Rev. 21:1 might seem to refer to the destruction of the first creation and its replacement by a new creation. However, what follows suggests that this is not the case. John sees a new Jerusalem *coming down* out of heaven, presumably to the new earth, implying that our eternal existence is on this earth, not in some immaterial heaven. The nature of the event is explained in v. 5, in which the Greek word order is significant, 'See, *new* I am making all things'. Beasley-Murray[358] comments on the significance of this, 'the empha-

358. Beasley-Murray, *Revelation*, 312.

sis is on the newness which God imparts to his creation, and therefore to his creatures. He is not discarding them, but granting them to know the newness of life manifest in the risen Christ.' Similarly, Bauckham[359] says, 'the contrast between "the first heaven and the first earth", on the one hand and "the new heaven and the new earth" on the other, refers to the eschatological renewal of this creation, not its replacement by another.' What follows confirms this. The kings and the peoples of the nations bring 'their glory' into the New Jerusalem (vv. 24, 26). There is continuity with the first creation, and this is a continuity to which human endeavours in the first creation make their contribution. Also, there are elements in the picture which allude to the Garden of Eden — the river and the tree of life. God walked daily with Adam and Eve in the garden, and in John's vision God and the Lamb are permanently present in the city. So, this is the fulfilment of the purpose of God in creating humans as creatures who would enjoy continuous fellowship with their Creator. This has been made possible by 'the Lamb that was slain' (Rev. 5:6, 12).

Second Pet. 3:7-13 is a difficult passage to translate (as comparison of a few modern English translations will show) and to understand. Here we can only touch on a few key issues.[360] Probably *the* key issue is a textual one, concerning the final word of v. 10. Although many EVV adopt the reading 'will be burned up' there is little doubt among textual scholars that the best reading is 'will be found'. A second key issue is the meaning of the word στοιχεῖα *(stoicheia)* in these verses. The translation 'elements' leads many modern readers to presume that it refers to elements of which all physical things are composed. This is a possible meaning but in the context of how the word is used elsewhere in the NT (Gal. 4:3; Col. 2:8, 20) it is much more likely that it refers to (hostile) spiritual beings of some kind. This also fits with the fact that here Peter seems to be echoing Isa. 34:4, which refers to 'the host of heaven'.

The echoes of Isa. 34 in this passage suggest that the writer is influenced by the tradition of the Hebrew prophets in using *figurative* cosmic 'end of the world' language of 'normal' events within history which are seen as acts of God's judgement. So, we should be wary of taking the language as a literal account of the end of the physical cosmos. It is also important to note that the theme of this passage is God's final act of judgement (v. 7), not cosmological speculation about the end of the physical universe. Once we do this, things begin to fall into place. The verb 'to find' is used in the OT in judicial and quasi-judicial context of moral and judicial scrutiny. In the Bible a passive form of a verb can be used

359. Bauckham, *Theology,* 49.

360. Bauckham, *Jude, 2 Peter,* 298-335, provides a detailed discussion of the textual problem in v. 10 and the issues of interpretation in these verses.

to imply reference to God as the agent of the action. So, the end of v. 10 refers to the judgement of the earth and all the deeds done on it by God. To what, then, does the earlier part of the verse refer? In Isa. 34:4-5 judgement of the heavenly powers precedes judgement on earth. That may be what is in mind in 2 Pet. 3. What of the reference to 'fire' in vv. 10, 12? In the OT fire is used as a metaphor of judgement which does not simply destroy, but *purifies* (e.g. Isa. 1:21-26; Mal. 3:1-4). The language here of 'dissolving/melting' would fit with the figurative use of fire refining impure metals.

All this points to the primary reference of 2 Pet. 3:7-12 being to the ultimate act of God's judgement, which will purge the created order of all evil. Out of this act of judgement comes a new heaven and a new earth (v. 13). If taken strictly, the parallel with the Flood (vv. 5-6) suggests that while the event may be cataclysmic, there is still continuity with the worlds before and after the purifying judgement. There may be an implication of continuity in the Greek word used for 'new' (καινός, *kainos*) in v. 13 (and in Rev. 21:1). Although the earlier clear distinction between καινός (new in quality) and νέος (*neos*, previously non-existent) was blurred by the first century AD that distinction seems to be there in most uses of these words in the NT.[361] So, although 2 Pet. 3 is speaking of a radical transformation of the heaven and the earth, it is a renewal through transformation, not a total destruction of the old and its replacement by something quite different. Moreover, human activity in the present creation can contribute positively to the new creation. Therefore Christians have good reasons for getting involved in actions to preserve and enhance what is good in this creation because this is working with the grain of God's purposes for the creation and is part of the 'glory' of the nations which will be taken into the new creation.

Such an understanding of 2 Pet. 3:7-13 and Rev. 21:1 fits in with the general tenor of the Bible. It is significant that the hope for the future which arises in the OT and continues in the NT is not that of the Greeks — the escape of a non-material soul from 'prison-house' of the material body for an eternal existence in a 'spiritual' realm. Rather, it is the expectation of a *bodily* resurrection for existence in a renewed earth and heaven (Dan. 12:1-4; Isa. 65:17-25; 1 Cor. 15; Rev. 21–22). Exactly what that means is beyond our present understanding. Paul struggles with the concept of a resurrected 'spiritual body' in 1 Cor. 15:35-49. The only example we have is that of Jesus. In it we see both continuity (he was recognisable and had the scars of the crucifixion) and discontinuity (he could appear in a locked room). As in Rev. 21 he takes the 'glory' of his existence in this creation (the scars) into the new creation.

361. *NIDNTT* 2:669-70.

The implication of Heb. 2:6-9 is that whatever is done which is in accord with the 'creation mandates' (Gen. 1:26-28; 2:15), so that it accords with God's original purpose for the creation, will not be pointless, but will find its (transformed) place in the new creation. It is important, of course, to understand these mandates rightly. They are not a basis for thoughtless human exploitation of the rest of creation. Genesis 2:15 can be translated as 'to serve and preserve it (the garden)'. These two verbs are used together elsewhere only of priestly activity in the tabernacle (Num. 3:7-8; 8:26; 18:5-6). It is the language of looking after God's sanctuary.[362] It is not a licence to exploit and despoil the earth. Humans are to look after the earth as beings who 'image' God. That means acting in ways which reflect the character of God, displaying wisdom, justice, goodness, love and other godly traits. There is a firm theological basis here for thoughtful and discriminating Christian support for 'green' policies and actions.

What is said about Christ as the agent in creation goes beyond anything that is said of personified Wisdom. Creation is not only 'through him'. It is 'for him' (Col. 1:16; Heb. 2:10), he is the 'heir of all things' (Heb. 1:2). We might pick up on the implications of the use of the metaphor of 'heir of the creation' by using a parable:

> A man was left an estate as his inheritance by his father, but because he was away in a foreign country he appointed trustees to look after it until he could claim it. When he came to claim it he found they had smashed up the house, concreted over the beautiful garden to make a car park and polluted the lake so that it was a stagnant sewer. He was upset and angry at the way his inheritance had been ruined. How do you think he would deal with his trustees?

How will Christ feel when he comes to receive his inheritance — planet earth? How will you and I feel, having been appointed as his trustees, about our part in caring (or not caring) for it when he receives it? Surely if we love him, we will want to take good care of his inheritance until he claims it.

Wisdom and Creation

There is a general scholarly consensus that 'creation theology' is an important aspect of wisdom thinking in the OT. There is not agreement about its exact

362. Wenham, 'Sanctuary Symbolism in the Garden of Eden Story'.

role in wisdom thought. Dell[363] sums up the main positions saying, 'In general scholars saw creation either as the main element, following Zimmerli, or as just one element within the wisdom tradition; or, while seeing creation as the overarching principle in wisdom, found other themes that derive from it'. There are very few explicit references to creation in the Book of Proverbs. However, the frequency of references to an idea is not necessarily a guide to its importance. These few references could be evidence of an important underlying assumption or worldview. For this reason we will examine the explicit references, and a few less direct ones, in some detail.

Proverbs 3:19-20

The LORD founded the earth by wisdom,
established the heavens by skill.
By his knowledge the depths were split,
the clouds drop dew.

These two verses form a carefully constructed pair. Within each verse the couplet moves from below (the earth/the deeps) to above (the heavens/the clouds). The pair is linked by the parallelism of their opening words (The LORD by wisdom/by his knowledge) and the common theme of the LORD's creative activity. The preceding unit (3:13-18) is marked off by the *inclusio* of 'blessed'. A new lesson begins at v. 21. For this reason some commentators[364] see these verses as an originally independent poetic fragment. It should be noted, however, that the use of the pair 'wisdom//understanding' in v. 19 echoes its use in v. 13. Whatever the origin of the three sections 3:13-18, 19-20, 21-35 there is a development of thought here which, as von Rad[365] noted, is also found in 8:1-36:

3:13-18	8:1-21	In praise of wisdom
3:19-20	8:22-31	The role of Wisdom in creation
3:21-26	8:32-36	An appeal to follow Wisdom

This suggests that the different sections of ch. 3 have been put together deliberately. As we shall see, recognising this juxtaposition of the sections in ch. 3 helps in understanding the meaning of 3:19-20.

363. Dell, *Book of Proverbs*, 134.
364. For example: Whybray, *Proverbs;* Murphy, *Proverbs.*
365. Von Rad, *Wisdom in Israel*, 151, n. 4.

In these verses 'wisdom' is put in synonymous parallelism with 'skill' (תְּבוּנָה/*tĕḇûnâ*) and 'knowledge'. Although most EVV translate *tĕḇûnâ* as 'understanding', as Fox[366] notes, it refers to 'practical know-how and is best translated "good sense" in reference to human relations (as in 3:13) but "skill" in reference to craftsmanship'. Some commentators have seen in these verses implicit use of building something as a metaphor for God's creative activity. This has been discussed in detail by Van Leeuwen.[367] He shows that in both ancient Mesopotamian and Hebrew literature humans and gods build and provision temples, palaces and ordinary houses 'with wisdom'. He then argues that,[368] 'In the Bible, house building and filling is the fundamental metaphoric domain for divine creation. The thing known (house building) is used to help readers understand something less known, that is, wisdom, creation and divine activity.' He points out that well-known metaphors can be used in an implicit way by making partial use of them. In Prov. 3:19 the use of the terms 'wisdom', 'founded', 'established' and 'skill' implies the metaphor of building a house, and the following verse is about provisioning it. There is a striking parallel to these two verses within Proverbs, in 24:3-4, which Van Leeuwen translates as follows:

> *By wisdom* a house is built, *by skill* it is *established*.
> *By knowledge* (its) rooms are filled, with all (sorts of) wealth, precious and lovely.

He points to other, partial, parallels in references to the building of the tabernacle and the temple. With regard to the work on the tabernacle God promises to equip Bezalel for the task:

> I will fill him with God's spirit, *with wisdom, with skill, and with knowledge* in all (sorts of) workmanship. (Exod. 31:3)

Concerning building the temple we are told that

> (God) filled (Hiram) *with wisdom, with skill, and with knowledge* to do all (sorts of) workmanship in bronze. (1 Kgs. 7:14)

Van Leeuwen sees these examples as support for the view that the metaphor of building-providing is being used of creation in Prov. 3:19-20. If Van Leeuwen's

366. Fox, *Proverbs 1–9*, 159.
367. Van Leeuwen, 'Cosmos, Temple, House'.
368. Van Leeuwen, 'Cosmos, Temple, House', 72.

argument is accepted, and it is a strong one, it provides an answer to Whybray's[369] puzzlement at why v. 20 refers to the aspects of the created order that it does. In the Mesopotamian literature the provision of water is an element in the 'provisioning' aspect of the metaphor. This is not surprising given the climatic conditions of the region.

These verses probably assume the cosmology that was widespread in the ancient Near East which is referred to more explicitly elsewhere in the OT.[370] The earth was thought of as a flat disc supported by pillars. Above it the sky was seen as a dome, also supported by pillars, probably the mountains. The whole was surrounded by the cosmic ocean. The aspect of divine wisdom expressed in these verses is the controlled influx of water from this ocean through the springs in the earth and the dew that comes from the sky. Dew is mentioned here because it was a vital source of moisture in the dry summer months.

Because v. 20 speaks of the 'deeps' (תְּהוֹמוֹת/*tĕhômôt*) being 'broken open/divided' (נִבְקָעוּ/*nibqāʿû*) Perdue suggests that there may be allusion here to the imagery of creation through battle. He refers to the Akkadian story of Marduk slaying the leader of the chaos monsters, Tiamat, in battle and then splitting her in two to use her carcass in creating the earth and the sky. To support this he says,[371] '*Tĕhôm* in Hebrew, the deep or cosmic ocean . . . may be linguistically related to the Akkadian name for the chaos monster, Tiamat'. This, however, is unlikely. If the Hebrew word were derived directly from the Akkadian name one would expect *aleph* not *he* as the middle radical, and the feminine ending *-āh*. Von Soden[372] suggests that the Hebrew word is cognate to the Akkadian word *tiamatu* ('sea') from which the name is derived. Allusion to the battle with chaos is at most a distant echo here.

Related to this is the question of how we are to understand the tense of the verbs in these two verses. There is general agreement that v. 19 refers to the initial creation of the earth and the heavens. Waltke[373] sees a transition within v. 20, with v. 20b going beyond the initial creation of the world and its creatures to the sustaining of it by waters that are essential for life. Toy[374] takes the verbs in v. 19 as past, dealing with the creation of the world, but thinks that those in v. 20 are better taken as present, referring to God's on-going

369. Whybray, *Proverbs*, 69.

370. See: Keel, *Symbolism of the Biblical World*, 16-26; Walton, *Ancient Near Eastern Thought*, 165-78.

371. Perdue, *Wisdom and Creation*, 83.

372. Von Soden, *AHw* 3.1353-54.

373. Waltke, *Proverbs 1–15*, 261-62.

374. Toy, *Proverbs*, 71.

guidance of the world. Fox[375] makes the pertinent comment that, 'Though the welling up of springs and the descent of dew were events in the original creation, these processes continue as ongoing providential deeds that recall and renew creation.'

The Hebrew preposition ב has a range of possible meanings. In v. 19 von Rad[376] takes it to mean 'in' and so understands the verse to mean, 'Creation was raised by God to a state of wisdom or understanding', with the result that wisdom is understood as an attribute of the earth. This suggestion has found little support. The parallelism with v. 20, where 'knowledge' is clearly an attribute of God, makes it unlikely. Most commentators take the meaning of the preposition to be instrumental in both verses. This gives Wisdom a role in creation, though what that is is not made clear. Is Wisdom in these verses simply an attribute of God, or is the personification of Wisdom in 3:13-18 (in v. 16 she has hands) meant to be carried over to the next section so that Wisdom comes to be thought of as an agent? Whybray[377] thinks not, since the reference to 'hands' could be simply a figure of speech as it is with regard to Yahweh's creative 'hand' in Isa. 48:13. Also Boström[378] points out, 'The most natural way to interpret the passage is to take wisdom/understanding/knowledge as definite attributes or qualities of the Lord which can be referred to individually and which the Lord makes use of in acts of creation.'

Finally we can return to considering how the context of these two verses points to their meaning. They provide the reason why Wisdom can offer all the benefits listed in 3:13-18 and provide motivation to respond positively to the appeal to follow Wisdom in 3:21-26. The way to get the most out of life in this world is to understand how it works and to understand its rhythms and patterns. There is no better way to do this than to become acquainted with the Wisdom which produced the world in the first place. Living in accord with that Wisdom is the way to live in accord with the structure and purpose of creation.

Proverbs 8:22-31

We have noted above that Prov. 8:1-36 has the same three-fold structure as Prov. 3:13-26. An important difference between the two passages is that in Prov. 8

375. Fox, *Proverbs 1–9*, 160.
376. Von Rad, *Wisdom in Israel*, 155.
377. Whybray, *Proverbs*, 68.
378. Boström, *God of the Sages*, 50-51.

Wisdom is personified and, after the initial introduction, in which the father of the previous chapters is probably the speaker, she speaks in the first person.

In vv. 4-21 Wisdom speaks about herself. She stresses the value of the instruction she offers (8:4-11), describes her character (8:12-13) and speaks of the benefits she offers to society (8:14-16) and to individuals (8:17-21). In all this Wisdom speaks in the present tense. Although Wisdom continues to be the subject in 8:22-31, the focus shifts to the past and to Yahweh as the central character. This is signalled by his name being the opening word of v. 22. He is the subject of the active verbs in 8:22-29, which refer to his acts of creation. The result of this is that Wisdom's status is defined in relation to Yahweh and his actions in creation.

In the commentary we have argued that in 8:22-26 the origin of Wisdom is presented using the imagery of procreation, with the corollary that Yahweh is presented in a female role. However, the concern of these verses is not the 'how' of Wisdom's origin but the 'when'. In the commentary we have argued for translating v. 22a as 'Yahweh gave birth to me as the first of his works.' The statement in v. 22b then stands in synonymous parallelism with this, 'the first of his acts of old'. Verse 23 underlines this by asserting that Wisdom's origin predated that of the earth. This is expanded on in 8:24-26 by listing what did not exist when Wisdom came into being. The negative formulation of these verses is a feature of the opening of ancient Near Eastern creation stories. This has led to the suggestion that these stories might have provided a prototype for Prov. 8:22-31. Following a careful study of three non-biblical and two biblical creation texts Whybray cautions against this view. None of these texts resemble Prov. 8:22-31 in its form or purpose. He found no evidence of direct borrowing or the use of a common literary source. He concludes,[379]

> That a number of different creation stories or stories in which the creation of the world is mentioned should use negative temporal clauses of the kind we have investigated in order to indicate the absolute priority of the Creator, or the relative order of the various acts of creation, or for some similar purpose, is so natural that there is no need, in the absence of other evidence, to postulate the existence of a common tradition.

His caution seems to be well placed.

In 8:27-31 the focus changes from Wisdom's origin to her presence with Yahweh as he creates the earth. In the commentary we have argued for the following translation of v. 30:

379. Whybray, 'Proverbs VIII 22-31 and Its Supposed Prototypes', 513.

I was at his side as a (heavenly) sage.
I was filled with delight daily,
rejoicing always in his presence.

While the imagery used of Wisdom's origin is that of procreation, the creation of the earth seems to use the imagery of constructing a building, with terms such as: 'shaped' (v. 25), 'established' (vv. 27, 28), 'made firm' (v. 28), 'foundations' (v. 29). We've noted in the commentary how the listing of the creation of the features of the cosmos begins with the waters of the deep (v. 24a) and generally moves upwards to the sky (v. 27) and the clouds (v. 28) before descending again to the sea-shore and then finally the foundations of the earth (v. 29). As we commented there, this presents the creation as a coherent structure, not just an unconnected assemblage of parts. It implies that there is a plan, a pattern, to it all.

The significance of what these verses say about the origin of Wisdom before the creation of the earth and her presence with the Creator during the creation of the earth is that they support Wisdom's claim to be able to provide the benefits promised in 8:12-21 and give the basis for the appeal to heed her instruction in 8:32-36. They do this by establishing her position and authority in various ways. We repeat briefly the points made in the commentary.

- She has an intimate relationship with the Creator. She is his child and was at his side when he created the earth. That she is a sage or counsellor might imply that she embodies the principles and plan used in the creation.
- The significance of her origin before anything else and her presence during the creation of the earth is indicated by Eliphaz's taunt to Job: 'Are you the first man who was born, brought forth before the hills? Have you listened in the council of God and does wisdom belong to you alone?' (Job 15:7-8).
- Her observation of, and perhaps participation in, the plan and process of creation fits her to be the one who teaches humans how to live rightly in that creation. God's questions to Job are relevant here: 'Who is this that darkens counsel with words without knowledge? . . . Where were you when I laid the foundations of the earth?' (Job 38:2-4).
- For all these reasons, plus her delight in the creation and humans, it is Wisdom who is ideally suited to be the mediator between the Creator and his human creatures.

By the way that they relate Wisdom to creation Prov. 3:19-20 and 8:22-31 express something fundamental in the worldview of Israel's sages. What Kidner[380] says of Prov. 8 is true of both passages. Together they are 'an exposure of the main framework of [Proverbs'] thought'. They assert the status and authority of wisdom, and so of the wisdom tradition. Yee[381] writes: 'Woman Wisdom not only personifies God's own wisdom but also the human wisdom tradition itself. Divine and human wisdom find their unity in the personification of Woman Wisdom.' There is an order and pattern to creation that is known to wisdom. Proverbs 8:24-29 presents this in terms of the physical creation. In view of what Wisdom says about herself in moral terms in 8:7-8, the fact that she delights in the creation implies that there is moral pattern and purpose too. It is through coming to know Wisdom and heeding her instruction that humans can live lives in harmony with this order. This will be to live life as God intended it to be lived in his creation, and so to get the most out of life. However, this does not lead to a straightforward natural theology or to seeking 'oneness with nature' as the basis for a good life. Proverbs insists that 'the fear of Yahweh is the beginning of wisdom, and the knowledge of the Holy One is insight' (9:10). Trust in, and obedience to, Yahweh are preconditions for perceiving and understanding his plans and purposes to be seen in the patterns of his creation (3:5-6).

Proverbs about Poor People

With one exception (16:11), the relatively few explicit references to creation in Prov. 10–31 are to God as the Creator of human beings. There are four such proverbs which deal with the treatment of poor people.

Proverbs 14:31. This antithetical proverb condemns oppression of the poor person and encourages generosity towards him:

> Whoever oppresses the poor insults his maker,
> but whoever is kind to the needy honours him.

The word for 'the poor' (דַּל/*dal*) in v. 31a refers to people such as peasant farmers who are vulnerable to abuse at the hands of the powerful. The parallel term in v. 31b, 'the needy' (אֶבְיוֹן/*'ebyôn*), 'is used for people who are virtually destitute, the day labourers of the ancient world, completely dependent on others for their daily survival'.[382] These are not to be subjected to oppression of any kind.

380. Kidner, *Proverbs*, 52.
381. Yee, 'Theology of Creation in Proverbs 8:22-31', 90.
382. *NIDOTTE* 1:228.

Perdue[383] notes that the verb root used in v. 31a (עשק/*'šq*) is used in the OT of 'harsh treatment of the poor in a variety of ways: extortion, exploitation, defrauding them of their goods and rights, unremunerated labour, enslavement for debts, and the general neglect of their needs'. Instead of being treated like this they are to be treated with generosity. When applied to the way humans treat one another the verb used in v. 31b (חנן/*ḥnn*) refers to 'active kindness, or generosity exhibited particularly toward those in need'.[384]

Anyone who oppresses the poor person 'insults' (חֵרֵף/*ḥērēp*) his Maker. This verb is used repeatedly in the story of the messenger from the Assyrian King Sennacherib mocking Yahweh (2 Kgs. 19//Isa. 37). It is used of speech and behaviour which impugns God's name and reputation. In Isa. 65:7 it is used of idolatry. The opposite of this is to honour God by being generous to those in need.

'His Maker' is ambiguous. However, the fact that the nearest antecedent is 'the poor' and that in the parallel phrase the action is directed to 'the needy' makes it clear that 'his' refers to the poor person. Although in Proverbs poverty is sometimes presented as the result of laziness (10:4) or wickedness (13:25) the sages also recognised that it could be caused by social oppression (13:23). The striking thing about Prov. 14:31 is that there is no mention of any qualification of the poor person that would require one to support them. It is their poverty alone that calls for a response to treat them generously and not harshly. In the Mosaic Law commands to treat the poor and needy well are sometimes supported by reference to the Hebrews having been liberated by Yahweh from oppression in Egypt (e.g. Exod. 22:21; Lev. 19:33-34; Deut. 24:17-22). The sages, however, base their social ethics on their understanding of creation and providence. God is the Creator of both the rich and the poor, the powerful and the weak. All people deserve respect and support, even if they are mired in poverty, for whatever reason, because all are created by God.

Proverbs 17:5.

Whoever mocks the poor insults his maker;
whoever rejoices at calamity will not go unpunished.

The first line of this proverb is a slight variant on 14:31a. The word used for 'the poor' here (רָשׁ/*rāš*) is one that is used in the wisdom literature in contrast to 'the rich'. The form of 'oppression' is narrowed to verbal abuse, perhaps because this links more closely with 'insults his Maker'.

The second line broadens the message of the proverb to apply beyond the

383. Perdue, *Wisdom Literature*, 62.

384. *NIDOTTE* 2:204.

specific hardship of poverty to showing compassion to people suffering from any kind of calamity. The implication of the parallelism with the first line is that it is the Maker who will ensure that the person who delights in the misfortunes of others will experience appropriate consequences.

This proverb makes the same point as 14:31, that every human being, irrespective of wealth or circumstances, is worthy of respect because all are created by God.

Proverbs 22:2.

The rich and the poor meet together,
the LORD is the maker of them all.

In its form this proverb is simply a statement of fact. No explicit moral is drawn. That is left to the reader. The word for 'the poor' here is the same as in 17:5 and it stands in contrast to 'the rich' (עָשִׁיר/*ʿāšîr*). The previous proverb relativises riches by saying that they are of less value than a good reputation. This verse relativises them in another way, by saying that the rich and the poor have something in common — they are both created by God. Any more detailed understanding of the proverb depends on the exact meaning one puts on the general statement that the rich and poor 'meet together' (נִפְגָּשׁוּ/*nipgāšû*). Fox[385] lists eight possibilities that various commentators have offered:

1. It may refer to an incidental encounter on the street.
2. It might be a meeting when the poor approaches the rich for help.
3. They may meet in the sense of *clashing*.
4. It may refer to a legal adjudication in the city gate.
5. It may be a coming together in concord.
6. Their *stations* in life may meet when a rich man becomes poorer or a poor one richer.
7. It may be a statement that rich and poor are found side-by-side in every community.
8. The meeting may be life itself, which God has bestowed on all.

These are not all mutually exclusive, and choosing between them is not easy. Fox regards numbers 5, 7 and 8 as too broad in meaning for the verb used. He favours 1, which, he says may lead to 3 or 4. The emphasis then is on the fair treatment of all, but especially the poor, in the courts. Rather surprisingly he does not mention a meaning which is favoured by a number of recent commen-

385. Fox, *Proverbs 10–31*, 695.

tators and is expressed well by Whybray[386] when he says that the verb should 'be understood figuratively as meaning that rich and poor have something in common: their status as Yahweh's creatures (see Ps. 85:10 [Heb. 11] for a somewhat similar use of this verb).' This seems a plausible understanding of the proverb and gives it a meaning very similar to 14:31 and 17:5, namely that God has given both rich and poor the same status as humans created by him. The implication can then be drawn that for the rich to treat or regard the poor as less than human or as inferior to themselves is to commit the sin of insulting God.

Proverbs 29:13.

> The poor and the oppressor meet together,
> the LORD gives light to the eyes of both.

This proverb is a variant of 22:2. In the first line the more neutral term 'the rich' is replaced by 'the oppressor'. The second line means the same as 22:2b but expresses it differently. The phrase 'to give light to the eyes' means 'to give life to' (e.g. Ps. 13:3 [Heb. 4]). So, this proverb is an implicit condemnation of the oppression of the poor on the same basis as in 14:31a, namely that both the poor person and the oppressor are the creation of God and that therefore God is insulted by abuse of the poor. The following verse provides a positive example of how the poor should be treated by those who are powerful.

Conclusion. There is a clear and coherent theme which runs through all four of these proverbs about the treatment of poor people. It is that poor people share a common origin with rich people. Both were created by the same God. Therefore to oppress poor people is to insult God, while to recognise their status as fully fellow human beings is to honour God. As Whybray[387] comments, 'The theological implications of this thought are immense.'

Proverbs 16:4

> The LORD makes everything for its purpose,
> even the wicked for the evil day.

The syntax of v. 4a is ambiguous. Van Leeuwen[388] lists four possible translations.

386. Whybray, *Proverbs,* 318.
387. Whybray, *Proverbs,* 223.
388. Van Leeuwen, *Proverbs,* 158.

1. The LORD makes everything/all for its purpose.
2. The LORD makes everyone for his purpose.
3. The LORD makes everything/one for his purpose.
4. The LORD makes everything/one to answer him.

To this can be added McKane's[389] translation:

5. Yahweh has made everything in relation to its counterpart.

The word לַמַּעֲנֵהוּ *(lammaʿănēhû)* could be the noun for 'answer' (used in 16:1b) with prefixed preposition and third person masculine suffix. However, it could be the preposition לְמַעַן *(lĕmaʿan),* which expresses purpose ('for the sake of'), with the suffix. Boström[390] rejects McKane's translation on the grounds that it is doubtful whether the noun can signify a member of a pair and so mean 'counterpart'. Most commentators think that translation 4 is the least likely in context and favour translation 1.

This proverb is a statement that everything in the universe has a purpose, even the wicked. In the commentary we have noted that this proverb is part of a cluster on the theme of divine sovereignty and human planning. It states that the wicked, those who do not commit what they do to God, come under God's sovereignty. Fox[391] makes the point that one might have expected the proverb to say that God made the 'evil day' for the wicked. By putting it the other way round the sages make the proverb a put-down of the wicked: 'the evildoer (as a *type*) was created just to give God's grim judgements something to do, to keep them busy, as it were'. Most commentators agree that it should not be read as a statement of a deterministic metaphysical principle that God creates some people evil so that their fate might be evidence of divine justice. Rather, as Fox's emphasis indicates, it is about types of people or conduct and, as Clifford[392] puts it, it 'is simply an interesting way of stating that God deals with evil people'. His sovereignty encompasses them. Because he is the Creator he ensures that their ways will not prosper in his creation. However, the NIV translation of v. 4a, 'The LORD works out everything for his own ends', goes too far in trying to avoid a deterministic reading and making the proverb conform to Rom. 8:28.

This proverb touches on the problem of theodicy, of how to reconcile God's justice with the existence of evil in the world he created. It is evidence that

389. McKane, *Proverbs,* 235.
390. Boström, *God of the Sages,* 61.
391. Fox, *Proverbs 10–31,* 611.
392. Clifford, *Proverbs,* 158.

questions about the existence of evil and wicked people in the creation were a subject of debate among the Israelite sages.

Proverbs 20:12

> The hearing ear and listening eye,
> the LORD makes them both.

This proverb is a statement which doesn't make any explicit moral point. The ear and the eye are the two organs of perception which are referred to in Proverbs as playing a part in gaining wisdom. The use of the ear is mentioned far more often than the eye. In Prov. 1–9 there are frequent exhortations to heed the teaching of the father or the instruction of Wisdom. There are proverbs which make explicit mention of the use of the ear in gaining wisdom (e.g. 15:31; 18:15; 25:12). The importance of using the eyes rightly is stated in 4:25. Using the eyes to observe and learn is implied in 6:6-11 and 24:30-34. Fools, of course, misuse their ears and eyes (17:24; 23:9).

At least three different interpretations of this proverb have been proposed:

1. It asserts the reliability of these important organs of perception which are used in gaining wisdom, since they are created by God (McKane).[393]
2. It makes the point that the seeing and hearing that are needed to acquire wisdom are only possible because of God's good gift of eyes and ears (Longman).[394]
3. It carries the implication that since God created the ear and eye humans are accountable to him for how they are used. They should be used for the purpose of gaining wisdom (Waltke).[395]

Of these the third seems most likely in the general context of the Book of Proverbs. It is also supported by the immediate context. We noted in the commentary that this proverb is part of a cluster which is about discernment and character. The first two interpretations can, of course, be seen as added reasons for making good use of these organs of perception.

Some commentators support the view that the proverb is primarily about accountability to God by referring to Ps. 94:7-11. Here the psalmist responds

393. McKane, *Proverbs*, 547.
394. Longman, *Proverbs*, 380.
395. Waltke, *Proverbs, 15–31*, 141.

to those who think that they can act wickedly with impunity because they imagine God does not see what they are doing: 'He who planted the ear, does he not hear? He who formed the eye, does he not see?' However, the purpose of the psalmist is different from that of the sage, and it is not clear that there is a relevant parallel to be drawn.

Perdue[396] suggests that this proverb gives some insight into the epistemology of the sages. He says,

> Unlike the priests, whose special knowledge of God, time, history and the world came primarily through the casting of lots, or the prophets, whose ecstatic experiences and visions gave birth to their religious knowledge, the sages speak normally of organs of perception that observe, experience, analyze, reflect, imagine.

Perdue probably makes a too sharp division between these different traditions within Israelite religion. However, he makes a valid point about their different approaches to religious insight and understanding, one which gains some support from Jer. 18:18.

Proverbs 16:11

> Just balances and scales are the LORD's,
> all the weights in the bag are his work.

This 'Yahweh proverb' sits in a small cluster of proverbs about the king (16:10-15). The king is not mentioned, but part of a king's responsibility was to uphold the use of honest weights and measures (2 Sam. 14:26; Ezek. 45:9-12). Yahweh's concern with economic justice in the market-place is expressed in three other proverbs which brand false measures as an 'abomination' to Yahweh and just weights as a delight to him (11:1; 20:10, 23).

The word מַעֲשֵׂהוּ *(maʿăśēhû)*, 'his work', in v. 11b uses the same Hebrew root as is used to refer to God as 'Maker' in Prov. 14:31; 17:5; 22:2. It is reasonable, therefore, to take this proverb as one which refers to God as Creator. The proverb asserts that accurate and honest weights and measures are part of the order that God intends for his creation.

The requirement to use correct weights and measures is found in the Mosaic Law, where it is supported by an appeal to Yahweh as the God of the

396. Perdue, *Wisdom Literature*, 66.

exodus from Egypt (Lev. 19:35-36). In this proverb it is supported by appeal to Yahweh as Creator. Once again, as in Prov. 14:31, we see that the sages use a different basis for their social ethics from that found in the Law. They base it on their understanding of creation and providence.

Proverbs 27:23-27

In the commentary we have argued that this poem commends living in a sustainable way. Monetary wealth and social status are unreliable, depreciating assets (v. 24). In contrast to this a proper attention to agriculture can lead to a sustainable way of life.

Verse 25 refers to the use of grass as a sustainable food source for animals in an ancient Israelite context. The grass which grew rapidly after the first rains was harvested and used as hay. This made possible a second growth of grass on which the animals were pastured. Grass and other vegetation from the mountains was also harvested and used as hay. With this sustainable food source the flocks and herds became a sustainable resource for humans. They provided clothing, milk and meat. Any surplus could be sold, and this might provide the means to increase the size of the farm, maybe enabling the growth of crops that would be food for humans.

The interesting thing about this poem is that it shows an awareness of the existence and importance of sustainable ecosystems. This is one kind of pattern that God has put into his creation.

Proverbs 30:18-19

The interpretation of the details of this number proverb have been discussed in the commentary. Whatever conclusions are reached about the details, it is clear that, as Van Leeuwen[397] puts it, 'These verses portray simple wonder at marvellous phenomena in God's creation, culminating with the mystery of sexual love.' The examples of 'wonderful things' seem to have been chosen to encompass the whole range of creation. They cover the three major spheres of the creation: the air, the land and the sea, and also the human and non-human creatures. There is a sense of joyful awe at aspects of God's creation that are indescribable because they lie beyond the bounds of human comprehension. The element of joy expressed here by the sage can be related to the 'rejoicing'

397. Van Leeuwen, *Proverbs,* 254.

and 'delight' which Wisdom expressed with regard to God's creation (8:30-31). Also, this kind of awe can be seen as included within the wider awe that is 'the fear of Yahweh'.

This number proverb and those in 30:24-28, 29-31 give evidence of the careful observation of the natural world by the sages. An interest in the natural world was part of the wider wisdom tradition. There is evidence of it in the report of Solomon's wisdom in 1 Kgs. 4:33 [Heb. 5:13]. This report has been linked with the making of classified lists of natural phenomena, known as 'onomastica', by the sages in Mesopotamia and Egypt.[398] In the section 'Acts and Consequences in Proverbs' I argued that the Israelite sages were aware of the limitations of human wisdom with regard to understanding the moral order of the world. This proverb shows a recognition of a limit to human wisdom with regard to understanding the physical order. As Murphy[399] says, 'In view of the not uncommon charge that the sages were simplistic in their observations and teachings, this openness to wonder and the contemplation of one of the deepest mysteries in human relationship is not to be forgotten.'

In view of the importance of the imagery of 'the two ways' in Proverbs the use of the word 'way' in v. 19 is probably significant, especially since the next verse is about a wrong 'way' of sexual behaviour. The sages seem to see a single order encompassing all aspects of life because there is a single Creator of it all.

Reflection

It is time to return to the issue raised at the start of this section. Does the fact that there are only a few direct references to creation in Proverbs indicate that this was not an important concept for the sages, or are these references the tip of an iceberg that reveals an important presupposition? We have seen that, taken in their context, the passages which refer to wisdom's role in creation in Prov. 3:21-26 and 8:22-31 serve to establish the status and authority of wisdom. In doing so, they assert the status and authority of the wisdom tradition within Israelite Yahwism. They therefore do provide evidence of an important underlying presupposition held by the sages concerning the basis of the very enterprise in which they were involved. With regard to the other references to God as Creator, Boström[400] makes the important point that motivation clauses are not very common in the sentence literature and that therefore those that are

398. Gray, *I and II Kings*, 145.
399. Murphy, *Proverbs*, 235.
400. Boström, *God of the Sages*, 87.

used must be taken to be very significant. This is particularly so when the motivation given is theological and not solely pragmatic, based on the consequences of the particular behaviour or action under consideration. So, it is reasonable to take these few references to God as the Creator of humans as evidence of a fundamental tenet that the sages held to be of great importance.

Some scholars[401] have tried to read some significance into the fact that 'creation of the world' appears in Prov. 1–9 and 'creation of man' in Prov. 10–31. In fact the division is not total. Proverbs 8:22-31 refers to Lady Wisdom's delight in humans and implies their creation by Yahweh. The difference in the purposes of the references to creation in the two parts of the book is sufficient to explain the different emphases without need to postulate two traditions of separate origins.

Because the Israelite sages based their social ethics in a creation theology rather than rooting it in Israel's salvation-history traditions, it made it easier for them to share common ground with the wider ancient Near Eastern wisdom tradition. Commentators sometimes note parallels between the Hebrew proverbs and those from other ancient Near Eastern cultures, most notably of course *The Instruction of Amenemope.* From a Judeo-Christian perspective it is not surprising that sages observing and reflecting on what promotes a 'good life' for people made in the image of their Creator and living in the world he created — even in a 'post-Fall' situation — should come to some common conclusions. The Apostle Paul notes that Gentiles have some innate sense of God's law, even if they do not always follow it (Rom. 2:14-16). There is some important encouragement here for Christians who enter into the dialogue about social ethics today. Obviously a creation theology itself does not provide common ground in a modern secular society. However, because the dialogue is with other humans created in the image of God and living in the world created by God, there is ground for hope that some areas of agreement can be found in a common search for a 'good life', even though different religious and secular ideologies will differ somewhat in their understanding of what constitutes this. The fact that many proverbs adopt a 'consequentialist' approach without any explicit theological comment is a reason why some scholars have suggested that wisdom in Israel was originally 'secular'.[402] Such an approach, however, is consistent with a creation theology. Maybe it would be a fruitful one in seeking to find common ground in a secular society today.

The sages' search for patterns of 'acts and consequences' was based on a conviction that they lived in a planned and ordered world. This same convic-

401. See those mentioned by Boström, *God of the Sages,* 68.

402. See the discussion of this in the section 'God and Proverbs'.

tion motivated the early modern scientists in their search for patterns, 'laws of nature', in the material world. Collingwood expressed the conclusion of many historians and philosophers of science when he said concerning the Christian understanding of creation, 'The presuppositions that go to make up this "Catholic faith", preserved for many centuries by the religious institutions of Christendom, have as a matter of historical fact been the main or fundamental presuppositions of natural science ever since.'[403]

These 'presuppositions' included, but were wider than, the concept of 'natural law'. Trigg[404] sums them up when he says of the founders of modern science in the seventeenth century: 'they believed that their attempts to explain the workings of the material world rested on an ability to understand the regularities and orderliness given the world by a Creator, who had also given them the pale, but adequate, light of reason.' Trigg[405] notes that a common way of referring to human reason and its source in God in the seventeenth century was the phrase 'the candle of the LORD'. This was taken from the KJV translation of Prov. 20:27:

> The spirit of man is the candle of the LORD,
> searching all the inward parts of the belly.

Most commentators take this as referring to God's deep knowledge of humans, but some understand it to be a reference to human self-understanding as a gift from God.[406]

A striking example of the influence of Christian, biblically based, beliefs motivating one of the early modern scientists is a statement made by Johannes Kepler. Kepler is sometimes called 'the father of modern astronomy' because of his discovery and formulation of the three laws of planetary motion which bear his name. He arrived at them as a result of trying to find a geometrical shape that would fit the observational data of the motion of the planet Mars which had been obtained by the great Danish astronomer Tycho Brahe, whose assistant he became in Prague in 1600. Most 'natural philosophers' of the time, including Brahe, accepted Aristotle's view that all heavenly bodies moved in perfect circles with constant speed, and that the earth was the centre of the cosmos. Kepler had already broken with this orthodoxy by adopting Copernicus' proposal that the Sun is the centre of the system with the planets orbiting around it. Brahe's

403. Collingwood, *Essay on Metaphysics*, 127.

404. Trigg, 'Christian Roots of Scientific Reasoning', 47.

405. Trigg, 'Christian Roots of Scientific Reasoning', 32.

406. Murphy, *Proverbs*, 154.

data led him to question the assumption of circular motion. However hard he tried he could not make the data fit with circular orbits for the Earth and Mars. Both orbits were involved since the observations of Mars were made from the Earth. He spent some five years doing numerous calculations and recalculations of the orbits, trying different geometrical figures. We know he did at least 70 different calculations of the Earth's orbit alone. Eventually, he found a geometrical shape which did fit the data — the ellipse. This became his first Law of Planetary Motion: 'The orbit of a planet is an ellipse with the sun at one focus.' What motivated him to continue the search for the correct geometrical shape for so long without giving up? In his book *Harmonice Mundi* Kepler[407] explains what it was that sustained him for those five years. It was the conviction that

> Geometry, being part of the divine mind from time immemorial, from before the origin of things, being God Himself (for what is in God that was not God Himself), has supplied God with the models for the creation of the world and has been transferred to man together with the image of God. Geometry was not received inside through the eyes.

If one replaces the word 'geometry' here with 'wisdom' it becomes very clear that in what he says Kepler is alluding to two biblical passages about creation. The first part echoes what is said about wisdom in Prov. 8:22-31 and the second half echoes Gen. 1:26-27. Kepler is by no means alone among the early modern scientists in making it clear in his writings that Christian, biblical, beliefs motivated his scientific endeavours.[408] Because the Christian presuppositions of these early modern scientists have proved so fruitful for the last four centuries they have come to be taken for granted, and few scientists stop to think about them and where they come from. It is ironic that, because of the attacks on religion by a few vocal scientists who are atheists, many people think that science and Christianity are inevitably opposed to one another. As Trigg points out, the reality is that in the face of postmodernist challenges to their presuppositions most scientists find it hard to justify the scientific enterprise. He says,[409]

> Perhaps rather than being in retreat from the onward march of science, Christian doctrine itself is indispensable to it. Certainly, without the idea of an ordered creation, and a God-given rationality, it is difficult to see how science can be provided with the metaphysical grounding it clearly needs.

407. Caspar, *Kepler*, 271.
408. For other examples see Lucas, 'Biblical Basis for the Scientific Enterprise.'
409. Trigg, 'Christian Roots of Scientific Reasoning,' 48.

The creation theology of the Israelite sages has wider relevance than they could ever have imagined.

The sages sense of wonder and delight about the mystery and beauty of the physical creation is also something worth pondering. If humans are simply the outcome of a purposeless process it is not obvious why we should be able to appreciate beauty. Conan Doyle[410] comments on the significance of this ability in one of his stories about Sherlock Holmes. As usual Dr. Watson is the storyteller:

> [Sherlock Holmes] walked past the couch to the open window and held up the drooping stalk of a moss rose, looking down at the dainty blend of crimson and green. It was a new phase of his character to me, for I had never before seen him show any keen interest in natural objects.
>
> 'There is nothing in which deduction is so necessary as in religion', said he, leaning his back against the shutters. 'It can be built up as an exact science by the reasoner. Our highest assurance of the goodness of Providence seems to me to rest in the flowers. All other things, our powers, our desires, our food, are all really necessary for our existence in the first instance. But this rose is an extra. Its smell and its colour are an embellishment of life, not a condition of it. It is only goodness which gives extras, and so I say again that we have much to hope from the flowers.'

Conan Doyle goes too far when he says that religion can be 'built up as an exact science' by deduction. But he is right to point to beauty as one of those features of the natural world that gives us good reason to believe in the existence of a good Providence. It is hard to explain the existence of our ability to appreciate and enjoy the beauty of flowers or stars in purely materialistic, mechanistic terms. It seems unnecessary for mere existence, and to have no particular survival value. However, it can reasonably be seen as a pointer, a sign-post, to our having been created by a God who wants us to enjoy the world in which we live.

Beauty seems to have another function besides giving us enjoyment. Quite a number of scientists, especially in the physical sciences, argue that beauty is a guide to truth. The beauty they are talking about is a special kind of beauty — what they call 'mathematical beauty'. Paul Dirac, one of the founders of quantum physics, used to tell his students to look for 'beautiful equations' because they were likely to be true.[411] When asked what led him to one of his

410. Conan Doyle, *Complete Sherlock Holmes,* 455-56.

411. Polkinghorne, *One World,* 45-46.

greatest achievements, the 'relativistic equation of the electron', his answer was that it was the beauty of the equation. Now it is amazing that humans should be able to appreciate the beauty of sub-atomic quantum systems, but what is even more amazing is that that sense of beauty should lead to the understanding of nature at deeper and deeper levels in the micro-world. It was the relativistic equation of the electron which predicted the existence of anti-matter — something no one had ever thought of before. It was not long after the prediction that its existence was proved during the study of cosmic rays. This, too, cannot be explained simply as the result of being shaped by an impersonal process of 'the survival of the fittest' in the macro-world. Why should the human mind be able to appreciate such beauty? Might it be because we were created in the image of the Creator of the universe, as the Bible teaches, and so are able to share God's appreciation and enjoyment of the world?

A number of prominent scientists who are not Christian believers recognise that science raises questions which cannot be answered from within science and which therefore point to the need for a metaphysical basis for science. Paul Davies,[412] a professor of theoretical physics who subsequently held chairs in the philosophy of science in Australia and the USA, has written, 'though science may explain the world, we still have to explain science. The laws which enable the universe to come into being spontaneously seem themselves to be the product of exceedingly ingenious design.' According to Martin Rees,[413] Professor of Astrophysics at Cambridge University, British Astronomer Royal and a past President of the Royal Society, 'The pre-eminent mystery is why anything exists at all. What breathes life into the equations of physics, and actualized them in a real cosmos? Such questions lie beyond science, however; they are the province of philosophers and theologians.' Taking delight in creation and pursuing where that leads just might bring people into contact with Lady Wisdom.

Words in Proverbs and the New Testament

It is arguable that the category of sins that is mentioned most often in the Bible is sins of speech. This is certainly true in Proverbs. The fact that three of the lessons in Prov.. 1–9 are about the dangers of adultery (5:1-23; 6:20-35; 7:1-27) might lead the superficial reader to think that this is the major concern of the book. It is certainly an important concern for the father who is giving instruction to

412. Davies, *Superforce*, 243.
413. Rees, *Our Cosmic Habitat*, xi.

a young man apparently about to start out on adult life. However, in the book as whole more than twice as much space, measured in terms of the number of verses, is given over to sins of speech than to sexual sins. Murphy[414] estimates that about 20 per cent of Prov. 10–29 deals with the topic of speech. Waltke[415] notes that 'two semantic domains stand out prominently in contrasting the wise/righteous and fools/wicked: communication and wealth' (on the subject of wealth see the section 'Wealth and Poverty in Proverbs').

Of the seven sins which are listed in Prov. 6:16-19 as 'an abomination' to the LORD two are explicitly misuses of speech: 'a lying tongue' (general dishonesty of speech) and 'a false witness who utters lies' (perjury in court). Another misuse of speech is implied with the mention of 'one who lets loose conflict among brothers'. Elsewhere in Proverbs such conflict is attributed to people who misuse speech:

> A perverse person spreads strife,
> and a whisperer separates close friends. (16:28)
>
> Without wood the fire goes out,
> and without a whisperer quarrelling ceases. (26:20)
>
> Drive out the scoffer and quarrelling will go out,
> and discord and abuse will cease. (22:10)

'Lying lips' are again said to be 'an abomination to the LORD ' in 12:22, and in 24:9 the scoffer is declared to be 'an abomination to humankind'.

Why is speech, and the way we use it, so important? One reason is that it is a capability which clearly distinguishes humans from other creatures. Other animals can communicate using sounds, and plants can communicate using chemical signals, but none seem to have a 'language' which allows the breadth, flexibility and subtlety of communication which is possible with human speech. Among other things this allows us to pass on our learning and experience. Human culture can therefore develop and grow. Speech plays a crucial role in the formation and development of social relationships. Communication leads to the formation of communities. For a community to develop and function well there has to be good, reliable communication. Without it people cannot trust each other. That is why the proverbs quoted above condemn lying and other misuses of speech so strongly:

414. Murphy, *Proverbs*, 258.
415. Waltke, *Proverbs 1–15*, 101-102.

By the blessing of the upright a city is exalted,
but by the mouth of the wicked it is destroyed. (11:11)

Another reason for the importance of words concerns the nature of God. The God of Israel is a God who speaks. God spoke, and creation came into being. God called Abraham and the story of salvation began. God spoke to the rabble of Hebrew slaves at Sinai, giving them what in Hebrew are called 'the ten words', the Ten Commandments, and the people of God came into being. Down through their chequered history God spoke to them through the prophets. This reason appears indirectly in Proverbs in the guise of personified Wisdom who calls out to and speaks to humans. In Prov. 8:6-9 she describes the nature of her words, which might be summed up in the phrase, 'All the words of my mouth are righteous' (v. 8a). Like the LORD she hates perverse speech (8:13). Humans have to use words to communicate with God, and since the LORD hates 'a lying tongue' it is not surprising that

The LORD is far from the wicked,
but he hears the prayer of the righteous. (15:29)

As we shall see, the sages are very concerned about good communication — 'good' in two senses. Most importantly it must be 'good' in content, honest and reliable. It also needs to be 'good' in the sense of being presented well, so that it is attractive and persuasive. The sages consider good communication so valuable that they compare it to precious metals (10:20; 25:11-12) and precious jewels (20:15).

The Power of Words

'Death and life are in the power of the tongue' (18:21a). This statement about the power of words is part of a proverb-pair concerning the consequences of speech. Although there is some debate about the detailed understanding of the pair (see the commentary on these verses) there is a clear statement here of the power of words.

One context in which speech can literally lead to death or life is the witness given in court for a case for which the penalty is capital punishment. This is the subject of the following proverbs:

A truthful witness saves lives,
but one who spreads lies is deceitful. (14:25)

> Like a club, a sword, or a sharp arrow,
> is a man who bears false witness against his neighbour. (25:18)

The weapons listed in 25:18a are clearly all instruments of death. The proper administration of justice in any judicial system depends on the honesty of witnesses in court. This is no doubt why the Ten Commandments include a prohibition against false witness (Exod. 20:16; Deut. 5:20). It is therefore understandable that there are several proverbs about the importance of this in the Book of Proverbs (6:12; 12:17; 14:5, 25; 19:5, 9, 28; 21:28; 24:28; 25:18). Some of them are quite similar in wording, suggesting they may be variants of a common popular saying. Three proverbs warn that a false witness 'will not go unpunished' (19:5, 9) or 'will perish' (21:28). These may be statements of how seriously the courts view perjury. However, since false witness is an abomination to the LORD there may be the implication that, whether or not the court detects the perjury, there will be divine retribution for the offence.

Apart from this literal meaning, words can bring life or death in a metaphorical sense of being life-enhancing or life-diminishing. It is a theme in Prov. 1–9 that heeding the father's teaching, his words, is the way to have a good life. For example, he says (4:20), 'My son, pay attention to my words', and gives a motivation:

> For they are life to those who find them,
> and healing to all their flesh. (4:22)

The 'mouth' of the righteous is said to be 'a fountain of life' (10:11a). The same imagery is used in another proverb:

> The teaching of the wise is a fountain of life,
> that one may turn away from deadly snares. (13:14)

Those who recognise the truth of this will listen and give heed to the teaching of the wise even when it comes in the uncomfortable form of 'life-giving reproof' (15:31). The double-sidedness of the power of words is brought out in a proverb which evokes the strong image of the tree of life:

> A healing tongue is a tree of life.
> but when perverse it breaks the spirit. (15:4)

Other proverbs also contrast the positive and negative effects of words:

> There is one whose gossip is like sword thrusts,
> but the tongue of the wise brings healing. (12:18)

Proverbs 12:6a compares the words of the wicked to a deadly ambush, and in 10:6, 11 they are linked with violence (see the commentary on these verses). The godless use their words to try to destroy their neighbours (11:9). This probably refers to character assassination, but could refer to perjury in court (see the commentary on this verse). The words of a worthless person are compared to a scorching fire (16:27). Lying to someone is seen as an expression of hatred:

> A lying tongue hates those it crushes,
> and a flattering mouth works ruin. (26:28)

Verse 28a may be another reference to character assassination. This is not the only proverb which speaks of the harmful effect of flattery:

> A man who flatters his neighbour
> spreads a net for his feet. (29:5)

Building up someone's ego falsely only sets them up for a fall, so is a subtle form of character assassination. For this reason the flatterer is compared unfavourably with the person who is willing to tell others what they might find to be unpalatable truths:

> Whoever rebukes a person will afterwards find more favour
> than one who flatters with the tongue. (28:23)

Proverbs 15:4 (quoted above) refers to a possible negative emotional and psychological effect of words. Other proverbs speak of the positive emotional and psychological effects they can have:

> Anxiety in a man's heart depresses him,
> but a good word gives him joy. (12:25)

> Like a honeycomb are pleasant words.
> Sweetness to the soul and healing for the bones. (16:24)

As well as having a pleasant taste, honey was thought to have medicinal value. Pleasant words not only give an emotional lift, they can bring healing to the core of one's being (the bones in Hebrew thought). An appropriate word, spoken at the right time, can bring joy to both the speaker and the hearer (15:23).

One of the themes of Proverbs is the fact that people reap the reward and punishment for what they say. There is some debate about the meaning of Prov. 12:13, but it is generally taken to say that those who commit sins of speech will find that they cause trouble for themselves. The righteous, by contrast, presumably because their speech is truthful, can get themselves out of troublesome situations:

> In the transgression of the lips is an evil snare,
> but the righteous escapes from trouble.

Prov. 14:3 expresses much the same idea, though the translation of v. 3a given requires emending the Hebrew (see the commentary on this verse):

> By the mouth of a fool comes a rod for his back,
> but the lips of the wise will preserve them.

There is a mini-portrait of the way fools make problems for themselves by their words in 18:6-7. The GNB translation brings out the humour of it:

> When some fool starts an argument,
> he is asking for a beating.
> When a fool speaks, he is ruining himself;
> he gets caught in the trap of his own words.

Because of the powerfulness of words there is some onus on the hearers to be careful about what they listen to, and how they respond. They must not be naive and credulous:

> The simple believe everything,
> but the prudent give thought to their steps. (14:15)

It is a sad fact that all too often we enjoy listening to some juicy gossip, and are all too ready to believe it:

> The words of a gossiper are like tasty morsels;
> they go down into the inner parts of the body. (18:8)

The danger is that once accepted and believed the gossip will not be easily forgotten, but remain imprinted on the mind to influence our behaviour. That is why the sages say that listening to such a person is as bad as being one:

An evildoer is one who listens to wicked lips,
and a liar one who gives ear to a mischievous tongue. (17:4)

Of course, to benefit from good words one has to be teachable (see 15:31 quoted above). As noted in the section 'Characters in Proverbs', a characteristic of both fools and scoffers is that they lack humility and are unteachable.

The Weakness of Words

The sages recognised that there is a limit to the power of words. One limiting factor is the one just mentioned — the unteachability of some people:

A rebuke goes deeper into an understanding person
than a hundred blows into a fool. (17:10)

But the problem may be deeper than understanding:

By mere words a servant is not corrected,
for though he understands, he will not respond. (29:19)

The problem may lie in a stubborn will that does not want to accept what has been understood.

Another weakness of words is that they are no substitute for action:

In all work there is profit,
but utterances of the lips tend only to poverty. (14:23)

The importance of diligence, of working to get things done, is a major theme in Proverbs. On this see the section 'Wealth and Poverty in Proverbs' and the subsection 'The Sluggard'.

Words can be rendered powerless by the person who uses them:

Like a lame person's legs which dangle
is a proverb in the mouth of fools. (26:7)

The effective use of proverbs requires the wisdom to know which proverb is appropriate for a given situation or person.

The sages were aware that words can be used as a smokescreen, or a surface glaze, to hide the true attitudes or motives of the speaker (26:23-26, see the commentary on these verses). Therefore the listeners need to use their discretion to see through this. The sages are confident that such hypocrisy will eventually be exposed.

Words and Character

The ultimate origin of words is in a person's 'heart':

> The heart of the wise instructs his mouth,
> and adds persuasiveness to his lips. (16:23)
>
> The lips of the wise spread knowledge,
> but the hearts of fools, not so. (15:7)

In Hebrew the 'heart' (לֵב, לֵבָב/*lēb, lēbāb*) is not used metaphorically of the centre of the emotions, as is the case in English. Rather, as Fox[416] puts it, the heart in Hebrew 'is the locus and organ of thought and the faculty of understanding. It is also the organ of psychological experiences that we currently classify as emotions.' It is the centre of a person's inner life.[417] As one would expect, therefore, a person's words express their character:

> The tongue of the wise commends knowledge,
> but the mouths of fools pour out folly. (15:2)

The intimate connection between the person and their words is emphasised in Proverbs by the frequent mention of the body parts 'mouth', 'lips' and 'tongue' to refer to words and speech. They are used much more frequently than the abstract nouns. See further on this theme in the character studies in the section 'Characters in Proverbs'.

Using Words Wisely

The sages have a lot to say about what the characteristics of the right, or wise, way to use words are.

Honest. Since 'Lying lips are an abomination to the LORD' (12:22) and he

416. Fox, *Proverbs 1–9*, 109.
417. *NIDOTTE* 2:749.

hates 'a lying tongue' (6:17), it is clear that a primary characteristic of the right use of words is that they should be honest, should tell the truth. Personified Wisdom declares that 'my mouth will utter truth' (8:7). The purpose statement at the beginning of the section in Proverbs entitled 'The Words of the Wise' includes the following:

> To let you know truth, words that are reliable,
> that you may bring back reliable words to the one who sent you. (22:21)

This, of course, is especially important in a judicial context:

> He who declares the truth speaks honestly,
> but a false witness speaks lies. (12:17)

A particular test of honesty in words is the willingness to give honest words of rebuke when it is appropriate. There is a proverb pair on this subject (see the commentary on these verses):

> Better an open rebuke
> than a love that is hidden.
> Faithful are the wounds of a friend,
> profuse are the kisses of an enemy. (27:5-6)

Sometimes, at least, the rebuke will come to be appreciated (28:23, quoted above). The exact meaning of the metaphor in 24:26 is unclear:

> He kisses the lips,
> the person who replies with honest words. (24:26)

It probably means that telling someone the truth is the most genuine sign of affection (see the commentary on this verse).

Restrained. The sages were very much of the opinion that, where words are concerned, less is better:

> In many words there is no lack of transgression,
> but whoever restrains his lips is prudent. (10:19)

Given the power of words for good or ill and the fact that we are imperfect people and bound to say something that is wrong, hurtful or harmful in some way or other from time to time, it makes good sense to restrain ourselves from speaking when it is unnecessary. Another reason for being watchful about what we say is that words may not only harm others but also the speaker (see above):

> The one who guards his mouth and tongue
> keeps himself out of trouble. (21:23)

Those who do not do this may bring ruin on themselves:

> The one who guards his mouth preserves his life;
> he who opens wide his lips comes to ruin. (13:3)

In the opinion of the sages the person who speaks impulsively, without restraint, is worse off than a fool:

> Do you see someone who is hasty with words?
> There is more hope for a fool than for him. (29:20)

Thoughtful. It follows from what has just been said, that words should be used thoughtfully:

> The heart of the righteous ponders how to answer,
> but the mouth of the wicked pours out evil things. (15:28)

As noted above, the Hebrew use of the word 'heart' approximates to the English use of the word 'mind'. Hence the translation of the GNB: 'Good people think before they answer'. There is a modern English saying which is similar in meaning to this proverb: 'Engage the brain before opening the mouth.'

One particular way of failing to think before speaking is to be a good talker but a poor listener. As a result what is said may seem irrelevant or even foolish. In any case such people may seem self-opinionated because of their failure to listen carefully to others:

> The one who answers before listening,
> his is the folly and the shame. (18:13)

Fitting. If a word is spoken with due thought it is more likely to fit the occasion or the person to which it is addressed. It is important to the sages that words are not only correct in their content, but they are also fitting for the context in which they are spoken. They need to be spoken at the right time and place:

A man gets joy from the answer of his mouth,
and a timely word, how good it is! (15:23)

There is a proverb pair which brings this out using striking, and beautiful, imagery:

Like apples of gold in settings of silver
is a word fitly spoken.
Like a gold earring or an ornament of fine gold
is a wise person who reproves to a listening ear. (25:11-12)

A proverb does have value in itself, like a golden apple. Nevertheless, when it is used on the right setting its value is greatly enhanced. All that value is wasted, however, unless there is a listening ear, ready to welcome the wise words, even if they are words of reproof. For the person ready to heed it, the one who is able to give such reproof is as valuable as golden jewellery.

Persuasive. Two proverbs, both in a small cluster about various kinds of speech (16:20-24, see the commentary), use the phrase 'increases learning' (יֹסִיף לֶקַח/*yōsîp leqaḥ*). There is some debate about the meaning of this phrase but it is generally taken in to refer to the persuasiveness of the words used:

The wise of heart are called discerning,
and sweetness of lips increases learning. (16:21)

The wise man's heart gives insight to his mouth,
and increases learning on his lips. (16:23)

The second proverb makes the link between character and words that is discussed above. A thoughtful, wise person is more likely to be persuasive in speaking than other people. The first proverb makes the point that presentation is important as well as content. The 'sweetness' in this proverb cannot refer to the 'smooth words' of the flatterer which the sages condemn. It might refer to the right use of rhetoric or to the attitude with which the words are spoken:

By patience a ruler can be persuaded,
and a soft tongue can break a bone. (25:15)

The imagery of v. 15b is a striking way of saying that gentleness or tenderness can break through seeming stubborn resistance. The first half of the proverb is a particular example of this.

Humble. The sages counsel against boasting about oneself and one's achievements:

> Let another praise you and not your own mouth,
> a stranger and not your own lips. (27:2)

It is difficult to have a relatively objective assessment of one's own strengths and weaknesses. Someone else's view (and this is all that 'stranger' means here) is less likely to be biased. The following is another proverb on the theme of humility:

> A man's pride brings him low,
> but a humble spirit gains honour. (29:23)

There is ambiguity in another proverb about a person's praise:

> A crucible is for silver and a furnace for gold,
> and a man is tested by his praise. (27:21)

The second part of the proverb can be taken in two ways. It could mean that how a person responds to praise is a test of character or that the amount and nature of praise that people get from others reveals their character. The ambiguity may be intentional. The first part of the proverb is identical to 17:3a, which is followed by a reminder of who is the ultimate judge of character, 'and the LORD tests hearts'.

Calm. The sages prized calmness and self-control in all things, including the use of words:

> Whoever restrains his words is a knowledgeable person,
> and he who has a cool spirit is an understanding person. (17:27)

In Egyptian wisdom literature[418] the terms 'hot' and 'cool' are used metaphorically of two different personality types. The ideal person is 'cool' and calm, controlling emotion and speech. The 'hot' person readily loses his temper and provokes strife. Slowness to anger, 'keeping your cool' to use a modern English idiom, is commended in Proverbs:

> Whoever is slow to anger has great understanding,
> but the quick-tempered exalts folly. (14:29)

418. Fox, *Proverbs 10–31,* 598; Waltke, *Proverbs 16–31,* 64.

The difference between the reactions mentioned in this proverb is that self-control enables one to ignore insults and other provocations instead of simply 'seeing red' and giving vent to one's anger (12:16; 19:11). It is not that the wise lack emotions but that they express them as and when is appropriate rather than letting them take over and cloud their judgement. Someone who cannot do that is in a dangerous state:

> A city breached without a wall
> is a man without self-control. (25:28)

He is not able to make considered decisions and cope with life as he should. Also, by playing on his emotions other people can manipulate him.

Conclusion. This final characteristic of the wise use of words brings us back to the fact that the sages in ancient Israel were not just concerned to pass on knowledge and skills which would enable one to have a good life. They were concerned about the formation of good people.

James 3:1-12

Murphy[419] comments that 'The power of the tongue is, as we say, proverbial, and one of the most famous descriptions is contained in the epistle of James, Jas 3:1-12. This is in genuine continuity with Old Testament sapiential thought.'

James does indeed have some strong things to say about our use of words, the control of our tongues. He begins with a warning to teachers about being judged by what they say. This is understandable in the light of some words of Jesus: 'I tell you, on the day of judgement people will give account for every careless word they speak, for by your words you will be justified, and by your words you will be condemned' (Matt. 12:36-37).[420] James, of course, is addressing those who have specific teaching responsibility in the church. Today that would include people such as preachers, those who teach children and young people, home-group leaders and those who lead Bible studies. However, it applies more widely than that because many church members have some teaching responsibility at various times: pastoral visitors, parents, those giving counsel to friends. In any case, it is clear that from v. 2 onwards James is addressing all his readers, not just teachers, as he begins what he has to say with, 'For we all . . .'

419. Murphy, *Proverbs*, 259.

420. NT quotations are from the ESV unless otherwise indicated.

The importance of the tongue. Why is how we use words so important? James uses two illustrations to answer this. He compares the tongue to a bridle and to a rudder. Each is something comparatively small that is used to control something much larger than itself — a horse or a ship. Small though it is, the tongue can utter words that can have huge effects.

'Death and life are in the power of the tongue' says Prov. 18:9. As has been noted above, that can be literally true in some judicial situations in countries which still have capital punishment. But, as also noted, the writers of Proverbs had a wider meaning in mind. Proverbs 11:9 says, 'With their mouths the godless would destroy their neighbours'. People's lives can be destroyed by malicious accusations, hurtful gossip, verbal bullying and in other ways. On the other hand, people's lives can be enhanced by words of encouragement, wise counsel and sound teaching. Looking back over their lives most people can probably think of examples of both helpful and harmful words in their own personal development. That should make us aware of the importance of how we use words. Do we use them to build people up, or to knock them down, to give life or death?

The power of the tongue. James goes on to speak of the power of the tongue using a number of vivid comparisons. In doing so, for reasons which he doesn't explain but no doubt had to do with the pastoral situations he knew he was addressing, he concentrates on the destructive power of the tongue:

- He compares it to a small fire which becomes a major forest fire (vv. 5b-6). He has probably picked up this imagery from the Book of Proverbs:

  Scoffers set a city aflame. (29:8)

  For lack of wood the fire goes out,
  and where there is no whisperer quarrelling ceases. (26:20)

  Scoundrels concoct evil,
  and their speech is like a scorching fire. (16:27)

  Some people use words in an inflammatory way. Others keep stoking the fire, and then there are those who use words as a weapon, like a flame-thrower.
- He compares the tongue to an untamed beast that rampages about, causing destruction (vv. 7-8a).
- He calls the tongue a source of poison (v. 8b). This is imagery that is found in some of the Psalms. In Ps. 140:3 the psalmist says of evildoers, 'They make their tongues sharp as a snake's, and under their lips is the venom of vipers.'

The inconsistency of the tongue. James moves from talking about the power of the tongue to point out that we are very inconsistent in the way we use it (v. 9). He again seems to be echoing the Book of Proverbs in what he says. For example, in the Book of Proverbs we read, 'Those who mock the poor insult their Maker' (17:5). We use our tongues to praise and worship God but then use them to harm those whom God has made in his own image. James uses two examples to drive home the inconsistency of this:

- You wouldn't expect a spring of water to produce pure, fresh drinkable water one minute and undrinkable salty water the next.
- You wouldn't expect a fig tree to produce olives or grapes.

Both of these examples are probably rooted in sayings of Jesus:

- Hear and understand, it is not what goes into the mouth that defiles a person, but what comes out of the mouth; this defiles a person. . . . But what comes out of the mouth proceeds from the heart, and this defiles a person. (Matt. 15:10-20)
- You will recognize them by their fruits. Are grapes gathered from thorn bushes, or figs from thistles? So, every healthy tree bears good fruit, but the diseased tree bears bad fruit. (Matt. 7:16-17)

This, I think, shows us what James is getting at by his illustrations, and indeed in this whole section about the tongue. How we use words reveals something about the kind of person we are. There is a strong link between speech and character. This, as discussed above, is a theme in the Book of Proverbs. Just before talking about the tongue James has dealt with the issue of faith and *works* (2:14-26). He has stressed that a saving faith shows itself in good works. Now he is making a point about faith and *words.* A saving faith should show itself in a good use of words. In fact James has already made this point in 1:26: 'If anyone thinks he is religious, and does not bridle his tongue but deceives his hearts, this person's religion is worthless.' But is 'bridling' of the tongue possible?

Controlling the tongue. The tone of what James has said in vv. 5b-12 is so negative that one might be left feeling that the situation is hopeless. But this isn't the case.

- First, James's comment in 1:26 indicates that this is not really the case. What he says here implies that someone who is truly 'religious', truly a Christian, *can* bridle the tongue. His use of the imagery of the bridle in what he says about words in 3:2-3 must be understood in the light of what he has already said in 1:26.

- Second, when he says in 3:2, 'if anyone does not stumble in what he says, he is a perfect man' the word translated as 'perfect' (τέλειος, *teleios*) is the same word that he has used in 1:4 where it is, rightly, usually translated as 'mature'. Here James is saying that it is possible for Christians to become 'mature' through coping with life with the help of the wisdom that God gives. So, it is possible to learn to control the tongue properly.
- Third, there is v. 8. Although this is sometimes translated as 'but no one can tame the tongue', what James actually says is, 'but *no human being* can tame the tongue' (as in the ESV). James is not saying that the tongue is beyond all control, but seems to imply that to do this one needs more than human strength, that is, the help, the grace of God

What does proper control of the tongue mean in practice? James doesn't go into any detail about this. No doubt he would agree with what is said above about what the sages commend as the wise use of words.

But how is it possible to do all this? The only answer is — by the grace of God. James has said that in ch 1. There he reminds his readers that God has given us a new birth, with a new power to live as God's children (1:18, 21). Moreover, God has promised to give us the good gifts we need to cope with life, in particular his wisdom (1:5, 17). For whatever reason, James doesn't mention the Holy Spirit as such, but it is the work of the Holy Spirit within us that he is talking about.

Ephesians 4:17–5:20

James is not the only writer in the NT to deal with the matter of the right and wrong use of words. It is quite a common topic in the Pauline letters. One place where it is dealt with in some detail is Eph. 4:17–5:20. This comprises a distinct section of ethical teaching within the letter. It is, however, ethics grounded in theology. In 4:1 the readers are urged to 'walk in a manner worthy of the calling to which you have been called'. Following that there is a section on the importance of maintaining the unity of the church as 'the body of Christ'. The exhortation to walk in a worthy manner is picked up again in 4:17: 'you must no longer walk as the Gentiles do'. The reason for this is the radical change that happens when one becomes a true follower of Christ. This is described in terms of 'putting off' an 'old self' and 'putting on' a 'new self'. Although the language might evoke the imagery of changing clothes, the use of 'old self/new self' indicates that what is being referred to is not a mere surface change, but a radical inner change of a person's nature. The imagery may derive from the practice of removing clothes before entering the water for Christian baptism and being dressed in new clothes afterwards. In Gal. 3:27 Paul says, 'For as many of you as were baptized into Christ have put on Christ', and in Rom. 13:12-14, 'let us cast off the works of darkness and put on the armour of light. Let us walk properly as in the daytime . . . put on the Lord Jesus Christ.' However, we do not know enough about early Christian baptismal practice to be sure that it does lie behind Eph. 4:22-23. Besides the 'put off/put on' language, two other forms of language are used in this section of Ephesians to express the radical change that marks becoming a Christian. In 5:7-14 the readers are urged to 'walk as children of light' who have left the darkness of their former way of life, using the light/darkness imagery that is also used in Rom. 13:12-14. Then in 5:16-17 they are urged to walk 'not as unwise but as wise' and admonished to 'not be foolish'. This is language which is reminiscent of Proverbs with its wise-foolish contrast and its imagery of the two ways.

As Paul[421] moves to discuss the practical implications of this radical change in terms of moral behaviour, the first thing he says concerns the use of words: 'Therefore, having put away falsehood, let each one of you speak the truth with his neighbour, for we are members one of another' (4:25). We have seen above that one of the characteristics of the right use words in Proverbs is honesty. Here Paul adds a particular Christian motivation for this, the fact that we are all members of the body of Christ. His next admonition (4:26-27) is about anger and quotes Ps. 4:4a from the LXX text (where it is Ps. 4:5). Anger is usually expressed in words, and we have seen that the control of anger is an important theme in Proverbs. Although the next admonition (4:28) does not refer to the use of words, it does deal with another kind of honesty — doing 'honest work' instead of thieving and sharing the proceeds with those in need. This is similar to the stress in Proverbs on the importance of gaining wealth by diligent work and not by devious means and the admonitions to care for the needy (see the section 'Wealth and Poverty in Proverbs'). When Paul goes on to contrast 'corrupting talk' with the kind of talk that should characterise Christians (4:29) there are again echoes of Proverbs. Christian talk should 'fit the occasion' which, as we have noted, is one of the characteristics of the good use of words in Proverbs. It should also be 'good for building up' and 'give grace to those who hear'. This is a good description of the kinds of things which Proverbs says about the words of the wise — that they impart knowledge, wisdom, life

421. I am assuming that in some sense he is the ultimate author of Ephesians. See the commentaries for discussion of the authorship of this letter.

and healing. The list of types of speech that are to be 'put away' (4:31) includes the kinds of speech that are characteristic of the various 'bad characters' in Proverbs — the wicked, the fool, the scoffer, the whisperer (see the section 'The Characters of Proverbs). In vv. 30 and 32 Paul adds two specific Christian motivations, which will be discussed later.

The call to be 'imitators of God, as beloved children' is reminiscent of the father teaching his son in Prov. 1–9 with the father urging the son to listen to his teaching and obey it. The section in 5:3-7 is primarily about sexual behaviour, which also features in Proverbs, but speech also figures within it. When Paul said that sexual sins and covetousness 'must not even be named among you' he might have meant that this kind of behaviour should not occur among Christians.[422] However, the following verse and v. 12 suggest that he meant that such sins should not even be talked about among Christians. Now that goes somewhat against the grain of modern Western society with its stress on openness and freedom of speech. However, every society has recognised that this freedom has to be used responsibly, and that there need to be curbs on irresponsible use of it. Many countries have laws against inciting racial hatred, or violence, and laws against pornography. These are laws against the misuse of language. Paul is getting at something even more fundamental than that. He is reminding us that simply talking about some things, that is, making them the subject of general discussion, can make them seem acceptable, just part of the way things are. As a result we may stop taking them seriously as things that are evil. What Prov. 18:8 and 26:22 say about the attractiveness of the 'delicious morsels' of salacious gossip is relevant here, as the attention given to stories about the sexual (mis-) behaviour of prominent people in the mass media illustrates. What Paul is seeking to prevent is not serious discussion of issues of sexual behaviour but, as v. 4 indicates, prurient discussion of sexual misbehaviour which ultimately trivialises it.

It might seem strange that Paul puts thanksgiving as the antidote to the three wrong kinds of speech he lists in 5:4. However, the following verse provides a clue to this when it equates covetousness with idolatry. When we covet something we give it the central place in our desires that God should have. The same can be true with uncontrolled sexual desire. Thanksgiving is a way of reminding ourselves of our dependence on a good and generous God and that nothing should be allowed to usurp God's place in our desires. Stott[423] suggests that there may be another reason why Paul calls for thanksgiving here. He suggests that Paul is setting thanksgiving in opposition to vulgarity as a way of

422. Brachter and Nida, *Handbook,* 125-26.

423. Stott, *God's New Society,* 192-93.

expressing alternative Christian and pagan attitudes to sex. He says, 'All God's gifts, including sex, are subjects for thanksgiving, rather than for joking. To joke about them is bound to degrade them; to thank God for them is the way to preserve their worth as the blessings of a loving Creator.' Paul adds a specifically Christian motivation for not getting involved in sexual immorality and covetousness. They are the object of God's wrath and exclude people from the kingdom of Christ and God. The 'empty words' of v. 6 are the words of those who deny that these sins have that much importance.

In 5:8-14 the darkness/light contrast is introduced. This has been anticipated by mention of the 'darkened understanding' of the Gentiles in 4:18. The change may happen here because of the reference to the wrath of God in v. 7 and the association of dark/light imagery with the Day of the LORD in the OT in Amos 5:18. The 'works of darkness' in v. 11 might refer back specifically to the sins listed in v. 3, but the probable link back to 4:18 suggests that the reference is wider than that to the general way of life depicted in 4:18-19, 22. It may be that v. 12 is saying much the same thing as v. 3. However, in the context of vv. 11 and 13 with their reference to the 'natural' power of light to expose what is in the darkness some commentators suggest a different meaning. Lincoln,[424] for example, refers to the warnings in Prov. 9:7 and 15:12 that scoffers are impervious to verbal correction. Christians should not talk about these kinds of shameful deeds, and in any case doing so would have no effect on those doing them. He therefore argues that what is being said here is that the exposure of the works of darkness mentioned in v. 11 is to be brought about not by verbal reproof but by the behaviour of Christians as children of the light: 'As they refuse to join in evil actions and display a different quality of life, they cast their illuminating beam into the dark recesses of the surrounding society and will invariably show up its immoral practices for what they are.'

In 5:15-20 the language changes again, this time to the wise-foolish contrast. Its mention of debauchery as a result of drinking too much wine could bring Prov. 23:29-35 to mind. Paul contrasts being 'filled with the Spirit' with being drunk with wine. One of the things about getting drunk is that it affects how people speak. They lose control and say things they would not normally say, often telling dirty jokes and using bad language that they would not use when sober. Eventually their speech becomes incoherent, and they cannot communicate any more. You should not be like that, says Paul. The Spirit that fills *you* will enable you to speak in ways that will build one another up as you help each other keep your focus on God and what pleases him. He specifically mentions worship and thanksgiving (vv. 19-20). Often we have a very narrow

424. Lincoln, *Ephesians,* 330.

view of what it means for someone to be 'filled with the Spirit', limiting it to a few special experiences or gifts. Here Paul is telling us that one mark of true fullness of the Holy Spirit is the way we talk and what we talk about. This takes us back to 4:30 and Paul's warning to 'not grieve the Holy Spirit of God'. The preceding verse shows that what Paul has in mind here is that letting 'corrupting talk' come out of our mouths rather than using 'fitting' talk to build one another up is what will grieve the Holy Spirit.

How is it possible to make sure that we do use words rightly? The first part of Paul's answer in this passage is much the same as what we saw in James. It is implied in the command in 5:1: 'Therefore be imitators of God, as beloved children.' Christians are children of God. Children share something of the nature of their parents and have a natural tendency to copy their parents. This is particularly true if the family is a loving one and the relationship a good one. So, the stronger our relationship with God, the more natural it will be for us to use words rightly. Second, we have the power of the Holy Spirit to enable us to live as we should as 'children of light', provided we do not grieve the Spirit but are filled with the Spirit.

Conclusion

From these two passages we can see that NT writers share the Israelite sages' concern about the right use of the human power and gift of speech. Also, when they deal with this subject they stand firmly in the OT wisdom tradition. The sages, James and Paul all speak of the tongue and the mouth when referring to words and speech. In their days speech was by far the major form of communication. Only a small minority of people could read or write with any fluency. Today, of course, we have a wide range of means of communication, written and electronic. What the biblical writers say about the importance of the power of the tongue applies to the use of words in all these means of communication too. They have greatly increased the power of words to influence people for good and ill. As a result it is all the more important that we take seriously our responsibility to use words wisely.

Bibliography

Aitken, K. T. *Proverbs*. DSB. Edinburgh: St Andrews Press, 1986/Leicester: IVP, 1996.

Albertz, R. *A History of Israelite Religion in the Old Testament Period*. 2 vols. London: SCM, 1994.

Albright, W. F. 'The Goddess of Life and Wisdom'. *AJSL* 36 (1919): 258-94.

———. 'Some Canaanite-Phoenician Sources of Hebrew Wisdom'. Pp. 1-15 in *Wisdom in Israel and the Ancient Near East: Presented to H. H. Rowley*. Edited by M. Noth and D. W. Thomas. VTSup 3. Leiden: Brill, 1955.

Aletti, J. N. 'Séduction et parole en Proverbs I–IX'. *VT* 27 (1977): 129-44.

Alexander, D. (ed.). *Can We Be Sure about Anything? Science, Faith and Postmodernism*. Leicester: Apollos, 2005.

Alster, B. *Proverbs of Ancient Sumer*. 2 vols. Bethesda, MD: CDL, 1997.

Andreasen, N.-E. A. 'The Role of the Queen Mother in Israelite Society'. *CBQ* 45 (1983): 179-94.

Atkinson, D. *The Message of Proverbs*. Leicester: IVP, 1996.

Attridge, H. W., et al. (eds.). *Of Scribes and Scrolls: Studies on the Hebrew Bible, Intertestamental Judaism, and Christian Origins Presented to John Strugnell*. Lanham, MD: University Press of America, 1990.

Barr, J. *The Semantics of Biblical Language*. Oxford: Oxford University Press, 1962.

Barré, M. L. (ed.). *Wisdom, You Are My Sister*. Washington, DC: Catholic Biblical Association of America, 1997.

Barrett, C. K. *The Gospel According to John*. London: SPCK, 1956.

Barton, S. C. (ed.). *Where Shall Wisdom Be Found?* Edinburgh: T&T Clark, 1999.

Bauckham, R. *Jude, 2 Peter*. WBC. Waco, TX: Word, 1983.

———. *The Theology of the Book of Revelation*. Cambridge: Cambridge University Press, 1993.

Beasley-Murray, G. R. *The Book of Revelation*. NCB. London: Oliphants, 1974.

Bellis, A. O. 'The Gender and Motives of the Wisdom Teacher in Proverbs 7'. Pp. 79-91 in *Wisdom and Psalms*. A Feminist Companion to the Bible (2nd series). Edited by A. Brenner and C. Fontaine. Sheffield: Sheffield Academic Press, 1998.

Berlin, A. *The Dynamics of Biblical Parallelism*. Grand Rapids, MI: Eerdmans, 2008 (rev. ed.).

Bernhardt, K.-H. (ed.). *Schalom: Studien zu Glaube und Geschichte Israels: Festschrift Alfred Jepson*. Stuttgart: Calwer, 1971.

Bledsoe, S. A. 'Can *Ahiqar* Tell Us Anything about Personified Wisdom?' *JBL* 132 (2013): 119-37.

Blenkinsopp, J. 'The Social Context of the "Outsider Woman" in Proverbs 1–9'. *Bib* 72 (1991): 457-73.

Boström, G. *Proverbiastudien: Die Weisheit und das fremde Weib in Sprüche 1–9*. Lund: Gleerup, 1935.

Boström, L. *The God of the Sages: The Portrayal of God in the Book of Proverbs*. Coniectanea Biblica, Old Testament Series 29. Stockholm: Almqvist & Wiksell, 1990.

Brachter, R. G., and E. A. Nida. *A Translator's Handbook on Paul's Letter to the Ephesians*. London: United Bible Societies, 1982.

Brenner, A. 'Proverbs 1–9: An F Voice?' Pp. 113-30 in *On Gendering Texts*. Edited by A. Brenner and F. van Dijk-Hemmes. Leiden: Brill, 1993.

Brenner, A. (ed.). *A Feminist Companion to the Bible* 5. Sheffield: Sheffield Academic Press, 1994.

——— (ed.). *A Feminist Companion to Wisdom Literature*. Sheffield: Sheffield Academic Press, 1995.

Brenner, A., and F. van Dijk-Hemmes (eds.). *On Gendering Texts*. Leiden: Brill, 1993.

Brenner, A., and C. Fontaine (eds.). *Wisdom and Psalms*. A Feminist Companion to the Bible (2nd series). Sheffield: Sheffield Academic Press, 1998.

Bricker, D. P. 'The Doctrine of the "Two Ways" in Proverbs'. *JETS* 38 (1995): 501-17.

Brown, R. E. *The Gospel According to John*. AB. Garden City, NY: Doubleday, 1971.

Brown, W. P. *Character in Crisis: A Fresh Approach to the Wisdom Literature of the Old Testament*. Grand Rapids, MI: Eerdmans, 1996.

Bryce, G. E. 'Another Wisdom-"Book" in Proverbs'. *JBL* 91 (1972): 145-57.

———. 'Omen-Wisdom in Ancient Israel'. *JBL* 94 (1974): 19-37.

Budge, E. W. *Facsimiles of Egyptian Hieratic Papyri in the British Museum*. 2nd series. London: British Museum, 1923.

Byargeon, R. W. 'The Structure and Significance of Prov. 9:7-12'. *JETS* 40 (1997): 367-75.

Calvin, J. *Institutes of the Christian Religion*. Translated by H. Beveridge. London: James Clarke, 1962.

Camp, C. *Wisdom and the Feminine in the Book of Proverbs*. Sheffield: Almond, 1985.

———. 'What's So Strange about the Strange Woman?' Pp. 17-32 in *The Bible and the Politics of Exegesis*. Edited by D. Jobling et al. Cleveland, OH: Pilgrim, 1991.

Campbell, E. E. *Ruth*. AB. Garden City, NY: Doubleday, 1975.

Carmody, D. L. *Biblical Woman: Contemporary Reflections on Scriptural Texts*. New York: Crossroad, 1989.

Caspar, M. *Kepler*. New York: Dover, 1993.

Charlesworth, J. H. (ed.). *The Old Testament Pseudepigrapha*. vol. 2. London: Darton, Longman & Todd, 1985.

Clements, R. E. 'The Concept of Abomination in the Book of Proverbs'. Pp. 211-25 in *Texts, Temples and Traditions*. Edited by M. V. Fox et al. Winona Lake, IN: Eisenbrauns, 1996.

Clifford, R. J. 'Observations on the Texts and Versions of Proverbs'. Pp. 47-61 in *Wisdom, You Are My Sister*. Edited by M. L. Barré. Washington, DC: Catholic Biblical Association of America, 1997.

———. J. *Proverbs*. OTL. Louisville, KY: Westminster John Knox, 1999.
Clifford, R. J. (ed.). *Wisdom Literature in Mesopotamia and Israel*. Atlanta, GA: SBL, 2007.
Clifford, R. J., and J. J. Collins (eds.). *Creation in the Biblical Traditions*. Washington, DC: Catholic Biblical Association of America, 1982.
Cohen, A. *Proverbs*. London/Jerusalem/New York: Soncino, 1995 (rev. 2nd ed.).
Collingwood, R. G. *An Essay on Metaphysics*. Oxford: Oxford University Press, 1947.
Collins, J. J. *Jewish Wisdom in the Hellenistic Age*. Edinburgh: T&T Clark, 1998.
Conan Doyle, A. *The Penguin Complete Sherlock Holmes*. Harmondsworth: Penguin, 1982.
Cook, J. 'The Dating of Septuagint Proverbs'. *ETL* 69 (1993): 383-99.
Cook, J. *The Septuagint of Proverbs: Jewish or Hellenistic Proverbs?* VTSup 69. Leiden: Brill, 1997.
Cotterell, P., and M. Turner. *Linguistics and Biblical Interpretation*. London: SPCK, 1989.
Crenshaw, J. L. 'The Three Main Contexts of Israelite Learning'. Pp. 205-16 in *The Sage in Israel and the Ancient Near East*. Edited by J. G. Gammie and L. G. Perdue. Winona Lake, IN: Eisenbrauns, 1990.
———. *Old Testament Wisdom: An Introduction*. Louisville, KY: Westminster/John Knox, 1998 (rev. ed.).
Crenshaw, J. L. (ed.). *Studies in Ancient Israelite Wisdom*. New York: Ktav, 1976.
———. (ed.). *Theodicy in the Old Testament*. London: SPCK, 1983.
Davies, P. *Superforce*. London: Unwin, 1985.
Day, J. 'Foreign Semitic Influence on the Wisdom of Israel'. Pp. 55-70 in *Wisdom in Ancient Israel: Essays in Honour of J. A. Emerton*. Edited by J. Day, R. P. Gordon and H. G. M. Williamson. Cambridge: Cambridge University Press, 1995.
Day, J., R. P. Gordon and H. G. M. Williamson (eds.). *Wisdom in Ancient Israel: Essays in Honour of J. A. Emerton*. Cambridge: Cambridge University Press, 1995.
Day, P. L. (ed.). *Gender and Difference in Ancient Israel*. Minneapolis, MN: Fortress, 1989.
Delkurt, H. *Ethische Einsichten in der alttestamentlichen Spruchweisheit*. BTS 21. Neukirchen-Vluyn: Neukirchener Verlag, 1984.
Dell, K. J. *The Book of Proverbs in Social and Theological Context*. Cambridge: Cambridge University Press, 2006.
Dodd, C. H. *The Interpretation of the Fourth Gospel*. Cambridge: Cambridge University Press, 1972.
Driver, G. R. 'Problems in "Proverbs"'. *ZAW* 50 (1932): 141-48.
———. 'Misreadings in the Old Testament'. *WO* 1 (1948): 234-48.
———. 'Problems in the Hebrew Text of Proverbs'. *Bib* 32 (1951): 173-97.
Dunn, J. D. G. *The Epistles to the Colossians and to Philemon*. NIGTC. Carlisle: Paternoster, 1996.
———. 'Jesus: Teacher of Wisdom or Wisdom Incarnate?' Pp. 75-92 in *Where Shall Wisdom Be Found?* Edited by S. C. Barton. Edinburgh: T&T Clark, 1999.
Eichrodt, W. *Theology of the Old Testament*. 2 vols. London: SCM, 1961/1967.
Eissfeldt, O. *Der Maschal im Alten Testament*. BZAW 24. Giessen: Töpelmann, 1913.
———. *The Old Testament: An Introduction*. Oxford: Blackwell, 1965.
Ellingworth, P. *The Epistle to the Hebrews*. NIGTC. Carlisle: Paternoster, 1993.
Emerton, J. A. 'The Teaching of Amenemope and Proverbs XXII 17–XXIV 22: Further Reflections on a Long-Standing Problem'. *VT* 51.4 (2001): 431-65.
Estes, D. J. *Hear, My Son: Teaching and Learning in Proverbs 1–9*. Leicester: Apollos/IVP, 1997.

Exum, J. C., and H. M. G. Williamson (eds.). *Reading from Right to Left: Essays on the Hebrew Bible in Honour of David J. A. Clines*. JSOTSup 373. London: Sheffield Academic Press, 2003.

Finamore, S., and J. Weaver (eds.). *Wisdom, Science and the Scriptures: Essay in Honour of Ernest Lucas*. Oxford: Centre for Baptist History and Heritage/Regent's Park College, 2012.

Foster, B. R. *Before the Muses*. Bethesda, MD: CDL, 2005 (3rd ed.).

Fox, M. V. 'Words for Wisdom'. *ZAH* 6 (1993): 149-69.

———. 'World Order and Ma'at: A Crooked Parallel'. *JANESCU* 23 (1995): 37-48.

———. 'The Social Location of the Book of Proverbs'. Pp. 227-39 in *Texts, Temples and Traditions*. Edited by M. V. Fox et al. Winona Lake, IN: Eisenbrauns, 1996.

———. '*'amon* Again'. *JBL* 115 (1996): 699-702.

———. *Proverbs 1–9*. AB. New York: Doubleday, 2000.

———. 'Like Grapes of Gold Set in Silver: An Interpretation of Proverbial Clusters in Proverbs 10:1–22:16. By Knut Martin Heim.' *HS* 44 (2003): 267-72.

———. 'The Rhetoric of Disjointed Proverbs'. *JSOT* 29 (2004): 165-77.

———. *Proverbs 10–31*. AB. New Haven, CT: Yale University Press, 2009.

———. 'From Amenemope to Proverbs: Editorial Art in Proverbs 22,17–23,11'. *ZAW* 126 (2014): 76-91.

Fox, M. V. et al. (eds.). *Texts, Temples and Traditions: A Tribute to Menachem Haran*. Winona Lake, IN: Eisenbrauns, 1996.

Franklyn, P. 'The Sayings of Agur in Proverbs 30: Piety or Scepticism?' *ZAW* 95 (1983): 235-52.

Fritsch, C. T. 'The Treatment of the Hexaplaric Signs in the Syro-Hexaplar of Proverbs'. *JBL* 72 (1953): 169-81.

Gammie, J. G. 'The Theology of Retribution in the Book of Deuteronomy'. *CBQ* 32 (1970): 1-12.

Gammie, J. G., and L. G. Perdue (eds.). *The Sage in Israel and the Ancient Near East*. Winona Lake, IN: Eisenbrauns, 1990.

Gerleman, G. *Studies in the Septuagint III: Proverbs*. Lund: Gleerup, 1956.

Gese, H. *Lehre und Wirklicheit in der alten Weisheit*. Tübingen: Mohr, 1958.

Gibson, J. C. L. *Canaanite Myths and Legends*. Edinburgh: T&T Clark, 1978 (2nd ed.).

Gilbert, M. (ed.). *La Sagesse de l'Ancien Testament*. BETL 51. Leuven: Leuven University Press/Gembloux: Duculot, 1979.

Gillingham, S. E. *The Poems and Psalms of the Hebrew Bible*. Oxford: Oxford University Press, 1994.

Golka, F. W. *The Leopard's Spots: Biblical and African Wisdom in Proverbs*. Edinburgh: T&T Clark, 1993.

———. 'Wisdom by (the) People for (the) People: Eine Antwort an J. A. Loader'. *ZAW* 112 (2000): 78-79.

Grabbe, L. L. *Wisdom of Solomon*. London: T&T Clark, 2003.

Gray, J. *I and II Kings*. OTL. Philadelphia, PA: Westminster, 1970 (2nd rev. ed.).

Greene, M. *The Great Divide*. London: London Institute for Contemporary Christianity, 2010.

Greenfield, J. C. 'The Seven Pillars of Wisdom (Prov. 9:1): A Mistranslation'. *JQR* 76 (1985): 13-20.

Gressmann, H. 'Die neugefundene Lehre des Amen-em-ope und die vorexilische Spruchdichtung Israels'. *ZAW* 42 (1924): 272-96.

Grollenberg, L. H. 'A propos de Prov. VIII,6 et XVII,27'. *RB* 59 (1952): 40-43.
Habel, N. C. 'The Symbolism of Wisdom in Proverbs 1–9'. *Int* 26 (1972): 131-57.
Hallo, W. W. (ed.). *The Context of Scripture*, vol. 1: *Canonical Compositions from the Biblical World*. Leiden: Brill, 1997.
Hanson, R. P. C. *The Search for the Christian Doctrine of God: The Arian Controversy, 318-81*. Grand Rapids, MI: Baker Academic, 2005.
Harrington, D. J. *Wisdom Texts from Qumran*. London: Routledge, 1996.
Hatton, P. T. H. *Contradiction in the Book of Proverbs*. Aldershot: Ashgate, 2008.
Hatton, P. T. H. 'A Cautionary Tale: The Acts-Consequence "Construct"'. *JSOT* 35 (2011): 375-84.
Heim, K. M. *Like Grapes of Gold Set in Silver: An Interpretation of Proverbial Clusters in Proverbs 10:1–22:16*. BZAW 273. Berlin/New York: de Gruyter, 2001.
———. 'A Closer Look at the Pig in Proverbs xi 22'. *VT* 58 (2008): 13-27.
———. 'Personified Wisdom in Early Judaism'. Pp. 56-71 in *Wisdom, Science and the Scriptures: Essay in Honour of Ernest Lucas*. Edited by S. Finamore and J. Weaver. Oxford: Centre for Baptist History and Heritage/Regent's Park College, 2012.
Hess, R. S., and D. T. Tsumura (eds.). *I Studied Inscriptions from Before the Flood*. Winona Lake, IN: Eisenbrauns, 1994.
Hildebrandt, T. A. 'Proverbial Pairs: Compositional Units in Proverbs 10–29'. *JBL* 107 (1988): 207-24.
———. 'Proverbial Strings: Cohesion in Proverbs 10'. *Grace Theological Journal* 11 (1990): 171-85.
Hoglund, K. G., et al. (eds.). *The Listening Heart: Essays in Wisdom and the Psalms in Honor of Roland E. Murphy*. JSOTSup 58. Sheffield: JSOT Press, 1987.
Houston, W. J. 'The Role of the Poor in Proverbs'. Pp. 229-40 in *Reading from Right to Left*. Edited by J. C. Exum and H. G. M. Williamson. London: Sheffield Academic Press, 2003.
———. *Contending for Justice*. London: T&T Clark, 2006.
Hubbard, D. A. *The Preacher's Commentary: Proverbs*. Nashville, TN: Thomas Nelson, 1989.
Hugenberger, G. P. *Marriage as a Covenant: A Study of Biblical Law and Ethics Governing Marriage Developed from Malachi*. VTSup 52. Leiden: Brill, 1994.
Humphreys, W. L. 'The Motif of the Wise Courtier in the Book of Proverbs'. Pp. 177-90 in *Israelite Wisdom: Theological and Literary Essays in Honour of Samuel Terrien*. Edited by J. G. Gammie et al. Missoula, MT: Scholars Press, 1978.
Hurowitz, V. A. 'The Seventh Pillar — Reconsidering the Literary Structure and Unity of Proverbs 31'. *ZAW* 113.2 (2001): 209-18.
Irwin, W. A. 'Where Shall Wisdom Be Found?' *JBL* 80 (1961): 133-42.
Irwin, W. H. 'The Metaphor in Prov. 11,30'. *Bib* 65 (1984): 97-100.
Jobling, D., P. L. Day and G. T. Sheppard (eds.). *The Bible and the Politics of Exegesis*. Cleveland, OH: Pilgrim, 1991.
Kassis, R. A. *The Book of Proverbs and Arabic Proverbial Works*. VTSup 74. Leiden: Brill, 1999.
Kayatz, C. *Studien zu Proverbien 1–9*. WMANT 22. Neukirchen-Vluyn: Neukirchener Verlag, 1966.
Keel, O. *The Symbolism of the Biblical World*. New York: Seabury, 1978.
Keel, O., and C. Uehlinger. *Gods, Goddesses and Images of God in Ancient Israel*. Translated by T. Trapp. Minneapolis, MN: Fortress, 1998.
Kelly, J. N. D. *Early Christian Doctrines*. London/New York: Continuum, 2004 (5th rev. ed.).

Kidner, D. *Proverbs*. TOTC. London: IVP, 1964.
Kimilike, L. P. *Poverty in the Book of Proverbs: An African Transformational Hermeneutic of Proverbs on Poverty*. New York/Oxford: Peter Lang, 2008.
Kitchen, K. A. 'Proverbs and Wisdom Books of the Ancient Near East: The Factual History of a Literary Form'. TynBul 28 (1977): 69-119.
Knox, W. L. 'The Divine Wisdom'. *JTS* 38 (1937): 230-37.
Koch, K. 'Gibt es ein Vergeltungsdogma im Alten Testament'. *ZTK* 52 (1955): 1-42.
Koch, K. 'Is There a Doctrine of Retribution in the Old Testament?' Pp. 57-87 in *Theodicy in the Old Testament*. Edited by J. L. Crenshaw. London: SPCK, 1983.
Lambert, W. G. *Babylonian Wisdom Literature*. Winona Lake, IN: Eisenbrauns, 1996.
Lane, W. L. *Hebrews 1–8*. WBC. Dallas, TX: Word, 1991.
Lang, B. *Wisdom and the Book of Proverbs: An Israelite Goddess Redefined*. New York: Pilgrim, 1986.
Lichtenstein, M. 'The Banquet Motif in Keret and in Prov 9'. *JANESCU* 1 (1968/69): 19-31.
Lichtenstein, M. H. 'Chiasm and Symmetry in Proverbs 31'. *CBQ* 44 (1982): 202-11.
Lichtheim, M. *Ancient Egyptian Literature*. 3 vols. Berkley, CA: University of California Press, 1973-1980.
———. 'Instruction of Amenemope'. Pp. 115-22 in *The Context of Scripture*, vol. 1: *Canonical Compositions from the Biblical World*. Edited by W. W. Hallo. Leiden: Brill, 1997.
Lincoln, A. T. *Ephesians*. WBC. Dallas, TX: Word, 1990.
———. *The Gospel According to John*. BNTC. London: Continuum, 2005.
Lindenberger, J. *The Aramaic Proverbs of Ahiqar*. Baltimore, MD: Johns Hopkins University Press, 1983.
———. 'Ahiqar'. Pp. 479-507 in *The Old Testament Pseudepigrapha*, vol. 2. Edited by J. H. Charlesworth. London: Darton, Longman & Todd, 1985.
Loader, J. A. 'Wisdom by (the) People for (the) People'. *ZAW* 111 (1999): 211-33.
Longman III, T. *Proverbs*. Grand Rapids, MI: Baker, 2006.
Luc, A. 'The Titles and Structure of Proverbs'. *ZAW* 112 (2000): 252-55.
Lucas, E. C. *Exploring the Old Testament*, vol. 3: *The Psalms and Wisdom Literature*. London: SPCK, 2003.
———. 'A Biblical Basis for the Scientific Enterprise'. Pp. 46-68 in *Can We Be Sure about Anything?* Edited by D. Alexander. Leicester: Apollos, 2005.
———. 'The New Testament Teaching about the Environment'. Pp. 195-212 in *The Bible and Christian Ethics*. Edited by D. E. Singh and B. C. Farr. Oxford: Regnum/Eugene, OR, 2013.
Luther, M. *Luther's Works*, vol. 44. Edited by J. Atkinson. Philadelphia, PA: Fortress, 1966.
Maier, C. 'Conflicting Attractions: Parental Wisdom and the "Strange Woman" in Proverbs 1–9'. Pp. 92-108 in *A Feminist Companion to Wisdom Literature*. Edited by A. Brenner. Sheffield: Sheffield Academic Press, 1995.
Malchow, B. V. 'A Manual for Future Monarchs'. *CBQ* 47 (1985): 238-45.
Marcus, R. 'The Tree of Life in the Book of Proverbs'. *JBL* 62 (1943): 117-20.
Masenya, M. 'Proverbs 31:10-31 in a South African Context: A Reading for the Liberation of African (Northern Sotho) Women'. *Semeia* 28 (1997): 55-68.
McCreesh, T. P. 'Wisdom as Wife: Proverbs 31:10-31'. *RB* 92 (1985): 25-46.
McGrath, A. E. *Christian Spirituality*. Oxford: Blackwell, 1999.
McKane, W. *Proverbs*. OTL. Philadelphia, PA: Westminster, 1970.

Metzger, B. M. *An Introduction to the Apocrypha*. New York: Oxford University Press, 1977.
———. *A Textual Commentary on the New Testament*. Stuttgart: United Bible Societies, 1994 (4th rev. ed.).
Moore, C. A. *Daniel, Esther and Jeremiah: The Additions*. AB. Garden City, NY: Doubleday, 1977.
Moore, R. D. 'A Home for the Alien: Worldly Wisdom and Covenantal Confession in Proverbs 30,1-9'. *ZAW* 106(1994): 96-107.
Murphy, R. E. *Wisdom Literature*. FOTL 13. Grand Rapids, MI: Eerdmans, 1981.
———. 'The Personification of Wisdom'. Pp. 222-33 in *Wisdom in Ancient Israel: Essays in Honour of J. A. Emerton*. Edited by J. Day, R. P. Gordon and H. G. M. Williamson. Cambridge: Cambridge University Press, 1995.
———. *The Tree of Life: An Exploration of Biblical Wisdom Literature*. Grand Rapids, MI: Eerdmans, 1996 (2nd ed.).
———. *Proverbs*. WBC. Nashville, TN: Thomas Nelson, 1998.
———. 'Wisdom and Yahwism Revisited'. Pp. 191-200 in *Shall Not the Judge of All the Earth Do What Is Right?* Edited by D. Penchansky and P. L. Redditt. Winona Lake, IN: Eisenbrauns, 2000.
Naré, L. *Proverbes salomoniens et proverbs mossi: Etude comparative à partir d'une nouvelle analyses de Pr 25–29*. Frankfurt/Berne: Peter Lang, 1986.
Nel, P. J. 'The Genres of Biblical Wisdom Literature'. *JNSL* 9 (1981): 129-42.
Newsom, C. A. 'Woman and the Discourse of Patriarchal Wisdom: A Study of Proverbs 1–9'. Pp. 142-60 in *Gender and Difference in Ancient Israel*. Edited by P. L. Day. Minneapolis, MN: Fortress, 1989.
Niccacci, A. 'Proverbi 22.17–23.11'. *SBFLA* 29 (1979): 42-72.
Nickelsburg, G. W. E. *Jewish Literature between the Bible and the Mishnah*. London: SCM, 1981.
Noth, M., and D. W. Thomas (eds.). *Wisdom in Israel and the Ancient Near East: Presented to H. H. Rowley*. VTSup 3. Leiden: Brill, 1955.
O'Brien, P. T. *Colossians, Philemon*. WBC. Waco, TX: Word, 1982.
O'Connor, M. P. *Hebrew Verse Structure*. Winona Lake, IN: Eisenbrauns, 1980.
Oesterley, W. O. E. *An Introduction to the Books of the Apocrypha*. London: SPCK, 1935.
Otwell, J. H. *And Sarah Laughed: The Status of Women in the Old Testament*. Philadelphia, PA: Westminster, 1977.
Peels, H. G. L. 'Passion or Justice? The Interpretation of *b^{e}yôm nāqām* in Proverbs VI 34'. *VT* 44 (1994): 270-74.
Penchansky, D., and P. L. Redditt (eds.). *Shall not the Judge of All the Earth Do What Is Right? Studies on the Nature of God in Tribute to James L. Crenshaw*. Winona Lake, IN: Eisenbrauns, 2000.
Perdue, L. G. 'Cosmology and the Social Order in the Wisdom Tradition'. Pp. 457-78 in *The Sage in Israel and the Ancient Near East*. Edited by J. G. Gammie and L. G. Perdue. Winona Lake, IN: Eisenbrauns, 1990.
———. *Wisdom and Creation: The Theology of Wisdom Literature*. Nashville, TN: Abingdon, 1994.
———. *Proverbs*. Interpretation. Louisville, KY: Westminster John Knox, 2000.
———. *Wisdom Literature: A Theological History*. Louisville, KY: Westminster John Knox, 2007.

Pleins, J. D. 'Poverty in the Social World of the Wise'. *JSOT* 37 (1987): 61-78.
———. *The Social Visions of the Hebrew Bible*. Louisville, KY: Westminster John Knox, 2001.
Plöger, O. *Sprüche Salomos (Proverbia)*. BKAT 17. Neukirchen-Vluyn: Neukirchener Verlag, 1984.
Polkinghorne, J. *One World: The Interaction of Science and Theology*. London: SPCK, 1986.
Porter, S. E., et al. (eds.). *Crossing the Boundaries: Essays in Biblical Interpretation in Honour of Michael D. Goulder*. Leiden: Brill, (1994).
Preuss, H. D. 'Das Gottesbild der ältesten Weisheit Israels'. VTSup 23 (1972): 117-45.
Rad, G. von. *Old Testament Theology*. 2 vols. Edinburgh: Oliver & Boyd, 1962/1965.
Rad, G. von. *Wisdom in Israel*. London: SCM, 1972.
Ray, J. D. 'Egyptian Wisdom Literature'. Pp. 17-29 in *Wisdom in Ancient Israel: Essays in Honour of J. A. Emerton*. Edited by J. Day et al. Cambridge: Cambridge University Press, 1995.
Rees, M. *Our Cosmic Habitat*. Princeton, NJ: Princeton University Press, 2003.
Ringgren, H. H. *Word and Wisdom: Studies in the Hypostatization of Divine Qualities and Functions in the Ancient Near East*. Lund: Ohlsson, 1947.
Roth, W. M. W. 'The Numerical Sequence x/x+1 in the Old Testament'. *VT* 12 (1962): 307-11.
———. Numerical Sayings in the Old Testament. VTSup 13. Leiden: Brill, 1965.
Ruffle, J. 'The Teaching of Amenemope and Its Connection with the Book of Proverbs'. *TynBul* 28 (1977): 29-68.
Sandmel, S. *Philo of Alexandria: An Introduction*. Oxford: Oxford University Press, 1979.
Sandoval, T. J. *The Discourse of Wealth and Poverty in the Book of Proverbs*. Leiden: Brill, 2005.
Schroer, S. *Wisdom Has Built Her House*. Collegeville, MN: Liturgical Press, 2000.
Schwáb, Z. 'The Sayings Clusters in Proverbs: Towards an Associative Reading Strategy'. *JSOT* 38 (2013): 59-79.
Scott, R. B. Y. 'The Study of the Wisdom Literature'. *Int* 24 (1970): 20-45.
———. 'Folk Proverbs of the Ancient Near East'. Pp. 417-26 in *Studies in Ancient Israelite Wisdom*. Edited by J. L. Crenshaw. New York: Ktav, 1976.
Sheriffs, D. *The Friendship of the Lord*. Carlisle: Paternoster, 1996.
Shupak, N. 'Female Imagery in Proverbs 1–9 in the Light of Egyptian Sources'. *VT* 61 (2011): 310-23.
Singh, D. E., anad B. C. Farr (eds). The Bible and Christian Ethics. Oxford: Regnum/Eugene, OR: Wipf & Stock, 2013.
Sinnott, A. M. *The Personification of Wisdom*. Aldershot: Ashgate, 2005.
Skehan, P. W., and A. A. Di Lella. *The Wisdom of Ben Sira*. AB. New York: Doubleday, 1987.
Skladny, U. *Die älteten Spruchsammlungen in Israel*. Göttingen: Vandenhoeck & Ruprecht, 1962.
Snell, D. C. *Twice-Told Proverbs and the Composition of the Book of Proverbs*. Winona Lake, IN: Eisenbrauns, 1993.
Soden, W. von (ed.). *Akkadisches Handwöterbuch* III. Wiesbaden: Otto Harrassowitz 1981.
Spanier, K. 'The Queen Mother in the Judean Royal Court: Maacah — A Case Study'. Pp. 186-95 in *A Feminist Companion to the Bible* 5. Edited by A. Brenner. Sheffield: Sheffield Academic Press, 1994.
Stott, J. R. W. *God's New Society: The Message of Ephesians*. Leicester: IVP, 1979.
Thomas, D. W. 'A Note on *Lîqqahat* in Proverbs 30:17'. *JTS* 42 (1941): 151-55.
Tov, E. 'Recensional Differences between the Masoretic Text and the Septuagint of Proverbs'.

Pp. 43-56 in *Of Scribes and Scrolls*. Edited by H. W. Attridge et al. Lanham, MD: University Press of America, 1990.

Toy, C. H. *The Book of Proverbs*. ICC. Edinburgh: T&T Clark, 1899.

Trigg, R. 'The Christian Roots of Scientific Reasoning'. Pp. 30-48 in *Can We Be Sure about Anything?* Edited by D. Alexander. Leicester: Apollos, 2005.

Valler, S. 'Who Is *ʾēšet Ḥayil* in Rabbinic Literature?' Pp. 85-97 in *A Feminist Companion to Wisdom Literature*. Edited by A. Brenner. Sheffield: Sheffield Academic Press, 1995.

Van Leeuwen, R. C. *Context and Meaning in Proverbs 25–27*. SBLDS 96. Atlanta, GA: Scholars Press, 1988.

———. 'Proverbs 30:21-23 and the Biblical World Upside Down'. *JBL* 105 (1986): 599-610.

———. 'Wealth and Poverty: System and Contradiction in Proverbs'. *HS* 33 (1992): 25-36.

———. 'The Background to Proverbs 30:4aα'. Pp. 102-21 in *Wisdom, You Are My Sister*. Edited by M. L. Barré. Washington, DC: Catholic Biblical Association of America, 1997.

———. *Proverbs*. New Interpreter's Bible 5. Nashville, TN: Abingdon, 1997.

———. 'Cosmos, Temple, House: Building and Wisdom in Mesopotamia and Israel'. Pp. 67-90 in *Wisdom Literature in Mesopotamia and Israel*. Edited by R. J. Clifford. Atlanta, GA: SBL, 2007.

Waltke, B. K. 'Does Proverbs Promise Too Much? *AUSS* 34 (1996): 319-36.

———. *The Book of Proverbs 1–15*. NICOT. Grand Rapids, MI: Eerdmans, 2004.

———. *The Book of Proverbs 15–31*. NICOT. Grand Rapids, MI: Eerdmans, 2005.

Walton, J. H. *Ancient Near Eastern Thought and the Old Testament*. Grand Rapids, MI: Baker Academic, 2006.

Washington, H. C. *Wealth and Poverty in the Instruction of Amenemope and the Hebrew Proverbs*. SBLDS 142. Atlanta, GA: Scholars Press, 1994.

———. 'The Strange Woman (אשה זרה נכרה) of Proverbs 1–9 and Post-Exilic Judean Society'. Pp. 163-71 in *A Feminist Companion to the Wisdom Literature*. Edited by A. Brenner. Sheffield: Sheffield Academic Press, 1995.

Watson, G. W. E. *Classical Hebrew Poetry*. Sheffield: JSOT Press, 1986 (2nd ed.).

Weber, M. *The Protestant Ethic and the Spirit of Capitalism*. Translated by T. Parsons. London: Unwin, 1971.

Weeks, S. *Instruction and Imagery in Proverbs 1–9*. Oxford: Oxford University Press, 2007.

Wenham, G. J. 'Sanctuary Symbolism in the Garden of Eden Story'. Pp. 399-404 in *I Studied Inscriptions from Before the Flood*. Edited by R. S. Hess and D. T. Tsumura. Winona Lake, IN: Eisenbrauns, 1994.

Westermann, C. 'Weisheit in Sprichwort'. Pp. 73-85 in *Schalom: Studien zu Glaube und Geschichte Israels: Festschrift Alfred Jepson*. Edited by K.-H. Bernhardt. Stuttgart: Calwer, 1971.

———. *Roots of Wisdom*. Edinburgh: T&T Clark, 1995.

Whybray, R. N. *Wisdom in Proverbs*. London: SCM, 1965.

———. 'Proverbs VIII 22-31 and Its Supposed Prototypes'. *VT* 15 (1965): 504-14.

———. *The Intellectual Tradition in the Old Testament*. BZAW 135. Berlin: de Gruyter, 1974.

———. 'Yahweh-Sayings and Their Contexts in Proverbs 10,1–22,16'. Pp. 153-65 in *La Sagesse de l'Ancien Testament'*. Edited by M. Gilbert. BETL 51. Leuven: Leuven University Press and Gembloux: Duculot, 1979.

———. *Wealth and Poverty in the Book of Proverbs*. JSOTSup 99. Sheffield: Sheffield Academic Press, 1990.

———. *The Composition of the Book of Proverbs*. JSOTSup 168. Sheffield: JSOT Press, 1994.

———. *Proverbs*. NCB. London: Marshal Pickering, 1994.

———. 'The Structure and Composition of Proverbs 22:17–24:22'. Pp. 83-96 in *Crossing the Boundaries: Essays in Biblical Interpretation in Honour of Michael D. Goulder*. Edited by S. E. Porter et al. Leiden: Brill, 1994.

———. *The Book of Proverbs: A Survey of Modern Study*. Leiden: Brill, 1995.

Williams, J. G. 'The Power of Form: A Study of Biblical Proverbs'. *Semeia* 17 (1980): 35-58.

Williams, R. *Arius: Heresy and Tradition*. London: Darton, Longman & Todd, 1987.

Williams, R. J. 'The Alleged Semitic Original for the Wisdom of Amenemope'. *Journal of Egyptian Archaeology* 47 (1961): 100-106.

Wilson, F. M. 'Sacred or Profane? The Yahwistic Redaction of Proverbs Reconsidered'. Pp. 313-34 in *The Listening Heart: Essays in Wisdom and the Psalms in Honor of Roland E. Murphy*. Edited by K. G. Hoglund et al. JSOTSup 58. Sheffield: JSOT Press, 1987.

Winston, D. *The Wisdom of Solomon*. AB. New York: Doubleday, 1979.

Witherington III, B. *Jesus the Sage: The Pilgrimage of Wisdom*. Minneapolis, MN: Augsburg Fortress, 1994.

———. *The Jesus Quest: The Third Search for the Jew of Nazareth*. Carlisle: Paternoster, 1995.

Wolters, A. *The Song of the Valiant Woman: Studies in the Interpretation of Proverbs 31:10-31*. Carlisle: Paternoster, 2001.

Wright, C. J. H. 'The Israelite Household and the Decalogue: The Social Background and Significance of Some Commandments'. *TynBul* 30 (1979): 101-24.

Wright, G. E. *God Who Acts: Biblical Theology as Recital*. London: SCM, 1952.

Wyatt, N. *Religious Texts from Ugarit*. Sheffield: Sheffield Academic Press, 1998.

Yee, G. A. 'The Theology of Creation in Proverbs 8:22-31'. Pp. 85-96 in *Creation in the Biblical Traditions*. Edited by R. J. Clifford and J. J. Collins. Washington, DC: Catholic Biblical Association of America, 1982.

———. '"I Have Perfumed My Bed with Myrrh": The Foreign Woman (*'iššâ Zārâ*) in Proverbs 1–9'. *JSOT* 43 (1989): 53-68.

Yoder, C. R. 'The Woman of Substance (אשת־חיל): A Socioeconomic Reading of Proverbs 31:10-31'. *JBL* 122 (2003): 427-47.

———. *Proverbs*. Abingdon Old Testament Commentaries. Nashville, TN: Abingdon, 2009.

Yonge, C. D. *The Works of Philo*. Peabody, MA: Hendrickson, 1997 (new ed.).

Index of Authors

Index of Scripture and Other Ancient Literature